Design and Analysis of
Reliable and
Fault-Tolerant
Computer Systems

Design and Analysis of
Reliable and
Fault-Tolerant
Computer Systems

Mostafa Abd-El-Barr
Department of Information Science
Kuwait University, Kuwait

Imperial College Press

ICP

Published by

Imperial College Press
57 Shelton Street
Covent Garden
London WC2H 9HE

Distributed by

World Scientific Publishing Co. Pte. Ltd.
5 Toh Tuck Link, Singapore 596224
USA office: 27 Warren Street, Suite 401-402, Hackensack, NJ 07601
UK office: 57 Shelton Street, Covent Garden, London WC2H 9HE

British Library Cataloguing-in-Publication Data
A catalogue record for this book is available from the British Library.

DESIGN AND ANALYSIS OF RELIABLE AND FAULT-TOLERANT COMPUTER SYSTEMS

ISBN-13   978-1-86094-668-4
ISBN-10   1-86094-668-2

Printed in Singapore

To the memory of my mother and my father.

— Mostafa Abd-El-Barr

Preface

Fault tolerance, reliability, and availability are becoming major design issues nowadays in massively parallel distributed computing systems. Examples of systems in which fault tolerance is needed include mission-critical, computation-intensive, transactions (such as banking), and mobile/wireless computing systems/networks. High performance, measured in terms of speed and computing power, is essentially used as major design objective for such systems. It is however conceivable that great loss of crucial transactions can take place due to a small system/component error. The emergence of new paradigms, such as mobile/wireless computing, requires the introduction of new techniques for fault tolerance. It is therefore prudent that the issue of fault tolerance become among the set of design objectives of current and future computing systems.

A number of pressing challenges need to be faced in designing high performance computing systems. One such challenge is minimizing the performance loss due to the incorporation of fault tolerance techniques. Another challenge is to maximize the mean-time between failures (MTBF) of transaction-related systems, e.g., banking and airfare reservation systems. Yet another more critical challenge is to eliminate system interruptions due to fault(s) during the mission time of mission-critical systems, such as space crafts. These and other challenges require new innovative techniques for achieving fault tolerance in computing and networking systems.

My interest and commitment to the area of fault tolerance and reliability analysis started at the time when I was enrolled, as a doctoral candidate at the University of Toronto in Canada, in a graduate course entitled "Fault-Tolerant Computing". The course was taught by my PhD thesis advisor Professor Zvonko Vranesic; a well known name in the area of Fault Tolerance and Testability Analysis. It was then that I came to realize the importance of reliability and fault tolerance not only in computing but also in day to day life. Just imagine the devastation resulting from a situation such as an error prone elevator control circuitry in a 50-story building, or an error prone circuitry in a space craft sent to space with humans onboard, or even a small error in the control circuitry of an atomic reactor. It is clear that such possible situations make design for fault tolerance and reliability as important as design for optimization and/or performance gains.

The material presented in this book is meant to guide the design of computer systems with fault tolerance and reliability as basic design objectives. The book is an attempt to complement earlier efforts made by other colleagues on the same subject. It is comprehensive in its coverage and covers recent developments in the design of fault-tolerant and reliable systems, including mobile/wireless networking and distributed systems. The material presented in the book represents the outcome of more than twenty years of teaching undergraduate and graduate courses on Fault-Tolerant Computing and Reliability Engineering at institutions in Canada, Saudi Arabia, and Kuwait. During this period, I have developed my own class notes and improved it over the years based on the feedback obtained from my students and fellow colleagues. The material presented in the book has been class-tested. It evolved out of the class notes for the University of Saskatchewan's (Canada) CMPT 874, the King Fahd University of Petroleum and Minerals, Saudi Arabia (KFUPM) COE 421, COE 523 & CSE 641, and the Kuwait University (KU) ECE 564. The experiences gained in these courses have been incorporated into this book.

The book is divided into six parts. Each part consists of a number of chapters. Part I deals with the fundamental concepts involved in fault analysis. This part consists of three chapters: Fundamental Concepts, Fault Modeling, Simulation & Diagnosis, and Error Correcting Codes. The main objective in this part is to introduce the reader to the basic concepts in fault detection and correction. A number of fundamental concepts, simple reliability, and fault tolerance mathematical relations that will be used throughout the book are introduced in Part I of the book.

While Part I of the book deals primarily with a system consisting of a single component, Part II is devoted to a discussion of the fundamental issues related to fault tolerance and reliability analysis of computer systems consisting of more than one component. This part consists of three chapters: Fault Tolerance in Multi-Processor Systems, Fault-Tolerant Routing in Multi-Computer Systems, and Fault Tolerance and Reliability in Hierarchical Interconnection Networks. The discussion in these chapters spans a number of issues including the fault tolerance aspects of bus structures, fault tolerance and reliability features in simple multi-computer architectures, such as the hypercube and the mesh, and finally the achievement of various degrees of fault tolerance using hierarchical networks.

The reliability and fault tolerance of computer networks/distributed systems is the main theme in Part III of the book. These systems are characterized by having a number of processing units (nodes) collaborate together and execute a given task while being connected over a number of geographically distributed locations. Mobile/Wireless systems are good examples of distributed systems. Part III consists of four chapters: Fault Tolerance and Reliability of Computer Networks, Fault Tolerance in High Speed Switching Networks, Fault Tolerance in Distributed Computing Systems, and Fault Tolerance in Mobile Networks. With the present advances is VLSI/WSI technology, it is now economically feasible to implement massive parallel processor arrays consisting of a large number of fine-grained regular processing elements (PEs). The advantages offered by PEs include low assembly cost, high reliability, and high performance. Part IV of the book is dedicated to the discussion of the reliability and yield enhancement of array processors. This part consists of three chapters: Reliability and Yield Enhancement of VLSI/WSI Circuits, Design of Fault-Tolerant Processor Arrays, and Algorithm-Based Fault Tolerance Techniques.

Mission-critical systems incorporate massive parallel complex computing systems in solving real-time and computation-intensive problems. A small mistake in such systems can lead to devastating losses of human life. It is prudent in designing such systems to incorporate a sizeable degree of fault tolerance and reliability by incorporating redundant processing elements. These redundant elements can be used to replace faulty ones. In performing such replacement, the system needs to be switched periodically to what is known as the *diagnostic mode.* During this mode, detection of faulty processing element(s) is performed. As the complexity of the diagnosed systems increases, the amount of data that needs to be analyzed also increases. Part V of the book is concerned with System Level Diagnosis. Part VI of the book is used to present two fault-tolerant and highly reliable/available practical systems. These are the Redundant Array of Independent Disks (RAID) systems and the TANDEM highly available systems, including a brief discussion on achieving high availability in Client/Server Computing paradigm.

Students in Computer Engineering, Information/Computer Sciences, and Electrical Engineering should find this book useful for their program of study. The majority of these programs include undergraduate as well as graduate courses in Fault-Tolerant Computing and Reliability Analysis of Computer Systems. Selected chapters can be used to offer core/elective courses in these disciplines. We offer the following suggestions: A one-semester course on "Introduction to Fault-Tolerant Computing" may cover Part I (three chapters), Chapter 4 (part of Part II), Chapter 7 (part of Part III) and Chapter 12 (part of Part IV). Another one-semester course on "Fault Tolerance and Reliability Analysis of Computer Networks" may cover Chapters 1 and 2 (part of Part I), Chapter 4 (part of Part II) and Part III (four chapters). Yet a third one-semester course on "Reliability and Fault Tolerance of Multi-Processor Systems" may cover Chapters 1 and 2 (part of Part I), Part II (three chapters), Chapter 8 (part of Part III) and Part IV (three chapters). In addition, selected individual chapters can be used to offer special topic courses with different emphasis. Above all, the book can also be used as a comprehensive reference for designers of fault-tolerant and reliable computer systems.

The book assumes that students studying fault tolerance must have had exposure to a basic course in logic design and a course on college-level probability/statistics. No other academic background is assumed of the readers in order to grasp, understand, and digest the material presented in the book and be able to apply what is presented in real life designs. Every possible effort was made to make the book self-contained. Any feedback/comments are welcome on this aspect or any other related aspects. Comments can be sent to me through the publisher or directly to my emails: mostafa@cfw.kuniv.edu or mostafa@ccse.kfupm.edu.sa.

Mostafa Abd-El-Barr
KFUPM (Saudi Arabia) 2003 &
CFW, Kuwait University 2004-2006

Acknowledgements

I owe much to a number of my undergraduate and graduate students for their help in correcting and improving the material presented in the book. To name a few, I would like to thank S. Bambang, A. Zakir, G. Hashim, K. Hawashim, E. Ghanim, F. Ashraf, F. Daud, T. Sommani, M. Shenwari, S. Joma'a and T. Gahtani. Special thanks to Lenore Betts and Steven Patt, Editors Imperial College Press for their help in making this book a reality.

Finally, and most importantly, I would like to thank my wife Medical Professor Ebtesam Abd-El-Basset, for tolerating all the long hours I spent on writing this book. Special thanks go to members of my immediate family: my sons Drs. Muhammad, Abd-El-Rahman, and Ibrahim & my daughters-in-law Dr. Mai and Mariam. Special love goes to the little Mariam (my grand-daughter).

Contents

Chapter 1

Fundamental Concepts in Fault Tolerance and Reliability Analysis

This chapter introduces the main issues related to the design and analysis of fault-tolerant systems. Our coverage starts with an introduction to faults and their characterization. We then discuss the main issues related to redundancy, including hardware, software, time, and information redundancies. The chapter also covers the fundamental issues related to reliability modeling and evaluation. In particular, the combinatorial reliability model is discussed in details.

1.1 Introduction

Computer systems are becoming complex in both their design and architecture. It is not unusual to have a computer system that consists of hundreds and maybe thousands of interacting software and hardware components. Computer systems are developed over a period of time. They usually go through a number of phases (stages) starting from the specification phase, through the design, prototyping, and implementation phases and finally the installation phase. A fault can occur during one or more of these phases. A *fault* is defined as a physical defect that takes place in some part(s) of a system. A fault that occurs during one development stage can become apparent only at some later stage(s). Faults manifest themselves in the form of *error(s)*. When an error is encountered during the operation of a system, it will lead to a *failure*. A system is said to have failed if it cannot deliver its intended function. Figure 1.1 shows a simple example that illustrates the three terms.

Example

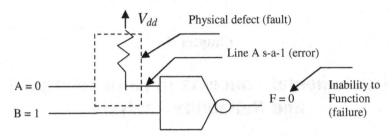

Fig. 1.1: The relationship among fault, error, and failure.

Faults can be characterized based on a number of attributes. These include the cause, duration, nature, extent, and value. Table 1.1 summarizes the relationship between these attributes and the type of faults.

Table 1.1: Fault characterization.

Cause	Duration	Nature	Extent	Value
Specification Mistake	Permanent	Hardware	Global	Determinate
Design Mistake	Transient	Software	Local	Indeterminate
Implementation Mistake	Intermittent			
Component Defects				
External Disturbance				

A fault is said to be *permanent* if it continues to exist until it can be repaired. Software bugs are classified as permanent faults. A *transient fault* is one that occurs and disappears at an unknown frequency. A lightening hitting a transmission line causes a transient fault. An *intermittent* fault is one that occurs and disappears at a frequency that can be characterized. A loose contact due to bad soldering can cause an intermittent fault. Fault causes can lead to either software or hardware errors. These in turn can lead to a failure of the system in delivering its intended function.

Based on the level targeted, different techniques can be used to deal with fault(s). These include fault *avoidance*, fault *masking*, and fault *tolerance*. Fault avoidance refers to the techniques used to prevent the occurrence of faults, e.g. quality control (design review, component screening, testing, etc.) and shielding from interference (radiation, humidity, heat, etc.). Fault masking refers to the techniques used to prevent faults from introducing errors, e.g. error correcting codes, majority voting, etc. A fault-tolerant system is a system that continues to function correctly in the presence of hardware failures and/or software errors. A typical fault-tolerant system shall include the following attributes: Fault detection, location, containment, and recovery.

In dealing with faults, a method is needed to model their effect(s). A fault model is a logical abstraction that describes the functional effect of the physical defect. Fault modeling can be made at different levels (ranging from the lowest physical geometric level, up through the switch level, gate level and finally to the functional level). The lower the level of modeling, the more computationally intensive (expensive) the method needed for detecting such fault. The higher the level for fault modeling, the less accurate it is in representing the actual physical defect. The stuck-at gate-level fault model represents a tradeoff between cost and accuracy. It is not as accurate as, but it is less expensive, compared to the switch level fault model. An example of the switch level fault model is the transistor stuck-open (short).

In a given system, failures due to the occurrence of fault(s) take place at a given rate. A failure rate of a system, λ, is defined as the expected number of failures of the system per unit time.

The *Reliability*, R(t), of a system is defined as the conditional probability that the system operates correctly throughout the interval $[t_0, t]$ given that it was operating correctly at t_0. A relationship between reliability and time that has been widely accepted is the exponential function, i.e., $R(t) = e^{-\lambda t}$. The *mean-time-to-failure* (*MTTF*) of a system is defined as the expected time that a system will operate before the *first* failure occurs. The relationship between the *MTTF* of a system and its failure rate λ can be expressed as $MTTF = \dfrac{1}{\lambda}$.

Whenever a given system fails, it may be possible to bring it back to function through a process called *system repair*. Repair of a system requires the use of a workshop characterized by a repair rate, μ. The repair rate is defined as the average number of repairs that can be performed per unit time. The *mean-time-to-repair* (*MTTR*) of a system is defined as the expected time that the system will take while in repair (being unavailable). The relationship between the *MTTR* of a system and the repair rate μ can be expressed as $MTTR = \dfrac{1}{\mu}$. During its operation, a system can be either available or unavailable (in repair). The *Availability* of a system, $A(t)$, is defined as the probability that the system is operating correctly at instant t. The relationship between the steady state availability of a system, A_{ss}, and the *MMTF* and the *MTTR* can be expressed as $A_{ss} = \dfrac{MTTF}{MTTF + MTTR}$.

The expected level of service delivered by a given system can be specified in terms of the extent to which the service is offered. When no service degradation can be tolerated, e.g. space missions, a *highly reliable* system is demanded. When short service degradation can be tolerated, e.g. banking systems, a *highly available* system is demanded.

In addition to reliability and availability, a number of other attributes can be used to characterize a given system. Among these *maintainability* and *Safety* are defined next. We define maintainability, $M(t)$, as the probability that a failed system will be restored to operation within time t. The relationship between maintainability and time can be expressed as $M(t) = 1 - e^{-\mu t}$. On the other hand, the safety of a system, $S(t)$, is defined as probability that the system either performs correctly or discontinues without disturbance to other systems.

1.2 Redundancy Techniques

In order for a system to deliver its expected service in the presence of errors caused by faults, some extra (redundant) resources are needed. *Redundancy* can be included in any, or a composite, of the following forms.

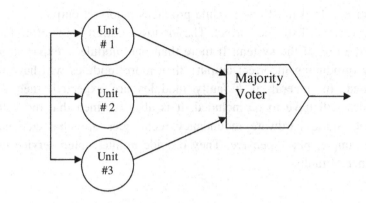

Fig. 1.2: Static HWR (TMR).

1.2.1 *Hardware Redundancy*

This refers to the inclusion of some extra hardware such that concurrent computations can be voted upon, errors can be masked out, or duplicate (spare) hardware can be switched automatically to replace failed components. Three forms of hardware redundancy can be identified. These are Static (Passive), Dynamic (Active) or Hybrid redundancy. In view of Fig. 1.2, Static redundancy requires fault masking; Dynamic redundancy requires fault detection plus replacement of faulty module(s), while Hybrid redundancy requires both fault masking and replacement.

1.2.1.1 *Passive (Static) Hardware Redundancy*

According to this technique, the effects of faults are essentially masked with no specific indication of their occurrence, i.e., these effects are hidden from the rest of the system. A representative of this technique is demonstrated via the use of the *N-Modular Redundancy* (NMR). Figure 1.2 shows the basic arrangement for a *Triple-Modular Redundancy* (TMR). In this case, three identical modules are used. They perform the same computation at the same time. Their outputs are fed to a majority voter. The output of the voter will be correct if at least two of its inputs are correct. If at most one module produces incorrect output, the output of the voter will still be correct. The incorrect output is therefore hidden from the rest of the system. If more than one module is expected to be faulty (producing incorrect output), then more modules will have to be included. In general, if k faulty modules are expected, then $2k+1$ modules will have to be included. It is also assumed that the voter is perfect. Static hardware redundancy techniques are characterized by being simple, but expensive. They provide uninterrupted service in the presence of faults.

1.2.1.2 *Active (Dynamic) Hardware Redundancy*

This technique involves removal, or replacement, of the faulty unit(s) in the system, in response to system failure. The process is usually triggered either by internal error detection mechanisms in the faulty unit(s) or by detection of errors in the output(s) of these units. Figure 1.3 shows the basic arrangement for the *standby sparing*. In this arrangement, each unit is provided to the input of an *N to* 1 *Switch* together with a faulty/not-faulty indication. This fault indication can be obtained by using a duplex system. A duplex system uses two identical modules and a comparator. The comparator checks the output of the two modules and indicates the existence of a fault whenever the two outputs are different.

The final output of the switch can be the output of any of the available units as long as the output of that unit is accompanied by a not-faulty indication, call that the *Primary Unit* (PU). As soon as the accompanied signal to the output of the PU indicates a faulty output, the switch will stop routing the output of that unit to the system output and switch to one of the other units, call them *Spare Units* (SUs). The process is repeated until all SUs are exhausted. *Hot Standby Sparing* refers to the case whereby spare units are powered, operate in Synchrony with the on-line unit(s) and is ready to take over at any times. *Cold Standby Sparing* refers to the case whereby spares are powered only when needed.

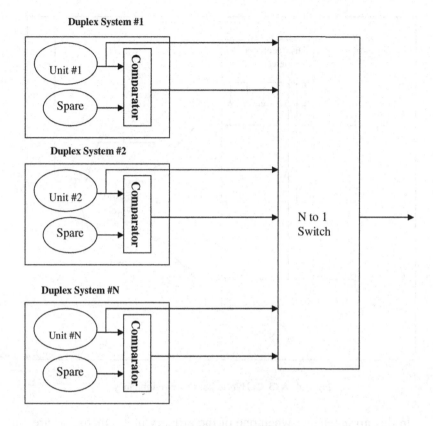

Fig. 1.3: Standby dynamic HWR.

During the switching time, no output should be provided at the output of the system. This system output interruption is a characteristic of the dynamic hardware redundancy techniques. The output of the system is interrupted and no output will be available. Dynamic hardware redundancy techniques are characterized as being inexpensive, but are only suitable for systems that can be interrupted for short time periods.

1.2.1.3 *Hybrid Hardware Redundancy*

This technique combines the advantages of the passive and the active redundancy. Figure 1.4 shows the basic arrangement for the hybrid hardware redundancy based on the TMR system.

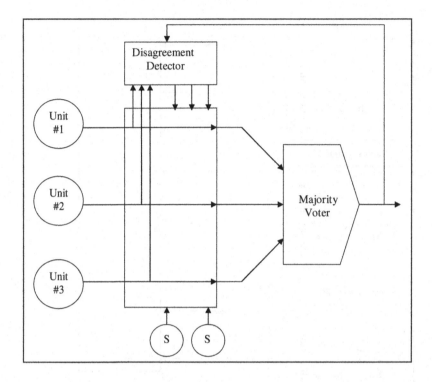

Fig. 1.4: A (3, 2) Hybrid hardware redundancy.

In this arrangement, when one of the primary units (there are three in the figure) fails, it is replaced by a spare (there are two in the figure), so that the basic *TMR* configuration can continue. Identification of the failed unit is made by feeding the output of the majority voter back to a disagreement detector whose job is to compare the voter's output with the outputs produced by the three primary units. Any disagreement with a PU output will indicate that this unit should be replaced by a spare. This replacement is made while the system is not interrupted, i.e., the correct output is still routed to the rest of the system.

In the general case, where N primary units are used and K spare units are included, called (N, K) system, the system can tolerate the failure of up to $K + \left\lfloor \dfrac{N}{2} \right\rfloor$ units. The advantage of this system is that it hides the effect of faults (fault masking) while replacing faulty units with spare ones (reconfiguration). This system is far more expensive than the static hardware redundancy technique. The system should be used in critical applications, such as space applications.

1.2.2 *Software Redundancy*

This refers to the use of extra code, small routines or possibly complete programs, in order to check the correctness or the consistency of the results produced by a given software. A number of software techniques are used. Some of these techniques have their hardware counterpart techniques.

1.2.2.1 *Static Software Redundancy Techniques*

1. **N-version programming (NVP):** The idea behind this technique is to independently generate $N>2$ functionally equivalent programs "VERSIONS" for the same initial specification of a given task. This is usually achieved by having N individuals (or groups) that work independent to achieve the stated specifications in terms of the algorithms and programming languages used. In the case of 3VP, majority voting is performed on the results procedure by 3 independent programs. The assumption is that the original specification provided to the three programming teams is not flawed. NVP is similar to the hardware majority voting. NVP is expensive, difficult to maintain, and its repair is not trivial.

2. **Transactions:** Here the software is treated as a transaction. Consistency checking is used at the end of the transaction. If the conditions are not met, then restart. The transaction should work the second time around. For a given computation, consistency checking can be performed by inserting assertions to check the results of the computations. As long as the assertion is true, no fault has occurred; otherwise a fault is detected.

3. **Ad-Hoc Techniques:** These are techniques that are application-dependent. For example, a consistency checking on a bank withdrawal can be made by checking that the amount of money withdrawn from any bank machine does not exceed a certain known a priori amount and that the aggregate amount withdrawn by any customer during the 24 hours period from all bank machines does not exceed his/her allowed maximum amount per day. In the case of instruction execution, a check can be made to ensure that no attempt is made by the processor to execute any of the $(2^n - 2^k)$ invalid instructions (assuming that k bits are actually used out of the available n bits op-code). A processor trying to execute any of the invalid instructions is called a *Run Away Processor*. Yet another example for consistency checking is to compare obtained performance with predicted performance based on an accurate model.

1.2.2.2 *Dynamic Software Redundancy Techniques*

1. **Forward Error Recovery:** In this case, the system will continue operation with the current system state even though it may be faulty. Real-time applications with data collected from a sensor can tolerate missing response to the sensor input.

2. **Backward Error Recovery:** Use previously saved correct state information at the starting point after failure. A copy of the initial data (database, disk, files, etc.) is stored as the process begins. As the process executes, it makes a record of all transactions that affect the data, this is called *Journalizing*. Some subset of the system state is saved at specific points (*check points*) during execution, including data, programs, machine state, etc., that is necessary to the successful continuation and completion of the process past the check point. Rollback is used to recover from failure after repair. This technique is called *Check-pointing*. The primary process records its state on a duplex storage module. When the secondary takes over, it starts by reading the recorded status. This is called checkpoint-restart

technique. The main disadvantage is the need for long repair time, i.e., the time needed to read the status. The use of Checkpoint-restart will yield a highly reliable, but not a highly available system. Alternatively, the primary process can send its status in the form of messages to the secondary process. When the secondary process takes over, it gets its current state from the most recent message. This is called checkpoint-message technique. The main disadvantage of the checkpoint-message is the danger resulting from missing any, or some, of the sent messages to the secondary process. A seemingly more appropriate techniques is called *Persistent*. According to this technique, all state changes are implemented as transactions. When the Secondary takes over, it starts in the null state and has the transaction mechanism undo any recent uncommitted state changes.

3. **Use of Recovery Blocks:** Use of three software elements:

    1. A primary routine to execute critical software functions

    2. An acceptance test routine, which tests the output of the primary routine after each execution.

    3. An alternate routine which performs the same as the primary routine (maybe less efficient or slower) and is invoked by the acceptance test upon detection of failure.

    4. For real-time programs, the Recovery Block should incorporate a watchdog timer to initiate Q if P does not produce acceptable result(s) within the allocated time.

4. **Some Other Software Fault Detection Techniques**

A number of software faults can be detected using techniques that are similar to those used to detect hardware faults. One of the techniques that have been widely used is the *Watchdog Timers*.

According to this technique, a watchdog daemon process is used. The task of the daemon process is to check the status of a given application, i.e., whether the application is alive. This is achieved by periodically sending a signal to the application and checking the return value.

1.2.3 *Information Redundancy*

This refers to the addition of redundant information to data in order to allow fault detection, fault masking, or possibly fault tolerance. Examples of added information include error-detecting and error-correcting codes that are usually added to logic circuits, memories, and data communicated over computer networks. In presenting the basic issues related to information redundancy, we will make use of a number of definitions and theorems. These are presented below.

The term *Code Word* (CW) is used to mean a collection of symbols representing meaningful data. Symbols are grouped according to a predefined set of rules. The term *Error Detecting Code* (EDC) is used to indicate a code that has the ability to expose error(s) in any given data word. Exposure of an erroneous data word is achieved by showing the invalidity of the decoded data word. Based on the principles discussed above, an EDC can be used to initiate a reconfiguration (replacement) process. The term *Error Correcting Code* (ECC) is used to indicate a code that has the ability that if an error has been detected, then it is possible to determine what the correct data would have been. An ECC can be used for masking the effect of errors. Two code words can be distinguished based on their *Hamming Distance* (HD), defined as the number of bits in which the two words differ. For example, the HD between the two code words 0010 and 0101, abbreviated as HD (0010,0101), is HD (0010,0101) = 3. It should be noted that a HD = 1 between two code words, will mean that one word can be changed into the other by flipping one bit. The term *Code Distance* (CD), of a given set of code words, is used to mean the minimum *HD* between any two code words in that set. Notice that for a given set of code words, if the CD = 2, then any single bit error will change a code word into an invalid code word (the minimum distance becomes 1 and not 2). A code having $CD = 3$ has the ability to expose any single or any double error, i.e., any single or double error will be detected. However, only a single error can be corrected. In general, we can state that in order to detect d errors, then $CD \geq (d + 1)$, to detect and correct t, or fewer errors, then $CD \geq 2t + 1$, and to detect d and correct t, or fewer errors, then $CD \geq t + d + 1$, where $t \leq d$.

Consider, for example, a code consisting of the three code words {10101, 01001, 01110}. This code has a code distance $CD = 3$. If, due to errors, in a word-oriented communication system the word (01100) is received, it will be concluded that there are errors because 01100 is not a valid code word. Since $CD = 3$, then any single error can be corrected. One way to correct this erroneous word is to EXOR it with each of the valid code words, i.e., $01100 \oplus \begin{cases} 10101 & = 11001 \rightarrow HD = 3 \\ 01001 & = 00101 \rightarrow HD = 2 \\ 01110 & = 00010 \rightarrow HD = 1 \end{cases}$

We see that $HD(01100, 01110) = 1$, so the originally transmitted word must have been 01110.

Table 1.2 shows the ED and EC ability for three different example codes.

Table 1.2: The ED and EC ability for three different example codes.

Code	Code distance	Detection ability	Correction ability
{00, 11}	2	1	0
{000, 111}	3	2 or fewer	1
{0000, 1111}	4	{3} or {2 or fewer}	{0} or{1}

It should be noted that the code {000, 111} can detected 2 or fewer errors and correct none or can correct only one error, but not both. Similarly, the code {0000, 1111} can detect 3 errors and correct none or alternatively it can detect 2 or fewer errors and correct only one error.

In addition to the detection/correction ability of a code, i.e., the CD of a code, codes can be characterized based on a property called *separability.* If the data information and the detection/correction information are separable, the resulting code is called a *separable code*; otherwise the code is *non-separable*. We will introduce a number of codes, starting with error detecting codes and followed by error correcting codes.

1.2.3.1 *Error Detecting Codes*

These codes usually have less overhead than the error correcting codes but they lack any error correcting capability. We will discuss four different techniques for error detection: Parity codes, Borden codes, Berger code and Bose Code.

(1) Parity Codes

Single bit odd (even) parity: Addition of one extra bit such that the total number of 1's is odd (even). This simple code has applications in data storing/retrieving in/from computer main memory. The basic scheme used for this is shown in Fig. 1.5.

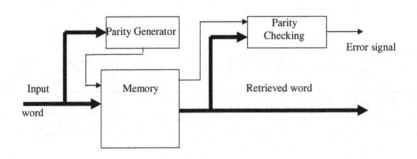

Fig. 1.5: Parity checking in computer main memory.

In this case, before storing a word in the memory, a parity generator is used to compute the parity bit required. Then both the original word and the computed parity bit are stored in the memory. On retrieval, a parity checker is used to compute the parity based on the data bits stored. The computed parity bit and the stored parity bit are compared by the parity checker and an error signal is set accordingly, i.e., if the computed and stored parity bits match, then the retrieved word is assumed to be correct; otherwise the retrieved word is assumed to be in error. It should be noted that for n bit data, there are 2^n possible data words. The addition of 1 parity bit will result in a total of 2^{n+1} possible words. Among these there is $\dfrac{2^{n+1}}{2}$ words with odd number of 1s and $\dfrac{2^{n+1}}{2}$ words with even number of 1s. For odd (even) parity, only those words with odd (even) number of 1's are valid code words. In the presence of a single error, an odd (even) parity code word will change into an even (odd) parity and thus, the error will be detected. Although simple, but the simple parity code has limited fault detection ability, i.e., it can only detect the occurrence of single errors. The occurrence of double errors will escape the detection unobserved. In general, simple parity codes have the ability to detect the occurrence of only odd number of errors. The occurrence of even number of errors will not be detected by simple parity codes.

(2) Borden Codes

Borden code is a general formulation for a wide range of error detecting codes. In general, Borden codes are non-separable error detecting codes. They are characterized by the following definition:

Definition

If $C_{m/n}$ is the set of codes of length n for which exactly m bits are ones, then the union of all such codes with m being the set of values congruent to $\lfloor n/2 \rfloor \bmod(d + 1)$ is known as the Borden (n, d) code.

Example: Suppose that we would like to construct the Borden (5,2) code. We first have to compute the quantity $\lfloor n/2 \rfloor \bmod(d + 1) = \lfloor 5/2 \rfloor \bmod(3) = 2$. This means that m belongs to the set $\{0,2,4\}$. Thus any word of length 5, of which either no bits, two bits, or four bits are 1 belongs to this Borden code. Here are all the possibilities: (00000,00011,00110,01100,11000,00101,01010,10100,01001,10010,10001,11110,11101,11011,10111,01111}

The Borden (n, d) can detect d unidirectional errors (errors that cause either a 0 $\rightarrow$ 1 or 1 $\rightarrow$ 0 transition, but not both). It is the optimal code for all d-unidirectional error detecting codes. It is also interesting to observe the following special cases:

If $d = 1$, the Borden code becomes the well-known parity code.

If n = 2d, we get a special kind of code called the k/2k (or k out of 2k) code.

(3) Berger Code

The Berger error detecting code is a separable code capable of detecting all unidirectional errors. It is formulated by appending check bits to the data word. The check bits constitute the binary representation of the number of 0's in the data word. For example, for a 3 bit long data word, we need 2 bits for the check. Table 1.3 shows the valid Berger code words.

Table 1.3: Valid Berger code words.

Data word	Check bits	Codeword
000	11	00011
001	10	00110
010	10	01010
011	01	01101
100	10	10010
101	01	10101
110	01	11001
111	00	11100

As can be seen, the Berger code is simpler to deal with than the Borden codes. However, the Bose code is more efficient than the Berger code. This is shown below.

(4) Bose Code

The Bose code provides the same error detecting capability that the Berger code does, but with fewer check bits. It requires exactly r extra bits for a 2^r data word. Bose codes are generated according to the following rules:

If the number of zeros in the data word is 0 or 2^r, then complement the first 2^{r-1} data bits and append $2^{r-1} -1$ in the check bit locations.

If the number of zeros in the data word is between 2^{r-1} and $2^r -1$, then append the binary representation of this number (as in Berger codes).

If the number of zeros is between 1 and $2^{r-1} -1$, append this number minus one as a check symbol.

Table 1.4 shows an example for constructing Bose code with 4 data bits.

Table 1.4: An example Bose code with 4 data bits.

Data word	Check bits	Codeword
0000	01	110001
0001	11	000111
0010	11	001011
0011	10	001110
0100	11	010011
0101	10	010110
0110	10	011010
0111	00	011100
1000	11	100011
1001	10	100110
1010	10	101010
1011	00	101100
1100	10	110010
1101	00	110100
1110	00	111000
1111	01	001101

1.2.3.2 *Error Correcting Codes*

In this section, we discuss a number of error correcting codes. These are codes that have the ability not only to detect the existence of a fault, but they have also the ability to locate the errors and hence allow for correcting these errors.

Hamming Codes

Hamming codes are the earliest linear error correcting codes. They consist of "k" data bits and "r" check bits such that $k = 2^r - r - 1$, $n = 2^r - 1$, $r \geq 3$. Hamming codes are usually referred to as Hamming (n, k) codes. Thus, for r = 3, we have the Hamming (7,4) code. Hamming codes can be used to correct single errors or detect double errors but not both simultaneously.

The parity checker matrix, *H*, for the Hamming code can be formed by filling the columns of the *P* matrix with all the nonzero binary combinations that do not appear in the columns of the neighboring identity matrix. For example, for Hamming (7,4), the following binary combinations are used for the identity matrix (001,010,100), which leaves us with the following combinations that can be put in any order in the *P* matrix (011,101,110,111). Thus, the parity checker matrix may appear as shown below.

$$H = \begin{pmatrix} 1 & 0 & 0 & 1 & 1 & 0 & 1 \\ 0 & 1 & 0 & 1 & 0 & 1 & 1 \\ 0 & 0 & 1 & 0 & 1 & 1 & 1 \end{pmatrix}$$

Given the forms of the *generator matrix* G and the H matrix, we can construct the *G* matrix by mapping the identity matrix and the *P* matrix to their correct positions (in the *H* matrix, the *P* matrix is transposed):

$$G = \begin{pmatrix} 1 & 1 & 0 & 1 & 0 & 0 & 0 \\ 1 & 0 & 1 & 0 & 1 & 0 & 0 \\ 0 & 1 & 1 & 0 & 0 & 1 & 0 \\ 1 & 1 & 1 & 0 & 0 & 0 & 1 \end{pmatrix}$$

Now, to encode a message, we multiply the message by the generator matrix. To decode the received message, we multiply the received vector by the transpose of the parity check matrix. If the syndrome is zero, then the received vector is assumed correct, otherwise the syndrome will be used to access a table containing the error vectors.

Example: The following steps show the encoding and decoding of a message according to the Hamming code.

$$\vec{m} = (0011)$$

$$\vec{c} = \vec{m}G = \begin{pmatrix} 0 & 0 & 1 & 1 \end{pmatrix} \begin{pmatrix} 1 & 1 & 0 & 1 & 0 & 0 & 0 \\ 1 & 0 & 1 & 0 & 1 & 0 & 0 \\ 0 & 1 & 1 & 0 & 0 & 1 & 0 \\ 1 & 1 & 1 & 0 & 0 & 0 & 1 \end{pmatrix} = \begin{pmatrix} 1 & 0 & 0 & 0 & 0 & 1 & 1 \end{pmatrix}$$

To decode:

$$\vec{c} = (1000011)$$

$$\vec{s} = \vec{c}H^T = \begin{pmatrix} 1 & 0 & 0 & 0 & 0 & 1 & 1 \end{pmatrix} \begin{pmatrix} 1 & 0 & 0 \\ 0 & 1 & 0 \\ 0 & 0 & 1 \\ 1 & 1 & 0 \\ 1 & 0 & 1 \\ 0 & 1 & 1 \\ 1 & 1 & 1 \end{pmatrix} = \begin{pmatrix} 0 & 0 & 0 \end{pmatrix}$$

Since the syndrome is zero, the codeword is accepted as valid. If, however, an error occurred, say, the received message was (1010011), then we would get a nonzero syndrome as shown below.

$$\vec{c} = (1010011)$$

$$\vec{s} = \vec{c}H^T = \begin{pmatrix} 1 & 0 & 1 & 0 & 0 & 1 & 1 \end{pmatrix} \begin{pmatrix} 1 & 0 & 0 \\ 0 & 1 & 0 \\ 0 & 0 & 1 \\ 1 & 1 & 0 \\ 1 & 0 & 1 \\ 0 & 1 & 1 \\ 1 & 1 & 1 \end{pmatrix} = \begin{pmatrix} 0 & 0 & 1 \end{pmatrix}$$

This syndrome is used to index a table that will output an error vector. This vector is added to the received message to get the corrected message. To construct the syndrome table, we note that an error in a certain column in the received message correspond to adding the corresponding row in H^T. The Syndrome Table for the Hamming code is shown in Table 1.5.

Table 1.5: Syndrome Table for Hamming code.

Error vector	Syndrome
1000000	100
0100000	010
0010000	001
0001000	110
0000100	101
0000010	011
0000001	111

1.2.3.3 *SEC-DED Codes*

The Hamming codes discussed above can correct a single error or detect double errors, but not both simultaneously. Although it is quite useful in cases where only a single error is of significant probability, it does carry the hazard of miscorrecting double errors. To solve this, we may introduce an extra parity bit. This parity bit will change the appearance of the *H* matrix and the *G* matrix. This extra parity bit will be appended to the beginning of the codeword. For a Hamming (7,4) code, the *H* matrix would become as shown below.

$$H = \begin{pmatrix} 0 & 1 & 0 & 0 & 1 & 1 & 0 & 1 \\ 0 & 0 & 1 & 0 & 1 & 0 & 1 & 1 \\ 0 & 0 & 0 & 1 & 0 & 1 & 1 & 1 \\ 1 & 1 & 1 & 1 & 1 & 1 & 1 & 1 \end{pmatrix}$$

As can be seen, we added the first column and the last row to the original *H* matrix. When we perform the decoding, we transpose *H* and the first column becomes the first row. Thus, the first three columns of the syndrome will not be affected by the parity bit. The final column consists of all 1's. This means that now an entire parity check bit will be appended to the syndrome. The parity bit depends on all data bits and parity bits. Thus, it cannot be part of the *G* matrix but rather has to be appended manually after performing a regular Hamming encoding.

To perform the decoding of SEC-DED Hamming codes, we separate the resulting syndrome into the regular Hamming syndrome (s), and the parity check bit (p). Decoding then takes place as shown below.

If $p = 0$ and $\vec{s} = 0$, then no errors have occurred.

If $p = 1$, a single error occurred and we can correct it as shown previously.

If $p = 0$ and $\vec{s} \neq 0$, then a double error have occurred and is not correctable.

Using the SEC-DED codes, we are guaranteed that a double error will not be miscorrected but will rather be just reported as a double error. This is very useful in cases where double errors are not too probable but nevertheless have some significant probability.

Cyclic Codes

The second class of codes we will discuss is the cyclic codes. These are linear codes with an added property. The added property is that a rotation of any valid codeword is also a valid codeword. For example, (000000000, 110110110, 011011011, 101101101) is a valid cyclic code, since it is linear and the rotation criteria holds. This property facilitates the design of decoder circuits.

Cyclic codes can be constructed using the same matrix method that was used for Hamming codes. A closer look at the G matrix format will reveal that each row of the G matrix represents a valid codeword, and that all code words are made of combinations of these rows. Thus, if the rows of the generator matrix are rotations of a certain vector, then any combination of these rows can be expressed as rotations of a different combination of rows. The general structure of the G matrix in this case will become as shown below.

$$G = \begin{pmatrix} g_0 & g_1 & \cdot & \cdot & \cdot & g_{n-k} & 0 & 0 & 0 \\ 0 & g_0 & g_1 & \cdot & \cdot & \cdot & g_{n-k} & 0 & 0 \\ \cdot & \cdot & \cdot & \cdot & \cdot & \cdot & \cdot & \cdot & \cdot \\ \cdot & \cdot & \cdot & \cdot & \cdot & \cdot & \cdot & \cdot & \cdot \\ \cdot & \cdot & \cdot & \cdot & \cdot & \cdot & \cdot & \cdot & \cdot \\ \cdot & \cdot & \cdot & \cdot & \cdot & \cdot & \cdot & \cdot & \cdot \\ 0 & 0 & 0 & 0 & g_0 & g_1 & \cdot & \cdot & g_{n-k} \end{pmatrix}$$

Thus, the characteristics of the G matrix are all encapsulated in the vector $g_0 g_1 \ldots g_{n-k}$. If we represent this vector and the message vector as polynomials, then a very efficient means of representing cyclic codes can be used.

Polynomial Representation of Binary Vectors

We can represent any binary vector by a polynomial of a degree less than the number of bits of the vector by 1. In this polynomial $f(x)$, each term gets as its weight a digit from the binary vector, with the highest power term getting its weight from the most significant bit of the binary vector, e.g., $(11001) = x^4 + x^3 + 1$ and $(00111) = x^2 + x + 1$. As in the GF(2) arithmetic, addition can be performed as $x^a \pm x^a = 0$. The following two examples illustrate the multiplication and division of polynomials.

$$A = (11001) = x^4 + x^3 + 1 \text{ and } B = (00111) = x^2 + x + 1$$

$$A * B = (x^4 + x^3 + 1)(x^2 + x + 1) = x^6 + x^5 + x^2 + x^5 + x^4 + x + x^4 + x^3 + 1$$

$$= x^6 + x^3 + x^2 + x + 1$$

$$
A/B = x^2 + x + 1 \overline{\smash{)}\, x^4 + x^3 + 1} \quad \overset{\textstyle x^2 + 1}{}
$$

$$\underline{x^4 + x^3 + x^2}$$

$$x^2 + 1$$

$$\underline{x^2 + x + 1}$$

$$x$$

$$\Rightarrow A = (x^2 + 1)B + x$$

The idea of cyclic coding involves adding redundancy to the original data vector by multiplying it with the polynomial whose coefficients are $g_0 g_1 \ldots g_{n-k}$ (discussed earlier). This polynomial is known as the *generator polynomial* and has degree $r = k\text{-}n$. The product constitutes the codeword and has exactly n bits (with the polynomial representing it having power less than or equal n-1).

If we suppose that the generator polynomial $g(x)$ is a factor of $x^n + 1$. In this case $x^n + 1 = g(x)h(x)$. If this criterion is met, then we can mathematically express the encoding and decoding process of the cyclic code as follows:

To encode a message $m(x)$ into a codeword $c(x)$, we multiply the two polynomials:

$$c(x) = m(x)g(x)$$

To decode a codeword $c(x)$, we divide the two polynomials:

$$m'(x) = c(x)/g(x)$$

Since the decoded message may differ from the original message, we need some means of error checking. Consider the following modulo multiplication result for a valid codeword:

$$c(x)h(x)\bmod(x^n+1) = m(x)g(x)h(x)\bmod(x^n+1)$$
$$= m(x)(x^n+1)\bmod(x^n+1) = 0$$

However, if the codeword is invalid, then one can express the codeword as $c'(x) = c(x) + e(x)$, where $e(x)$ is an error vector. In this case, the modulo multiplication becomes:

$$c'(x)h(x)\bmod(x^n+1) = c(x)h(x)\bmod(x^n+1) + e(x)h(x)\bmod(x^n+1)$$
$$= e(x)h(x)\bmod(x^n+1)$$

The significance of this result is that the resulting quantity depends only on the error vector and can be thus taken as a syndrome for error correction. The syndrome can then be used to address a lookup table which will reveal the error vector. This method is quite general and can be used in any cyclic code. In the following section, we will look at a more specific case of cyclic code implementation, namely, the *systematic cyclic codes*.

Generating and Decoding Systematic Cyclic Codes

It is useful to generate a separable version of the cyclic codes. This can be accomplished if we insert parity bits according to some rules such that the resulting codeword maintains its cyclic characteristic. If we agree to append the parity bits at the least significant positions instead of the most significant, then we can get a systematic cyclic code by setting:

$$c(x) = x^r m(x) + x^r m(x)\bmod g(x)$$

The first term is nothing more than a shift by r bits to accommodate the parity bits. The actual parity bits are the ones represented by $x^r m(x)\bmod g(x)$. Note that the encoding here is different from the general case where we multiply by the generating polynomial. In this case, we construct the parity bits by dividing the shifted message by the generating polynomial and appending the remainder to the message. This division can be realized in hardware by the divider circuit shown in Fig. 1.6.

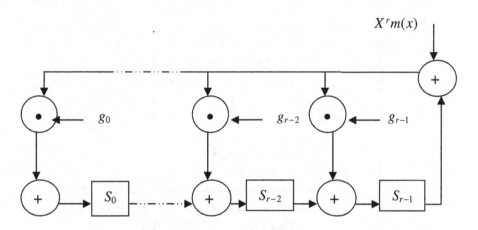

Fig. 1.6: Divider circuit.

In this circuit, the shifted message is passed through the circuit. If the shifted message enters MSB first, then after k steps, the remainder can be taken in parallel from the intermediate latches. The encoded message can be constructed by appending these parity bits to the original message.

The syndrome for this encoding is calculated by dividing a shifted version of the codeword by the generating polynomial. For a valid codeword, this translates mathematically to:

$$x^r c(x) \bmod g(x) = \left[x^r \bmod g(x) \right] \left[x^r m(x) \bmod g(x) + x^r m(x) \bmod g(x) \right]$$
$$= 0$$

For an invalid codeword, the resulting syndrome will be:

$$s(x) = x^r c'(x) \bmod g(x) = x^r (c(x) + e(x)) \bmod g(x) = x^r e(x) \bmod g(x)$$

which depends only on the error vector, as in the general non-separable case. Each error vector will have a syndrome associated with it. Thus, a hardware design for the decoder would be possible using a division circuit and a syndrome lookup table. A block diagram of such a design is shown in Fig. 1.7.

$X^rV(x)$

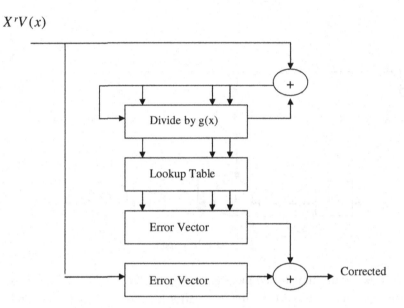

Fig. 1.7: Decoding circuit for systematic cyclic code.

1.2.3.4 *CRC Codes*

The CRC (Cyclic Redundancy Check) codes are cyclic codes that lack error correction capability but can be used to detect errors. They are often used as complementary circuits for other error correcting circuits. They are mainly used to detect miscorrections of the decoder, as was pointed out previously.

CRC codes are used extensively in microcomputer systems. They are used to detect errors in floppy disks and compact disks. Selecting a certain CRC code requires selecting a generator polynomial. CRC polynomials are usually selected from a family of polynomials called *primitive polynomials.* A primitive polynomial is any polynomial g(x) of degree r-1 that satisfies the following two conditions:

$$g(x)\mod(x^{2^{r-1}}-1)=0$$

$$g(x)\mod(x^m-1)\neq 0,\ m<2^{r-1}-1$$

There are various standard CRC polynomials that have been tested to achieve a high error detection capability. These standards are issued by organizations such as IEEE and are adopted by manufacturers for different types of communication media and devices. Table 1.6 shows some of the standard CRC polynomials.

Table 1.6: Some standard CRC polynomials.

Name	Max block length	Degree	Polynomial (in octal)
CRC-24	1023	24	140050401
CRC-32A	1023	32	50020114342
CRC-12	2047	12	14017
CRC-SDLC	16383	16	320227

From: Applied Coding and Information Theory for Engineers, Richard Wells.

1.2.3.5 *Convolution Codes*

Convolution codes differ greatly from the previous encoding methods, perhaps not in the mechanism and implementation but definitely in the use. In all previous cases, the encoder would take blocks of data (of length k) and add some redundancy to it. Convolution codes, however, can work on streams of data of different lengths. This is useful when we would like a high code rate (k/n) and would also like good error correcting capability. For this reason, convolution codes are generally used in noisy channels with high error rates. Convolution codes are implemented using shift registers that are arranged such as to form a finite impulse response (FIR) circuit. FIR circuits (or channels) have a finite response to a single input. This is unlike IIR (infinite impulse response) channels, that have an infinite memory of a single input.

FIR circuits can be constructed using shift registers. Convolution codes use these FIR circuits to add a certain amount of redundancy to the input. An example of a convolution encoder is shown in Fig. 1.8.

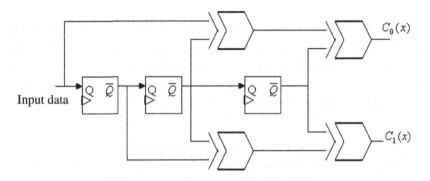

Fig. 1.8: An example of a convolution encoder.

In this figure, the input data stream passes through the register stages shown. The two outputs are interleaved in a certain way and sent. In this case, for each input bit there are two output bits, one coming from $c_0(x)$ and the other one from $c_1(x)$. The code ratio for this encoder (k/n), however, is slightly below the expected 0.5 ratio. This is because we need to flush out the contents of the registers when we are done encoding a certain length of data stream (called a frame). The extra bits from the registers are also sent with the code, lowering the code ratio. For this reason, it is good to choose high values for the frame length such that the overhead of sending the flushed values is minimal.

Following is an example of encoding a data stream using the convolution encoder of Fig. 1.8.

Example 7: We want to send the following data stream (1001101) using the encoder of Fig. 1.8. We will denote the values on the flip flops by S_0, S_1 and S_2. The following equations and table can be used to determine the outputs $c_0(x)$ and $c_1(x)$:

$S_0^+ = input$

$S_1^+ = S_0$

$S_2^+ = S_1$

$c_0 = S_1 + S_2 + input$

$c_1 = S_0 + S_1 + S_2$

Time	Input	S_0	S_1	S_2	C_0	C_1
0	?	0	0	0	0	0
1	1	1	0	0	1	0
2	0	0	1	0	0	1
3	1	1	0	1	0	1
4	1	1	1	0	0	0
5	0	0	1	1	1	0
6	0	0	0	1	0	0
7	1	1	0	0	0	1
8	0	0	1	0	0	1
9	0	0	0	1	1	1
10	0	0	0	0	1	1

The three final inputs are not part of the data but are deliberately inserted to flush the contents of the shift register. If the output is interleaved such that the bit from c_0 is sent first, then the output stream would look like this: (10010100100001011111). The code ratio is: 7/20 $= 0.35 < 0.5$

1.2.4 *Time Redundancy*

Time redundancy refers to the repetition of a given computation a number of times and a comparison of the results to determine if a discrepancy exists. The existence of a discrepancy between subsequent computations indicates the existence of transient or intermittent faults. The basic scheme used is shown in Fig. 1.9.

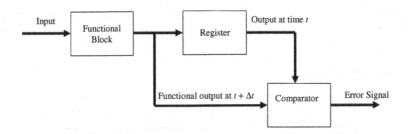

Fig. 1.9: Time redundancy basic scheme.

In this scheme, all intermittent and transient fault occurring in either of the computation steps at times t and $t + \Delta t$, but not both, can be detected. No permanent faults can be detected.

1.2.4.1 *Permanent Error Detection with Time Redundancy*

A similar arrangement can be used to detect permanent faults in a functional bock. Consider, for example, the arrangement shown in Fig. 1.10. According to this arrangement, the computation using the input data is first performed at time t. The results of this computation is then stored in a register. The same data is used to repeat the computation, using the same functional block at time $t + \Delta t$. However, this time the input data is first encoded in some way. The results of the computation is then decoded and the results are compared to the results produced before. Any discrepancy will indicate a permanent fault in the functional block.

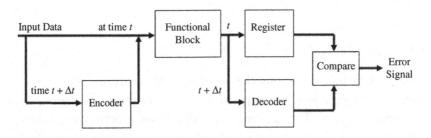

Fig. 1.10: Permanent fault detection scheme.

Assume that the input data is called x, the functional computation is called F, the encoding is called E, and the decoding is called D, then given that there is no permanent fault in the functional block, we can write the following relation $D(F(E(x))) = F(x) \; \forall \; x$. If D and E are properly chosen such that a failure in F will effect $F(x)$ and $F(E(x))$ differently, thus making the output of time and at time $t + \Delta t$ not equal, then an error signal will be produced. The above condition requires the following to be true: $D(E(x)) = x$, i.e. D and E are inverse of each other. Consider, for example, the case whereby the encoding of the input data is just the complementation of the input and that the decoding is just the complementation of the output from the functional block, i.e., $\overline{F(\overline{x})} = F(x)$. This arrangement is shown in Fig. 1.11.

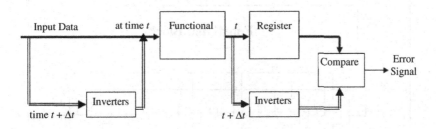

Fig. 1.11: Example encoding/decoding.

The above mentioned property is that of what is known as *self-dual function*. Using this property, it can be seen that for a self-dual function, the application of the input x will produce an output that is the complement of the output produced if this input is followed by the complement, i.e., $\overline{x}$. Therefore, if the output of the functional block in response to an input x is 1(0), then the output of the same functional block in response to an input $\overline{x}$ will be 0(1). This is called *alternating logic*. In order to be able to detect the existence of a permanent fault in a functional block that is self-dual using alternating logic is to try to find at least one input combination for which the fault will not produce alternating output.

The above discussion shows that it is possible to detect the existence of a permanent fault using alternating logic only if the function realized by the functional block under test possesses the self-duality property. It is, however, possible to generalize this observation to include those non-self-dual function. This is because of the following general observation: any non-self dual function of n variables can be converted into a function of n + 1 variable that is self dual and therefore can be realized by an alternating logic circuit.

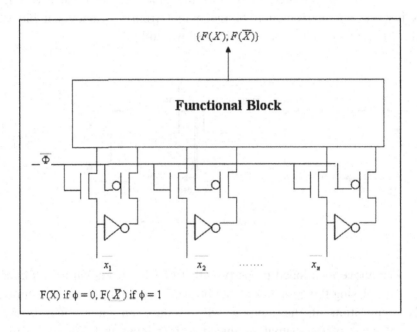

Fig. 1.12: A possible scheme for alternating logic.

The scheme shown in Fig. 1.12 indicates that if the control input $\Phi = 0$ then the functional block will compute F(X), while if $\Phi = 1$ then the functional block will compute $F(\overline{X})$ instead.

Recomputing with Shifted Operands (RESO)

This method uses the basic time redundancy techniques discussed above in achieving concurrent fault detection in arithmetic logic units (ALUs). In this case, shift operations are used as the encoding functions. For example, a shift left operation can be used as the encoding function while a shift right operation can be used as the decoding function. Figure 1.13 shows an illustration of an ALU designed to allow such encoding/decoding to be realized.

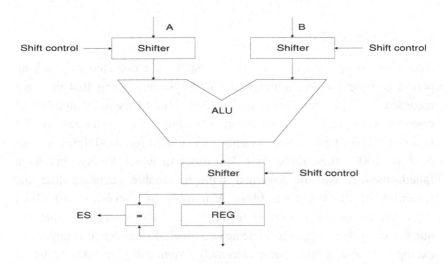

Fig. 1.13: RESO in an ALU.

It should be noted that RESO technique assumes bit-slice organization of the ALU.

1.3 Reliability Modeling and Evaluation

Reliability modeling aims at using abstract representation of systems as means for assessing their reliability. Two basic techniques have been used. These are the empirical and the analytical techniques (see Fig. 1.14).

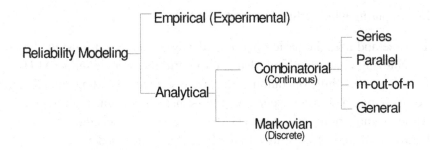

Fig. 1.14: Reliability modeling.

1.3.1 *Empirical Models*

According to this model, a set of N systems are operated over a long period of time and the number of failed systems during that time are recorded. The percentage of the failed system to the total number of operated systems, N, is used as an indication of the reliability of the systems. For example, if the systems are operated for 1000 times and out of those 1000 times, there were 100 times in which the systems have failed, then it will be assumed with reasonable accuracy that the reliability of the system is 90%. A number of concerns exist about the accuracy of the empirical model. One such concerns is that the number of systems required to achieve a level of confidence is large. For example, it would have been extremely expensive if a 1000 on-board processing systems of the space shuttle has to be built such that the reliability could be experimentally determined. In addition, the time required for the experiment may be too long to afford. For example, using the exponential failure rate for a system with reliability of 0.97 will mean a failure rate of approximately, $\lambda = 10^{-8}$ failures per unit time.

1.3.2 *The Analytical Technique*

The analytical model is based on the use of the probability of failure of individual components of a given system in order to arrive at a measure for the probability of failure of the overall system. The overall failure probability of a system will depend not only on the individual failure probability of its individual components but also on the way these components are interconnected in order to form the overall system. Two techniques exist for computing a system reliability according to the analytical technique. These are the *Combinatorial* (Continuous) and the Markov (Discrete) models. These are discussed below.

(1) Combinatorial (Continuous) Model

According to this technique, the number of ways in which a system can continue to operate, given the probability of failure of its individual components, is enumerated. A number of models exist for the interconnection among the system's components. These are summarized in Table 1.7. Shown also in the table are the corresponding expression of system reliability $R(t)$ in terms of the reliability of the individual components of the system.

Table 1.7: Reliability models.

Technique	Reliability equation
1. Series	$R_{series}(t) = \displaystyle\prod_{i=1}^{N} R_i$
2. Parallel	$R_{parallel}(t) = 1 - \displaystyle\prod_{i=1}^{N}(1-R_i)$
3. Series/Parallel	$R_{sp}(t) = \displaystyle\prod_{i=1}^{N} R_{parallel_i}$ $R_{parallel_i}$ is the reliability of the ith group
4. Parallel/Series	$R_{ps}(t) = 1 - \displaystyle\prod_{i=1}^{N}(1 - R_{series_i})$ R_{series_i} is the reliability of the ith group
5. M out of N	$R_{MoN} = \displaystyle\sum_{i=0}^{N-M}\binom{N}{i}(1-R)^i * R^{N-i}$
6. Exact	$P_{system} = (P_{system}|A)P_A + (P_{system}|\bar{A})(1-P_A)$
7. Approximate	$R_{system} \leq 1 - \displaystyle\prod_{i=1}^{n}(1 - R_{path_i})$ n is the number of paths from input to output

In modeling systems according to the combinatorial model, a reliability block diagram (RBD) is formed. The RBD shows the connection among the system's components from the reliability point of view (as opposed to the functionality view point).

We provide some more details on the model presented under exact above. This model is extremely useful in modeling complex systems by de-synthesizing them into simpler ones. The theorem according to which such model is formed is called *Bay's Theorem*. The theorem states that for a given system consisting of 2 or more modules, select one module (any module) and call it module *A*. Two mutually exclusive events occur. These are

1. The system with *A* working ($P_{system}|A$)
2. The system with *A* not working ($P_{system}|\bar{A}$)

The probability of the system working P_{system} can then be expressed as shown in the table above, i.e., $P_{system} = (P_{system}|A)P_A + (P_{system}|\bar{A})(1-P_A)$, where P_A is the probability that module A is working while $(1-P_A)$ is the probability that module A is not working. The following example illustrates the use of the theorem.

Example 8: Consider the RBD shown in Fig. 1.15. It is required to compute the overall relaibility of the system in terms of the reliability of its individual components using the Bay's theorem. In the given RBD, we can choose module 5 as module *A* and redraw the RBD under the two conditions

1. The system with A working
2. The system with A not working

The relaibility of each of the resulted sub-systems can now be computed as follows.

$R_{A\ is\ OK} = [1-(1-R1)(1-R2)][1-(1-R3)(1-R4)]R5$
$R_{A\ is\ Faulty} = [1-(1-R1*R3)(1-R2*R4)](1-R5)$

One of the main versatility of Bay's theorem is that it can be applied recursively to each of the sub systems, if needed be.

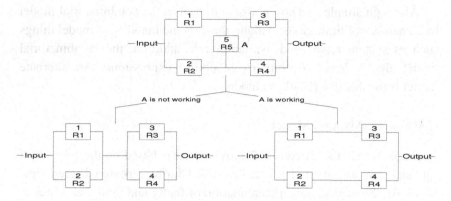

Fig. 1.15: Example RBD for applying Bay's theorem.

An approximate model

The approximate model provides an upper bound on the reliability of a given system in terms of the reliability of its components. The model assumes that the system consists of parallel paths from input to output and computes the relaiblity using the parallel model. Consider, for example, the reliability block diagram (RBD) shown in Fig. 1.15. The approximate (upper bound)reliability between the input and the output of the system represented by this RBD can be computed assuming that there exists four (parallel) paths as folows:

Path #1: consisting of components 1 and 3.
Path #2: consisting of components 1, 5, and 4.
Path #3: consisting of components 2 and 4.
Path #4: consisting of components 2, 5, and 3.

Therefore, the approximate (upper bound) reliability between the input and the output of the system is computed as

$$R \leq 1 - \prod_{i=1}^{4}(1 - R_{path_i}) \leq 1 - (1 - R_1 R_3)(1 - R_1 R_5 R_4)(1 - R_2 R_4)(1 - R_2 R_5 R_3)$$

Although simple and straightforward to use, the combinatorial model has a number of limitations. Among these, is the inability to model things such as system repair and availability. In addition, the combinatorial model always leads to complex relaibility expressions. An alternate model is the discrete (Markov) model.

(2) Discrete (Markov) Model

In simple terms, the discrete (Markov) model is based on the concept of sate and state transition. These are recorded during repeated discrete time slices, Δt. System state is a combination of faulty and fault-free states of its components. State transition shows the changes in the system's state as time progresses. Consider, for example, the case of a system consisting of a single module (component), as shown in Fig. 1.16. At any given time, the module can exists in one of two states, i.e., Fault-free or Faulty. We can draw a state diagram for that module as follows.

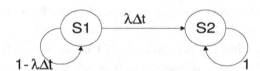

Fig. 1.16: A single component system states with no repair.

In that state diagram, circles represent states and arcs represent state transitions. State S1 represents the fault-free state while state S2 represents the faulty state. The failure rate of the module is assumed to be λ. The versatility of the discrete model becomes clear if we assume the case of having repair (with repair rate μ) for the same single module system. In this case, the state transition diagram will become as shown in Fig. 1.17.

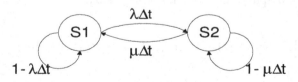

Fig. 1.17: A single component system states with repair.

It is now possible to write probability equations relating the state of the system at a given time t and that at a subsequent time $t + \Delta t$. These are shown below.

$$P_1(t+\Delta t) = (1-\lambda\Delta t)*P_1(t)+\mu\Delta t*P_2(t)$$
$$P_2(t+\Delta t) = \lambda\Delta t*P_1(t)+(1-\mu\Delta t)*P_2(t)$$

Writing this in a matrix form will result the following.

$$\begin{bmatrix} P_1(t+\Delta t) \\ P_2(t+\Delta t) \end{bmatrix} = \begin{bmatrix} 1-\lambda\Delta t & \mu\Delta t \\ \lambda\Delta t & 1-\mu\Delta t \end{bmatrix} \begin{bmatrix} P_1(t) \\ P_2(t) \end{bmatrix}$$

or simply $\underline{P}(t+\Delta t) = \underline{A}* \underline{P}(t)$, where $\underline{A}$ is called the state transition matrix. This matrix form can be used to compute the probability of the system existing in a given state at any time. For example, $\underline{P}(0+\Delta t) = \underline{A}*\underline{P}(0)$, where $\underline{P}(0)$ is the initial state of the system. Similarly, $\underline{P}(2\Delta t) = \underline{A}*\underline{P}(\Delta t) = \underline{A}* \underline{A} *\underline{P}(0) = \underline{A}^2 *\underline{P}(0)$. In general $\underline{P}(n\Delta t) = \Delta t) = \underline{A}^n *\underline{P}(0)$.

Example

Consider the case of a TMR. The state diagram is shown in Fig. 1.18 (assuming that $X = \lambda\Delta t$).

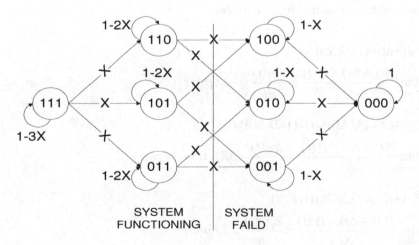

SYSTEM FUNCTIONING | SYSTEM FAILD

Fig. 1.18: TMR state diagram.

This can be reduced to 3 states as follows:

S3: State whereby three modules are working
S2: State whereby two module are working
SF: State whereby 1 or 0 module is working (Failure state)

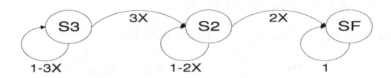

Writing the probability equation in the matrix form will result in the following.

$$\begin{bmatrix} P_3(t+\Delta t) \\ P_2(t+\Delta t) \\ P_F(t+\Delta t) \end{bmatrix} = \begin{bmatrix} 1-3X & 0 & 0 \\ 3X & 1-2X & 0 \\ 0 & 2X & 1 \end{bmatrix} \begin{bmatrix} P_3(t) \\ P_2(t) \\ P_F(t) \end{bmatrix} \text{ and } \underline{P}(0) = \begin{bmatrix} 1 \\ 0 \\ 0 \end{bmatrix}$$

It should be noted that the shorter the Δt period, the accurate the model. The case whereby $\Delta t = 0$ leads to the continuous model. Consider, for example the case of the TMR. The following mathematical treatment shows how to obtain the reliability equations starting from those obtain from the discrete model.

P$_3$(t+Δt)=(1-3$\lambda\Delta$t)P$_3$(t)

$$\lim_{\Delta t \to 0} \frac{P_3(t+\Delta t) - P_3(t)}{\Delta t} = \frac{dp_3(t)}{dt} = -3\lambda p_3(t)$$

P$_2$(t+Δt)=(3$\lambda\Delta$t)P$_3$(t)+(1-2$\lambda\Delta$t)P$_2$(t)

$$\lim_{\Delta t \to 0} \frac{P_2(t+\Delta t) - P_2(t)}{\Delta t} = \frac{dp_2(t)}{dt} = 3\lambda p_3(t) - 2\lambda p_2(t)$$

P$_F$(t+Δt)=(2$\lambda\Delta$t)P$_2$(t)+P$_F$(t)

$$\lim_{\Delta t \to 0} \frac{P_F(t+\Delta t) - P_F(t)}{\Delta t} = \frac{dp_F(t)}{dt} = 2\lambda p_2(t)$$

The above three simultaneous partial differential equations can be solved using *Laplace* and the inverse *Laplace* transforms as follows.

$S*P_3(S)-P_3(0) = -3\lambda*P_3(S)$, i.e., $P_3(S)=1/(S+3\lambda)$ and $P_3(t) = e^{-3\lambda t}$

$S*P_2(S)-P_2(0) = 3\lambda*P_3(S) -2\lambda*P_2(S)$, i.e., $P_2(t) = 3e^{-2\lambda t} -3e^{-3\lambda t}$

$S*P_F(S)-P_F(0) = 2\lambda*P_2(S)$, i.e., $P_F(t) =1-3e^{-2\lambda t} +2e^{-3\lambda t}$

$P_{TMR} = 1-P_F = 1-(1-3e^{-2\lambda t} +2e^{-3\lambda t}) = 3e^{-2\lambda t} -2e^{-3\lambda t}$

This same result would have been obtained using the continuous model.

The versatility of the discrete model can be displayed by considering the effect of factors such as the fault coverage (FC), C. The FC is defined as the ratio of the number of faults that a diagnostic system can detect to the total number of possible faults occurring in a given module. The above discussion assumes that C = 1. However, if C < 1 then there will be some more states to be considered in the state transition diagram. These states correspond to the case(s) whereby the fault has occurred but was not detected. Consider, for example, the single module system with fault coverage C < 1. The new state transition diagram will become as shown below.

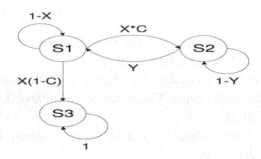

$X = \lambda\Delta t, Y = \mu\Delta t$

S1: The system is working

S2: The system is faulty, and the fault was detected by the diagnostic system

S3: The system is faulty, and the fault was not detected by the diagnostic system

The *availability* of the system can then be computed as the probability of being in S1 = $P_1(t)$. The *safety* of the system is the probability of being in S1 or S2 = $P_1(t)+P_2(t)$. The un-safety of the system is the probability of being in S3 = $P_3(t)$.

1.4 Summary

The main objective of this chapter has been to introduce the reader to the some of the fundamental concepts in fault tolerance and reliability analysis. In fulfilling this objective, we have introduced the main issues related to the design and analysis of fault-tolerant systems. We have also discussed different types of faults and their characterization. A detailed discussion on redundancy and its basics forms, i.e., hardware, software, time, and information has been conducted with illustrative examples. In addition, we have covered the fundamentals of reliability modeling and evaluation techniques. These include the combinatorial and the discrete (Markov) reliability modeling.

References

Books

[1] Pradhan, D. (Editor), Fault-Tolerant Computer System Design, Prentice-Hall PTR, New Jersey, 1996.
[2] Pradhan, D. and Avresky, D. (Editors), Fault-Tolerant Parallel and Distributed Systems, Computer Society Press, Los Alamitos, California, 1995.
[3] Jalote, P., Fault Tolerance in Distributed Systems, Prentice-Hall PTR, New Jersey, 1994.

Websites

[1] http://elib.uni-stuttgart.de/opus/volltexte/2000/616/pdf/Diss.pdf
[2] http://www.omg.org/news/meetings/workshops/presentations/embedded-rt2002/03-1_Garon-Narasimhan_FTTutorial-OMGWkshp-2002.pdf

[3] http://www.csee.wvu.edu/~katerina/Teaching/CS-757-Fall-2003/Fault-Tolerance.pdf

[4] http://www.cs.vu.nl/~ast/books/ds1/07.pdf

[5] http://www.ecs.soton.ac.uk/~lavm/papers/fta-europar2002.pdf

[6] http://wwwhome.cs.utwente.nl/~krol/publications-krol/proefschrift/ts1m.pdf

[7] http://www.idi.ntnu.no/~noervaag/IDI-TR-6-99/IDI-TR-6-99.pdf

[8] http://www.cin.ufpe.br/~prmm/wellington/00995536_wjs.pdf

[9] http://ii.pmf.ukim.edu.mk/ciit/2001/papers/2Ciit-24.pdf

Chapter 2

Fault Modeling, Simulation and Diagnosis

In this chapter, we consider the issues related to fault modeling, diagnosis, and simulation. The chapter begins with some introductory material related to fault modeling. We cover issues such as logical fault modeling, fault detection and redundancy, fault equivalence and dominance, and single stuck-at and multiple stuck-at faults. Our coverage then continues with a discussion on logic simulation and its different types. This is followed by a detailed discussion covering a number of fault simulation techniques, such as serial, parallel, deductive, concurrent and differential fault simulation. We also introduce a number of advanced fault simulation techniques, such as parallel pattern and critical path tracing. Our coverage ends with a discussion of the basic concepts related to fault sampling. Our coverage in this chapter concludes with a brief introduction to the issues related to fault diagnosis, such as combinational fault diagnosis, fault dictionary, fault location, and sequential fault diagnosis.

2.1 Fault Modeling

It has been indicated in Chapter 1 that faults are the manifestation of physical defects in the behavior of a component/system. Logical faults are therefore the abstraction (modeling) of the physical defects. Logical fault modeling lead to a number of benefits. These benefits include reducing complexity, since a number of physical defects can be modeled using the same logical fault; achieving technology-independent modeling, since one logical fault model could be applicable to a number of different technologies; and achieving abstraction, since logical fault

44

tests may be used for physical faults whose effect is not totally understood.

Logical faults can be categorized as explicit or implicit. Explicit faults may be enumerated while implicit faults cannot be enumerated but are identified by a number of given characterizing properties. Logical faults may also be categorized as structural or functional. Structural faults modify the interconnections among components (but not the functions of components), while functional faults modify the function(s) performed by components (but not the interconnection among them).

Modeling can be made at different levels (ranging from geometrical up to the functional levels) depending on a number of factors, such as cost and accuracy. The lower the level of modeling, the more computationally intensive the fault detection becomes but the more expensive the modeling is. Figure 2.1 shows a schematic of the different levels of fault modeling.

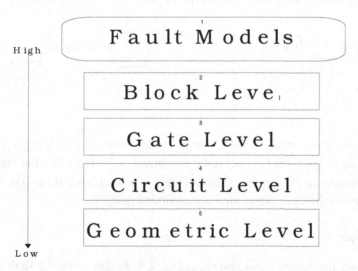

Fig. 2.1: Fault modeling levels.

Consider an *n-input* fault-free combinational circuit C whose output is F. It will be assumed that the presence of a fault f transforms C into a different circuit C_f with a new output realized function $F_f(x)$. This situation is shown in Fig. 2.2.

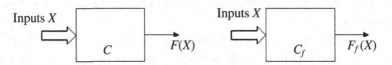

Fig. 2.2: Fault-free and faulty combinational circuits.

If t represents a specific input vector, called test vector, and $F(t)$ represents the response of C, then test vector t is said to detect fault f iff $F(t) \neq F_f(t)$.

Using a similar reasoning, consider an *n-input* fault-free sequential circuit *SC* with an initial state q and output sequence $F(X)$. It will be assumed that the presence of a fault f transforms *SC* into a different circuit SC_f with a new output sequence $F_f(X)$. This situation is shown in Fig. 2.3. The main difference between the case of a combinational and a sequential circuit is the need for a sequence of tests in the latter case as compared to a single test in the former case.

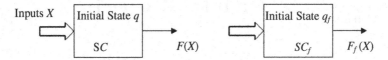

Fig. 2.3: Fault-free and faulty sequential circuits.

In a given circuit, a line whose value under test t changes in the presence of the fault f is said to be *sensitized* to the fault f by the test t. A path composed of sensitized lines is called a *sensitized path*. The test t propagates the fault effect along a sensitized path.

Example

Consider the logic circuit shown in Fig. 2.4. In this circuit, a fault $x/1$ is sensitized by the value 0 on line x. A test $t = 1011$ is simulated, both without and with the fault $x/1$. The results of the simulation are different in the two cases. The fault is detected since the output values in the two cases are different. A path from the faulty line x is sensitized (bold lines) to the primary output of the circuit.

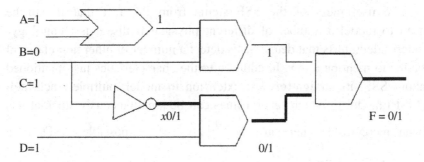

Fig. 2.4: Path sensitization.

There exists a number of structural fault models. These include the following.

Stuck-at fault model: In this case, a line l is assumed to be stuck at a fixed logic value v, $\bar{v} \in \{0,1\}$. Two stuck-at faults exists: a line l is stuck-at-1 ($l/1$ *or* l s-a-1) or line l is stuck-at-0 ($l/0$ or l s-a-0). A short between ground (s-a-0) or power (s-a-1) and a signal line are examples of stuck-at faults.

Bridging fault model: This represents the case of shorts between signal lines. A short between two signal lines can be modeled as the ANDing (ORing) of the functions realized by the lines depending on the technology used.

The Single Stuck-Fault model (SSF) is the *standard* or *traditional* fault model. It has been extensively used for modeling single stuck-at faults in digital circuits. If the number of possible SSF sites is n, then there are $2n$ possible SSFs. This is because each site can be s-a-0 or s-a-1. The number of sites in which SSF may occur can be computed using the following formulae.

$$n = \sum_{i=1}^{m} (1 + f_i - q_i)$$

$$q_i = \begin{cases} 1 & if \ f_i = 1 \\ 0 & if \ f_i > 1 \end{cases}$$

m = signal sources and f_i = fan-out count of signal s_i. For example, in Fig. 2.4, m = 9 and n = 11.

The usefulness of the SSF stems from the fact that it can be used to model a number of different physical faults; it is technology-independent; tests that detect SSFs detect a number of other non-classical faults; to mention a few. In addition to the characteristics just mentioned about SSF, its straightforward extension to model multiple stuck-fault (MSF) model in which several lines can be simultaneously stuck-at has been recognized. There are $\sum_{i=1}^{n} \binom{n}{i} \times 2^i = 3^n - 1$ possible MSFs in a circuit having n SSF sites.

A fault f is said to be detectable if there exists at least one test t that detects f, otherwise, f is an undetectable fault. It should be noted that the presence of an undetectable fault f may prevent the detection of another fault g, even then when there exists a test which detects the fault g.

Example

Consider the gate level circuit shown in Fig. 2.5. In this figure, the fault $b/1$ is undetectable. The test $t = 1101$ detects the fault $a/0$. However, in the presents of $b/1$, the test t is not any more able to detect the fault $a/0$.

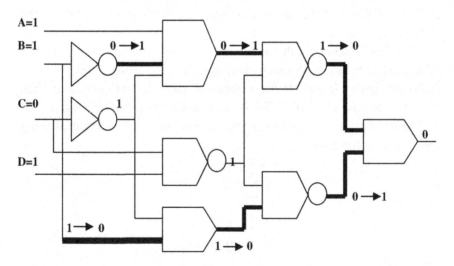

Fig. 2.5: Example gate level circuit.

Example

The test $T = \{1111, 0111, 1110, 1001, 1010, 0101\}$ detects every SSF in the circuit in Fig. 2.6. Let f be $b/1$ and g be $c/1$. The only test in T that detects the single faults f and g is 1001. However, the multiple fault $\{f, g\}$ is not detected because under the test vector 1001, f masks g and g masks f.

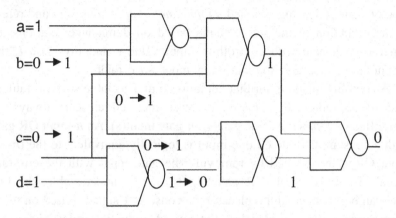

Fig. 2.6: Example gate level circuit.

Let T be the set of all tests that detect a fault f. We say that a fault g functionally *masks* fault f iff the multiple fault $\{g\&f\}$ is not detected by any test $t \in T$. Also, two faults f_i and f_j are said to be *equivalent* if every test that detects f_i also detects f_j and vice versa, i.e. the test sets of f_i and f_j are identical. The s-a-0 faults on the inputs and output of a 2-input AND gate are equivalent. In addition to fault masking and fault equivalence, there is the important issue of fault dominance. Let T_f be the set of all tests that detects a fault f. We say that a fault g *dominates* the fault f iff g and f are functionally equivalent under T_f. If fault g dominates fault f then the test t that detects f will also detect g. Fault dominance is important because by deriving a test to detect f we automatically obtain a test that detects g as well. One criterion for choosing a fault model is that of having its faults dominated by a number of other faults. This is because the test set for detecting the faults of the chosen model will also detect those other faults. The single stuck-at fault model (SSF) discussed above possesses such property.

Fault collapsing refers to the reduction of the set of faults need to be analyzed. Two types of fault collapsing. The first is called *Equivalence Fault Collapsing* and refers to the reduction in the set of faults based on equivalence relations. In general for a gate with a controlling input value c and inversion i, all input s-a-c faults and the output s-a-$(c \oplus i)$ are functionally equivalent. This makes the number of single stuck-at faults that need to be considered for an n-input gate to be (n + 2). The second type of fault collapsing is called *Dominance Fault Collapsing* and refers to the reduction in the set of faults based on dominance relations. In general for a gate with controlling input value c and inversion i, the output fault s-a-$(\overline{c} \oplus i)$ dominates any input s-a-$\overline{c}$ fault.

A combinational circuit that contains an undetectable stuck-at fault is said to be redundant. This is because such circuit can always be simplified *by removing* some gate(s) or gate input(s). An n-input OR gate with a constant 0 value on one input is logically equivalent to the $(n$-$1)$-input OR gate obtained by removing the gate input with the constant signal. Similarly, if an OR gate input s-a-1 is undetectable, the OR gate can be removed and replaced by a constant 1 signal. Based on these observations, we can develop the set of reduction rules shown in Table 2.1.

Table 2.1: Reduction rules for a number of basic logic gates.

Undetectable fault	Reduction rule
OR (NOR) input s-a-0	Remove input
OR (NOR) input s-a-1	Remove gate and replace by 1(0)
AND (NAND) input s-a-1	Remove input
AND (NAND) input s-a-0	Remove gate, replace by 0(1)

A number of other fault models exists in practice. These are Transistor Stuck-Open (Stuck-On) Faults, Functional Faults (Decoders, Multiplexers, Adders, RAMs, ROMs, Counters), Delay Faults (Gate Delay, Path Delay, etc.), Memory Faults (Parametric, Functional, Pattern Sensitive, Cell Coupling, etc.), PLA Faults (missing/extra transistor,

Cross-point, Break, Bridging, etc.), and State Transition Faults. Interested readers should consult one of the textbooks on fault modeling.

2.2 Fault Simulation

Fault simulation is the process of determining the fault coverage, either as fraction or as a percentage of the modeled faults detected by a given set of inputs (test vectors) as well as finding the set of undetected faults in the modeled circuit. A fault simulator accepts as inputs the circuit, a specified sequence of test vectors, and a fault model. Figure 2.7 shows the main components of a fault simulator.

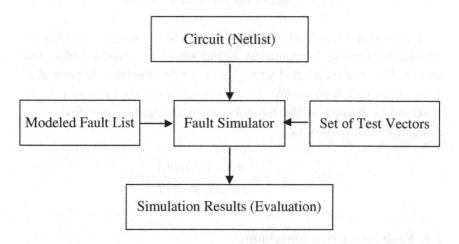

Fig. 2.7: Main components of a fault simulator.

The figure shows that a fault simulator requires as input the circuit description (netlist), the modeled fault list, and the set of test vectors. The output of a fault simulator consists of the fault coverage, defined as the ratio between the number of detected faults and the total number of simulated faults, and the set of undetected faults.

Logic level models for circuits are widely used as the circuit input to fault simulators. These can be enhanced with switch-level models for MOS circuits. The fault model used in majority of fault simulators is the single stuck-at model. This also can be enhanced using stuck-open and path delay in order to accommodate for transistor stuck-open and delay faults in MOS circuits.

The basic concept of fault simulation is shown in Fig. 2.8.

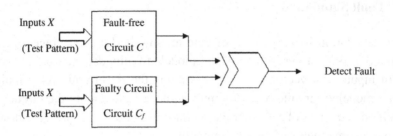

Fig. 2.8: Basic concept of fault simulation.

The output of a fault simulator is measured using a number of parameters. One such parameters is the set of undetected faults. The smaller the set of undetected faults, the better the simulator. In particular, a measure called *fault coverage* is used to measure such property. Fault coverage is defined as the fraction (or percentage) of modeled faults detected by test vectors, i.e.,

$$fault\ coverage = \frac{detected\ faults}{simulated\ faults}100\%$$

2.3 Fault Simulation Algorithms

In this section, we introduce a number of fault simulation algorithms. In particular, we cover issues related to the serial, parallel, deductive, concurrent, and differential simulators.

2.3.1 *Serial Fault Simulation Algorithm*

According to this technique, true-value simulation is performed across all vectors and outputs saved. Faulty circuits are simulated one-by-one by modifying the circuit and running true-value simulator. Simulation of a faulty circuit stops as soon as fault is detected.

Serial Algorithm in a Nutshell

According to this technique, the following steps are performed.

(a) Simulate fault-free circuit and save responses,
(b) Repeat the following steps for each fault on the fault list

b.1 Modify the net-list by injecting one fault,
b.2 Simulate modified net-list, (one vector at a time)
b.3 Compare obtained response with saved response,
b.4 In case of discrepancy, declare fault as detected and stop simulation; otherwise fault is declared as undetected.

The main advantages of the serial fault simulators are its simplicity and its ability to simulate most faults, including analog faults. The main disadvantage is the need for prohibitively long CPU time.

2.3.2 *Parallel Fault Simulation*

The main idea behind a parallel fault simulator is to take advantage of the available bit-parallelism in logical operations of a digital computer in processing computer words. For example, in a 64-bit word computer, it is possible to simulate up to 64 different copies of the simulated circuit, each bit can represent the status of a circuit such that if the circuit is fault-free, then the corresponding bit will be 1; otherwise the bit will be 0. In general, if the computer word size is N, then N-1 copies of faulty circuit are also generated. For a total of M faults in the circuit, $\lceil M/(N-1) \rceil$ simulation runs will be needed. It is therefore possible to consider that this type of simulators achieve a speedup of about N-1 over serial fault simulators.

Parallel fault simulators are most effective in simulating faults that are modeled using the stuck-at fault model, circuits consisting of only one type of gates, signals that assume a 0 or a 1 values, and when all gates have the same delay (zero or one unit). The disadvantages of this simulator are the inability to simulate accurate rise and fall delays of signals and the inability to simulate circuits with non-Boolean logic.

Example

Consider the circuit in Fig. 2.9. Assuming that a computer word consisting of 11 bits is available, then Table 2.2 shows an illustration of how parallel simulation is performed.

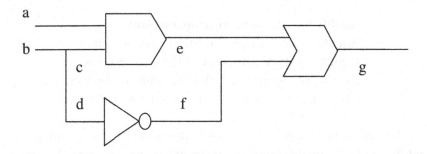

Fig. 2.9: Example of parallel fault simulation.

Table 2.2: Parallel fault simulation.

	FF	a/0	b/0	c/0	d/0	e/0	e/1	f/0	f/1	g/0	g/1
a=1	1	0	1	1	1	1	1	1	1	1	1
b=1	1	1	0	1	1	1	1	1	1	1	1
c=b	1	1	0	0	1	1	1	1	1	1	1
d=b	1	1	0	1	0	1	1	1	1	1	1
e=ab	1	0	0	1	1	0	1	1	1	1	1
$f=\bar{d}$	0	0	1	0	1	0	0	0	1	0	0
g=e+f	1	**0**	1	1	1	**0**	1	1	1	**0**	1

According to table, only the following faults are detectable: a/0, e/0, and g/0.

2.3.3 *Deductive Fault Simulation*

This type of simulators differ from the previous two types in the sense that only the fault free circuit is simulated. Faulty circuits are deduced from the fault-free one. The simulator processes all faults in a single pass using true-value simulation. This property makes the simulator to be extremely fast. It should, however, be noted that major modifications are required in order to be able to handle cases such as variable rise/fall delays and multiple signal states.

A vector is simulated in true-value mode. A deductive procedure is then performed on all lines in level-order from inputs to outputs. The fault list L_A is defined as the set containing the name (or index) of every fault that produces an error on line A when the circuit is in its current logic state. Fault lists are to be propagated from the primary inputs (*PIs*) to the (*POs*). A fault list is generated for each signal lines, and updated as necessary with every change in the logic state of the circuit. List events occur when a fault list changes. Instead of keeping all signal values, as in the Parallel Fault Simulation, only those bits that are different from the good (fault free) values are kept in deductive fault simulation. Figure 2.10 shows an illustration of fault list propagation in the case of a 2-input AND gate.

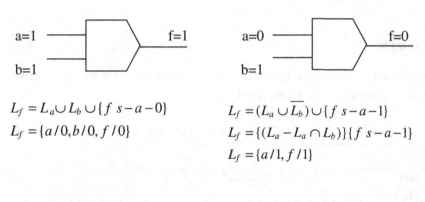

$$L_f = L_a \cup L_b \cup \{f\ s-a-0\}$$
$$L_f = \{a/0, b/0, f/0\}$$

$$L_f = (L_a \cup \overline{L_b}) \cup \{f\ s-a-1\}$$
$$L_f = \{(L_a - L_a \cap L_b)\}\{f\ s-a-1\}$$
$$L_f = \{a/1, f/1\}$$

$$L_f = L_a \cap L_b \cup \{f\ s-a-1\}$$

Fig. 2.10: Fault list propagation rules for 2-input AND gate.

Table 2.3 presents a list of the rules of fault list propagation assuming a number of logic gates.

Table 2.3: Fault list propagation rules.

Gate type	A	B	C	Output fault list
AND	0	0	0	$(L_a \cap L_b) \cup c_1$
	0	1	0	$(L_a \cap L_b) \cup c_1$
	1	0	0	$(L_a \cap L_b) \cup c_1$
	1	1	1	$(L_a \cup L_b) \cup c_0$
OR	0	0	0	$(L_a \cup L_b) \cup c_1$
	0	1	0	$(L_a \cap L_b) \cup c_0$
	1	0	0	$(L_a \cap L_b) \cup c_0$
	1	1	1	$(L_a \cap L_b) \cup c_0$
NOT	0	-	1	$(L_a \cup c_0$
	1	-	0	$(L_a \cup c_1$

Example

Figure 2.11 shows how to deduce the faults detected for the shown two input circuit under the given input test vector.

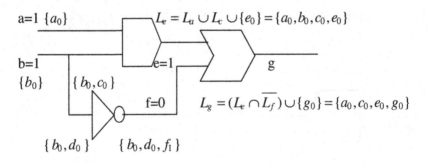

$$L_g = (L_e \cap \overline{L_f}) \cup \{g_0\} = \{a_0, c_0, e_0, g_0\}$$

Fig. 2.11: Example of deductive fault simulation.

2.3.4 *Concurrent Fault Simulation*

This technique extends the event-driven simulation method to simulation of faults. The main idea is that a fault is only simulated when it causes some lines to carry a different value than the corresponding one in the fault-free circuit. As in the deductive fault simulation, a fault list is associated with each element. An entry in the list contains the fault and the input-output value of the gate induced by the fault. An illustration is shown in Fig. 2.12. The process is illustrated in Table 2.4.

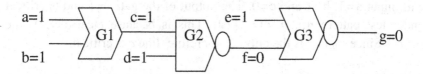

Fig. 2.12: Concurrent fault simulation example.

Table 2.4 Concurrent fault simulation process.

G1	a	b	c		G2	c	d	f		G3	e	f	g
	1	1	1			1	1	0			1	0	0
a/0	0	1	1		c/0	0	1	1		c/0	1	1	0
b/0	1	0	1		d/0	1	0	1		d/0	1	1	0
c/0	1	1	0		f/1	1	1	1		f/1	1	1	0
										e/0	**0**	**0**	**1**
										g/1	**1**	**0**	**1**

The main advantages of concurrent fault simulation are its efficiency and its flexibility in simulating diverse of faults.

2.3.5 *Critical Path Tracing*

A line l with value 0(1) is said to be critical under test pattern t iff t detects the fault line l s-a-1(0). In this case, 0(1) is called the critical

value of that line. By finding the critical lines under a test *t*, it is possible
to know the faults detected by *t*. For instance, if a line *l* has value 1 and is
critical under test *t*, then the fault line *l* s-a-0 can be detected by *t*. Fault
simulation by critical path tracing determines those critical lines by a
back-tracking process starting from the primary outputs and proceeding
backward toward the primary inputs of the circuit. For a *NAND (AND)*
gate, an input with a value 0 is called a controlling input (CI). This is
because a value 0 at an input of a NAND (AND) gate determines
completely the output of the gate. Similarly, an input with a value 1 is a
CI for a NOR (OR) gate. Consider, for example, a 3-input NAND gate
with input a=1, b=1 and c=0. The output of the gate f=1 and is critical
under test pattern $t(a, b, c) = (110)$. This is because *t* can detect line
f s-a-0. Since input *c* is the only CI, therefore, line *c* is critical.

Example

Consider the circuit shown in Fig. 2.13. The figure shows the fault
simulation result for that example circuit under test vector $t(a, b, c, d)$
$= (0011)$. The critical lines in the circuit are shown in bold.

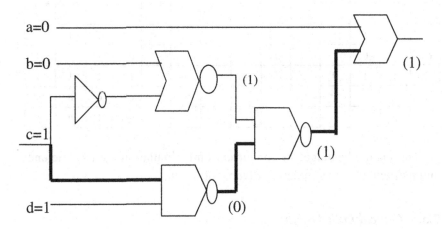

Fig. 2.13: Critical path simulation example.

2.4 Fault Diagnosis

Fault diagnosis (FD) is defined as the process of locating fault(s) in a given circuit. Two main fault diagnosis processes can be employed. These are the *top-down process* and the *bottom-up process*. In the *top-down approach*, large units such as Printed Circuit Boards (PCBs) are first diagnosed. Faulty PCBs are then tested in a repair center to locate the faulty ICs. In the *bottom-up approach*, components are first tested and only fault-free ones are used to assemble higher level systems. The top-down approach is suitable to use while the system is in operation, while the bottom-up approach is suitable to use while the system is in manufacturing. As a rule of thumb in fault diagnosis, if it costs one unit cost to test an IC, the cost of locating the same defective IC when mounted on a PSB and of repairing the board is about ten units; when the defective board is plugged into a system, the cost of finding the fault and repairing the system is hundred units.

As indicated in Chapter 1, repairing a CUT requires the replacement of the faulty component(s) with spare component(s). In performing such replacement, we do not try to identify the actual fault inside the CUT. Consider, for example, the case of having the results of a test conducted on a CUT such that it was not possible to distinguish between two suspected replaceable units (RUs), call these U1 and U2. In this case, it is possible to proceed to identify the faulty unit in a sequential form as follows. Replace one of the RUs, say U1, with a good unit and perform the test again. If the new output results are correct, then the faulty RU was the replaced one; otherwise, the faulty RU is U2. This type of fault diagnosis is called *sequential diagnosis*. Combinational and sequential fault diagnoses are explained below.

2.4.1 *Combinational Fault Diagnosis*

According to this approach, fault simulation is used to determine the possible responses to a given test in the presence of faults. This step helps constructing what is known as the *fault table* (FT) or *fault dictionary* (FD). To locate faults, a match, using a table look-up, between the actual results of test experiments and one of the precomputed (expected) results stored in FT (FD) is sought. A *fault table* is a matrix $FT = \|a_{ij}\|$ where columns F_j represent faults, rows T_i represent test patterns. In this matrix $a_{ij} = 1$ if the test pattern T_i detects fault F_j, otherwise $a_{ij} = 0$. If this table look-up is successful, the FT (FD) provides the corresponding fault(s).

The actual result of a given test pattern is indicated as a 1 if it differs from the precomputed expected one, otherwise it is 0. The result of a test experiment is represented by a vector $E = |e_i|$ where $e_i = 1$ if the actual result of the test patterns does not match with the expected result, otherwise $e_i = 0$. Each column vector f_j corresponding to a fault F_j represents a possible result of the test experiment in the case of the fault F_j.

Depending on the quality of the test patterns used for carrying out a test experiment, three cases are possible. These are:

Total Match: In this case, the test result E matches with a single column vector f_j in FT. This result corresponds to the case where a single fault F_j has been located. In other words, maximum diagnostic resolution has been obtained. *Diagnostic resolution* (DR) is used to define the degree of accuracy to which faults can be located in the circuit under test (CUT).

Partial Match: The test result E matches with a subset of column vectors $\{f_i, f_j \dots f_k\}$ in FT. This result corresponds to the case where a subset of indistinguishable faults $\{F_i, F_j \dots F_k\}$ has been located. Faults that cannot be distinguished are called *Functionally equivalent faults* (FEFs).

No Match: The test result E does not match with any column vectors in FT. This result corresponds to the case where the given set of vectors does not allow to carry out fault diagnosis. The set of faults described in the fault table must be incomplete (in other words, the real existing fault is missing in the fault list considered in FT).

Example

Consider the FT shown in Table 2.5.

Table 2.5: Example Fault Table (FT).

	F_1	F_2	F_3	F_4	F_5	F_6	F_7		E_1	E_2	E_3
t_1	0	0	0	0	1	1	0		1	0	0
t_2	0	0	0	1	0	0	1		0	1	0
t_3	0	1	0	1	0	1	1		0	1	1
t_4	0	0	1	0	0	1	0		1	0	0
t_5	0	1	1	0	1	0	0		1	0	1

F_2 is located

F_4 and F_7 are indistinguishable

No match

There are a total of seven faults F_j and five tests t_i. The results of conducting three test experiments E_1, E_2, E_3 are also shown. E_1 corresponds to the first case where no match is found, i.e., diagnosis is not possible, E_2 corresponds to the second case where a subset of two indistinguishable faults (F_4 and F_7) is located, and E_3 corresponds to the third case where a single fault F_2 is located.

2.4.2 *Sequential Fault Diagnosis Methods*

In sequential fault diagnosis the process of fault location is carried out step by step, where each step depends on the result of the diagnostic experiment at the previous step. Sequential experiments can be carried out either by observing only output responses of the CUT or by pinpointing by a special probe also internal control points of the CUT (*guided probing*). Sequential diagnosis procedure can be graphically represented as *diagnostic tree*.

A diagnostic tree consists of the fault nodes FN (rectangles) and test nodes TN (circles). A FN is labeled by a set of not yet distinguished faults. The starting fault node is labeled by the set of all faults. To each FN k a TN is linked labeled by a test pattern t_k to be applied next. Every test pattern distinguishes between the faults it detects and the ones it does not. The task of the test pattern t_k is to divide the faults in FN k into two groups - detected and not detected by t_k faults. Each test node has two outgoing edges corresponding to the results of the experiment of this test pattern. The results are indicated as *passed* (P) or *failed* (F). The set of faults shown in a current fault node (rectangle) are equivalent (not distinguished) under the currently applied test set.

Example

The diagnostic tree shown in Fig. 2.14 represents the FT shown in Table 2.5.

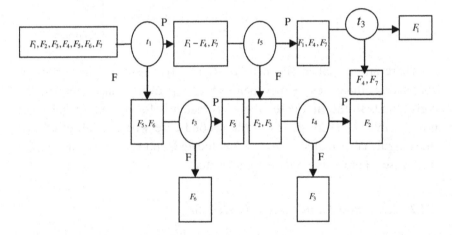

Fig. 2.14: Diagnostic tree.

To improve the fault resolution of a given test set T, it is necessary to generate tests to distinguish among faults equivalent under T. Consider the problem of generating a test to distinguish between faults F1 and F2. Such a test must detect one of these faults but not the other, or vice versa.

Example

Consider the circuit shown in Fig. 2.15.

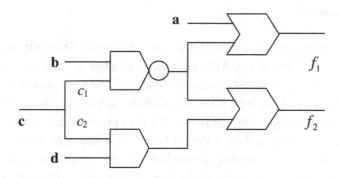

Fig. 2.15: Example circuit.

There are two faults in the circuit: $F1$: c_1 **s-a-0** and $F2$: d s-a-1. The fault $F1$ may influence both outputs, f_1 and f_2, the fault $F2$ may influence only the output f_2. A test pattern $t(a, b, c, d) = (0010)$ activates $F1$ up to the both outputs, and $F2$ only to f_2. If both outputs are erroneous, then it will be concluded that $F1$ is present, and if only the output f_2 is erroneous, then it will be concluded that $F2$ is present.

Guided-probe testing extends the testing process by monitoring internal signals in the CUT via a probe which is moved (usually by an operator) following the guidance provided by the test equipment. The principle of guided-probe testing is to back trace an error from the primary output where it has been observed during edge-pin testing to its physical location in the CUT. Probing is carried out step-by-step. In each step an internal signal is probed and compared to the expected value. The next probing depends on the result of the previous step.

A diagnostic tree can be created for the given test pattern to control the process of probing. The tree consists of internal nodes (circles) to mark the internal lines to be probed, and of terminal nodes (rectangles) to show the possible result of diagnosis. The results of probing are indicated as *passed* (P) or *failed* (F).

Typical faults located are opens and defective components. An open between two points A and B in a connection line is identified by a mismatch between the error observed at B and the correct value measured at A. A faulty device is identified by detecting an error at one of its outputs, while only correct values are measured at its inputs.

2.5 Summary

In this chapter, we have considered the issues related to fault modeling, diagnosis, and simulation. After covering a number of basic concepts and terminology, we covered issues such as logical fault modeling, fault detection and redundancy, fault equivalence and dominance, and single stuck-at and multiple stuck-at faults. We then provided a brief discussion on logic simulation and its different types. This has been followed by a detailed discussion covering a number of fault simulation techniques, such that serial, parallel, deductive, concurrent, differential fault simulation, and critical path tracing. We concluded our coverage in this chapter with a brief introduction to the issues related to fault diagnosis, such as combinational fault diagnosis, fault dictionary, fault location, and sequential fault diagnosis. Our coverage in this first introductory part continues in the next chapter, which introduces the basic concepts related to error control and self checking circuits.

References

Books

[1] S. Mourad, "Principles of Testing Electronic Systems", Wiley Inter-Science, 2000.
[2] M. Abramovici, M. Breuer, and A. Friedman, "Digital Systems Testing and Testable Design", IEEE Press, 1990.

Journals and Conference Proceedings

[1] Margit Aarna, jaan Raik and Raimund Ubar, "Parallel Fault Simulation of Digital Circuits." Tallinn technical University.
[2] William Rogers and Jacob Abraham, "High level Hierarchical Fault Simulation Techniques." March. 1985: 89-97.
[3] Kristian Wiklund, "A gate-level simulation toolkit." Chalmers University of Technology. 1-6. "Fault Simulation" Addison Wesley Longman, Inc 1997.

[4]   C. J. Shi and M. W. Tian, "Efficient DC fault simulation of nonlinear analog circuits", Design, Automation and Test in Europe Conference (DATE '98), Paris, France, Feb. 23-26, 1998.

[5]   M. Zwolinski, A. D. Brown and C. D. Chalk, "Concurrent analogue fault simulation", pp. 42-47, in Proc. 3rd IEEE International Mixed-Signal Testing Workshop, 1997.

[6]   J. Vlach and K. Singhal, *Computer Methods for Circuit Analysis and Design*, Van Nostrand Reinhold, New York, 1983.

[7]   T. M. Niermann and W. T. Cheng and J. H. Patel, "PROOFS: A Fast, Memory Efficient Sequential Circuit Fault Simulator," *IEEE Trans.On Computer-Aided Design*, pp. 198-207, Feb. 1992.

[8]   H. K. Lee and D. S. Ha, "HOPE: An Efficient Parallel Fault Simulatorfor Synchronous Sequential Circuits," *Proc. 29th ACM/ IEEE Design Automation Conference*, pp. 336-340, June 1992.

[9]   S. Ghosh, "Behavioral-Level Fault Simulation," *IEEE Design and Test of Computers*, pp. 31-42, June 1988.

[10] S. Gai, F. Somenzi, M. Spalla, "Fast and Coherent Simulation with Zero Delay Elements," IEEE Transactions on CAD/ICAS, Vol. CAD-6, no. 1, January 1987, pp. 85-92.

[11] E. Ulrich, "Concurrent Simulation at the Switch, Gate and Register Levels," Proc. International Test Conference, Philadelphia (PA), November 1985.

[12] S. Gai, F. Somenzi, and E. Ulrich, "Advanced Techniques for Concurrent Multilevel Simulation," Proc. IEEE Int. Conf. on CAD, Santa Clara, CA, Nov. 1986, pp. 334-337.

[13] M. Abramovici, M.A. Breuer, K. Kumar, "Concurrent Fault Simulation and Functional Level Modeling," Proc. 14th Design Automation Conference, June 1977, pp. 128-137.

[14] Jeff Rearick and Janak H. Patel, "Fast and Accurate Bridging Fault Simulation," Int. Test Conf., 1993, pp. 54-62.

[15] J. M. Acken and S. D. Millman, "Fault Model Evolution for Diagnosis: Accuracy vs. Precision," IEEE Custom Int. Circ. Conf., 1992, pp. 13.4.1-13.4.4.

[16] M. Abd-El-Barr, C. McCrosky, and W. Li, "Less Expensive Test Patter Generation Technique", IEE Proc.-Computers and Digital Techniques, Vol. 143, No. 1, January 1996, pp. 17-22.

Chapter 3

Error Control and Self-Checking Circuits

This chapter aims at introducing the basic issues related to the design and analysis of a variety of techniques that are used for error detection and correction in digital systems. Error detection and correction (EDC) is one of the widely studied fields in fault tolerance. Different techniques have been and are still being devised for EDC, with the aim of implementing a digital system that is as fail-safe as possible. The need for EDC techniques has become more and more important as the level of integration in digital systems continues to increase, sometimes by orders of magnitude. This increase in integration allows for larger and more complex digital systems to be forged, thereby increasing the chances of failure and malfunction. Different phenomena tend to facilitate failures of large integrated digital systems. Some of these include: increased parasitic capacitances as a result of extreme integration, increased noise susceptibility, and higher risk of system failure that is due to the large number of subcomponents. Without EDC techniques, contemporary digital systems would be more prone to failure and the advancement in design technology would have to halt for the sake of reliability and stability of the system.

The need for EDC does not end at the chip or memory level. There is an equal need for EDC techniques in digital communication channels. Data traveling through communication channels suffers corruption due to ambient noise. The matter gets worse as we go higher in bandwidth. Communication channels contain highly uncorrelated noise that is often modeled by white noise, i.e. one that is evenly distributed along the frequency spectrum. As more bandwidth of the channel is consumed, a larger portion of the white noise is filtered in with the data, which causes

66

higher data corruption rate. By introducing error detection codes, we can arbitrarily reduce the average probability of error on a communication channel.

We start our coverage in this chapter with a discussion on the issues related to design and implementation of a number of error detecting and correcting codes. This is followed by a discussion on the design and analysis of self-checking circuits.

3.1 Error-Detecting/Error-Correcting Codes

Numerous error-detecting and error-correcting codes have been developed over the years. In Chapter 1, we have introduced the basic issues related to error coding. In this section, we cover a number of other issues that are related to the same topics. We advise the reader to consult the information provided in Chapter 1 before proceeding further in this Chapter.

A unidirectional error is said to have occurred if all transitions are either 0 to 1 or 1 to 0, but not both, in any given data word. The type of transition is not known a priori. This means that one data word may have a unidirectional error of 1 to 0 type, while another data word may have a unidirectional error of 0 to 1 type. This type of faults is most likely to occur in ROMs.

Classification of codes can also be made based on the amount of redundancy involved. A parameter called *redundancy ratio* is defined below.

Redundancy Ratio

$$= 100\% - \frac{The\ number\ of\ codewords\ in\ the\ codeword\ space}{The\ number\ of\ words\ in\ the\ word\ space}$$

If there is a total of n bits in a word, then

$$Redundancy\ Ratio = 100\% - \frac{The\ number\ of\ codewords}{2^n}$$

Two broad classifications of codes are made based on the above criterion. These are shown below.

(1) Systematic and Separable Codes: Here the check bits are appended after the information bits. In such code, each of the 2^n data information symbols appear as part of the code word. The advantage of systematic codes are that encoding/decoding and data manipulation can be done in parallel. The main disadvantage, however, is its high redundancy ratio, i.e., the availability of less number of code words in the code space compared to the total number of words in the word space. Examples of systematic codes include parity and two-rail codes. These are discussed later in this chapter.

(2) Non-Systematic Codes: Here information bits and the check bits cannot be distinguished. The advantage of these codes is that they are less redundant than systematic codes. The disadvantage is that encoding/decoding and data manipulation is these codes are more involved. Examples of non-systematic codes include m-out-of-n and Borden codes.

Two important concepts associated with code are the *weight* of an error and the *distance* of the code words. These are defined below.

Definition: The Hamming weight of a vector X, denoted by $w(X)$, is the number of non-zero components of X.

Definition: The Hamming distance between two vectors X and Y, denoted by $d(X,Y)$, is the number of components in which they differ.

Example

If $X = <1,0,1,1>$ and $Y = <0,1,1,0>$ are two vectors, then $w(X) = 3$ and $w(Y) = 2$ and $d(X,Y) = 3$. It should be noted that $d(X,Y) = w(X \oplus Y) = 3$ where $\oplus$ is the Binary Exclusive-OR operation.

The occurrence of an error, will cause a code word X to change into another word $X' = X \oplus E$ where E is a non-zero *error vector*. In this case, the *weight of the error* is defined as the *Hamming weight of E*. Consider, for example, an error that changes $X = <1,0,1,1>$ into $X' = <1,0,0,1>$ has the error vector $E = <0,0,1,0>$. The weight of that error is 1. An error of weight 1 is referred to as a *single error*. An error of weigh 2 is referred to as a *double error* and so on.

Definition: The *minimum distance* of a code S is defined as the minimum of the Hamming distances between all possible pairs of code words of S.

If a code has a minimum distance of $d+1$, then it can detect all errors with weight d or less. An error is undetectable if it changes some code word X into another valid code word Y. Since code words are at least distance $d+1$ apart, this can only happen if the error has weight $d+1$ or more. Consider, for example, a code that consists of only two code words $\{00,11\}$. In this case $w(00 \oplus 11) = 2$. A single error in any of the two code words will produce an invalid word, i.e., 01 or 10, and thus will be detected. A double error in any of the two code words, on the other hand, will produce a valid code word, and thus will not be detectable.

Consider the case of a code that has a minimum distance of $2c+1$. In this case, any error of weight c or less in a code word X will produce an erroneous word X' that can be correctly associated with X, since no code word would be closer to X than X'. Consider, for example, a distance-3 code consisting of $\{111,000\}$. Assume that a single error occurs in the middle bit of the word 111 and changed it to 101. In this case, $d(111 \oplus 101) = 1$ while $d(000 \oplus 101) = 2$. Since code word 111 is closer to 101 than word 000 to 101, therefore, the word 101 will be corrected to 111. Notice however that if a double error occur such that 111 becomes 010, then $d(111 \oplus 010) = 2$ while $d(000 \oplus 010) = 1$ indicating incorrectly that the erroneous word 010 should be corrected to 000.

It is possible to have codes that can correct a certain number of errors and detect an additional number of errors. Empirically, if the minimum distance of a code is $2c+d+1$ then that code can correct c errors and detect $c+d$ errors. In this case, words within a distance c of a code word are associated with that code word, and if any such word is received, correction takes place. Words that are further than c but within $c+d$ will be recognized as errors but correction cannot be made. Words that are more $c+d$ distance from a code word, may be "corrected", but unfortunately to the wrong code word.

For a code with a given minimum distance, the choice of using the code to detect errors, correct errors or both will depend on the policy of the decoder used to interpret the code. For example, a code with minimum distance 5 can be used to detect quadruple errors and correct no errors, or to detect double errors and correct a single error.

Sample Codes

(1) **Parity Code:** Such code has been introduced in Chapter 1 (please refer to Chapter 1). Here, we would like to consider increasing the capability of a parity code. This can be achieved by adding more *redundant* bits to the original *information bits*. For example, a single-error correcting code can be constructed for n-bit information word by adding k redundant check bits. The error-correcting capability of the resulting code will be such that $2^k \geq n + k + 1$. For example, for a 11-bit code with one-bit error correcting capability then $k \geq 4$. The n information bits and the k check bits are intermingled to form an $(n+k)$-bit word, i.e., $w_{n+k}, w_{n+k-1}, \ldots, w_2, w_1$. The location of the check bits in the word is determined by $w_{2^i}, 0 \leq i \leq k - 1$. For example, if $n = 11$ and $k = 4$, then the bits w_1, w_2, w_4, and w_8 will be the check bit locations.

Consider the case of $n = 6$. The number of check bits k must be 4 in order to satisfy the inequality $2^k \geq n + k + 1$. Therefore the total number of bits would be 10. The location of the check bits would be $w_{2^i}, 0 \leq i \leq k - 1$, i.e., w_1, w_2, w_4, and w_8. The values of the check bits can be computed, given the information bits, using the following equations.

$$w_1 \oplus w_3 \oplus w_5 \oplus w_7 \oplus w_9 = 0$$
$$w_2 \oplus w_3 \oplus w_6 \oplus w_7 \oplus w_{10} = 0$$
$$w_4 \oplus w_5 \oplus w_6 \oplus w_7 = 0$$
$$w_8 \oplus w_9 \oplus w_{10} = 0$$

Consider the case of having information bit as follows: $w_3 = 1$, $w_5 = 0$, $w_6 = 1$, $w_7 = 1$, $w_9 = 0$, $w_{10} = 1$. The check bits can be computed as follows:

$$w_1 \oplus 1 \oplus 0 \oplus 1 \oplus 0 = 0, i.e., w_1 = 0$$
$$w_2 \oplus 1 \oplus 1 \oplus 1 \oplus 1 = 0, i.e., w_2 = 0$$
$$w_4 \oplus 0 \oplus 1 \oplus 0 = 0, i.e., w_4 = 0$$
$$w_8 \oplus 0 \oplus 1 = 0, i.e. w_8 = 1$$

Therefore, the encoded word would be 1011100100. If an error occurs in w_6, thus making the word to become 1011000100, then re-computing w_1, w_2, w_4, w_8 would produce 0110 which is the binary equivalent of 6, i.e., the position where the error occurred. Thus, the bit can be corrected.

Parity codes found most of their applications in memory systems. They can be used in the form of bit-per-byte, bit-per-word, and overlapping parity. The redundancy ratio of the code will depend on which of these forms is used. For example, the redundancy ratio of the simple bit-per-word is 50%. For an overlapping parity code having n information bits and k parity bits, the ratio would be $1 - \dfrac{2^2}{2^{n+k}}$.

(2) **Two-rail Code:** This code consists of two rails $X = (x_1, x_2, \ldots, x_n)$ and $Y = (y_1, y_2, \ldots, y_n)$, where $y_i = \overline{x}_i, 1 \le i \le n$. The X rail can be thought of as carrying the information part while the Y rail carries the detection part. A two-rail code can be used to detect any unidirectional error. This is because a unidirectional error can change the bits in X and/or those in Y such that the fixed relationship between x_i and y_i will be no longer valid. In addition, the code can detect any symmetric error

which does not affect the same corresponding bits in X and Y. For example, let $X = 01101100$ and $Y = 10010011$. Let the symmetric error be such that X becomes $X' = 01011100$ and Y to become $Y' = 10110011$. It can be seen that such error can be detected by the two-rail code since the relation $y_i = \overline{x}_i$ is no longer valid. The redundancy ratio of the two-rail code is given by $1 - \dfrac{2^n}{2^{2n}} = 1 - \dfrac{1}{2^n}$. For $n=8$, the redundancy ratio is 99.6%. When $n=16$, the redundancy ratio becomes 99.9985%. It is clear that such code is not efficient. Therefore, more efficient code capable of detecting unidirectional errors are often preferred. Some of these are discussed below.

Sample All-Unidirectional Error-Detecting (AUED) Codes

Code that can detect all possible unidirectional errors are called *all-unidirectional Error-detecting* (AUED) codes. Unidirectional errors are dominant in VLSI circuits. Let X and Y be two vectors. We define $N(X,Y)$ to be the number of bits in which X has 1 and Y has 0. For example, if $X = 1010$ and $Y = 0111$ then $N(X,Y) = 1$ and $N(Y,X) = 2$. If $N(X,Y) \geq 1$ and $N(Y,X) \geq 1$, then X and Y are said to be *unordered*, else they are *ordered*. X is said to *cover* Y, if $N(X,Y) \geq 1$, and $N(Y,X) = 0$. If vector X covers Y then the two vectors are said to be *ordered*. There is no covering relationship between a pair of unordered vectors. If two vectors are unordered, then no unidirectional error can change one vector into the other. But, if they are ordered, then one vector can be changed into the other by a unidirectional error.

For example, if $X = 01101011$, $Y = 11011110$ and $Z = 01001100$, then unidirectional error that changes the 2nd, 5th and 8th bit (from right to left) of Y to 0's will change Y to Z and vice versa. Notice that Y and Z are ordered and that Y covers Z. Notice also that X and Z are unordered. There is no unidirectional error which can change X to Z or Z to X. The above observation can be generalized to say that in order for a code to be AUED, every pair of code words should be unordered. Many AUED codes have been designed to satisfy this condition. Two most well-know unidirectional error-detecting codes: (1) m-out-of-n codes and (2) Berger codes.

m-out-of-n Code: This is a non-systematic (the information bits can not be separately identified from the check bits) and unordered code (for any two code works X and Y, $N(X,Y) \geq 1$ and $N(Y,X) \geq 1$). It consists of code words each is n-bit long out of which exactly m bits are 1s. Therefore, in the m-out-of-n code each code word has weight m. Since all code words have the same weight m, this code is also called a *constant weight* code.

There are $\binom{n}{m} = C_m^n = \dfrac{n!}{(n-m)!m!}$ code words in the code space.

Example

Let $X = 01101011$ and $Y = 11010110$ be two code words in a 5-out-of-8 code. The number of code words in the code space is $\binom{8}{5} = C_5^8 = \dfrac{8!}{(8-5)!5!} = 56$ words. Notice that $N(X,Y) = 3$ and $N(Y,X) = 3$.

If there are unidirectional errors in a code word, the erroneous word will have weight more than m in the case of 0 to 1 errors, and less than m in the case of 1 to 0 errors. In both cases unidirectional errors can be detected.

Example

Suppose that in a 3-out-of-6 code, a code word $X = 101010$ has been subject to unidirectional 0 to 1 error such that $X_{error} = 111110$. Notice that each of the second and the forth bits has change from 0 to 1. The new word X_{error} has a weight of 5, not 3. Therefore, the error will be detected. Similarly, if X has been subject to a 1 to 0 unidirectional error such that $X_{error} = 001000$, then the weight of the new words is 1, not 3 and the error can be detected. The number $\binom{n}{m} = C_m^n = \dfrac{n!}{(n-m)!m!}$ is maximized when $m = \left\lfloor \dfrac{n}{2} \right\rfloor$ or $\left\lceil \dfrac{n}{2} \right\rceil$. Thus, $\left\lfloor \dfrac{n}{2} \right\rfloor$-out-of-n or $\left\lceil \dfrac{n}{2} \right\rceil$-out-of-n codes are considered the most efficient codes. It has been shown that the k-out-of-$2k$ code is optimal among all AUED codes. The redundancy ratio of k-out-of-$2k$ is computed as:

$$1 - \frac{\frac{(2k)!}{(k!)^2}}{2^{2k}} = 1 - \frac{(2k)!}{(k!)^2 2^{2k}}$$

For k = 16 (n=32), the redundancy ratio is 86%.

Berger codes: Berger codes are (separable codes) formed by appending a number of check bits to each word of information. The check bits are the binary representation of the number of 0's in the information word. For example, if 1010100 is the given information word, then the check bits will be 100. This is because there are four zeros in the information word. In fact, if there are n bits in the information word, then the count of 0's can vary from 0 to n. Thus the number of check bits k in the check word is given by $k = \lceil \log_2(n + 1) \rceil$. If $n = 2^k - 1$, the code is called a *maximal-length* Berger code. Table 3.1 shows an example for encoding 3-bit information using Berger code.

Table 3.1: A Berger code encoding example.

Information symbol	Check symbol
000	11
001	10
010	10
011	01
100	10
101	01
110	01
111	00

The capability of the Berger code to detect unidirectional errors can be explained as follows.

1. If there are unidirectional errors in the information part, the number of zeros in the information part of the corrupted word will be greater than the check value in the case of 1 to 0 errors and less than the check value in the case of 0 to 1 errors.

2. If the check part has unidirectional errors, the number of zeros in the information part of the corrupted word will be less than the check value in the case of 0 to 1 errors and greater than the check value in the case of 1 to 0 errors.

3. Finally, if both the information and the check parts have unidirectional errors, the number of zeros in the information part of the corrupted word will increase in the case of 1 to 0 errors and decrease in the case of 0 to 1 errors. On the other hand, the check value of the corrupted word will decrease in the case of to 1 to 0 errors and increase in the case 0 to 1 errors. So in both the cases the number of zeros in the information part can not be the same as the value of check part in the corrupted.

The redundancy ratio of the code is computed as $1 - \dfrac{1}{n+1}$ when $n=2^k-1$. If the number of information bits is small, the redundancy of a Berger code is high. The redundancy is 50% or greater if the number of information bits eight or less.

Sample *t*-UED Codes

The *t*-UED codes can be considered as a subclass of AUED codes. It is highly unlikely in VLSI circuits that more than *t* bits of data word will have unidirectional errors. In such cases, one can use *t*-unidirectional error-detecting codes instead of AUED codes. The *t*-UED codes have less redundancy than the AUED codes and hence are preferred when AUED capability is not required.

Like AUED codes, *t*-UED codes must satisfy some conditions. A code C is *t*-UED if and only if for all vectors $X,Y \in C$, either X and Y are *unordered* or $d(X,Y) \geq t+1$, when one covers the other. If two code words are unordered, then no unidirectional error can change one into the other. If they are ordered, then it takes a unidirectional error in at least t + 1 bits to change one into the other. A number of *t*-UED codes have been presented in the literature. We discuss one of these below.

Borden code: This is a non-systematic t- UED code. The code consists of all length n words whose weight is congruent to $\lfloor n/2 \rfloor \mod(t+1)$. The code is usually denoted as $C(n,t)$. For example, let $n = 11$ and $t = 3$. Then, among $\{0,1,2,3,4,5,6,7,8,9,10\}$ there are three integers $\{1,5,9\}$ whose modulus of $(t+1)$ are 1. Therefore, the three subsets $C_1 (11,3) = \{1\text{-out-of-}11\}$, $C_2 (11,3) = \{5\text{-out-of-}11\}$, and $C_3 (11,3) = \{9\text{-out-of-}11\}$ constitute the set $C(11,3)$. We say that $C(11,3) = C_1(11,3) \cup C_2(11,3) \cup C_3(11,3)$. The only way a unidirectional error can change one code word into another is by changing the code word from set C_j, $j \neq i$. This would require a unidirectional error in at least four bits $> t$.

It has been shown that the Borden code is the optimal among all t-UED codes. In other words, no other t-UED code with less redundancy exists.

Convolution Codes

Block error correcting codes serve well in memory and digital logic systems. They provide limited help in a number of multimedia systems and communications. Space imaging and video transmission benefit more from convolution codes since they can operate on differing sizes of data. The trend is now on finding cost-effective solutions for convolution decoder circuitry and more efficient algorithms. The issue of convolution codes has been touched on briefly in Chapter 1. In this section, we provide a detailed coverage of convolution codes: their design and analysis.

In all previous cases, an encoder would take blocks of data (of length k) and add some redundancy to it. Convolution codes, however, can work on streams of data of different lengths. This is useful when we would like a high code rate (k/n) and would also like good error correcting capability. For this reason, convolution codes are generally used in noisy channels with high error rates. Convolution codes are implemented using shift registers that are arranged such as to form a finite impulse response (FIR) circuit. FIR circuits (or channels) have a finite response to a single input. This is unlike IIR (infinite impulse response) channels, that have an infinite memory of a single input.

FIR circuits can be constructed using shift registers. Convolution codes use these FIR circuits to add a certain amount of redundancy to the input. An example of a convolution encoder is shown in Fig. 3.1. It should be noted that this same example has been introduced in Chapter 1. We use it here as an entry point to a more elaborate discussion on convolution codes.

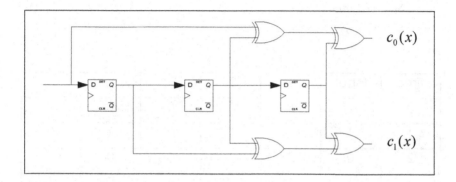

Fig. 3.1: A convolution encoder.

In this figure, the input data stream passes through the register stages shown. The two outputs are interleaved in a certain way and sent. In this case, for each input bit there are two output bits, one coming from $c_0(x)$ and the other one from $c_1(x)$. The code ratio for this encoder (k/n), however, is slightly below the expected 0.5 ratio. This is because we need to flush out the contents of the registers when we are done encoding a certain length of data stream (called a frame). The extra bits from the registers are also sent with the code, lowering the code ratio. For this reason, it is good to choose high values for the frame length such that the overhead of sending the flushed values is minimal.

Following is an example of encoding a data stream using the convolution encoder of Fig. 3.1.

Example

Suppose that it is required to send the data stream (1001101) using the encoder shown in Fig. 3.1. We will denote the values on the flip flops by

S_0, S_1 and S_2. The following equations and table can be used to determine the outputs $c_0(x)$ and $c_1(x)$:

$$S_0^+ = input$$
$$S_1^+ = S_0$$
$$S_2^+ = S_1$$
$$c_0 = S_1 + S_2 + input$$
$$c_1 = S_0 + S_1 + S_2$$

Time	Input	S_0	S_1	S_2	C_0	C_1
0	?	0	0	0	0	0
1	1	1	0	0	1	0
2	0	0	1	0	0	1
3	1	1	0	1	0	1
4	1	1	1	0	0	0
5	0	0	1	1	1	0
6	0	0	0	1	0	0
7	1	1	0	0	0	1
8	0	0	1	0	0	1
9	0	0	0	1	1	1
10	0	0	0	0	1	1

The three final inputs are not part of the data but are deliberately inserted to flush the contents of the shift register. If the output is interleaved such that the bit from c_0 is sent first, then the output stream would be (10010100100001011111). The code ratio is: 7/20 = 0.35 < 0.5

Performance Measure of Convolution Codes

As mentioned previously, convolution codes are used for high error correction capability. In order to measure the performance of a certain convolution encoder, we need to develop a model for it. In the following section, we will model the encoder of Fig. 3.2 and obtain its error correcting capability. Note that the metric for this remains to be the Hamming distance between code words. It is the discovery of this Hamming distance that is the purpose of this section.

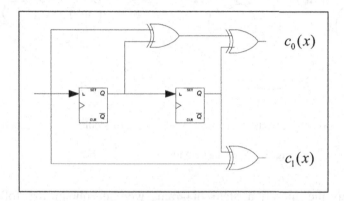

Fig. 3.2: Two stage convolution encoder.

Figure 3.2 shows a two stage convolution encoder. This encoder can be designed as a state machine whose state diagram is shown in Fig. 3.3. There are a total of 2^n states for an encoder with n stages. For this encode, it is required that we start at state 0 (all registers hold value 0) and end at that same stage as well. With this restriction, we need to find the minimum code distance between any two code words. This will necessities tracing all possible paths of a certain length (depending on our frame size) that start and finish at state 0. To accomplish this, we will assign three variables: L, N and D to the links. Each link will be assigned a variable D with a power equal to the number of 1's in the output code segment of that link. Each link will also be assigned the variable N with a power equal to that of the number of 1's in the input, in this case it would be either 1 or 0. Finally, the variable L with power 1 will be assigned to all links. This variable simply counts the number of links traversed and would thus give us a measure for the frame length. The values in part (b) of the figure show the assignments to the links. We have also removed the loop on state 0 and introduced a replica of state 0 that should be visited when any encoding process has finished.

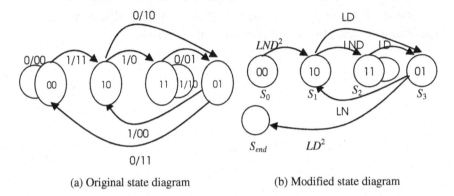

(a) Original state diagram   (b) Modified state diagram

Fig. 3.3: State diagram for the encoder in Fig. 3.2.

From the modified state diagram, we can obtain the following equations (assuming that $S_0=1$):

$$\begin{pmatrix} -1 & 0 & JN \\ JND & JND-1 & 0 \\ JD & JD & -1 \end{pmatrix} \begin{pmatrix} S_1 \\ S_2 \\ S_3 \end{pmatrix} = \begin{pmatrix} -JND^2 \\ 0 \\ 0 \end{pmatrix}$$

$$S_{end} = JD^2 S_3$$

Solving these equations for S_{end} using Kramer's rule, we get:

$$\Delta = -1(1-JND) + JN(J^2ND^2 - JD(JND-1)) = JND(1+J)-1$$

$$\Delta S_3 = -JND^2(JD)$$

$$S_3 = \frac{\Delta S_3}{\Delta} = \frac{J^2ND^3}{1-JND(1+J)} \Rightarrow S_{end} = \frac{J^3ND^5}{1-JND(1+J)}$$

This quantity found (called the transfer function) has all the information of the convolution encoder of Fig. 3.2. If we perform long division on the quantity obtained, we will get an infinite number of terms, each having certain powers of D,J and N. Each one of these terms refers to one of the possibilities of traversing the graph starting and ending at state 0. For example, if one of the obtained terms was $J^5N^3D^9$, this would mean that there is a path with input Hamming weight of 3, output Hamming weight of 9, and taking 5 steps through the encoder. This information can tell us of the error correcting capability for a certain stream length. For example, one of the terms of the quotient is $J^4N^2D^6$. This means that for stream length of 4 (including flushing bits), there are inputs with Hamming weight of 2 that have output Hamming weight of 6. This would translate to a correcting capability of 2 errors.

3.2 Self-Checking Circuits

After discussing different methods of error control using redundancy, it is time to present a certain application of such error control schemes, namely, self checking circuits. We would like to have a circuit tested automatically for errors without the need for applying stimuli (test vectors). The idea is to add some circuitry to the original circuit (functional unit). This additional circuit will examine the output of the functional unit and determine whether there is an error in the functional unit. A block diagram of a self checking circuit is shown in Fig. 3.4.

The number of valid inputs to the functional block is chosen to be a subset of the entire input space of the functional block. For example, if the block has n bits, there are 2^n possible inputs. We will choose a subset 2^k of these inputs to be valid. This valid subset is known as the input codeword space of the block. Similarly, if the output space is 2^m then we choose 2^k possible outputs that will constitute the output codeword space. Thus, the purpose of the checking circuit is to ensure that the output word received belongs to the output codeword space. At this point, before we go into the design of self checking circuits, a few definitions are necessary.

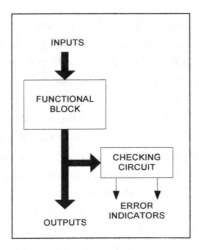

Fig. 3.4: General structure of self checking circuits.

Definition: A circuit is said to be **fault-secure** for a certain fault (or set of faults) if the circuit would not produce a non-codeword for any input belonging to the input code space.

Let F represents a set of faults for which a circuit is self-checking. Let X and Y_1 be respectively the input and output code spaces for the circuit. If Z is the output space and Y_2 is the set of non-code words then $Z = Y_1 \cup Y_2$. Let $x \in X$ be the input to the circuit and let the correct output of the circuit be $y_1 \in Y_1$. Assume that for the same input, the output of the circuit in the presence of a fault $f \in F$ be $y_1' \in Y_1$.

Fault security implies that if $y_1' \in Y_1$ then $y_1' = y_1$. In other words, the output of a faulty circuit cannot be a code word and at the same time be different from the correct code word output y_1. Therefore, if the output is a code word, then it is assumed to be correct. This is because the circuit is assumed to produce a non-code word in the presence of a fault.

Definition: A circuit is said to be **self-testing** for a set of faults if for at least one valid input, the faulty circuit produces a non-output codeword.

Self-testing property of a circuit ensures that for every fault $f \in F$, there is at least an input $x_2 \in X$ for which the resulting output is a non-code word $y_2 \in Y_2$, i.e., the presence of a fault is detected by the input x_2. In other words, the occurrence of any fault from the prescribed set will be detected by at least one member of the input set.

Definition: A circuit is said to be **code-disjoint** if it never produces non-codeword outputs for codeword inputs, and never produces codeword outputs for non-codeword inputs.

Definition: A checker circuit is said to be **totally-self-checking** (TSC) if it is fault-secure and self-testing, and code disjoint.

Totally self-checking circuits are desirable for the design of highly reliable systems. This is because during normal operation, any fault from a given set will cause detectable, erroneous output. A circuit is TSC under the following two assumptions.

Faults occur one at a time

Sufficient time interval between occurrence of any two faults is available so that all the required code word set can be applied to the circuit.

Subject to the above assumptions, a TSC circuit always produces a non-code word (not an incorrect code word) in the presence of a fault. The concepts of self-testing (ST), fault secure (FS) and TSC are illustrated in Fig. 3.5.

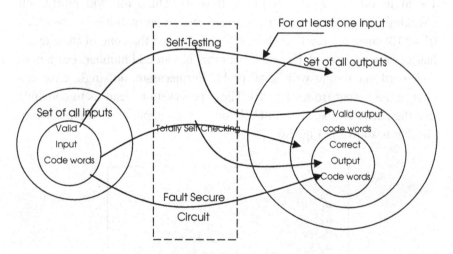

Fig. 3.5: Relationship among ST, FS, and TSC.

The final definition suggests that the checking circuit itself has an input and output code spaces. This is very true. In fact, the input code space for the checker is the output code space for our functional unit. For the output, we require that the output space consist of 2 bits, which gives 4 possible combinations. Two of them (10,01) are code words that indicate error-free operation. The other two (00,11) indicate faulty operation. The designer of the checking circuit must ensure these conditions for a given coding scheme. Also, to guard against a stuck-at fault on the output of the checker, we require that no single error can change a valid codeword of the checker to another valid codeword. In the following, we will present some examples of checking circuits for some known codes.

Gate Level Design of Self Checking Circuits

Parity Code Checker

To design a self checking circuit on a codeword with parity, we can split the input word into two sets, and pass each set into an XOR tree. The output of each set will be 1 if the corresponding set has an odd number of 1's in it, otherwise, the output will be 0. Thus, for odd parity self checking circuit, for a correct codeword, the output will have to be either 01 or 10, since the total number of 1's is odd and thus one of the subsets has an even number of 1's while the other has an odd number. For a non-codeword, the output will be 00 or 11. Furthermore, no single error can change the output from 01 to 10. These observations lead us to conclude that the parity checker is a TSC circuit. An example of a 10 input parity checker is shown in Fig. 3.6.

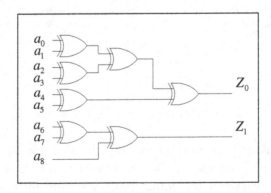

Fig. 3.6: 9-bit odd parity checker.

Two-Rail Checker

The two-rail checker is useful in itself and as a building block in other self checking circuits. The output of this circuit is either 01 or 10 if the input words (X,Y) are complementary; otherwise, the output becomes either 11 or 00. Figure 3.7 shows a 2-bit input two-rail checker. The two-rail checker shown in this figure is a TSC circuit for the following reasons:

The output is 01 for input (x_1,y_1,x_2,y_2) = 1001 or 0110 and is 10 for input 0101 or 1010. These are all the valid input code words.

All valid input code words can check all stuck-at faults of the circuit, so the circuit is self testing.

There is no single fault that could change an output of 01 to 10 or the other way around, which means that the circuit is fault secure.

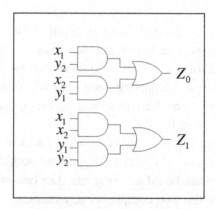

Fig. 3.7: Two rail checker for 2 bit input.

We can construct a two-rail checker for any number of inputs by connecting several 2-bit two-rail checkers in a tree. Figure 3.8 shows a 4-bit TRC.

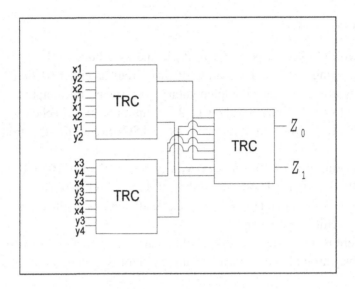

Fig. 3.8: A 4-bit tree TRC.

It is interesting to observe that the requirement of complementary inputs for the two-rail checker is not necessarily a limitation. This is because the output of a number of circuits can be restructures so as to become that of a comparing two words to determine if they are complementary. Consider, for example, the general structure of a separable code shown in Fig. 3.9.

The figure shows how a two-rail TSC checker can be used for checking such structure. The idea is to generate both the check bits and their complement from the information bits. The two-rail checker can the n be used to check the two complementary outputs, i.e., the check bits and their complement.

k out of 2k Codes

The design of a checker for the k out of 2k code is useful because many other coding techniques can be transformed to a 1 out of n code, which can then be transformed to a k out of 2k code. If we have a design for a checker for the k out of 2k code, then we effectively have a design for all of these codes.

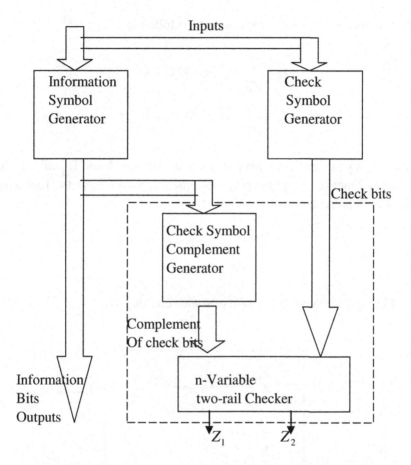

Fig. 3.9: The use of a two-rail checker for separable codes.

The k out of 2k code is defined as the set of 2k-bit words wherein the number of 1's are exactly k bits. This is a special case of the m out of n code. The reason we discuss this special case is that this is the only type of circuit for which a self-testing checker can be made. To design a checker for the k out of 2k (k/2k) code, we partition the input word into two subsets (A and B).

We then define the checker outputs as follows:

$$Z_0 = \sum_{i:odd}^{k} T(k_a \geq i)T(k_b \geq k - i)$$

$$Z_1 = \sum_{i:even}^{k} T(k_a \geq i)T(k_b \geq k - i)$$

where k_a and k_b are the number of 1's in the subsets A and B, and T is the majority function. For example, a 2/4 checker would have the following Boolean representation:

$$Z_0 = (x_0 + x_1)(x_2 + x_3)$$

$$Z_1 = x_1 x_2 + x_3 x_4$$

Figure 3.10 shows a diagram of such a circuit.

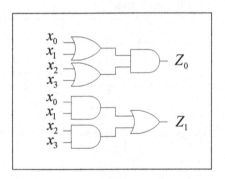

Fig. 3.10: A 2-out-of-4 Checker.

Now suppose we want to make a general m/n checker. The idea is to transform it to a 1-out-of n code, then transform that to a k/2k code, and finally, use the equations shown earlier to complete the checker. For example, if we want to build a 2/5 checker:

1. Since there are $\begin{pmatrix} 5 \\ 2 \end{pmatrix} = 10$ possible values for the 2/5 checker, we will transform this to a 1/10 code by getting all possible permutations.

2. Once the 1/10 code is ready, we need to transform it to a k/2k code. This code must have at least as many code words as the 1/10 has (which is 10). The minimum value of k is found to be 3, which means we need to construct a 3/6 code. Furthermore, each line of the 1/10 lines must contribute to 3 lines of the 3/6 code lines. There are many possible realizations of this circuit.

3. Finally, we apply the k/2k checking equations:

$$Z_0 = \sum_{i:odd}^{k} T(k_a \geq i)T(k_b \geq k - i)$$

$$= T(k_a \geq 1)T(k_b \geq 2) + T(k_a \geq 3)T(k_b \geq 0)$$

$$= (x_0 + x_1 + x_2)(x_3 x_4 + x_4 x_5 + x_3 x_5)$$

$$Z_1 = \sum_{i:even}^{k} T(k_a \geq i)T(k_b \geq k - i)$$

$$= T(k_a \geq 0)T(k_b \geq 3) + T(k_a \geq 2)T(k_b \geq 1)$$

$$= (x_3 x_4 x_5) + (x_0 x_1 + x_1 x_2 + x_2 x_3)(x_3 + x_4 + x_5)$$

The final circuit realization is shown in Fig. 3.11.

Universal TSC Model

The previous examples show the design of self checking circuits for certain classes of codes. What we will show here is a method to transform any gate level circuit to a self checking circuit that provides a two-rail output. The idea is based on using a universal totally self checking gate. This gate is a pair of 2 input AND and OR gate. If 2 two-rail input codes are fed to this circuit, the output is a two-rail code. Pagey and Al-Khalili have shown that this circuit is TSC for multiple stuck at faults. They have also shown that we can implement the

different types of logic gates by simply rearranging the way the input is
fed to the gates. If we can implement any logic gate as a universal TSC
module, then any circuit that can be described in gate level can
potentially be transformed into a TSC. Figure 3.12 shows the universal
TSC module.

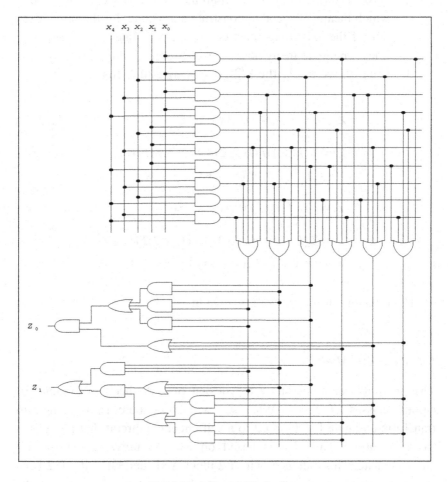

Fig. 3.11: A 2-out-of-5 checker.

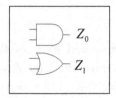

Fig. 3.12: A Universal TSC module.

Now we have all the required two-rail gates to implement a TSC circuit. However, this is not possible for all circuits. It has been shown that replacing each gate in a circuit with its TSC equivalent will yield a TSC circuit only if the circuit with multiple inputs and multiple outputs is fully testable for single stuck at faults. An example of such a circuit is a full adder. Figures 3.13 and 3.14 show a non-redundant full adder, followed by its two-rail TSC counterpart.

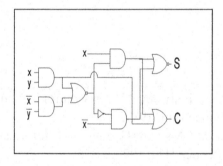

Fig. 3.13: A full adder cell.

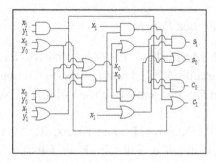

Fig. 3.14: A two rail TSC full adder.

3.3 Summary

In this chapter, we have presented some of the most widely employed schemes for error control coding. We have discussed several schemes for error detection and correction. We have also looked into self checking circuits and have seen how these can be built for some special cases. It is important to know that the methods discussed are by no means comprehensive. Many error control codes and self checking methods were not discussed. This field of research has gone so deep and has broadened so much that it would be impossible to discuss all of the methods used without writing an entire book on the subject. Each of the methods has its own virtues and is limited by its own drawbacks. It is entirely the decision of the designer of fault tolerant systems to select the type of error control coding (and self checking circuit, if applicable) to use for a particular application.

References

Books

[1] Rao, T. and E. Fujiwara. "Error Control Coding for Computer Systems". Prentice Hall, 1989.
[2] Wells, Richard. "Applied Coding and Information Theory for Engineers". Prentice Hall, 1999.
[3] Wakerly, J., "Error Detecting Codes, Self-Checking Circuits and Applications", 1978, North-Holland, ASIN 0444002561.

Journal and Conference Papers

[1] Lu, D. and McCluskey, E., "Quantitative Evaluation of Self-Checking Circuit", IEEE Transactions on Computer-Aided Design of Integrated Circuits and Systems, Volume 3, No. 2, pp. 150-155, April 1984.
[2] Bengtsson, T., Dubrova, E., and Krenz, R., "A Design Technique for High-Performance Self-Checking Circuits", http://klabs.org/richcontent/MAPLDCon01/Papers/E/E1_Bengtsson_P.pdf

[3]   Kia, S. and Parameswaran, "Design Automation of Self Checking Circuirs", Proceedings of the Conference on European Design Automation, France 1994, pp. 252-257.

[4]   Mohanram, K., Sogomonyan, E., Gossel, M. and Touba, N., "Synthesis of Low-Cost Parity-Based Partially Self-Checking Circuits", http://www-ece.rice.edu/~kmram/publications/iolts03.pdf

[5]   Jha, K., "Strong Fault-Secure and Strong Self-Checking Domino-CMOS Implementation of Totally Self-Checking Circuits", IEEE Transactions on Computer-Aided Design of Integrated Circuits and Systems, Volume 9, No. 3, pp. 332-336, March 1990.

[6]   Favalli, M. and Metra, C., "On the Design of Self-Checking Functional Units based on Shannon Circuits", Design, Automation and Test in Europe (DATE '99), March 1999, Munuch, Germany, pp.368-372.

[7]   Steininger, A., "Testing and Built-in Self-Test: A Survey", Journal of Systems Architecture, Elsevier Science Publishers, North-Hollan, http://www.ecs.tuwien.ac.at/lehre/vlsi-design/download/testing_jsa.pdf

[8]   Shirvani, P. and McCluskey, E., "Fault-Tolerant Systems in A Space Environment: The CRC ARGOS Project", http://crc.stanford.edu/crc_papers/CRC-TR-98-2.pdf

[9]   Burns, S. and Jha, N., "A totally Self Checking Checker for a Parallel Unordered Coding Scheme". IEEE Transactions on Computers. Vol. 43, No 4, April 1994.

[10] Pagey, S. and A. Al-Khalili. "Universal TSC Module and its Application to the Design of TSC Circuits". IEEE 1996.

[11] Rowaihy, Hosam. "A Survey on Some Linear Error Control Codes for Binary Systems". KFUPM, May 2001.

Websites

http://www.rel-net.co.uk/downloads/documents/Design%20Reliability%20Guide%206%20(Issue%202).pdf

Chapter 4

Fault Tolerance in Multiprocessor Systems

Multiprocessor systems are mostly designed based on performance measures such as speed. The issues of reliability and fault tolerance are sometimes overlooked as criteria for designing multiprocessor systems. Consider Table 4.1.

Table 4.1: MTBF in hours for a number of workstations.

Manufacturer	MTBF of one workstation	MTBF of 1000 MP nodes
DEC	35,872	35
HP	58,700	58
SUN	40,600	40
IBM	20,000	20

The table shows that the resulting MTBF for a multiprocessor system consisting of 1000 workstations is a little more than two days. This is clearly unaccountable. One can therefore conclude that multiprocessor systems are in real need of reliability/availability/fault tolerance features. It is possible to achieve fault tolerance in multiprocessors by using all forms of redundancy studied before. In particular, hardware and software redundancy techniques represent two such techniques. Multiprocessor systems include two main classes. These are shared – memory and distributed – memory systems. Figure 4.1 illustrates these two classes.

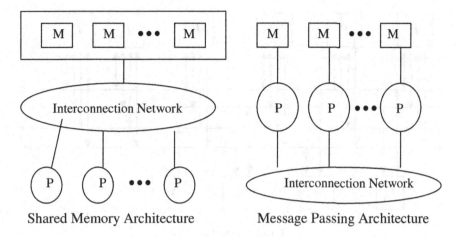

Shared Memory Architecture   Message Passing Architecture

Fig. 4.1: Multiprocessor systems.

4.1 Fault Tolerance in Interconnection Networks

As shown in Fig. 4.1, interconnection networks play a major role in connecting the different components of a multiprocessor system. Interconnection networks can be classified according to a number of criteria. These include the following.

1. Mode of operation: Synchronous versus asynchronous.
2. Control Strategy: Centralized versus distributed.
3. Switching Mechanism: Circuit versus packet switching.
4. Topology: Static versus dynamic.

Static interconnection networks (INs) include linear (1-D), ring (loop), tree, mesh, and hypercube networks. Dynamic INs include bus-based and switch-based networks. Bus-based networks include single-bus and multiple-bus networks. Switch-based networks include single-stage, multiple-stage, and cross-bar networks. Single-bus networks are the simplest among bus based networks. They possess the desirable feature of being easily expandable. However they suffer from a single point failure property, i.e., the failure of the bus will lead to the collapse of the whole system. Figure 4.2 shows the arrangement of a 2-out-of-4 bus system.

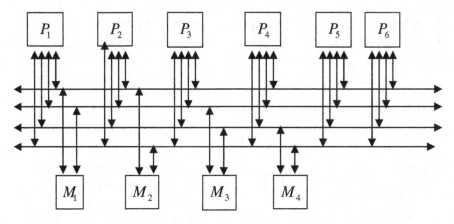

Fig. 4.2: Example multi-bus system.

In such arrangement, if a bus become faulty, the system can still operate as a (B-1)- bus system. The failure of B buses can cause the B-out-of-M system to collapse. Multi-bus based fault-tolerant multiprocessor systems such as Tandem Nonstop (a distributed memory systems which uses dual redundant buses) and the Stratus XA (a shared memory which uses dual buses).

Examples of redundant dual-bus commercial systems include the Tandem Nonstop/16, the stratus XA/R Series 300, and the Sequoia Series 400.

The cross-bar system is an example of a switch- based multiprocessor system. Figure 4.3 shows an illustration of a crossbar system.

Fault tolerance can be achieved in the cross-bar by adding extra row(s) and column(s) such that each input can be connected to more that one row and one column. In the case of a switch (cross-point) failure, the corresponding row and column are disconnected and the spare row and column are activated and the system can then reconfigured accordingly. Figure 4.4 shows an illustration of a $(4+1)\times(4+1)$ fault-tolerant crossbar system.

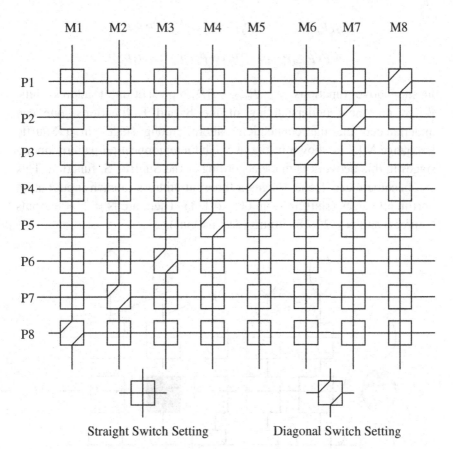

Fig. 4.3: A 8×8 crossbar system.

An N×N multi-stage interconnection network (MIN) consists of $\log_2 N$ stages of switching elements (SEs). Each SE has two inputs and two outputs. Each SE can exist in one four different states (see Fig. 4.5). Each stage consists of $\dfrac{N}{2}$ SEs. A number of MIN has been used in multiprocessor systems. Examples include the Omega, baseline, cube, and the Shuffle Exchange networks. We will use the Shuffle Exchange networks (SEN) in our discussion about the fault tolerance and reliability in MINS. In order to understand the operation of the Shuffle Exchange networks, one should understand two basic functions. These are the Shuffle, S, and the exchange, E, functions. These are introduced below.

$$S(P_{m-1}P_{m-2}\cdots P_1P_0) = P_{m-2}P_{m-3}\cdots P_1P_0P_{m-1}$$

$$E(P_{m-1}P_{m-2}\cdots P_1P_0) = P_{m-1}P_{m-2}\cdots P_1\overline{P_0}$$

In the above functions, $P_{m-1}P_{m-2}\cdots P_1P_0$ represent n-bit address bits. Based on one's understanding of the S and E functions, one can underhanded the interconnection pattern among stages in a Shuffle Exchange MIN as shown in Fig. 4.5. The interconnection pattern among stages in this network is made according to the Shuffle, S, function. This can become clear if one assigns a three bit address to each input/output port in all stages (starting from 000 to 111). There are $N = 2^3 = 8$ inputs (sources) and $N = 2^3 = 8$ outputs (destinations).

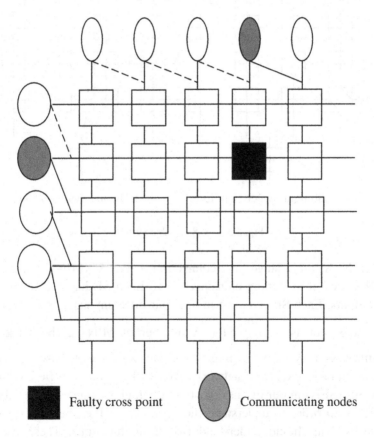

Fig. 4.4: A $(4 + 1) \times (4 + 1)$ fault-tolerant crossbar.

The network has three stages, each has $\dfrac{N}{2} = 4SEs$. The SEi in stage j will be denoted as SEij.

One of the main features of MINs is the existence of a unique path between each pair of source-destination. Another important feature is that the message is routed through the network according to the binary representation of the destination address. This can be achieved by using the following simple technique.

1. Each stage (from left to right) uses a bit from the destination address (from left to right).
2. A switch in stage i uses the stage's address bit to decide whether to send the message arriving at its input to the upper output (if the bit is 0) or to the lower output (if the bit is 1).

Figure 4.5 shows the unique path between input 101 and output 011, input (000) and output (101), and input (110) and output (010).

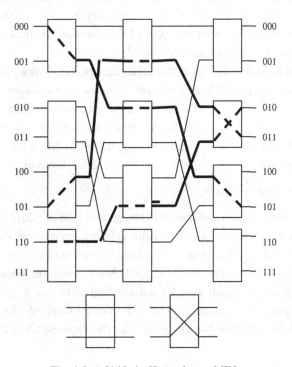

Fig. 4.5: A 8×8 shuffle exchange MIN.

Two measures can be used to assess the reliability of a MIN. The first is called the *Terminal Reliability* (TR(t)) and the second is called *Network Reliability* (NR(t)). These are defined as follows.

1. Terminal Reliability, TR(t) is defined as the probability that a given pair of input-output (source-destination) are connected.
2. Network Reliability, NR(t) is defined as the probability that all pairs of input-output (source-destination) are connected.

In computing the reliability of MINs, we will assume that links connecting the different stages are perfect and that only SEs are subjected to failure. We will also assume that when a SE is inoperable, i.e., connections between its input and output ports do not exist.

Recall that there exists a unique path in a MIN between any input-output pair. The number of SEs along that path is given by $n = \log_2 N$. All SEs along a given path from an input to an output must function in order for the path to be established. This is a characteristic of series system. Assume that each SE in a MIN has a reliability $R_{SE} = e^{-\lambda t}$. Therefore, the terminal reliability between any pair of input-output (source-destination) in an N×N MIN is given by $TR(t) = e^{-n\lambda t}$.

It should be noted that from the reliability point of view, the failure of any SE causes a possible connection between input-output pairs to be disrupted. Therefore, all *SEs* in the network are required to function in order to have all pairs of source-destination to be connected. This is a property of a series system. Thus, the network reliability can be computed as $NR(t) = e^{-k\lambda t}$, where k is the total number of *SEs* in the network, i.e., $k = \dfrac{N}{2} \log_2 N$.

The existence of a unique path between any pair of source-destination is considered a disadvantage from the reliability point of view. This is because the failure of a single SE along a path will cause that path to be inoperable. Therefore, the original MIN must be enhanced such that more than one path can be established between a given source-destination pair. This can be achieved if an extra stage of SEs is added to the original MIN. Consider, for example, the augmented MIN shown in Fig. 4.6.

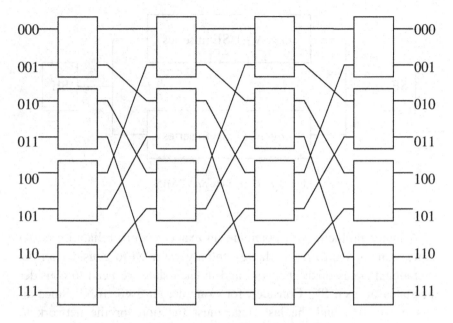

Fig. 4.6: Augmented shuffle-exchange MIN.

In this network, called the extra stage shuffle exchange network (SEN^+), two paths exist between any source-destination pair. This can be seen by considering that in the first stage (the added stage), a source will broadcast its message to both the upper and the lower outputs. The remaining stages use the same simple technique presented in connection with the SEN. This way two paths that are disjoint in the intermediate $n-1 = (log_2 N)-1$ stages but are joint in the first and the last stage are created by between any source-destination pair.

In order to compute the $TR(SEN^+)$, we use the Reliability Block Diagram (RBD) shown in Fig. 4.7.

The terminal reliability is given by

$$TR(t) = e^{-2\lambda t} \times (1 - (1 - e^{-(n-1)\lambda t}) \times (1 - e^{-(n-1)\lambda t})).$$

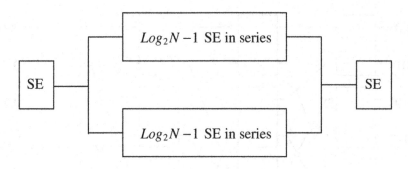

Fig. 4.7: RBD of the *SEN*⁺ MIN.

A major problem with obtaining an exact network reliability NR(t) expression for the *SEN*⁺ is that essentially we need to consider all the operational states of the network and in each state we need to consider the status of each SE. Consider, for example, an 8×8 SEN⁺. Since all SEs in the first and the last stage must function for the network to function, then we need to consider a total of 2^8 possible states. However, actual construction of the state space of the SEN⁺ will reveal that far less number of states need to be considered. It is possible to show that the NR(t) for an 8×8 SEN⁺ is given by the following expression:

$$NR(t)_{SEN^{+8\times8}} = 2 \times e^{-12\lambda t} + 4 \times e^{-14\lambda t} - 8 \times e^{-15\lambda t} + 3 \times e^{-16\lambda t}$$

An upper bound on the NR(t) of the SEN⁺ can be computed as follows.

1. Assume that the SEN⁺ consists of $\log_2 N + 1$ subsystems each consisting of $\dfrac{N}{2}$ SEs connected in Parallel.
2. The RBD for the SEN⁺ under this condition is shown in Fig. 4.8.
3. Based on the RBD, the upper bound on the NR(t) of the SEN⁺ is given by: $NR(t)_{SEN^{+upper}} \leqslant e^{-N\lambda t} \times (1 - (1 - e^{-\lambda t})^{N/2})^{n-1}$

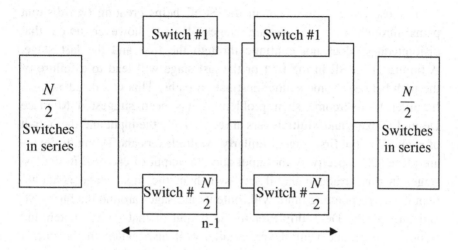

Fig. 4.8: RBD of the *SEN*$^+$ upper bound reliability computation.

A lower bound on the NR(t) of the SEN$^+$ can be computed as follows.

1. Assume that the SEN$^+$ consists of two parallel subsystems each consisting $\frac{N}{4} \times (\log_2 N - 1)$ SEs connected in series.
2. The RBD for the SEN$^+$ under such condition is shown in Fig. 4.9.
3. Based on the RBD, the lower bound on the NR(t) of the SEN$^+$ is given by: $NR(t)_{SEN^{+lower}} \geqslant e^{-N\lambda t} \times (1 - (1 - e^{-\frac{N}{4} \times (\log_2 N - 1)\lambda t})^2)$

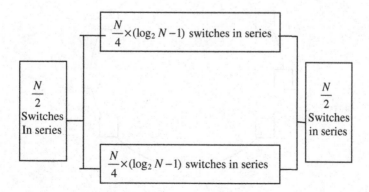

Fig. 4.9: RBD of the *SEN*$^+$ lower bound reliability computation.

The use of an extra stage in the SEN⁺ helps creating two disjoint paths through the intermediate stages. It was however noted that disjointedness does not continue through the first and the last stage. A failure of an SE in the first or the last stage will lead to a failure of the path between some source-destination paths. This is a disadvantage. In order to overcome such problem it has been suggested to place De-multiplexers and Multiplexers at respectively the input and the output of each SE in the first stage. Similarly, Multiplexers and De-multiplexers are placed at respectively the input and the output of each SE in the last stage. In this arrangement, if any switch in the input stage is faulty, then the corresponding input will route its messages around the faulty SE and through the De-multiplexer to the output of that faulty switch and through the output Multiplexer. Similarly, if any switch in the output stage is faulty, then the De-multiplexer at the input of that faulty switch will route the messages arriving at its input around the faulty switch and to the final destination through the output Multiplexer.

4.2 Reliability and Fault Tolerance in Single Loop Architectures

In this section, we discuss the issues related to the reliability and fault tolerance of loop architectures (ring). A schematic for the basic ring network is shown in Fig. 4.10.

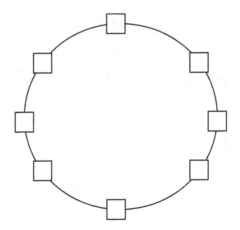

Fig. 4.10: A schematic for the basic ring network.

The basic ring architecture is essentially a series of workstations connected in a point-to-point manner to form a loop. From the reliability and fault tolerance point of view, the properties of the ring architecture are similar to those of a series system. The basic ring architecture suffers from the inability to tolerate any single node (or link) failure. In other words, the basic ring architecture suffers from what is know as single point failure (SPF). This is because a single failure in a node or a link will lead to the failure of the whole architecture. Assume that ring architecture consists of N nodes connected in series. The reliability of the architecture is therefore given by $R_{basic}(t) = e^{-N\lambda t}$ and the meantime to failure $MTTF_{basic} = \dfrac{1}{N\lambda}$.

Two variances to the basic ring scheme are presented in this chapter. Each presented schemes is capable of tolerating node and/or link failures. These are presented below.

Bypass-Switch Ring Network

In this case, each node is provided with a bypass switch (see Fig. 4.11).

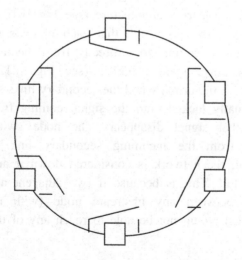

Fig. 4.11: A schematic of the bypass switch network.

When a node fails, the bypass switch closes in order to isolate that node from the ring and thus maintains data-path continuity. The terminal reliability between any pair of nodes in the bypass switch architecture, assuming that the bypass switches are perfect, is given by

$$R_{bypass}(t) = e^{-2\lambda t} * \sum_{j=0}^{N-2} \binom{N-2}{j} (1 - e^{-\lambda t})^j * e^{-\lambda(N-2-j)t}$$

In the above expression, $e^{-2\lambda t}$ represents the probability that both of the communicating nodes are working (non-faulty), the term $(1 - e^{-\lambda t})^j$ represents the probability that j of the remaining (N-2) nodes have failed, and the term $e^{-\lambda(N-2-j)t}$ represents the probability that (N-2-j) nodes are working (non-faulty). It should be noted that in case that the bypass switches are subject to failure, then their failure rate has to be taken into consideration in developing the terminal reliability equation.

The Braided Ring Architecture

In this case, the basic ring architecture (see Fig. 4.10) is augmented by a set of secondary links such that each node is bypassed by a secondary link and that link goes directly from the node's upstream neighbor to its downstream neighbor (see Fig. 4.12). Each node transmits over both the primary and the secondary links simultaneously. A node is normally locked onto the signal coming from its primary link. In case that signal disappears, the node switches into the signal coming from the incoming secondary link. According to this arrangement, the network is considered down if and only if two adjacent nodes fail. This is because if two adjacent nodes fail, then communication between any upstream node (with respect to the two failing nodes) would not be able to reach any of the downstream node(s).

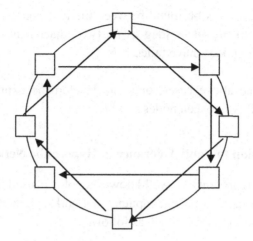

Fig. 4.12: A schematic of the braided ring network.

In order to be able to develop the terminal reliability between any two communicating nodes in the braided ring network, one has first to consider the network as consisting of three set of nodes. These are:

(1) The two communicating nodes $S_1 = \{i, i+j\}$; node i sending to i+j
(2) The supper stream set consisting of nodes $S_2 = \{i+j+1, i+j+2, ..., N\}$
(3) The down stream set consisting of node $S_3 = \{i+1, i+2, ..., i+j-1\}$

In analyzing the working conditions of the braided network, one can observe the following possible cases:

(1) nodes i and j are neighboring nodes: in this case, the cardinality of S_2 is N-2 and the cardinality of S_3 is 0. All remaining nodes are upper stream nodes with respect to nodes i and j.
(2) There exists one node in the down stream set, i.e., $S_3 = \{i+1\}$. The failure of this downstream node does not affect the communication between nodes i and j, *i.e.*, this downstream node does not contribute to the terminal reliability between i and j.
(3) A path can always be found between the two nodes i and j through the downstream set as long as no two adjacent nodes, out of the downstream nodes, have failed.

(4) A path can always be found between the two nodes i and j through the upper stream set as long as no two adjacent nodes, out of the upper stream nodes, have failed.

Based on the above cases, one can develop the expression for the terminal reliability between nodes i and j.

4.3 Introduction to Fault Tolerance in Hypercube Networks

A hypercube represents a well-known topology used in connecting distributed memory multi-computer networks. An n-dimensional hypercube, is defined recursively as follows:

$$Q_n = \begin{cases} O_0 & , \quad n = 0 \\ K_2 \times Q_{n-1}, & n > 0 \end{cases}$$

Where Q_0 is a trivial graph with one node, K_2 is the complete graph with two nodes, and $\times$ is the product operation of two graphs. Address of a node is specified by $S_n S_{n-1} S_{n-2} ... S_2 S_1$, where $S_i \in \{0,1\}$. Figure 4.13 shows a 4-cube architecture.

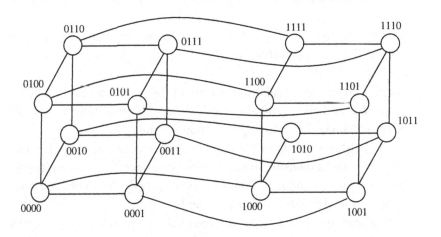

Fig. 4.13: A 4-cube architecture.

The Hamming distance between two addresses $S_n S_{n-1} S_{n-2} ... S_2 S_1$ and $D_n D_{n-1} D_{n-2} ... D_2 D_1$ in a Q_n is defined as follows:

$$H(s,d) = \oplus_{i=1}^{n} h(u_i, w_i), \text{ where } h(u_i, w_i) = \begin{cases} 1, & u_i \neq w_i \\ 0, & u_i = w_i \end{cases}$$

and $\oplus_{i=1}^{n} h(u_i, w_i)$ represents n sequential exclusive-or operations.

A path between a source node s and a destination node d in a hypercube is specified by a coordinate sequence. The coordinate sequence contains all the dimensions which need to be traversed to reach d from s. The dimensions traversed need not to be ordered. If $[c1, c2, ..., ck]$ is such coordinate sequence of a path in Q_n starting from s and going to d and k = $H(s,d)$ then the path ends at d if and only if $e^{c_1} \oplus e^{c_2} \oplus ... \oplus e^{c_k} = d_{/s}$, where $d_{/s}$ represents the relative address of node d with respect to that of node s and is equal to $d \oplus s$ and $e^j = e_n e_{n-1} ... e_1$ is a bit stream of length n with only $e_j = 1$.

Example

Suppose that in a 4-dimensional cube, the source is $s = 0110$ and the destination is $d = 1000$ and that the coordinate sequence is [3, 4, 2]. We calculate k = $H(s,d)$ = 3, $e^{c_1} = e^3 = 0100$, $e^{c_2} = e^4 = 1000$, $e^{c_3} = e^2 = 0010$. Hence, $\oplus_{i=1}^{3} e^{c_i} = 0100 \oplus 1000 \oplus 0010 = 1110$ and $d_{/s} = 1000_{/0110} = 1110$. Therefore, the right hand side and the left hand side are equal and hence the path is correct.

An important property of a hypercube is the availability of a number of paths between any pair of nodes. Consider, for example, any pair of nodes s and d in a cube Q_n such that $H(d,s)=k$. There are exactly n disjoint paths of length less than or equal to $k+2$ between s and d. Of these, k disjoint paths are of length k and $(n-k)$ disjoint paths are of length $k+2$. It should be noted that disjoint paths share no common links among them. This is important for fault tolerance since the failure of a path does not lead to the failure of any of the disjoint paths. Consider, for example, the case of a 4-cube. Assume that the source node address is 0000 and the destination address is 0111. The Hamming distance is 3 and therefore there are three paths of length 3 and one path of length of length 5. Thus, if the number of faulty components f links and g nodes is less than n, then there is at least one path of length less than or equal to $k+2$ between any two non-faulty nodes s and d where $k=H(d,s)$.

Fault-Tolerant Basic Block (FTBB) — Based Hypercube

In this section, we present a number of fault-tolerant hypercube architectures using redundancy.

Approach #1

In this approach, a fault-tolerant hypercube architecture is created using fault-tolerant modules together with decoupling networks and soft switches. A fault-tolerant module consists of m active nodes and k spare nodes. A group of k level decoupling networks as shown in Fig. 4.14 is used to connect one fault tolerant module to another.

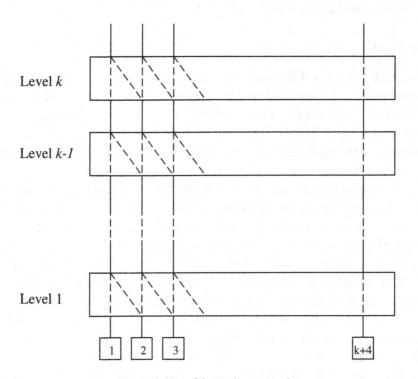

Fig. 4.14: Use of decoupling networks.

When none of the modules have failed, dotted connections shown in Fig. 4.14 are not used. When a node fails, the fault-tolerant module is reconfigured using the soft switches so as to bypass the failed node and replace it with a spare node. Connections between nodes of one module and another are established as follows. Given a module with k spare nodes, let i-1 be the number of nodes that have failed and replaced during the operation of the system. When another active node fails, the level i decoupling network is reconfigured by switching the link that connects to the failed node and all links to the right of it, one position to the right. For example, with three spares, we show the connections in Fig. 4.15 after node 3 has failed.

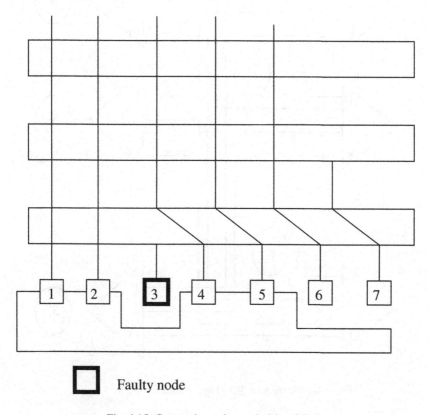

Faulty node

Fig. 4.15: Connections after node 3 has failed.

Approach #2

Consider a FTBB with M primary nodes $P_1,...,P_M$ and K spare nodes $S_1,...,S_K$ using full spare utilization, i.e., any spare can replace and primary node within an FTBB. The switching logic for reconfiguration in this case uses multiplexers and demultiplexers as shown in Fig. 4.16.

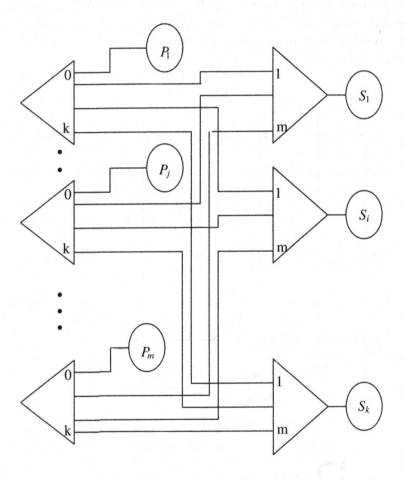

Fig. 4.16: Switching logic within an FTBB.

In this figure, it is assumed for simplicity that multiplexers and de-multiplexers can multiplex and de-multiplex lines, respectively. Specifically, a 1-to-(K+1) de-multiplexer is used for each P_j to divert when needed the links of P_j to S_i. Also, an M-to-1 multiplexer is used for each S_i to connect it to the appropriate links. If a primary node P_j is non-faulty, then the de-multiplexer is set to select the 0th output. In case P_j is faulty, the replacement of P_j by S_i requires that the de-multiplexer associated with P_j be set to its *ith* output and the multiplexer associated with S_i be set to select its *jth* output. The scheme can also support spare failures.

Approach #3

This scheme, called the *node spare scheme*, uses spare nodes attached to specific nodes in the cube using specific embedding techniques. The hypercube in this scheme consists of two types of nodes, called the P and the S nodes. The P and S nodes have different internal architectures. Figure 4.17(a) shows the internal details of a normal processing node (the P node) of a hypercube.

The P node consists of a computation processor (CPU) connected through an internal bus to a local memory and message routing logic consisting of a DMA unit and a $(d+1) \times (d+1)$ crossbar switch for a 2^d processor hypercube.

Figure 4.17(b) shows an S node consisting of two copies of the CPU and local memory connected to two internal busses. The DMA and message routing logic is shared between the two processing units, one of which is active under normal conditions; the other is a standby spare. Under failure of any processing element either within the S node or in a nearby P node, the spare processor/memory/bus from the corresponding S node is brought on line.

A perfect embedding for allocation of S nodes in the cube requires that each P node is adjacent to exactly one S node in the cube. A perfect embedding is a 3 cube is shown in Fig. 4.18. An algorithm for reconfiguration in the presence of primary node failure is used such that an S node will replace the failed P node.

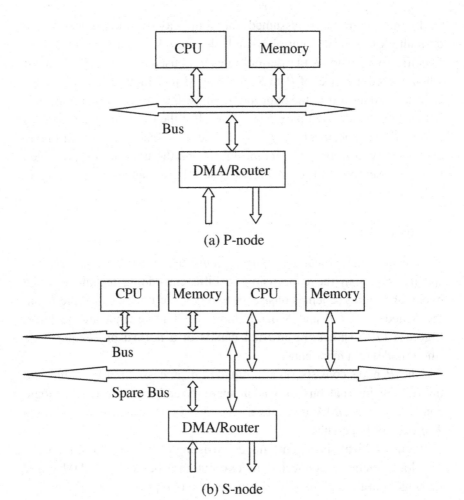

(a) P-node

(b) S-node

Fig. 4.17: Architecture of the *P* and *S* nodes.

Approach #4

For connecting very large number of processors, the link cost of a hypercube becomes prohibitively expensive and therefore hierarchical interconnection network (HINs) schemes are used in this approach. A homogeneous two level Binary Hypercube/Binary Hypercube (BH/BH) HIN is shown in Fig. 4.19.

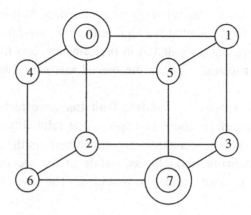

Fig. 4.18: A perfect embedding in a 3 cube.

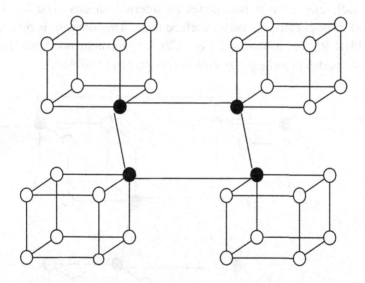

Fig. 4.19: A BH/BH HIN with a cluster size of 8.

Each level 1 network is called a *cluster*. A cluster of size 8 and two levels have been found to be optimal for connecting very large number of processors in a BH/BH network under a cost/performance tradeoff. Although it results in a reduction in the number of links, a HIN does not seem to possess good fault tolerance characteristics. Major disadvantages of HINs include the potential for high traffic rates on inter-cluster links, and thus the potential degradation in performance, and the potential for diminished fault tolerance due to the special role played by the interface nodes.

It should be noted that standard fault tolerance techniques can be applied to the interface nodes to improve the reliability of the BH/BH networks. Two specific techniques are shown here. In the first technique, the level two network is duplicated, while in the second technique, a standby spare interface node is provided. The two techniques are described below.

Replication Techniques

Here each cluster uses two nodes as interface nodes. The level two network is duplicated for each interface node. This network is referred to as BH/BH-RS and is shown in Fig. 4.20. It is recommended that the two interface nodes in a cluster be kept as far apart as possible.

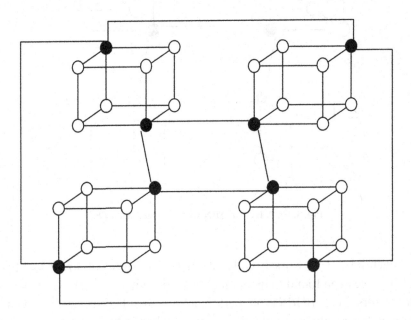

Fig. 4.20: A BH/BH-RS network with a cluster size of 8.

Standby Spare Interface Node Technique

Since interface nodes are the most vulnerable, a standby spare for each interface node in the network is used. One node is normally operational and the other serves as a spare. If a failure of the interface node occurs, the spare takes over. This technique is referred to as BH/BH-SI.

It is clear that the BH/BH-RS technique uses more links as compared to the BH/BH-SI. However, the BH/BH-SI technique requires fault detection of the interface nodes and extra spare nodes. It is possible to show that the fault tolerance and the performance of the BH/BH-RS are substantially better, justifying the increased link cost.

In Chapter 5, we discuss some issues that are related to fault-tolerant routing algorithms in hypercube. In the next Section, we discuss sub-cube reliability in hypercube.

Sub-Cube Reliability in Hypercube

According to the sub-cube reliability measure, the reliability is computed in terms of the number of disjoint sub-cubes that can be embedded in a d-cube in the presence of node and/or link failures. In particular, the ability of a hypercube to embed a $(d-1)$ sub-cube (the largest fault-free sub-cube in a d-cube) in the presence of failures is considered. When component failures (nodes and links) occur, the topology of the hypercube may change. For example, when a single node failure occurs in a d-cube it is no longer possible to have a functional d-cube but a functional $(d-1)$-sub-cube could be found (embedded). For the purpose of discussion in this section, we assume that the node failure obey the exponential failure law with node failure rate denoted by λ_n. Links are considered perfect.

Consider the embedding of a fault free $(d-1)$-sub-cube in a d-cube in the presence of node failure. A single node failure will always leave an undamaged $(d-1)$-sub-cube but two node failures could destroy all $(d-1)$-sub-cubes. For example, if node 0 and node $(N-1)$ fail, there is no way of embedding a $(d-1)$-sub-cube. A fault free $(d-1)$-sub-cube exists if and only if all failures occur such that they can be enclosed in an i sub-cube with $i < d$.

Define S_i as the system state whereby all node failures that have occurred could be enclosed in a maximal i sub-cube, i.e., a lower order sub-cube that encloses all failed nodes does not exist. In terms of functional cubes, state S_i can be characterized as embedding $(d\text{-}i)$ disjoint fault free sub-cubes of order $(d\text{-}1)$, $(d\text{-}2)$, ..., i, respectively. The state diagram along with the transition rates (the number of ways a transition can take place) is shown in Fig. 4.21. State S_d means that all failures have occurred in a maximal d cube so that no embedding of $(d\text{-}1)$-sub-cube is possible. S_* represents the fault free initial state or perfect state.

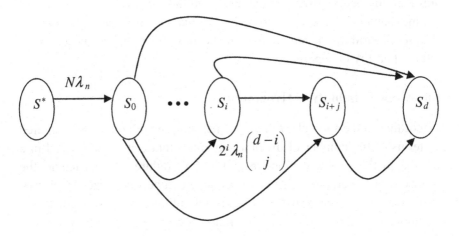

Fig. 4.21: State diagram.

Consider the state transition from state S_* to state S_0. A single node failure can cause such transition. Therefore, the transition rate is $N\lambda_n$. Now, consider the state transition from state S_i to state S_{i+j}. State S_i signifies that all failures have occurred within i sub-cubes. This takes up i dimensions of the d. Label these dimensions as faulty. The remaining $(d\text{-}i)$ dimensions are fault free. State S_{i+j} signifies that all failures have occurred in a $(i+j)$ sub-cube. This labels $(i+j)$ dimensions as faulty. The transition from S_i to state S_{i+j} means that additional j dimensions becomes faulty out of the fault free $(d\text{-}i)$ dimensions. j dimensions out of the $(d\text{-}i)$ can be chosen in $\binom{d-i}{j}$ ways. Considering one of these ways we see that the original faulty i dimensions could take up values either 0s of 1s (total of 2^i ways). Each of the different ways represents the address of the nodes which can fail to cause the transition. Therefore, the transition rate is labeled as $\binom{d-i}{j} 2^i \lambda_n$.

Figure 4.22 shows the system state diagram for a 3 FTBB under node failure model.

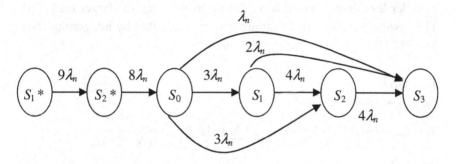

Fig. 4.22: System state diagram for a 3 FTBB under node failure model.

Let the probability of being in state S_i at time t be $P_i(t)$. The state equations for this system are given as follows.

$$\partial P_* / \partial t = -\lambda_n N P_*,$$
$$\partial P_0 / \partial t = -\lambda_n (N-1) P_0 + \lambda_n N P_*,$$

$$\partial P_i / \partial t = -\lambda_n (N - 2^i) P_i + \sum_{j=0}^{i-1} \lambda_n 2^j \binom{d-j}{i-j} P_j, 0 < i \le d$$

The initial conditions are $P_*(0) = 1$ and $P_i(0) = 0$ for all $i > 0$.

It can be shown by induction on i that the solution to this system of equations is as follows.

$$Pi(t) = (-1)^{i+1} \binom{d}{i} 2^{d-i} e^{-\lambda n N t} + \binom{d}{i} \sum_{m=0}^{i} (-1)^{i-m} \binom{i}{m} 2^{d-m} e^{-(N-3m)\lambda n t}$$

Let us define the reliabilities as follows

$R_*(t) = P_{*(t)}$,
$R_0(t) = P_0(t) + R_*(t)$ and
$R_i(t) = P_i(t) + R_{i-1}(t)$, for all i.

Thus $P_i(t)$ is the probability that all failures are enclosed in an *i* sub-cube. $R_i(t)$ is the probability that all failures have occurred in a sub-cube of order less than or equal to i. The probability $R_i(t)$ is larger than $P_i(t)$. The system's mean time to failure can be evaluated by integrating $R_i(t)$. The MTTF is given by the expressions

$T_* = 1/N\lambda_n$,
$T_0 = T_* + 1/(N-1)\lambda_n$ and
$$T_i = T_{i-1} + (-1)^{i+1}\binom{d}{i}\frac{1}{2^i \lambda_n} + \binom{d}{i}\sum_{m=0}^{i}(-1)^{i-m}\binom{i}{m}\frac{2^{d-m}}{(N-2^m)\lambda_n}$$

for $i > 0$.

4.4 Introduction to Fault Tolerance in Mesh Networks

An n-dimensional mesh is defined as an interconnection structure that has $K_0 \times \ldots \times K_{n-1}$ nodes where *n* is the number of dimensions of the network, and K_i is the radix of dimension *i*. Each node identified by an n-coordinate vector $(\chi_0, \chi_1, \ldots, \chi_{n-1})$. Where $0 \le \chi_i \le K_{i-1}$. Figure 4.23 shows a $3 \times 3 \times 2$ mesh network.

Parallel computers with mesh interconnection networks are able to efficiently support a number of scientific processing applications. A large number of distributed memory parallel computers utilizing mesh interconnection networks have been introduction in the literature. Example of these include MPP from Goodyear Aerospace, Paragon from Intel Scientific, T3D from Cray, and J − Machine from MIT. In this section, we present examples of fault-tolerant routing techniques used in mesh networks.

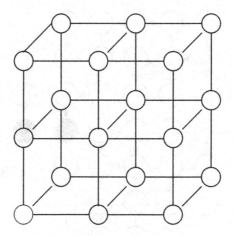

Fig. 4.23: A 3 × 3 × 2 mesh network.

The Turn Model

The fundamental concept used in the turn model is to prohibit the smallest number of turns in order to prevent cycles from taking place while routing. Consider the 2D mesh shown in Fig. 4.24. There are eight possible cycles. In this case, two turn need to be prohibited in order to prevent cycles. If the two turns to the west are prohibited, then the corresponding routing technique is called west first routing. Figure 4.24 shows the six turns allowed and the two turns prohibited in the case of west first routing in a 2D mesh. It should be noted that in order to travel to the west, a message must begin in that direction. Figure 4.25 shows an example path for the west-first routing algorithm using link fault model. It should be noted that the path is not minimal. It should also be noted that because cycles are avoided, west – first routing is deadlock-free.

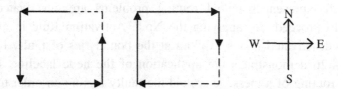

Fig. 4.24: The six turns allowed and the two turns prohibited in the West-First routing algorithm.

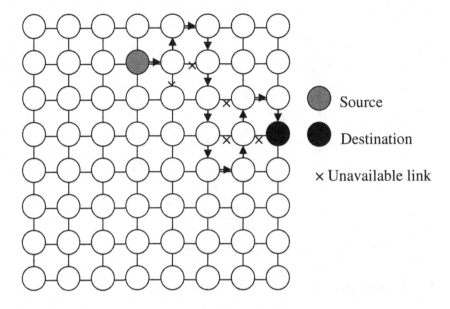

Fig. 4.25: West-first routing example in an 8 × 8 2D mesh.

Node Labeling Technique

In this technique nodes which cause routing difficulties are labeled. Nodes labeling strategy is based on the following two rules.

1. Node Deactivation Rule: in this case, a healthy node connected to two faulty nodes is deactivated and marked as faulty.
2. Node Activation Rule: In this case, a deactivated node connected to a healthy node is activated and marked as unsafe.

The technique starts by transforming faulty regions to rectangular regions. This can be achieved by applying the Node Deactivation Rule. Nodes that present potential routing problems are deactivated. The algorithm proceeds by applying the Node Activation Rule in order to activate deactivated nodes residing at the boundaries of faulty regions. Figure 4.26 demonstrates the application of the node labeling scheme and the routing of a message around the faulty regions in order to reach the destination. It should be noted that only node fault model is assumed in Fig. 4.26 (links are assumed to be perfect).

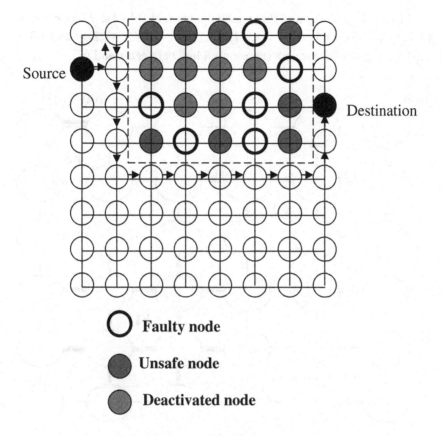

Fig. 4.26: Node labeling routing example in an 8 × 2D mesh.

Block-Fault-Model-Based Routing

According to this technique, each fault is assumed to belong to exactly one fault block. A set F of faulty nodes and links indicates a rectangular fault block, or f – region, if there is a rectangle connecting various nodes of the mesh such that:

1. The boundary of the rectangle has only fault-free nodes or links.
2. The interior of the rectangle contains all and only the components given by F.

Figure 4.27 illustrates three rectangular fault blocks: $F_1 = <(3,3)$, $(3,4)>$, $<(4,3), (4,4)>$, F2 $= <(1,1), (2,1)>$, $<(1,2), (2,2)>$, and F3 $= <(0,4), (0,5)>$ where $<x,y>$ represents a link between x and y.

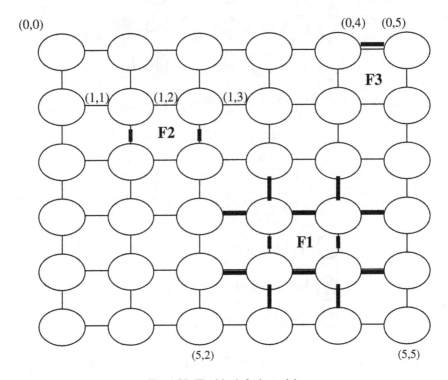

Fig. 4.27: The block fault model.

The complete fault set for the network in Fig. 4.27 is F_1 U F_2 U F_3. Conceptually, fault regions may be considered islands of faults in a sea of communication links and nodes. For each *f-region* in a network with faults, it is feasible to connect the fault free components around the region to form a ring or chain.

The faulty rings or *f-ring* of a given region consists of the fault free nodes and links that are adjacent (row-wise, column-wise or diagonally) to one or more components of the fault region. It should be noted that F_1 in Fig. 4.27 is an example of an *f-ring*. Forming a fault-ring around an *f-ring* is not possible when the *f-ring* touches one or more boundaries of the network. In this case, a *fault-chain* rather than an *f-ring* is formed around the *f-region*, F_3 in Fig. 4.27 represents such case.

Table 4.2 provides a summary of the main properties of the three mesh fault-tolerant routing techniques discussed above. The table shows the fault model used and the number of faults that can be tolerated. In multi-computer networks, faults can be of two types: node or link. A third hybrid fault type, called *block fault*, arises from a combination of both types. In Chapter 5, we elaborate more on these types of faults and discuss some ways to tolerate them.

Table 4.2: Main properties of mesh fault-tolerant routing techniques.

Technique	Fault model	Number of faults tolerated
Turn Model	Link	Any number as long as network remains connected
Node Labeling	Node/Link	< n
Block Model	Block	Any number as long as network remains connected

4.5 Summary

In this Chapter, we covered the basic issues related to the reliability and fault tolerance of multiprocessor interconnection networks. This includes both dynamic and static interconnection networks. In dynamic networks, we covered the reliability and fault tolerance issues related to bus (single and multiple), crossbar, and the multi-stage interconnection networks. In static networks, we covered the reliability and fault tolerance issues related to ring, hypercube, and mesh-connected networks. In ring networks, we covered both the basic ring and the bypass networks. In hypercube, we covered the FTBB and the sub-cube fault tolerance. In mesh-connected networks, we covered the turn model, the node labeling model, and the block fault model. Simple examples were provided in order to illustrate the basic concepts and the fault-tolerant routing algorithms used. In Chapter 5, we cover in more detail the issues related to the fault-tolerant routing in hypercube and mesh-connected networks.

References

[1] K. Al-Tawil, M. Abd-El-Barr, and F. Ashraf, "A Survey and Comparison of Wormhole Routing Techniques in Mesh Networks", IEEE Network, March/April 1997, pp. 38-45.

[2] S. Abraham and K. Padmanabhan, "Reliability of the hypercube", International Conference on Parallel Processing, II(4):7-19, Oct. 1988.

[3] A. El-Amawy and R. Raja, "Split sequence generation algorithms for efficient identification of operational subcubes in faulty hypercubes", Parallel Computing, 19(7):789-805, July 1993.

[4] P. Banerjee and M. Peercy, "Design and evaluation of hardware strategies of reconfiguring hypercube and meshes under faults", IEEE Transactions on Computers, 43(7):841-848, July 1994.

[5] Bruck et al., "Tolerating faults using subcube partitioning", IEEE Transactions on Computers, 41(5):599-605, May 1992.

[6] C. Das and J. Kim, "A unified task based dependability model for hypercube computers", IEEE Transactions on Parallel and Distributed Systems, 3:312-324, May 1992.

[7] S. Sultan and R. Melhem, "An efficient modular spare allocation scheme and its application to fault-tolerant binary hypercubes", IEEE Transactions on Parallel and Distributed Systems, 2(1):117-126, Jan. 1991.

[8] C. Yang et al., "A reconfigurable modular fault-tolerant hypercube architecture", IEEE Transaction on Parallel and Distributed Systems, 5:1018-1032, Oct. 1994.

[9] O. Ibe, "Reliability Comparison of Token-Ring Network Schemes", IEEE Transactions on Reliability, Vol. 41, no. 2, June 1992, pp.288-293.

Chapter 5

Fault-Tolerant Routing in Multi-Computer Networks

In this chapter, the architecture of the hypercube and that of the mesh multi-computer networks are briefly introduced. A number of algorithms that are used in routing messages in healthy hypercube and healthy mesh networks are then introduced. A number of routing algorithms for routing messages in faulty hypercube and faulty mesh networks are presented and analyzed.

5.1 Introduction

An n-dimensional hypercube, is defined recursively as follows:

$$Q_n = \begin{cases} O_0 & , & n = 0 \\ K_2 \times Q_{n-1}, & n > 0 \end{cases}$$

Where Q_0 is a trivial graph with one node, K_2 is the complete graph with two nodes, and $\times$ is the product operation of two graphs. Address of a node is specified by $S_n S_{n-1} S_{n-2} ... S_2 S_1$, where $S_i \in \{0,1\}$. Figure 5.1 shows a 4-cube architecture.

The Hamming distance between two addresses $S_n S_{n-1} S_{n-2} ... S_2 S_1$ and $D_n D_{n-1} D_{n-2} ... D_2 D_1$ in a Q_n is defined as follows:

$$H(s,d) = \oplus_{i=1}^{n} h(u_i, w_i), \text{ where } h(u_i, w_i) = \begin{cases} 1, & u_i \neq w_i \\ 0, & u_i = w_i \end{cases}$$

and $\oplus_{i=1}^{n} h(u_i, w_i)$ is the exclusive-or operation.

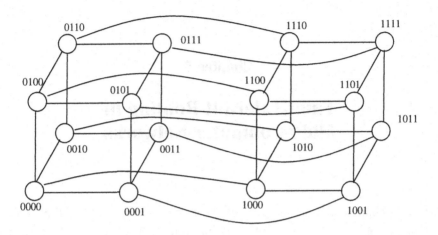

Fig. 5.1: A 4-cube architecture.

An n-dimensional mesh has $K_0 \times K_1 \times ... \times K_{n-1}$ nodes where n is the number of dimensions, denoted by $DIM_0, DIM_1, ..., DIM_{n-1}$, and K_i is the radix of dimension DIM_i, where $0 \geq i \geq n-1$. A node X is identified by an n-element vector $(x_0, x_1, ... x_{n-1})$, where $0 \geq x_i \geq K_i - 1$. Two nodes $X = (x_0, x_1, ... x_{n-1})$ and $Y = (y_0, y_1, ... y_{n-1})$ are connected in dimension i if and only if $x_i = y_i \pm 1$, and $x_j = y_j$ for all $i \neq j$. Each two neighboring nodes are connected by a bidirectional channel consisting of two unidirectional physical channels. Figure 5.2 shows an example of a $3 \times 3 \times 2$ mesh network.

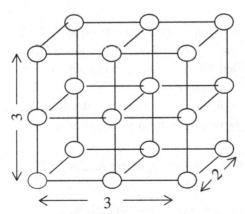

Fig. 5.2: A $3 \times 3 \times 2$ mesh network.

Table 5.1 shows a simple comparison between mesh and hypercube networks.

Table 5.1: Mesh versus hypercube.

	Mesh	Hypercube
Number of nodes	2^n	2^n
Total number of links	2×2^n	$n \times 2^n$
Diameter	$2^{\frac{n}{2}+1} - 2$	$\log_2 N$

The *e-cube routing* algorithm is widely used for routing messages in healthy mesh networks. According to this algorithm, messages are first routed along dimension DIM_0 and then along dimension along DIM_1, then along MID_2, and finally along DIM_{n-1}. Consider, for example, e-cube routing in a 6×6 mesh. In this case, a message starts to travel first along a row (row message) and then it changes its direction to travel along a column (a column message) until it reaches its destination, see Fig. 5.3.

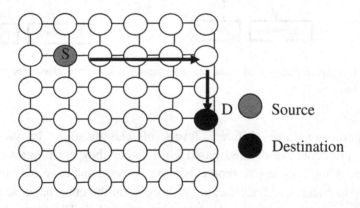

Fig. 5.3: The e-cube routing in a 6 × 6 mesh.

The e-cube algorithm provides deadlock free shortest-path routing. However, when faults exist in a mesh, messages may be misrouted to avoid faulty nodes/links.

Design Analysis

When the mesh or hypercube network becomes faulty, the simple e-cube or coordinate sequence algorithms may fail to route messages properly. Therefore, a number of adaptive algorithms have been introduced to achieve correct message routing in the presence of faulty (nodes or links) for both meshes and hypercube networks. A possible classification for the hypercube and mesh routing algorithms is shown in Fig. 5.4.

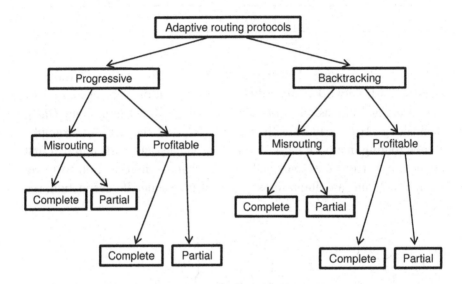

Fig. 5.4: A possible classification for adaptive routing algorithms in Hypercube & Mesh networks.

There are three different levels of classification. In the first level, protocols are divided based on whether they are progressive or backtracking. Progressive protocols move forward and have only limited ability to backtrack. Backtracking protocols, on the other hand, searches the network systematically, backtracking as needed. They store history information in the header to ensure that no path is searched more than once. In the second level, protocols are classified according to whether they are profitable or misrouting. Profitable protocols consider only those links for routing the message which are profitable. A profitable link is a link over which a message moves closer to its destination. A misrouting protocol considers both profitable and non-profitable links as candidates for routing decisions at each node. In the third level, protocols can be completely or partially adaptive. A completely adaptive protocol can use all paths in its class. It is not deterred by routing restrictions from establishing a path as the case in partial adaptive protocols.

The number of disjoint paths in an architecture can be used as a measure of the fault tolerance ability of that architecture. For an n-cube, there is a total of n disjoint paths. For a mesh network, there is a maximum of $2 \times n$ disjoint paths. For a wrap around mesh (torous), there is an exactly $2 \times n$ disjoint paths. This indicates that, in general an n-mesh is more fault-tolerant than an n-cube. The fault tolerance aspects of both meshes and hypercube are discussed below in some detail.

5.2 Fault-Tolerant Routing Algorithms in Hypercube

Several adaptive algorithms for routing in faulty hypercube exist in the literatures. Some of these are introduced below.

5.2.1 *Depth-First Search Approach*

This approach attempts to find the optimal path between the source and the destination nodes. It is characterized as being partially adaptive, misrouting, and progressive routing algorithm. The algorithm requires each node to know only the condition of its own links. It attempts to route messages along the optimal path, having a length equal to the hamming distance between the source and destination nodes. The algorithm guarantees routing only when the number of faulty elements (nodes and links) is less than n (the dimension of the cube).

According to the algorithm, each message takes the form

$$[ID, k, CS, message, Tag]$$

In this form, we have the following:

$CS = [c1, c2, c3, ..., ck]$, is called the *Coordinate Sequence* function and is used to store the dimensions that the message has to follow. The protocol tries to follow the *e*-cube pattern as much as possible, therefore the smallest dimension is tried first.

$Tag = t_n, t_{n-1}, ..., ..., t_1$, is used to keep track of the spare dimensions that have been used to bypass faulty components. It is initialized to all 0s at the source.

k: Indicates the remaining length of the path and is equal to 0 at the destination. If along routing no faulty links are encountered, k is decremented by 1 and the dimension in which routing is being done is removed from the coordinate sequence.

ID keeps track of the dimension along which routing was lastly performed.

If the smallest dimension specified by the coordinate sequence is blocked, the node tries to route the message in the next higher dimension as specified by the coordinate sequence. If there is no such dimension in the coordinate sequence, then misrouting is done. While misrouting, first the *tag* is updated to record the blocked dimensions as shown by the remaining coordinate sequence. The *tag* is then examined and the smallest dimension in which the tag shows a zero is selected for misrouting. The tag is then updated by adding a one in that dimension position in tag in which misrouting is done. The value k is incremented by one while misrouting. For each misrouting the data takes two additional hops to reach the destination. Spare dimensions specified in the *tag* are only used if faults are encountered in all the dimensions specified in the coordinate sequence. For each node, the algorithm can be explained as a sequence of steps in two parts, namely, the *routing section* and the *misrouting section*. These are explained below.

Routing Section

The value of k is checked, if it is 0, then destination has been reached; otherwise the following is done.

(a) The *CS* is scanned from lowest to highest dimension and whichever lowest dimension is found to be non-faulty is used to route the message.
(b) The previous value of the tag remains unchanged.
(c) The selected dimension is removed from the CS.
(d) The value of k is decremented by 1
(e) The packet is sent along the selected dimension.

Misrouting Section

(a) Store all dimensions remaining in the CS.
(b) The lowest dimension having its tag bit = 0 is identified.
(c) The tag in that dimension is updated to 1.
(d) The value of k is incremented.
(e) The dimension selected is included in the CS.
(f) The packet is sent along the selected dimension.

Example

Consider the 4-cube shown in Fig. 5.5. Faulty links are marked with (×). The message is assumed to start at source $S = 0110$ heading for destination $D = 1001$. The format of the message at the beginning is [0,4,[1,2,3,4], message, 0000]. The source node sends [0,3,[2,3,4], message, 0000] to node 0111. Node 0111 sends [0, 2, [3,4], message, 0000] to node 0101. This node finds that the third dimension blocked but the fourth dimension is open, so it sends [0,1, [3], message, 0000] to 1101. Now only one dimension remains in the coordinate sequence, i.e., dimension 3. However, this dimension is faulty and therefore misrouting starts and tag becomes 0100. When the tag is searched for minimum dimension spare link, it is found to be 1. So the tag now becomes 0101.

Since this is a misrouting, ID becomes 1 and k is incremented and the new coordinate sequence becomes [3,1]. Therefore [1,2,[1,3], message, 0101] is sent to node 1100. When ID is found to be 1 by node 1100, it sends [0,1,[1], message, 0101] not along the first dimension, but along the third dimension to node 1000. Again the first dimension out of node 1000 is found faulty, therefore misrouting is done along the spare dimension found in the tag. The second dimension of the tag is found open and therefore [2,2,[1,2], message, 0111] is sent to node 1010. This node will send [0,1,[1], message, 0111] to node 1011. The latter will send [0,0,[ ], message, 0111] to node 1001, the destination node. This completes the path. As can be seen, a path length of 8 is traversed.

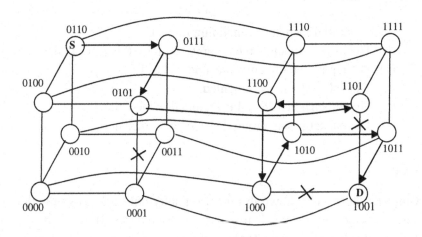

Fig. 5.5: Example 4-cube.

As can be seen from the above example, a path length larger than the smallest possible one was needed in order to route the message. This occurs because global knowledge about the network state was not available at each node. This is one of the shortcomings of the above algorithm.

In addition, it has been observed (through simulation studies) that the algorithm (Called A1 in the literature) left many of the routable packets un-routed when the number of faults is greater than or equal to n, the dimension of the hypercube. We present below a heuristic-based routing algorithm that can achieve on average shorter path length in routing messages around a hypercube and is able to route majority of the routable messages.

5.2.2 *Iterative-Based Heuristic Routing Algorithm*

This heuristic algorithm uses a total of five passes, numbered from 0 to 4. They are summarized in Fig. 5.6.

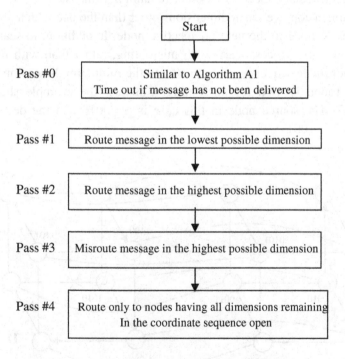

Fig. 5.6: The heuristic Algorithm passes.

In the first pass, if the message is not routed in the initial pass, another routing pass of the algorithm begins. The failure of the first pass is detected when the originator does not receive an acknowledgement from the destination node that it has received the message, within a pre-decided time interval. If this time interval elapses, the originator sends the same message again, after timing out. The new message will be sent with tag equal 0000 (in the case of a 4-cube). When the above scenario is followed, the message will be considered in pass 1.

One of the requirements of the heuristic algorithm is that the dimension to which a message is to be sent will be asked to return a dimension open vector of n bits (for n-cube). The bits of this vector will indicate the status of all the dimensions of the next node. After getting this information, each node will make sure that when it routes a message to an intermediate node, all its other remaining dimensions are open. By other dimension, we mean dimensions other than the one which connects the present node to the next prospective node. In addition, to search for new paths, the process starts with misrouting, rather than with routing. The coordinate sequence is searched and the minimum dimension where a 0 is found is tried for misrouting. Consider the example shown in Fig. 5.7. The source node in this case is $S = 0010$ and the destination node is $D = 1001$.

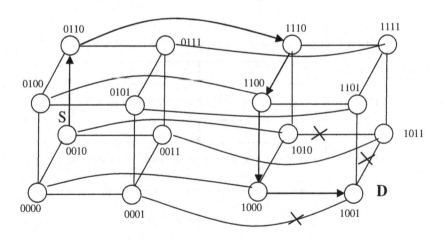

Fig. 5.7: Example 4-cube.

According to the algorithm shown in the previous sub-section, the following sequence of nodes will be followed $2 \rightarrow 3 \rightarrow 11 \rightarrow 3 \rightarrow 2 \rightarrow 0 \rightarrow 1$. This sequence will lead to the wrong conclusion that routing is not possible. The difficulty here is that the message is being sent to node 11 whose remaining links are all faulty. On the other hand, if the first pass of the heuristic algorithm, explained above, is used, then the following successful routing will be made: $2 \rightarrow 6 \rightarrow 14 \rightarrow 12 \rightarrow 8 \rightarrow 9$. This is because when node 2 times out, it will send a message with *tag* = 0000. Now the process begins with misrouting in the lowest possible dimension, which is dimension 3. By misrouting in dimension 3, the message will reach from node 2 to node 6 and then to the destination as shown in Fig. 5.7.

In the second pass, the originator node times out and sends a message with *tag* = 0000. According to the strategy adopted in the second pass, we do not route to a node whose remaining links are all faulty unless it is the last hop. The other strategy in this pass is that the routing begins not in the lowest dimension but in the highest dimension. Consider the example shown in Fig. 5.8. The source node in this case is S = 0000 and the destination is D = 1111.

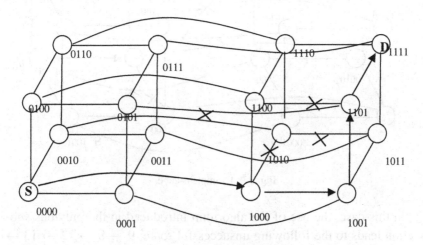

Fig. 5.8: Example 4-cube.

The use of the algorithm shown in the previous sub-section leads to the following unsuccessful route: $0 \to 1 \to 3 \to 2 \to 6$. On the other hand, if the proposed second pass is followed it will lead to the following successful routing: $0 \to 8 \to 9 \to 13 \to 15$. It should be noted that the minimum path length is achieved in this case.

In the third pass also the originator times out and sends the packet with empty *tag* (0000). When routing to a node we make sure that we route to a node where the remaining dimensions in coordinate sequence are open. For example, if the coordinate sequence is 1011 and a node is trying to route the message in the 1st dimension, the next node's dimensions denoted by 0011, dimension 3 and 4 should be open as in pass 2. The routing process starts with misrouting in the highest possible dimension. This is implemented as pass 3 of this algorithm. Consider the example shown in Fig. 5.9. The source node in this case is S = 1001 and the destination node is D = 0100.

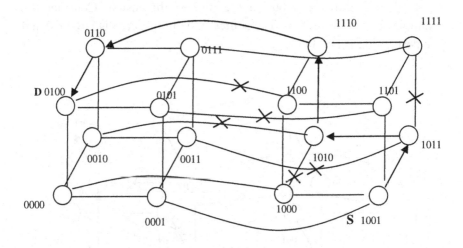

Fig. 5.9: Example 4-cube.

In this case, the use of the algorithm introduced in the previous sub-section leads to the following unsuccessful route: $9 \to 8 \to 12 \to 13 \to 15 \to 14 \to 12 \to 8$. On the other hand, if this pass is followed it will lead to the following successful routing: $9 \to 11 \to 10 \to 14 \to 6 \to 4$.

According to this pass, node 9 starts with misrouting in the highest possible dimension, which is node 2, and the message reaches from node 9 to node 11. Now we continue routing making sure that the node to which we send the message, has all the dimensions remaining in the coordinate sequence open. By doing so we are able to route the packet correctly.

In the fourth pass, also the originator times out and sends the same message with empty *tag*. As in previous pass, we route only to those nodes where the remaining dimensions are all open. The routing begins normally and not with misrouting. In the misrouting section every node makes sure not to misroute in a dimension in which the last routing took place. This can be accomplished by observing the dimension ID field. Consider the example shown in Fig. 5.10. The source node in this case is S = 0011 and the destination node is D = 1010.

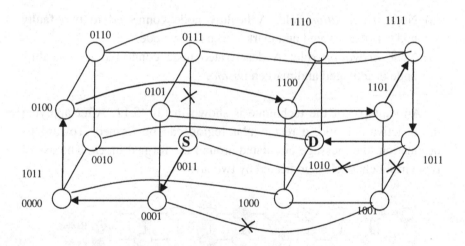

Fig. 5.10: Example 4-cube.

In this case, the use of the $A1$ algorithm leads to the following unsuccessful route: $3 \rightarrow 1 \rightarrow 0 \rightarrow 4 \rightarrow 6$. On the other hand, if this pass is followed it will lead to the following successful routing: $3 \rightarrow 1 \rightarrow 0 \rightarrow 4 \rightarrow 12 \rightarrow 13 \rightarrow 15 \rightarrow 11 \rightarrow 10$.

5.3 Routing in Faulty Mesh Networks

In this section, we present the basic ideas used in a number of algorithms that have been used to route messages in faulty mesh networks. It should be noted that message misrouting is the basic idea used in majority of these routing algorithms in order to avoid faulty nodes and/or links.

5.3.1 *Node Labeling Technique*

In this algorithm, each node is given a label to identify its status. The label given to a node can be one of four: *healthy, faulty, unsafe,* or *deactivated* node. Using these labels a faulty region can be converted to a rectangular region to facilitate routing decisions at each node. Node labeling technique is based on the following two rules:

(a) Node *deactivation* rule: A healthy node connected to two faulty nodes is deactivated and marked as a *faulty* node.
(b) Node *activation* rule: A deactivated node connected to a healthy node is activated and marked *unsafe*.

An example of the technique is shown in Fig. 5.11. After applying the deactivation rule, a rectangular region can be formed. Toward its destination, the message circulated around the formed block. The use of two virtual channels is indicated by two arrows.

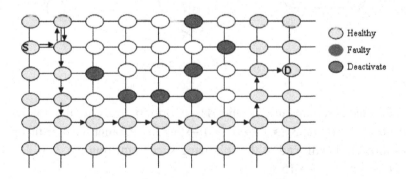

Fig. 5.11: Node labeling routing technique.

The e-cube routing algorithm for meshes is simple and provides the shortest path when routing messages. The problem with e-cube arises when there are faulty links in the mesh. Many algorithms have been proposed to tolerate faulty links. Most of these methods use virtual channels. A virtual channel is made up of a source buffer, a destination buffer, and some channel state. A virtual channel may share a physical communication channel with other virtual channels. Virtual channels are allocated a packet-by-packet.

Most of the algorithms presented above work when faulty regions do not overlap and when they do not touch the mesh boundaries. The following algorithm deals with non-convex faults.

5.3.2 *A FT Routing Scheme for Meshes with Non-convex Faults*

In a *convex-fault*, each connected set of faults has a convex shape, e.g., rectangular. Example of non-convex faults are: +, L, H and T shapes. In a *solid-fault*, any dimensional cross section of the fault region has contiguous faulty components. Solid faults include all convex faults and some non-convex faults, such as +, L and T, but not H. Figure 5.12 shows a non-solid fault, in which a cross along the row dimension indicates a discontinuity.

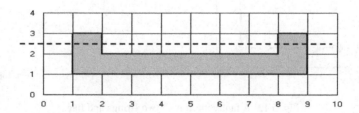

Fig. 5.12: A non-solid fault region.

An *f-ring* is a ring which consists of the fault-free nodes and channels that are adjacent (row-wise, column-wise or diagonally) to one or more components of the associated fault region. The four sides of a 2D mesh is labeled as East, West, South and North. A *row channel* connects two neighboring nodes in the same row. A *column channel* connects two neighboring nodes in the same column. A row channel is called a WE (respectively, an EW) channel if it directs from West to East (respectively from East to West). SN and NS channels are from South to North and from North to South respectively.

The algorithm consists of two main parts: (a) Determining Fault Rings and generating the flag bits and (b) Routing messages based on current node, destination node and flag bits.

Determining Fault Rings and Generating the Flag Bits

This part is executed each time there is a new faulty link. A fault ring, *f-ring*, can be formed around each fault region. It consists of the fault free nodes and channels that are adjacent to one or more components of the associated fault region. Figure 5.13 shows an example of 6 × 8 2D-mesh. The gray areas represent solid fault regions and the associated f-rings, denoted by R1 and R2.

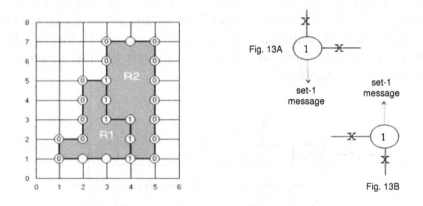

Fig. 5.13: A faulty mesh with two f-rings and flags.

A one bit flag is stored in each node. This bit is used by the routing algorithm. After determining fault rings, a procedure is executed in each node to determine the flag bit value. This procedure is shown in Fig. 5.14.

---

1. Initially, a node sets its flag to 0.
2. For each f-ring on which the node resides, do the following:
    2.1.   If both its west and south channels are faulty, then set its flag to 1 and send a set-1 message to its neighbor to the north. (See Fig. 5.13b)
    2.2.   If both its east and north channels are faulty, then set its flag to 1 and send a set-1 message to its neighbor to the south. (See Fig. 5.13a)
3. When a node receives a set-1 messages, it does the following:
    3.1   It sets its flag to 1.
    3.2   If the set-1 message is sent to it from the neighbor to the south (respectively, north) and its neighbor to the north (respectively, south) is also on the same f-ring, then set the set-1 message to the north (respectively, south). Otherwise, consume the set-1 message.

Fig. 5.14: Generation of flag bits.

A node's flag bit may be set to 1 with respect to any f-ring on which it resides. Figure 5.13 shows a two f-rings with the corresponding flag bits. The number in each node indicates the flag bit value. Note that the flag bits of the lower and upper boundaries of an f-ring is not shown since it is not important in the FT-routing algorithm. In Fig. 5.13, considering R1, the node (3,3) is set to 1 according to step 2.1 in the above table, after that a set-1 message is sent to nodes (3,4) and (3,5). Since nodes (3,6) and (3,7) are not parts of R1, they will not set their flag bit to 1, rather, they will consume the set-1 message. Node (4,3) is set to 1 according to 2.2, it then sends set-1 messages to the nodes (4,2) then (4,1).

Routing Messages Based on Current Node, Destination Node and Flag Bits

This part of the algorithm is executed each time a new message is needed to be routed from one node (source) to another (destination). The routing is done based on the *e-cube* routing scheme if there is no faulty link in the source-destination path. The e-cube algorithm routes a message along DIM0 (row) and then along DIM1 (vertical) in a 2D mesh.

The routing algorithm consists of two parts: initialization and hop advance (see Fig. 5.15). Initialization is executed one time at the beginning while the hop advance will be executed each time to route the message one hop in its way to the destination.

Initialization

Inputs: message (mg), source node (s0,s1) and destination node (d0,d1).
1. Set current node=source node or (c0,c1)=(s0,s1).
2. Set the type of the *mg* message as EW if s0>=d0 and as WE otherwise.

Hop advance

Inputs: message (mg), current node (c0,c1) and destination node (d0,d1).
1. If (c0,c1)=(d0,d1), consume *mg* and return.
2. Set message type as follows: if mg is a row message and c0=d0, then change its type to SN if c1<d1 or NS if c1>d1.
3. Set *mg* message status to *normal* in one of the following three cases, otherwise set to *misrouted*:
   - If *mg* is a *row* message and its e-cube hop is not blocked.
   - If *mg* is a *column* message, c0=d0, the e-cube hop is not blocked, and its previous status is *normal*.
   - If *mg* is a column message, c0=d0, the e-cube hop is not blocked, and its preceding node is not on the same column as the current node.
4. - If *mg*'s status is *normal*, then route *mg* along its e-cube hop.
   - If *mg*'s status is *misrouted*, route *mg* on the associated f-ring along the direction specified by Table 1. Use virtual channel *ch0* if mg's message type is *row*, *ch1* if SN, or *ch2* if NS.

Fig. 5.15: The FT routing algorithm.

Step-4 states that *normal* messages are routed along the e-cube hops. A misrouted message is routed along on an f-ring along a clockwise or a counterclockwise direction specified by Table 5.2. The function of the flag bit is to guide the row messages so that an EW (respectively, WE) message does not need to traverse a WE (respectively, EW) direction, (see Fig. 5.16). The case is different with column mess-ages, since an SN may traverse NS route and vice versa. For column messages, SN messages is misrouted in a clockwise direction, while NS is misrouted along a counter clockwise direction (see Fig. 5.17). Column message is more specific than row message since row message stops when $c0 = d0$, while column message finishes only when $(c0,c1) = (d0,d1)$, so NS (and respectively SN) can traverse a SN (and respectively, NS).

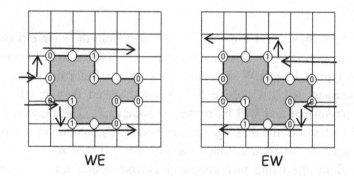

Fig. 5.16: WE and EW misrouted messages on f-rings.

Table 5.2: Misrouting directions.

Message type	Flag	Direction
Row Message	0	Clockwise
	1	Counter-clockwise
SN Message		Clockwise
NS Message		Counter-clockwise

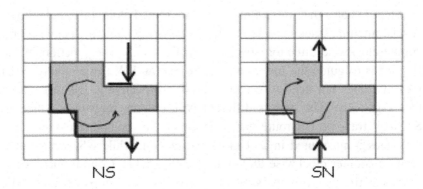

Fig. 5.17: NS and SN misrouted messages on f-rings.

Example

Figure 5.18 shows an FT-routing of message from the source S (6,3) to the destination D (2,0). First, the message is initialized to a row message and it's type is set to EW since s0 (=6) > d0(=2). Since the message is a row message and it's e-cube hub is not blocked then it's type will be set as *normal* and will be routed to node (5,3). The same will hold for left nodes until the message reaches node (3,3), in which it's type will be changed to misrouted. Since the *flag* bit is 1, the message will be routed along the f-ring in a counterclockwise direction until it reaches node (2,4). At node (2,4) message type will be changed to column message since c0(=2) = d0(=2) and it's type will be set to NS since c1(=4) > (d1=0). At node (2,4) the message type will be set to misrouted since the e-cube hub is blocked, then the message will be routed counterclockwise until it reaches node (2,2) in which message type is changed to normal since e-cube hub is not blocked and the preceding node is not in the same column as the current node. The message will then be routed along it's e-cub hubs until it arrives to the destination D (2,0).

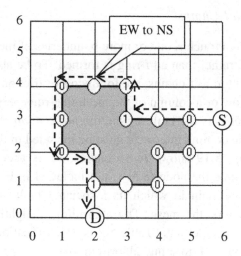

Fig. 5.18: Example.

5.4 Algorithm Extensions

The above FT-Routing algorithm can be extended to route messages in two cases. These are introduced below.

5.4.1 *Multidimensional Meshes*

A multidimensional version of the FT-Routing can be achieved by using the previous results of 2D meshes and the planner-adaptive routing technique [4]. Consider routing message from source $(s0, s1, \ldots, sn-1)$ to destination $(d0, d1, \ldots, dn-1)$. First, the message is routed on the 2D plane of dimensions DIM_0 and DIM_1, if $s_0 \neq d_0$. In this phase, a message my be WE or EW type. The first phase finishes when DIM0 of the address equals d0. We then enter the second phase in which the message in the 2D plane of dimensions DIM_1 and DIM_2 until $DIM_1 = d1$, and so on. Note that in each phase, the lower dimension corresponds to DIM_0 in the 2D mesh.

5.4.2 *Faults with f-Chains*

When a fault region touches one or more boundaries of the mesh, a fault-chain, or f-chain, rather than an f-ring is formed. To be able to apply the FT-routing algorithm to f-chains, the following restriction must be made to f-cahins: if a row or a column of the mesh that runs perpendicularly to the boundary intersects the fault region, the node at which the boundary and the row or the column intersects must be included in the fault region. For example, Fig. 5.19 shows two f-chains, F1 is accepted while F2 is not accepted since the node (8,5) is not included in F2 faulty region. A w-chain is an f-chain in which its associated faulty region touches the west boundary of the mesh. The algorithm is slightly modified by changing the *flag* bits setting. Table 5.2 is a modification to Table 5.1. Now, the previous FT-Routing algorithm may be applied but using Table 5.2.

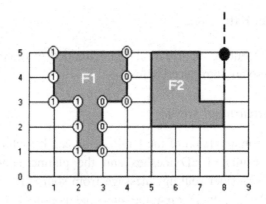

Fig. 5.19: 2D mesh with f-chains.

Table 5.2: Misrouting directions on f-rings and f-chains.

Message type	flag	f-ring and non w-chain	w-chain
Row	0	Clock	
	1	C-Clock	
SN		Clock	C-Clock
NS		C-Clock	Clock

5.5 Summary

In this chapter, we first introduced a number of algorithms that are used in routing messages in healthy hypercube and healthy mesh networks. This has been followed by a detailed explanation of several fault-tolerant routing algorithms for routing message in faulty hypercube and faulty mesh networks. We have also provided detailed analyses of these routing algorithms. In the next chapter, we will introduce a number of routing algorithms in hierarchical interconnection networks.

References

[1]   R.V. Boppana and S. Chalasani, "Fault-Tolerant Wormhole Routing Algorithms for Mesh Networks", *IEEE Trans. Computers*, vol. 44, no. 7, pp. 8480864, July 1995.

[2]   Y.M. Boura and C.R. Das, "Fault-tolerant Routing in Mesh Networks", *Proc. 1995 Int. conf. parallel processing*, vol. I, pp. 106-109, 1995.

[3]   S. Chalasani and R.V. Boppana, "Communications in multi-computers with non-convex faults", *IEEE trans. Computers*, vol. 46, no. 5, pp. 616-622, May 1997.

[4]   A.A. Chen and J.H. Kim, "Planar-Adaptive Routing: Low-Cost Adaptive Networks for Multiprocessors", *Proc. 19th Ann. Int'l Symp. Computer Architecture*, pp. 268-277, May 1992.

[5]   W.J. Dally and C.L. Seitz, "Dead-lock free message routing in multi-processor Interconnection networks", IEEE Trans. Computers vol. 36, no. 5, pp. 547-553, May 1987.

[6]   C.J. Glass and L.M. Ni, "Fault-Tolerant Wormhole routing in Meshes", *Proc. Int'l Symp. Fault-Tolerant Computing*, pp. 240-249, 1993.

[7]   Khalid M. Al-Tawil, Mostafa Abd-El-Barr, and Farooq Ashraf, "A Survey and Comparison of Wormhole Routing Techniques in Mesh Networks", *IEEE network*, 1997.

[8]   M.S. Chen and K.G. Shin, "Adaptive fault-tolerant routing in hypercube multicomputers", *IEEE Trans. On Computers* 39 (12) (1996) 130-138.

[9]   R.V. Boppana and S. Chalasani, "Fault-Tolerant Wormhole Routing Algorithms for Mesh Networks", *IEEE Trans. Computers*, vol. 44, no. 7, pp. 8480864, July 1995.

[10] Mostafa I. Abd-El-Barr, Mohammed M. Nadeem and Khaled Al-Tawil, "A heuristic-base wormhole routing algorithm for hybercube multicomputer networks", *Cluster Computing* 4, 253-262, 2001.

[11] M.S. Chen and K.G. Shin. Depth-first search approach for fault-tolerant routing in hypercube multiprocessors. *IEEE Trans. on Parallel and Distributed Systems*, pages 152–159, 1990.

[12] Q. Gu and S. Peng. Advanced fault-tolerant routing in hypercubes. In *Proc. of the International Symposium on Parallel Architectures, Algorithms and Networks (ISPAN'94)*, pages 189–196, 1994.

[13] T.C. Lee and J.P. Hayes. A fault-tolerant communication scheme for hypercube computers. *IEEE Trans. on Computers*, pages 1242–1256, 1992.

[14] G.-M. Chiu and S.-P. Wu. A fault-tolerant routing strategy in hypercube multicomputers. IEEE Trans. Comput., 45(2):143–155, February 1996.

[15] J. Bruck, R. Cypher, and D. Soroker. Fault-Tolerant in hyper-cubes using subcube partitioning. *IEEE Trans. on Computers*, pages 599–605, 1992.

[16] M.S. Chen and K.G. Shin. Depth-first search approach for fault-tolerant routing in hypercube multiprocessors. *IEEE Trans. on Parallel and Distributed Systems*, pages 152–159, 1990.

[17] A. H. Esfahanian. Generalized measures of fault tolerance with application to n-cube networks. *IEEE Trans. on Computers*, 38(11):1586–1591, 1989.

[18] Q. Gu and S. Peng. Node-to-node cluster fault-tolerant routing in star graphs. *Information Processing Letters*, 56:29–35, 1995.

[19] Q. Gu and S. Peng. Optimal algorithms for node-to-node fault-tolerant routing in hypercubes. *The Computer Journal*, 39(7):626–629, 1996.

[20] C.S. Raghavendra, P.J. Yang, and S.B. Tien. Free dimensions — an efficient approach to archieving fault tolerance in hypercube. *IEEE Trans. on Computers*, Vol. 44:1152–1157, 1995.

[21] S.B. Tien and C.S. Raghavendra. Algorithms and bounds for shortest paths and diameter in faulty hypercubes. *IEEE Trans. on Parallel and Distributed Systems*, pages 713–718, 1993.

[22] C.-L. Chen and G.-M. Chiu, "A fault-tolerant routing scheme for meshes with nonconvex faults", IEEE Trans. Parallel and Distributed Systems, Vol. 12, No. 5, May 2001, pp. 467–475.

Chapter 6

Fault Tolerance and Reliability in Hierarchical Interconnection Networks

Hierarchical Interconnection Networks (HINs) provide a framework for designing networks with reduced link cost. They take advantage of the locality of communication that exists in parallel applications. In this chapter, we present the main characteristics of a number of fault-tolerant HINs. These include HIN, BSN, HCN, HTN based on FFTB. We also provide an overall comparison among a number of these networks. The metrics used for comparison are node degree, network diameter and cost.

6.1 Introduction

Hierarchical interconnection networks (HINs) were introduced in an attempt to minimize message delay, reduce cost, and maximize network reliability and fault tolerance. HINs are networks having multiple levels, where lower level networks provide local communication and higher level networks facilitate remote communication. Fault tolerance is provided by either (1) duplicating the level-two network. This is called the *replication technique* or (2) by providing spare interface nodes. This is called the *standby spare technique*.

A hierarchical interconnection network can be defined as a network with distinct hierarchy of interconnections. At the lowest level, there exists clusters of individual nodes, with nodes in each cluster connected by a network. This network is called a level-one network. At the next level, groups of clusters are connected by a level-two network. The topology at each level can be the same or different. If the topologies at all levels are the same, then the network is called *homogenous HIN*; otherwise it is called a *heterogeneous HIN*. There can be any number of levels in HIN.

Depending on the way fault tolerance is provided, hierarchical interconnection networks can be classified as shown below.

Class #1: this includes HINs that use the replication technique. This technique aims at avoiding excessive traffic on inter-cluster links by duplicating the level-two network and having two or more interface nodes per cluster (see Fig. 6.1).

Class #2: this includes HINs that use the standby spare technique. In this technique, a standby spare interface node is provided to avoid the inter-cluster disconnection caused by interface node failure (see Fig. 6.2).

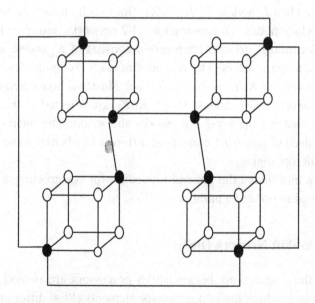

Fig. 6.1: The replication technique.

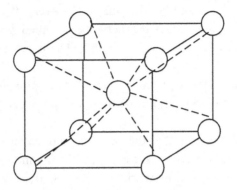

Fig. 6.2: The standby spare technique.

The general procedure for constructing a HIN is as follows. Assume that the total number of nodes in the network is N. Divide N into K_1 clusters, of N/K_1 nodes each. Each cluster of N/K_1 nodes is connected to form a level-1 network. The nodes in every cluster are ordered in the same way. Then I_1 nodes, $1 \leq I_1 \leq N/K_1$, from each cluster are selected to act as interface nodes. To construct level-2 networks, interface nodes are first divided into I_1 groups. Each group consists of K_1 nodes, which are from K_1 different clusters. The K_1 nodes of each group are again divided into K_2 clusters, of K_1/K_2 nodes each. Each cluster is connected to form a level-2 network, and I_2 nodes, $1 \leq I_2 \leq K_1/K_2$, are selected as the interface nodes to construct the level-3 networks and so on. The interconnection networks used to construct clusters at different levels may have the same or different topologies.

Having introduced the general procedure for constructing a HIN, we now proceed to present a number of HINs.

6.2 Block-Shift Network (BSN)

In BSN, the connections between two processors are named after the dimensions on which the two processor elements (PEs) differ and if they are connected by the links on these dimensions. For example, the link between PE 000 and PE 010 is named dimension-1 connection while the link between PE 010 and PE 100 is named dimension-2 connection. The following connection methods for the connections on dimensions i to j can be considered.

Concurrent-Connection: This connection takes place in the case whereby two processors whose addresses differ only in positions i to j are directly connected, i.e., bits i to j in one address can be changed in 1 step to reach another address. When $i = 0$ and $j = n$-1 (covering all dimensions), then the connection scheme corresponds to the fully connected topology.

Sequential-Connection: This connection takes place in the case whereby two processors whose addresses differ only in positions i to j can reach each other by changing bits i to j of their addresses one by one. Thus, for 2 processors with addresses differing in all bits from i to j, one needs unit-routes to send a message from one to the other. If only 1 bit is different in bits i to j, then 1 step is needed. When $i = 0$ and $j = n$-1, then the connection scheme corresponds to a hypercube topology.

Partial-Connection: Between the above two methods, other methods can be defined. For example, one can define a connection method in which the section (bits i to j) can change 2 bits at a time, 3 bits at a time, and so on. Assume that the section (bits i to j) has b bits, and can be divided into b/a subsections. A partial-connection can change a whole subsection into any pattern in 1 step by modifying 1 bit, 2 bits, ..., or a bits in the subsection.

6.2.1 *BSN Edges Groups*

BSN consists of 3 groups of edges:

Group #1: It connects nodes to their counterparts with addresses shifted cyclically positions left in 1 step, *i.e.*, it connects the processor at address $a_{n-1}a_{n-2}...a_1a_0$ to the processor at address $a_{n-b-1}a_{n-b-2}...a_1a_0a_{n-1}...a_{n-b}$. These connections are called *L-Shift links* and the data transfers over these links are called *L-Shift operations*. For example, if $b = 3$ then PE 0010011 must be connected to PE 0011001.

Group #2: It connects nodes to their counterparts with addresses shifted cyclically positions right in 1 step, *i.e.*, it connects the processor at address $a_{n-1}a_{n-2}...a_1a_0$ to the processor at $a_{b-1}a_{b-2}...a_1a_0a_{n-1}...a_{b+1}a_b$. These connections are called *R-Shift links* and the data transfers over these links are called *R-Shift operations*. For example, if $b = 3$ then PE 1010011 must be connected to PE 0111010.

Group #3: It contains the connections over the rightmost b dimensions. The links in group #3 are called *R-change links* and the data transfers over these links are called *R-change operations*. For example, if $b = 3$ then PE 0010000 could be connected to PE 0010001, PE 0010010, PE 0010011, PE 0010100, PE 0010101, PE 0010110 or PE 0010111.

6.2.2 *BSN Construction*

A block in BSN is defined as the nodes which are connected by the links in group #3 (R-change links). BSN has $N = 2^n$ nodes and in each step only a bits can be changed within the section of the rightmost b bits, and is labeled BSN(a, b). Changing these two parameters defines the network connection type as follows:

If $a = 1$ then the network BSN(1, b) has a sequential connection method and each block is a hypercube with 2^b nodes, see Fig. 6.3.

If $a = b$ then the network BSN(b, b) has a concurrent connection method over the last dimensions and contains 2^{n-b} blocks each with 2^b nodes, see Fig. 6.4.

Within each block is a complete graph (thin lines), and blocks are connected by either R-Shift or L-Shift links (thick lines which are double link), as shown in Fig. 6.4.

If $1 < a < b$ then the network has a partial connection method.

A number of existing networks can be considered as special cases of the BSN. For example,

BSN(1, 1) is the shuffle-exchange network.
BSN(1, n) is the n-dimensional hypercube.
BSN(n, n) is the fully-connected (complete) network.

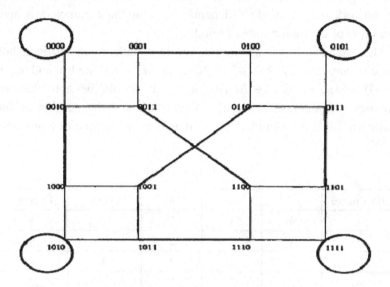

Fig. 6.3: A BSN(1, 2) with $N = 16$.

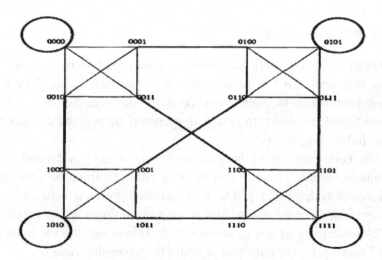

Fig. 6.4: A BSN(2, 2) with $N = 16$.

6.2.3 *BSN Degree and Diameter*

In BSN(a, b) of $N = 2^n$ nodes, the network degree (the maximum number of ports per node) is given by $(2^a - 1) * (b/a) + 2$. It should be noted that the network degree in BSN depends only on the parameters a and b regardless of the total number of nodes.

The diameter (the maximum shortest path, with distinct hops, between any two nodes) of BSN(a, b) of $N = 2^n$ nodes and degree $(2^a - 1) * (b/a) + 2$ is $(1 + (b/a)) * \lceil n/b \rceil$. It should be note that as b increases, the diameter of a BSN decreases, and the number of links increases. Table 6.1 summarizes the diameter and degree of a number of BSNs.

Table 6.1: BSN degree and diameter.

BSN figure	N	a	b	Degree	Diameter
1	4	1	2	4	6
2	4	2	2	5	4
3	3	1	2	4	6
4	3	2	2	5	4

6.2.4 *BSN Connectivity*

Connectivity of a network is defined as the minimum number of nodes or links that must fail for the network to be partitioned into 2 or more disjoint sub-networks. Network connectivity measures the resilience of a network and its ability to continue operation despite the existence of some failed components.

The node-connectivity between two nodes i and j is defined as the minimum number of nodes that must be removed from the network to disconnect nodes i and j. The node-connectivity of a network is the minimum node-connectivity value of all pairs of nodes. For example, the node-connectivity of a ring network is 2. This is because the failure of any 2 nodes prevents some pair of nodes from communicating.

Similarly, the link-connectivity between two nodes and is defined as the minimum number of links that must be removed from the network to disconnect nodes i and j. The link-connectivity of a network is the minimum link-connectivity of all pairs of nodes. The link-connectivity of a ring is also 2.

A network with node-connectivity, r, provides r disjoint paths between every pair of nodes in the network, thus has the ability to tolerate r-1 failures. Hence, higher node or link-connectivity increases the resilience of the network to failure. In addition to being a measure of network reliability, connectivity is also a measure of performance. Greater connectivity reduces the number of links that must be traversed to reach a destination node. Designing a network with higher connectivity and a constant number of connections per node is crucial since technology constraints limit the number of connections per node to a small value.

The node-connectivity of a BSN(1, b) is b. The node-connectivity of a BSN(b, b) is $2^b - 1$. The link-connectivity of a BSN(1, b) is b. The link-connectivity of a BSN(b, b) is $2^b - 1$. Therefore, both BSN with sequential connection method and BSN with concurrent connection method have optimal connectivity in the sense that the minimum degrees of the two networks are equal to the connectivity, i.e., b and $2^b - 1$, respectively.

Table 6.2 summarizes the node and link connectivity of a number of BSNs.

Table 6.2: BSN node-connectivity & link-connectivity.

BSN figure	a	b	Node-connectivity	Link-connectivity
1 & 3	1	2	2	2
2 & 4	2	2	3	3

6.2.5 BSN Fault Diameter

A fault diameter of a graph is defined as the diameter of a new graph generated after the faulty nodes & links are removed from the original graph.

An f-fault diameter of a graph is defined as the maximum of distances over all possible graphs that can occur with at most f faults.

The $(b-1)$-fault diameter of a BSN(1, b) is $2\lceil n/b \rceil + 2(b+1)*\lceil n/b \rceil$. The (2^b-2)-fault diameter of a BSN(b, b) is $6\lceil n/b \rceil$.

Table 6.3 summarizes the $(b-1)$-fault diameter of a BSN(1, b) and the (2^b-2)-fault diameter of a BSN(b, b).

Table 6.3: The BSN f-fault diameter.

BSN figure	n	a	b	(2^b-2) -fault diameter of a BSN(b, b)	$(b-1)$ -fault diameter of a BSN(1, b)
1	4	1	2	-	16
2	4	2	2	12	-
3	3	1	2	-	16
4	3	2	2	12	-

6.2.6 *BSN Reliability*

Reliability analysis could be intractable if many paths between any 2 nodes can have one or more links in common. Therefore, deriving a lower bound on 2-terminal reliability (also referred to as path reliability) by considering a subset of all available paths between two nodes in a network offers an important insight into the value of 2-terminal reliability of the network. As long as the lower bound is quite tight, it can be used to estimate the 2-terminal reliability of a network. The 2-terminal reliability between a source node s and a terminal node t is defined as the probability of finding a path entirely composed of operational links between them.

The 2-terminal reliability of BSN(b, b) is given by:

$$TR_{BSN(b,b)} = 1 - (1 - p^{4m})^{2^b - 1}, \quad m \equiv \lceil n/b \rceil$$

Where the probability of failure of all i paths of length j is $(1-p^j)^i$ and we already know that a block in BSN(b, b) is a complete network.

Therefore, $j = 4m$ since $2m$ links are internal within the blocks and $2m$ links are links between blocks. The number of disjoint paths in BSN(b, b) is $i = 2^b - 1$.

Similarly, the 2-terminal reliability of BSN(1, b) is given by:

$$TR_{BSN(1,b)} = 1 - (1 - p^{2m*(1+b)})^b, \quad m \equiv \lceil n/b \rceil$$

Where at most $2m*b$ links are internal within the block and $2m$ links exist between blocks. It should be noted that a node needs to traverse b links within a block to reach another node in the same block.

In the hypercube, only n of the $n!$ shortest paths are disjoint. Using a similar argument, 2-terminal reliability of a hypercube of size 2^n is given by:

$$TR_{cube} = 1 - (1 - p^n)^n$$

Table 6.4 shows the values for the 2-terminal reliability of the hypercube and BSN of moderate size $n=16$ for various b. The link operational rate is set to change from 0.90 to 0.98.

Table 6.4: 2-terminal reliability of BSN and hypercube.

P	Hypercube	BSN(2,2)	BSN(1,2)	BSN(4,4)	BSN(1,4)	BSN(8,8)	BSN(1,8)
0.90	0.962	0.099	0.012	0.953	0.057	1.000	0.166
0.92	0.992	0.194	0.036	0.989	0.134	1.000	0.334
0.94	0.999	0.359	0.099	0.999	0.296	1.000	0.598
0.96	0.999	0.612	0.262	0.999	0.580	1.000	0.876
0.98	1.000	0.892	0.614	1.000	0.905	1.000	0.994

6.3 Hierarchical Cubic Network (HCN)

A HCN(n, n) is a hierarchical network consisting of 2^n clusters, each of which is an n-dimensional hypercube. Each node of a HCN(n, n) is addressed by a pair of numbers (I, J), where I is an n-bit representing the cluster number and J is an n-bit representing the address of the node within a cluster. Each node in the HCN(n, n) has (n + 1) links connected to it. The links within a hypercube cluster are referred to as *local links* and the links between two clusters are referred to as *external links*.

The following set of rules can be used to construct a HCN(n, n) clusters connected by external links:

If $I \neq J$, a node (I, J) is connected to the node (J, I) using its external link, which is called *non-diameter link*. A node (I, I) is connected to the node (I', I'), where I' is the bitwise complement of I, using its external link, which is called *diameter link*. A HCN(2, 2) is shown in Fig. 6.5.

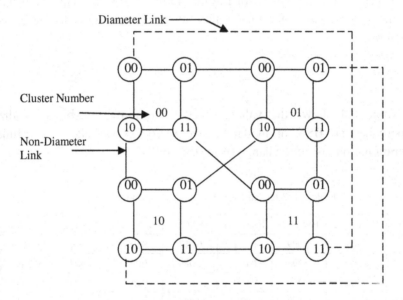

Fig. 6.5: A HCN(2, 2) network.

6.3.1 *HCN Degree and Diameter*

In HCN(n, n), the network degree (the maximum number of ports per node) is $n+1$ (n ports within the cube and one for the external link). The HCN(n, n) diameter (the maximum shortest path, with distinct hops, between any two nodes) is given by $n + \left\lfloor \dfrac{n+1}{3} \right\rfloor + 1$.

Following the definition given in the subsection above, we can show that the HCN fault diameter is given by $n + \left\lfloor \dfrac{n+1}{3} \right\rfloor + 5$ and that the 2-terminal reliability of HCN(n,n) is given by $TR_{HCN(n,n)} = 1 - (1 - p^n)^{n+1}$. Notice that there are a total of $n + 1$ node disjoint paths in a HCN(n, n).

6.4 HINs versus HCNs

6.4.1 *Topological Cost*

In general, the cost of a network can be expressed based on the node degree and diameter of the network. Networks with small node degree have large diameters, while networks with small diameters have nodes with large degrees. There is a tradeoff between the node degree and the diameter of a network. Therefore, a commonly used measure for the cost of a network is the product of the diameter and degree.

Table 6.5 shows the cost of BSN & HCN and Tables 6.6 & 6.7 show the cost when $n = 16$ for both HCN and BSN using different parameters.

Table 6.5: Network cost of BSN and HCN.

	Nodes	Degree	Diameter	Cost
BSN(a, b)	2^n	$(2^a - 1) \times (b/a) + 2$	$(1 + (b/a)) \times \lceil n/b \rceil$	$\left\lceil \dfrac{n}{b} \right\rceil \times \dfrac{2^a ab + 2^2 b^2 + ab - b^2 + 2a^2}{a^2}$
HCN(n,n)	2^{2n}	$n + 1$	$n + \left\lfloor \dfrac{n+1}{3} \right\rfloor + 1$	$(n+1) \times \left(n + \left\lfloor \dfrac{n+1}{3} \right\rfloor + 1 \right)$

Table 6.6: Topological cost BSN(b, b) and HCN(n, n) with $N = 65536$.

HCN(8, 8)	BSN(2,2)	BSN(4,4)	BSN(8,8)
108	80	136	1028

Table 6.7: Topological cost BSN(1, b) and HCN(n, n) with $N = 65536$.

HCN(8,8)	BSN(1,2)	BSN(1,4)	BSN(1,8)
108	96	120	180

It should be noted that for a given number of nodes, n, the cost of BSN varies based on the values of a and b, while it is constant for HCN. In addition, for $a = b$, the cost of BSN increases rapidly as the values of a & b increase and it becomes larger than that of HCN as $a = b \geqslant 4$. But for $a = 1$, the increase in the cost of BSN is not as rapid as it is in the case of $a = b$ but it is still larger than that of HCN as long as $b \geqslant 4$. The last column in Tables 6.6 and 6.7 shows a fast increase in the cost of BSN compared to that of HCN.

Table 6.8 shows the values for the 2-terminal reliability of BSN and that of HCN of moderate size ($N = 65536$). Table 6.9 shows 2-terminal reliability values for BSN (having $a = 1$) and HCN. The link operational rate of changes from 0.90 to 0.98. Figures 6.6 and 6.7 demonstrate the results of Table 6.8 and 6.9, respectively.

Table 6.8: 2-terminal reliability of BSN(b, b) and HCN(8, 8).

P	HCN(8, 8)	BSN(2,2)	BSN(4,4)	BSN(8,8)
0.90	0.994	0.099	0.953	1.000
0.92	0.998	0.194	0.989	1.000
0.94	0.999	0.359	0.999	1.000
0.96	1.000	0.612	0.999	1.000
0.98	1.000	0.892	1.000	1.000

Table 6.9: 2-terminal reliability of BSN(1, b) and HCN(8, 8).

P	HCN(8,8)	BSN(1,2)	BSN(1,4)	BSN(1,8)
0.90	0.994	0.012	0.057	0.166
0.92	0.998	0.036	0.134	0.334
0.94	0.999	0.099	0.296	0.598
0.96	1.000	0.262	0.580	0.876
0.98	1.000	0.614	0.905	0.994

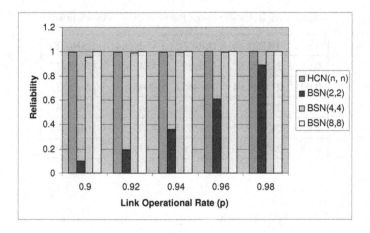

Fig. 6.6: Reliability of HCN(8, 8) and BSN(b, b).

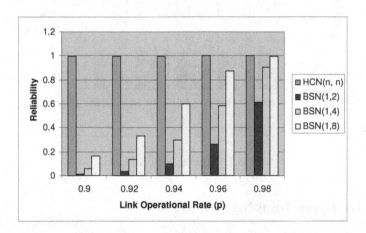

Fig. 6.7: Reliability of HCN(8, 8) and BSN(1, b).

The total number of links of BSN(b,b) is equal to $2^n * (2^b + 1)$, while the total number of links of HCN(n,n) is $2^{2n-1} * (n+1)$. Table 6.10 shows the product of the reliability and the number of links for HCN(8, 8) and BSN(b, b) and Fig. 6.8 illustrates these results.

Table 6.10 Reliability times the number of network links.

p	HCN(8,8)	BSN(2,2)	BSN(4,4)	BSN(8,8)
0.9	265420.8	294912	884736	15158477
0.92	271319.04	301465.6	904396.8	15495332
0.94	277217.28	308019.2	924057.6	15832187
0.96	283115.52	314572.8	943718.4	16169042
0.98	289013.76	321126.4	963379.2	16505897

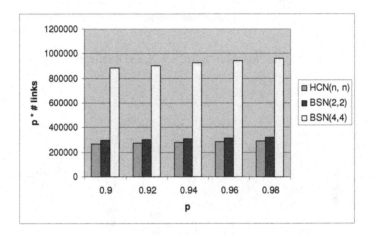

Fig. 6.8: Reliability × No. of Links.

6.5 The Hyper-Torus Network (HTN)

As explained above, a HIN consists of multiple levels. Networks at the lower level, called the basic-blocks or *cluster*, provide local communications, whereas networks at the higher level provide global communications. In the HTNs, the cluster network is a hypercube, while the level-two network is a torus topology. Figure 6.9 shows the general architecture of the HTN.

The Architecture of the cluster network used in the HTN is the 4-cube-based FTBB (Fault-Tolerant Building Block) having four spares, see Fig. 6.10.

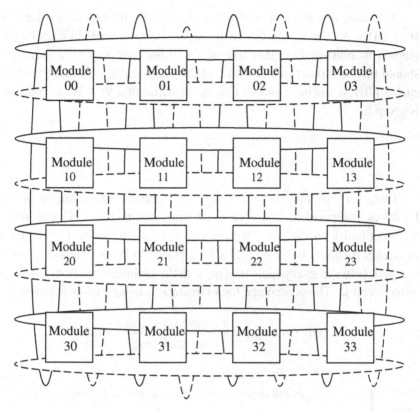

Fig. 6.9: General architecture of the HTN.

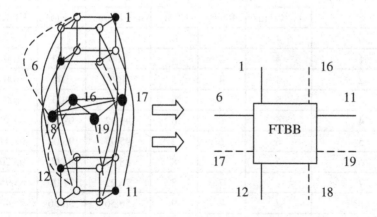

Fig. 6.10: The 4-cube based FTBB with four spares.

Assuming that the size of the torus is W × W, then there is a total of W^2 FTBBs. As can be seen there are eight interface nodes in each FTBB (shown in **bold** in Fig. 10), four in the main cube and four spares. It should be noted that there is a total of 20 nodes and a total of 42 links in each FTBB. It has been shown that the diameter of a W × W architecture is given by

$$8 \times \left\lfloor \frac{W}{2} \right\rfloor - 1$$

Table 6.11 summarizes the results obtained for the diameter of the FTBB as compared to that of a 4 × 4 torus and that of a 4-cube under different faulty conditions. The table also shows the percentage of fault coverage. It should be noted that a fault is said to be recoverable if there is a path between every fault-free node in the architecture; otherwise it is unrecoverable. The percentage fault coverage is computed as follows:

$$Fault\ Covergae = \frac{\#recoverable\ faults}{total\ \#of\ faults} \times 100$$

Table 6.11: Fault diameter and fault coverage in three architectures under different fault conditions.

Number of faults	Diameter			Fault coverage (%)		
	4 × 4 torus	4-cube	FTBB	4 × 4 torus	4-cube	FTBB
0	4	4	4	-	-	-
1	4	4	4	100	100	100
2	4	4	5	100	100	100
3	5	5	6	100	100	100
4	6	6	6	99.12	99.12	99.40
5	6	6	7	95.97	96.00	97.47
6	7	7	8	88.37	93.00	93.20
7	7	7	8	76.22	77.00	85.95
8	7	7	9	56.56	56.56	75.43
9	6	6	9	37.62	37.62	61.91

As can be seen from Table 6.11, for six or less faults, the fault coverage of the torus, the hypercube and the FTBB are nearly the same. However, as the number of faults increases beyond six, the FTBB recovers better from faults as compared to the other two architectures.

The reliability of the FTBB can be computed as follows. There is a total of 20 nodes in an FTBB, out of which 16 nodes are the hypercube nodes and the remaining four are spare nodes. Assume that in an FTTB, any 16 nodes function and communicate with each other. This means that the network should remain connected. Using the Combinatorial mode, we can write the reliability expression for the FTTB as follows:

$$R_{FTBB}(t) = r^{20}(t) + {}^{20}C_1 r^{19}(t)(1-r(t)) + {}^{20}C_2 r^{18}(t)(1-r(t))^2$$
$$+ {}^{20}C_3 r^{17}(t)(1-r(t))^3 + 4818 r^{16}(t)(1-r(t))^4$$

In this expression, $r(t) = e^{-\lambda t}$ is the reliability of a node and λ is the failure rate of a node. The first term of the expression stands for the event that all twenty nodes are functioning. The second term is the probability of the event that one node has failed and the remaining nineteen are functioning. The other terms can be explained in a similar way. The coefficient of the last term is less than ${}^{20}C_4$. This coefficient stands for the number of cases (the number occurrences of four faults) for which the network remains connected. This number has been arrived at using simulation.

The above reliability expression is to be compared to that of the 16-node hypercube which is given by $R_{HC}(t) = (r(t))^{16}$. It is clear that for the same node reliability, $r(t)$, the FTBB achieves higher reliability as compared to the hypercube. However, this is achieved at the expense of an increase in the number of node.

6.6 Summary

In this chapter, we presented a number of HINs. In particular, we have presented the main reliability and fault tolerance characteristics of the Block-Shift Network (BSN), Hierarchical Cubic Network (HCN), and the Hyper-Torus Network (HTN). A comparison among these networks has also been conducted. The metrics used for comparison include the network diameter, the fault coverage, and the reliability. The performance comparison shows that as the number of faults exceeds six, the FTBB has a higher probability to recover from those faults as compared to the other two architectures. The fault diameter of the FTBB is also larger than each of the other two architectures, particularly if the number of faults is seven or more. The improvement in the fault tolerance and reliability performance of the FTBB is achieved at the expense of a reasonable increase in the number of nodes and links.

References

[1] S. Dandamudi and D. Eager, "Hierarchical Interconnection Networks for Multi-computer Systems", IEE Transactions on Computers, Vol. 39, No. 6, June 1990, pp. 786-797.

[2] G. Jan, Y. Hwang, M. Lin, and D. Liang, "Novel Hierarchical Interconnection Networks for High performance Multi-computer Systems", Journal of Information Science and Engineering, Vol. 20, 2004, pp. 1213-1229.

[3] C. Sul, D. McLeod, and W. Pedrycz, "Reliable and fast reconfigurable Hierarchical Interconnection Networks for Linear WSI Arrays", IEEE Transactions on Very Large Scale Integration (VLSI) Systems, Vol. 1. No. 2, June 1993, pp. 224-228.

[4] Y. Shi, Z. Hou, and J. Song, "Hierarchical Interconnection Networks with Folded Hypercubes as Basic Clusters", 4th International Conference on High Performance Computing in Asia-Pacific Region, Vol. 1, 2000, pp. 134-137.

[5] M. Abd-El-Barr, F. Daud, and K. Al-Tawil, "A Hierarchical Fault-Tolerant Interconnection Network", 15th *IEEE Annual International*

Phoenix Conference on Computers and Communications, pp. 123-128, 27-29 March 1996.

[6]   Abd-El-Barr, M. H., and Hai, M. A., "Subcube Reliability of a Modular Fault-Tolerant Hypercube Architecture", Journal of Science and Engineering, Vol. 2, no. 1, 1996, pp. 7-25.

[7]   Y. Pan, "The block shift network: interconnection strategies for large parallel systems," Ph.D., Dep't Computer Science, University of Pittsburgh, 1991.

[8]   Y. Pan and H. Y. H. Chuang, "Properties and performance of the block shift network," *IEEE Trans. Circuits and Systems—I: Fundamental Theory and Applications*, vol. 44, pp. 93–102, Feb 1997.

[9]   Y. Pan, "Fault Tolerance in the Block Shift Network", *IEEE Trans. Reliability*, vol. 50, No. 1, March 2001, pp. 85–90.

[10] K. Ghose and K.R. Desai, "Hierarchical Cubic Network," *IEEE Trans. Parallel and Distributed Systems*, vol. 6, no. 4, pp. 427–435, Apr. 1995.

[11] K. Ghose and K.R. Desai, "The HCN: A Versatile Interconnection Network Based on Cubes", Proceedings of the Supercomputing Conference, 1989, pp. 426-435.

[12] K. Ghose and K.R. Desai, "Design and Evaluation of the Hierarchical Cubic Network", Proceedings of the 19th International Conference on Parallel Processing, Vol. 1, 1990, pp. 355-362.

[13] S. Wei and S. Levy, "Design and Analysis of Efficient Hierarchical Interconnection Networks", in *Proc. Supercomputing'91*, Nov 1991, pp. 390-399.

Chapter 7

Fault Tolerance and Reliability of Computer Networks

A number of techniques have been introduced to improve network reliability and fault tolerance. A number of algorithms have also been devised to calculate, or estimate, the reliability of a network. Some of these produces exact results while others produce approximate results. Some algorithms attempt at maximizing the reliability and fault tolerance of a network given some cost constraints. Some other algorithms attempt at minimizing the cost of a network subject to reliability and fault tolerance constraints.

Computer network reliability and fault tolerance is the main topic discussed in this chapter. We start our discussion by introducing a number of fundamental concepts. We then introduce the topic of fault tolerance and reliability of loop (ring) networks. The discussion then focuses on the issue of fault tolerance and reliability of general graph networks. In particular, we consider enumeration and iterative techniques. Important concepts such as all terminal and two-terminal reliability are discussed with examples. We also introduce some basic techniques for finding lower and upper bounds on network reliability with examples. We then cover the issues of optimization of network topology for improved reliability & fault tolerance followed by an introduction to the issue of maximizing network reliability by adding a single edge and design for reliability of networks.

7.1 Background Material

A computer network can be modeled as a non-directed graph $G(V, E)$, having a set of n vertices (nodes) $V = \{v_1, v_2, ..., v_n\}$ and a set of k edges (links) $E = \{e_1, e_2, ..., e_k\}$. Vertices represent processing nodes (computers) and edges represent communication links. Each link is assigned a pair of numbers. These represent respectively, the cost and reliability of the link. Unless otherwise indicated, nodes are assumed to be perfect. Link reliability is defined as the ability of the link to perform its function over a given period of time. The cost of a network includes material costs of the cabling, installation costs, and connection or terminal costs. Figure 7.1 shows an example of a four nodes, four links network graph.

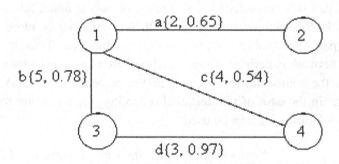

Fig. 7.1: Example graph of a network.

Two-terminal reliability is defined as the probability that a given pair of nodes in a network is connected. *All terminal reliability* is defined as the probability that each pair of nodes in the network can communicate with each other. All terminal reliability is especially important in the design of backbone networks whereby it is necessary for each pair of nodes to communicate with each other. *Network reliability* is defined as the probability that all nodes in a network are connected. It is concerned with the ability of each and every node to be able to communicate with all other nodes.

Network design can be stated as placing links among nodes in the network in such a way that the network reliability is maximized for a given cost. The problem can also be restated as: given a minimum required reliability, network design is concerned with the question of how to place links in the network such that the cost is minimized? In either case, the network reliability and cost are two conflicting objectives. A compromise has to be struck between the two. There exist a number of algorithms for solving this problem. These include heuristics, enumerative and iterative algorithms. A heuristic algorithm tries to find an acceptable solution to the problem based on a number of observations. It will not guarantee the optimality of the solution. A heuristic algorithm may fail to find a solution even if one exists.

A network is said to be fault-tolerant if in the presence of some fault(s), information from any source node to any destination node in the network can still be routed. In the context of two-terminal reliability, a network is considered fault-tolerant if there exists two or more totally disjoint paths between the given source-destination pair. Thus, a 1-fault-tolerant network is defined as one which retains a single established path between the source-destination pair in the presence of fault(s) in the network. In the case of two-terminal reliability, the following measure for fault tolerance, *FT*, can be used.

$$FT = 1 - \left[\frac{Number\ of\ common\ links\ between\ paths}{Total\ number\ of\ links\ present\ in\ the\ network} \right]$$

In the context of network reliability, the following measure for fault tolerance, *FT*, can be used.

$$FT = \frac{Number\ of\ nodes\ with\ degree\ \geq 2}{Total\ number\ of\ nodes\ in\ the\ network}$$

7.2 Fault Tolerance in Loop Networks

Loop (ring) networks represent the simplest and least expensive network topology. In such networks, a given node is connected to its down stream neighboring node in a unidirectional manner. From the reliability point of view, single-loop networks resemble series systems. As the number of nodes increases in a single-loop network, the reliability of the network decreases. In addition, single-loop networks are characterized by having single point failure. This means that the failure of a single link (or node) leads to the failure of the whole network. There exist a number of single-loop topologies. These include token-ring, bypass switch, and the braided ring, to mention a few. Figure 7.2 shows illustrations for these topologies.

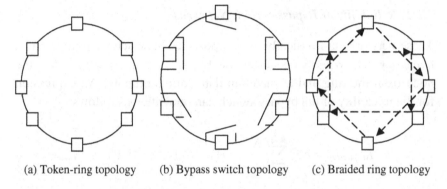

   (a) Token-ring topology   (b) Bypass switch topology   (c) Braided ring topology

Fig. 7.2: Different ring topologies.

7.2.1 *Reliability of Token-Ring Networks*

The token-ring network is essentially a series of work-stations connected in a point-to-point manner to form a loop. For the purpose of the simple analysis given here, a token ring network is considered to have several work-stations (N) and ONE file-server (FS), i.e. the network consists of ($N + 1$) **Nodes**. The stations send their requests to the FS and receive replies to these requests from the FS. Each node (including the FS, f) is considered as consisting of a workstation (w) and a port (p).The failure of any workstation, w, or its port (p), as well the failure of the FS (f) or its port causes the failure of the network. Based on the above assumptions, the reliability and the mean time to failure (MTTF) of a simple token ring are given by the following equations.

$$R_{Basic}(t) = e^{[-N(\lambda_w + \lambda_p)t]} \cdot e^{[-(\lambda_f + \lambda p)t]} = e^{[-(N(\lambda_w + \lambda_p) + \lambda_f + \lambda p)t]}$$

$$MTTF = \int_0^\infty R_{Basic}(t)\, dt = \frac{1}{[N(\lambda_w + \lambda_p) + \lambda_f + \lambda p]}$$

In the above equations, λ_w represents the failure rate of a workstation, λ_p represents the failure rate of a port, and λ_f represents the failure rate of file server.

7.2.2 Reliability of Bypass-Switch Networks

These networks are basically loop topologies in which each node has a bypass switch. When a node fails, the bypass switch closes to isolate the node from the ring and to maintain data-path continuity. An expression for the reliability of the bypass switch can be written as follows:

$$R_{bypass}(t) = e^{-\beta t} \sum_{j=0}^{N-1} \binom{N-1}{j}(1 - e^{-\alpha t})^j e^{-\alpha(N-1-j)t} e^{-j\lambda_s t} .$$

This can be explained as follows.

The probability that both the File Server and the tagged station and their ports are functioning is given by: $e^{-\beta t} = e^{-(\lambda_f + \lambda_w + 2\lambda_p)t}$. The probability that j workstations and their ports have failed is given by: $(1 - e^{-(\lambda_w + \lambda_p)t})^j$. The probability that the remaining (N-1-j) workstations and their ports have not failed is given by: $e^{-(\lambda_w + \lambda_p)(N-1-j)t}$. The probability that j switches have not failed is given by: $e^{-j\lambda_s t}$.

7.2.3 Double Loop Architectures

Double-loop networks are used to improve the reliability of single-loop topologies. They are derived from single-loop networks by introducing additional links between nodes. The effect of introducing redundant links in a network is to increase the number of paths among nodes, which in turn improves the fault tolerance aspects of the network. Additional links lead to a reduction in the network diameter and hence improves the delay of messages around the network. Figure 7.3 shows an illustration of a double-loop network.

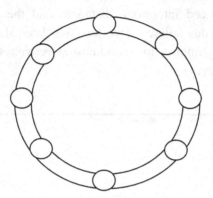

Fig. 7.3: Double-loop network.

In this topology, two or more independent loops each is operated in a unidirectional fashion are provided. When faults occur, the loops are reconfigured so as to maintain complete connectivity. Reconfiguration can be achieved by reversing direction of one or more links and/or operating one or more links in a bidirectional mode. Figure 7.4 shows two forms of the double loop Topology: the *self-heal* and the *bypass*.

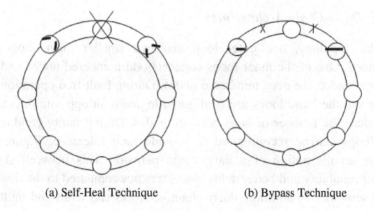

(a) Self-Heal Technique   (b) Bypass Technique

Fig. 7.4: Double-loop network.

7.2.4 *Multi-Drop Architectures*

This topology includes several loops interconnected using additional loops(s) in two or more level, see Fig. 7.5. The main advantages of these networks are reduced inter-node distances and the ability to tolerate multiple simultaneous failures. Two-level has been shown to be optimal from the reliability improvement and cost-effectiveness viewpoint in the multi-drop topology.

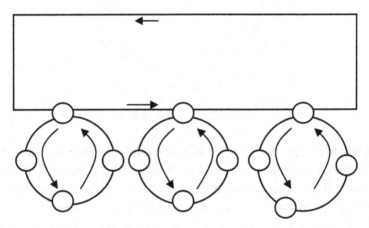

Fig. 7.5: Double-drop architecture.

7.2.5 *Daisy-Chain Architectures*

In this topology, one outer loop and two smaller inner loops are provided. One of the inner loops connects odd numbered nodes and the other connects the even numbered nodes. During fault-free operation the outer and the inner loops are configured logically in opposite directions to reduce the number of hops between nodes. During faulty conditions, the loops can be reconfigured to provide fault tolerance. Figure 7.6 shows an illustration of a daisy-chain network. This network shows higher reliability and better delay characteristics compared to the double-loop networks. In addition, daisy-chain networks can withstand multiple component failures.

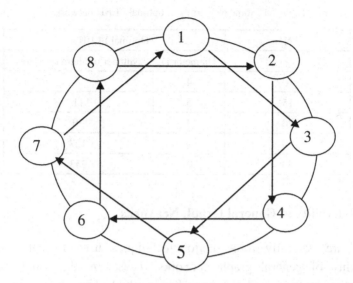

Fig. 7.6: A daisy-chain network.

The forward-loop backward-hop (FLBH) is a variant of the daisy-chain network. In its general form, a FLBH has node x connected to node $(x+1)$ and to node $(x-s)$mode N where N is the number of nodes in the network and s is the *skip distance of backward loop*. Different values of s result in different network properties such as diameter, delay, reliability and fault tolerance. It has been shown that optimal (or near optimal) network properties occur when $s = \sqrt{N}$. Optimal *FLBHs* have higher protection against both link and node failures. They provide larger number of alternate routes between two farthest nodes compared to regular daisy-chain networks. The increase in the number of alternate routes leads to a decrease in the network diameter, which in turn lead to an increase in the network terminal reliability. Table 7.1 relates the number of nodes, N, the diameter, D, and the number of alternate routes in optimal FLBH networks.

Table 7.1: Some properties of optimal FLBH networks.

N	Optimal FLBH	
	Diameter D	Number of alternate routes
10	4	7
15	5	11
20	7	30
30	9	127
40	10	253

7.3 Reliability of General Graph Networks

There are basically three major techniques used to calculate the reliability of general graph networks. These are the *exact* method, *estimation* method, and the *bounding* method. The exact method can be further classified as complete *state enumeration* and *factoring* (inclusive/exclusive) method. In this Section, we will cover the two exact methods, i.e., the complete state enumeration and the factoring methods in addition to the bounding method. These are explained below.

7.3.1 *The Exact Method*

Complete State Enumeration Method

The complete state enumeration (CSE) technique in calculating network reliability refers to the method in which the probabilities of all the possible outcomes are calculated. That is to say, to calculate the probability that all links are working. This is followed by calculating the probabilities that only a single link is not working and all the other links are working. Next, to calculate the probabilities that only 2 links are not working and all remaining links are working and so on. Finally, to calculate the probability that all links are not working. These probabilities are *mutually exclusive* (do not occur at the same time) and therefore, can be added up to form a cumulative probability. The name *enumerative technique* represents the fact that all possible outcomes are *"enumerated"*. Enumerating all those probabilities for large networks, is prohibitively expensive and therefore, it is practical to calculate the reliability of a network only to certain degree of accuracy.

Example

It is required to calculate, the probability of having nodes A and B (see Fig. 7.7) connected by enumerating all the possible paths between the two nodes under the following assumptions.

- Nodes are perfect (reliability = 1)
- Reliability of links are known (the number (0.98) next to a link is its reliability)
- Failures of different links are statically independent events.

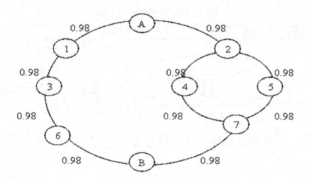

Fig. 7.7: Example seven node network.

Table 7.2 shows a number of steps in the required calculation.

Table 7.2: Reliability computation.

Conditional probability	Probability	Cumulative probability
All links are working	$R_0 = (0.98)^{10} \approx 0.8170728$	$R \approx 0.8170728$
Only one link down	$R_1 = 10*(0.02)(0.98)^9 \approx 0.1667496$	$R \approx 0.9838224$
Two links down	$R_2 = 45*(0.02)^2(0.98)^8 \approx 0.0153137$	$R \approx 0.9991361$
Three links down	$R_3 = 120*(0.02)^3(0.98)^7 \approx 0.0008334$	$R \approx 0.9999695$

Factoring Method

Under the factoring, we discuss a number of different possible methods.

The Parallel-Serial Reduction Method

The essence of this method is to reduce a complex network to a simple one in which the reliability could be easily calculated. It is usually the case that the network is reduced to the trivial case in which the source and destination nodes are having one link (of known reliability) between them. In presenting this method, we make the same assumptions mentioned above. Table 7.3 shows the two basic rules used.

Table 7.3 Reduction rules.

Connection type	Parallel	Series
Example	0.98 ... A — B ... 0.98 ⇓ A — 0.9996 — B	0.98 0.98 A — ○ — B ⇓ A — 0.9604 — B
Reliability	R= 0.98+0.98-0.98*0.98 = 0.9996	R=0.98*0.98=0.9604

Given a complex network, the above two simplifications can be used to reduce the network until one can arrive at the trivial network consisting of the source and destination and one link in between.

Example

Consider the network shown in Fig. 7.7. Using the series reduction, we can replace the path consisting of three links in series, with only one link having reliability $R = (0.98)^3 \approx 0.9223682$. The resulting network is shown in Fig. 7.8.

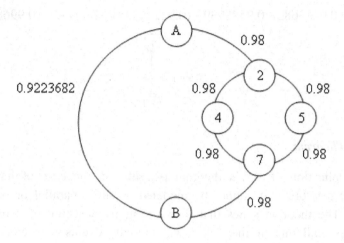

Fig. 7.8: A reduced network.

Now, we can replace the 2 parallel paths (2,4,7) & (2,5,7) with 2 parallel paths each with equivalent reliability of $R = (0.98)^2 = 0.9604$. The network is shown below.

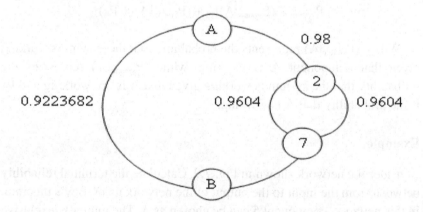

Similar steps can be used to further reduce the network until we arrive at the final reduced network shown below. The equivalent link between the two nodes is having reliability

$$R = 0.9223682 + 0.9588939 - (0.9223682 * 0.9588939) \approx 0.996809$$

Bay's Theorem

The application of Bay's theorem is useful in the case of having a general network that cannot be modeled as series-parallel or parallel-series. The theorem states that: For a system consisting of 2 or more modules, call one of them A. Two mutually exclusive events occur. These are

1. The system with A working
2. The system with A not working

The probability of the system working

$$P_{system} = (P_{system}|A)P_A + (P_{system}|\bar{A})(1-P_A)$$

Where $(P_{system}|A)$ represents the probability that the system is working given that component A is working, while $(P_{system}|\bar{A})$ represents the probability that the system is working given that A is not working and P_A is the probability that A is working.

Example

Consider the network shown in Fig. 7.9. Calculate the terminal reliability between from the input to the output of the network using Bay's theorem. In this network, component 5 can be chosen as A. The mutually exclusive cases (A is working and A is not working) are shown in the figure. Calculate the reliability as follows.

$R_{A\ is\ working} = [1-(1-R1)(1-R2)][1-(1-R3)(1-R4)]R5$
$R_{A\ is\ not\ working} = [1-(1-R1*R3)(1-R2*R4)](1-R5)$

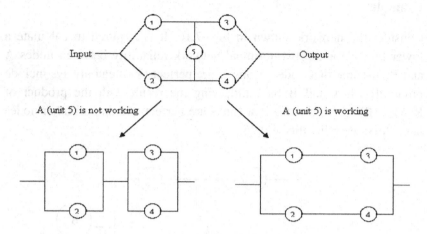

Fig. 7.9: Example network.

The required reliability is $R_{network} = (R_{A \text{ is working}})P_A + (R_{A \text{ is not working}})(1-P_A)$.

It should be noted that Bay's theorem can be applied recursively to sub networks.

7.3.2 Reliability Bounding

Two-Terminal Lower Bound

A lower bound on two-terminal network reliability is sometimes required. This is especially important in analyzing the worst-case scenario. The tighter the bound, the better the algorithm is.

Usually lower bound for two-terminal network reliability is found using the following steps:

1. Enumerate all the paths from source node to destination node.
2. Find non-overlapping paths.
3. Eliminate all other paths.
4. Compute the reliability (You will have only parallel paths).

Example

Consider the network shown in Fig. 7.10. It is required to calculate a lower bound for the two-terminal network reliability between nodes A and B. Assume that nodes A and B are perfect (You can always include reliability of A and B by multiplying the result with the product of R(A)*R(B)). Also assume that Links are perfect and that all other nodes have the same reliability = 0.95.

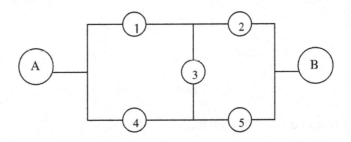

Fig. 7.10: Example network.

1. List of all paths from A to B: (1,2), (1,3,5), (4,3,2) and (4,5).
2. Find non-overlapping paths: (1,2) and (4,5)
3. Eliminate other paths: (1,3,5) and (4,3,2).
4. Remaining network is shown below.

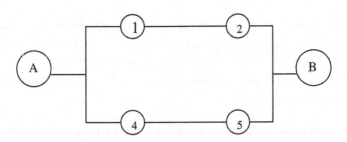

5. Compute the two-terminal reliability:

$$R \geq 1 - (1 - R^2) \bullet (1 - R^2) \geq 0.9905$$

It should be noted that the selection of different non-overlapping paths might lead to different lower bounds for the two-terminal reliability of a network.

Two-Terminal Reliability Upper Bound

It is sometimes desirable to compute an upper bound on two-terminal network reliability. Computing the upper bound can help finding how well a pair of nodes can communicate through the existing network compared to the ideal case (all paths are parallel). The following steps describe the method.

1. Enumerate all paths from source to destination.
2. Assume that all the paths are parallel. Draw a new network. (Duplicate any component that is shared by different paths)
3. Compute the reliability given the parallel paths. The resulting reliability is the upper bound.

Example

Consider the network shown in Fig. 7.11. It is required to calculate the upper bound on the two-terminal network reliability between nodes A and B. Assume that Links, A and B are perfect and that all nodes have the same reliability = 0.95

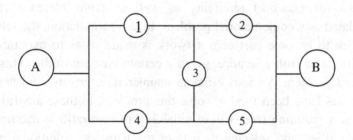

Fig. 7.11: Example network.

1. List of all paths: (1,2), (1,3,5), (4,3,5) and (4,5)
2. Assume that all paths are connected in parallel and redraw the new network.

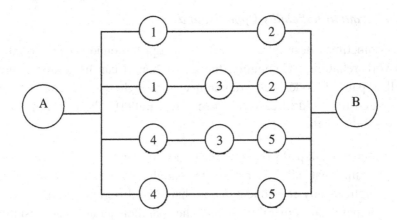

3. Compute the reliability:

$$R \leq 1-(1-0.95^2)^2 \bullet (1-0.95^3)^2 \leq 0.999807$$

7.4 Topology Optimization of Networks Subject to Reliability & Fault Tolerance Constraints

Topological layout of links in a computer network for optimizing terminal (or network) reliability as well as fault tolerance can be formulated as a combinatorial problem. In this formulation, the selection of a link to become part of a network is made so as to maximize the reliability and fault tolerance, given a certain cost constraint. This is an *NP-hard* problem. Various efficient enumerative, greedy, and heuristic techniques have been used to solve this problem. In these algorithms, a path (or a spanning tree) whose reliability to cost ratio is maximum is first identified and selected as part of the network. Additional path(s) whose reliability to cost ratio is maximum and which increases the fault tolerance of the network are added, one at a time, given that the cost constraint is not violated. In this section, we present two techniques, one enumerative and another iterative for the topology optimization of networks subject to reliability and fault tolerance constraints.

7.4.1 *Enumeration Techniques*

There has been a number of enumerative techniques presented in the literature. We present in this section a technique that takes both reliability and fault tolerance into consideration while optimizing the topology of a network. Two versions of the technique exist. The first one considers the two-terminal reliability in a networks and the second technique considers the network reliability.

Two-Terminal Reliability

The idea behind this technique is to start by enumerating all paths between the given pair of source-destination nodes. The reliability and the cost of each path are computed. The reliability of a path is defined as the product of the reliabilities of all links along that path, while the cost of the path is defined as the sum of the costs of the links along it. The path that has the maximum reliability to cost ratio is selected. The balance cost after the selection of the first path is computed. The cost and reliability of the remaining paths are also recomputed. The next path to be added is the one which satisfies the cost constraint while being maximally disjoint with the already selected path. The process is repeated until no more paths can be added. The steps of the algorithm are shown in Fig. 7.12. A more formal version of the algorithm is shown in Fig. 7.13.

The computations made in this algorithm are as follows.

$$p_c(i, j) = \begin{cases} c(j), \text{ the cost of link } j \text{ if it exists along path } i \\ 0 \quad \text{otherwsie} \end{cases}$$

$$p_r(i, j) = \begin{cases} p_j, \text{ the relaibility of link } j \text{ if it exists along path } i \\ 1 \quad \text{otherwise} \end{cases}$$

$$c(i) = \sum_{j=1}^{L} p_c(i, j), \text{ where } L \text{ is the number of links}$$

$$R(i) = \prod_{j=1}^{L} p_r(i, j) \quad \text{and} \quad D(i) = \frac{R(i)}{C(i)}$$

$$Ratio_{Disjoint}(i) = 1 - \frac{\text{Number of common links between paths}}{\text{Total number of links presence in the network}}$$

$Cost_{max}$ = maximum permissible cost for the network

$$\Delta D(i) = \frac{\Delta R(i)}{\Delta C(i)}, \Delta R(i) = \text{increment in reliability and } \Delta C(i) = \text{increament in cost}$$

Algorithm in a Nutshell

1. Determine all non-redundant paths between the source and destination nodes,
2. Determine the cost and reliability of each path,
3. Select the path whose reliability/cost ratio is maximum as the starting point, if its cost is less than the maximum permissible cost,
4. Compute the balance cost and do one of the following:
   (a) if the balance cost is zero, then the selected path is the optimal solution.
   (b) if the balance cost is < zero, then there is no solution.
   (c) if the balance cost is > zero, then do the following:
      • Remove all constituent links along the selected path from further consideration,
      • Arrange the remaining paths in an ascending order of their cost,
      • Remove those paths whose cost exceed the balance cost, if all paths are removed then stop; otherwise do the following:
      • Compute the reliability/cost ratio for each of the remaining paths,
      • Add the path whose reliability to cost ratio is maximum and which is maximally disjoint with existing path(s) to the network,
      • Stop either when the maximum permissible cost is reached or when all links are exhausted.

Fig. 7.12: Algorithm steps.

Algorithm: *Two-Terminal Optimization*

Step 1: Determine all the non-redundant paths between Source and Destination,

Step 2: Generate a path-cost matrix, P_c, and the path reliability matrix P_r,

Step 3: Generate the *Cost C* matrix,

Step 4: Generate the *Reliability R* matrix,

Step 5: Generate the D matrix such that $D(i) = \dfrac{R(i)}{C(i)}$ $\forall i$

Step 6: Choose k such that $D(k) \geq D(i)$ $\forall i$. Determine $C(k)$ and $R(k)$.

Step 7: Compute the balance cost as $\left| Cost_{\max} - C(k) \right|$

$$\begin{cases} if & \left| Cost_{\max} - C(k) \right| < 0, then\ D(k) = 0,\ go\ to\ step\ 6 \\ else-if & \left| Cost_{\max} - C(k) \right| = 0, then\ \text{the } kth\ path\ is\ the\ optimum\ solution, STOP \\ else-if & \left| Cost_{\max} - C(k) \right| > 0, then\ go\ to\ next\ step \end{cases}$$

Step 8: Remove used links and remove any path whose cost exceeds balance cost. If all paths are removed, then STOP; otherwise go to next step

Step 9: Generate the $\Delta D(i)$ matrix,

Step10: Generate the matrix $Ratio_{disjoint}$ and select the path with the maximum $Ratio_{disjoint}$. Break the ties in favor of the path having maximum $\Delta D(i)$ $\forall i$. Go to Step 6

End.

Fig. 7.13: Two-terminal reliability algorithm.

Example

Consider the seven nodes, eleven links network shown in Fig. 7.14 with links attributes as shown in the following table. Assume that the maximum permissible cost is 20 units. Use the above algorithm to find an optimal topology that maximizes the terminal reliability and fault tolerance between nodes S (node 5) and T (node 4).

Link	a	b	c	D	E	F	g	h	i	J	K
Cost	3.30	3.70	1.35	1.25	2.55	7.95	3.00	2.00	6.00	3.00	9.15
Reliability	0.84	0.76	0.90	0.89	0.94	0.73	0.76	0.92	0.49	0.90	0.78

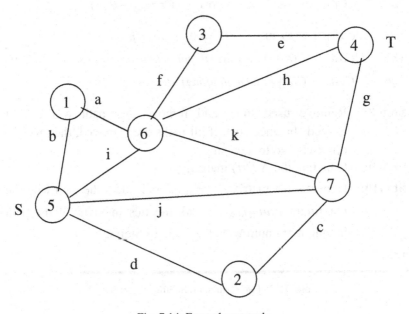

Fig. 7.14: Example network.

There 12 paths between S and T. These are: *abef, cdg, abh, efi, hi, gj, cdefk, abgk, cdhk, gik, efjk, and hjk*. The specifics of these paths are shown below.

$$
P_c(12\times11)=
\begin{bmatrix}
a & b & c & d & e & f & g & h & i & j & k \\
3.3 & 3.7 & 0.0 & 0.0 & 2.55 & 7.95 & 0.0 & 0.0 & 0.0 & 0.0 & 0.0 \\
0.0 & 0.0 & 1.35 & 1.25 & 0.0 & 0.0 & 3.0 & 0.0 & 0.0 & 0.0 & 0.0 \\
3.3 & 3.7 & 0.0 & 0.0 & 0.0 & 0.0 & 0.0 & 2.0 & 0.0 & 0.0 & 0.0 \\
0.0 & 0.0 & 0.0 & 0.0 & 2.55 & 7.95 & 0.0 & 0.0 & 6.0 & 0.0 & 0.0 \\
0.0 & 0.0 & 0.0 & 0.0 & 0.0 & 0.0 & 0.0 & 2.0 & 6.0 & 0.0 & 0.0 \\
0.0 & 0.0 & 0.0 & 0.0 & 0.0 & 0.0 & 3.0 & 0.0 & 0.0 & 3.0 & 0.0 \\
0.0 & 0.0 & 1.35 & 1.25 & 2.55 & 7.95 & 0.0 & 0.0 & 0.0 & 0.0 & 9.15 \\
3.3 & 3.7 & 0.0 & 0.0 & 0.0 & 0.0 & 3.0 & 0.0 & 0.0 & 0.0 & 9.15 \\
0.0 & 0.0 & 1.35 & 1.25 & 0.0 & 0.0 & 0.0 & 2.0 & 0.0 & 0.0 & 9.15 \\
0.0 & 0.0 & 0.0 & 0.0 & 0.0 & 0.0 & 3.0 & 0.0 & 6.0 & 0.0 & 9.15 \\
0.0 & 0.0 & 0.0 & 0.0 & 2.55 & 7.95 & 0.0 & 0.0 & 0.0 & 3.0 & 9.15 \\
0.0 & 0.0 & 0.0 & 0.0 & 0.0 & 0.0 & 0.0 & 2.0 & 0.0 & 3.0 & 9.15
\end{bmatrix}
$$

$$
P_r(12\times11)=
\begin{bmatrix}
a & b & c & d & e & f & g & h & i & j & k \\
0.84 & 0.76 & 1.0 & 1.0 & 0.94 & 0.73 & 1.0 & 1.0 & 1.0 & 1.0 & 1.0 \\
1.0 & 1.0 & 0.90 & 0.89 & 1.0 & 1.0 & 0.76 & 1.0 & 1.0 & 1.0 & 1.0 \\
0.84 & 0.76 & 1.0 & 1.0 & 1.0 & 1.0 & 1.0 & 0.92 & 1.0 & 1.0 & 1.0 \\
1.0 & 1.0 & 1.0 & 1.0 & 0.94 & 0.73 & 1.0 & 1.0 & 0.49 & 1.0 & 1.0 \\
1.0 & 1.0 & 1.0 & 1.0 & 1.0 & 1.0 & 1.0 & 0.92 & 0.49 & 1.0 & 1.0 \\
1.0 & 1.0 & 1.0 & 1.0 & 1.0 & 1.0 & 0.76 & 1.0 & 1.0 & 0.90 & 1.0 \\
1.0 & 1.0 & 0.90 & 0.89 & 0.94 & 0.73 & 1.0 & 1.0 & 1.0 & 1.0 & 0.78 \\
0.84 & 0.76 & 1.0 & 1.0 & 1.0 & 1.0 & 0.76 & 1.0 & 1.0 & 1.0 & 0.78 \\
1.0 & 1.0 & 0.90 & 0.89 & 1.0 & 1.0 & 1.0 & 0.92 & 1.0 & 1.0 & 0.78 \\
1.0 & 1.0 & 1.0 & 1.0 & 1.0 & 1.0 & 0.76 & 1.0 & 0.49 & 1.0 & 0.78 \\
1.0 & 1.0 & 1.0 & 1.0 & 0.94 & 0.73 & 1.0 & 1.0 & 1.0 & 0.90 & 0.78 \\
1.0 & 1.0 & 1.0 & 1.0 & 1.0 & 1.0 & 1.0 & 0.92 & 1.0 & 0.90 & 0.78
\end{bmatrix}
$$

$$C(12 \times 1) = \begin{bmatrix} 17.50 \\ 05.60 \\ 09.00 \\ 16.50 \\ 08.00 \\ \mathbf{06.00} \\ 22.25 \\ 20.15 \\ 13.75 \\ 18.15 \\ 22.65 \\ 14.15 \end{bmatrix} \quad R(12 \times 1) = \begin{bmatrix} 0.43807000 \\ 0.60876000 \\ 0.62228800 \\ 0.33623800 \\ 0.45080000 \\ \mathbf{0.68400000} \\ 0.42872400 \\ 0.37844352 \\ 0.57479760 \\ 0.29047200 \\ 0.48171240 \\ 0.72036000 \end{bmatrix} \quad D(12 \times 1) = \begin{bmatrix} 0.025032 \\ 0.108701 \\ 0.069143 \\ 0.020378 \\ 0.056350 \\ \mathbf{0.114000} \\ 0.019268 \\ 0.018781 \\ 0.041803 \\ 0.016003 \\ 0.021267 \\ 0.050908 \end{bmatrix}$$

Among these, path gj is selected as it has the highest reliability to cost ratio (D = 0.114). The reliability of this path (terminal reliability) is 0.684 and the cost is 6 units. The attributes of the potential set of remaining paths are shown below (paths that can be selected).

Path	cdg	abh	hi
Number of common links with already selected path (gj)	1	0	0
Fault tolerance measure	0.75	1.0	1.0

Among these paths *abh* and *hi* are potential candidates. Since *abh* has a better $\Delta D = \dfrac{\Delta R}{\Delta C}$, therefore, it is selected. The terminal reliability of the resulting network is 0.8696 and its cost is 15. The algorithm stops, since are no more possible paths to add. The resulting network is shown below. It consists of five nodes and five links.

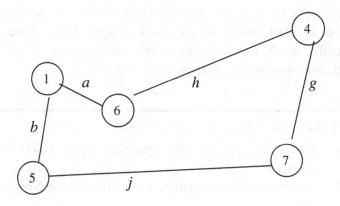

7.4.1.1 *Network Reliability*

In this section, a method for topological optimization of a computer network to maximize network reliability and fault tolerance is introduced. The basic idea is to enumerate the spanning trees (STs) of all network topologies. Among these STs, the one with the maximum reliability to cost ratio is selected as the starting point. The cost of a ST is computed as the sum of the costs of all constituent links and its reliability is computed as the product of the reliabilities of all constituent links. Additional STs are added depending on the balance cost. Among the STs that satisfy the cost criterion, the ST that is most disjoint from the existing ST(s) is added. The process continues until no more STs can be added. A formal explanation of the algorithm is shown in Fig. 7.15.

Example

Consider the network shown in Fig. 7.16. The network consists of six nodes and eight links and has the specifications shown in the following table. Assume that the maximum permissible cost is $Cost_{max} = 21$ units.

Link	A	B	C	D	E	f	g	H
Cost	2.0	3.0	3.0	3.0	4.0	3.0	4.0	3.0
Reliability	0.9	0.3	0.8	0.3	0.9	0.8	0.7	0.8

There are a total of 29 Spanning Trees. These are: abdeh, bcdeh, acdeh, bdefh, adefh, abefh, bdegh, adegh, abdgh, abdeg, abegh, bcefg, bcdfh, cdfha, acefh, bcegh, bcdeg, bcdgh, acegh, acdeg, acdgh, bdefg, adefg, abefg, abdfg, bcefg, abcfg, acefg, acdfg.

Algorithm *Network Reliability Optimization*

Step 1:   Enumerate all possible Spanning Trees (STs) in the network

Step 2:   Generate a *ST*-cost matrix, S_c, and the *ST* reliability matrix S_r

Step 3:   Generate the *Cost* matrix, C

Step 4:   Generate the *Reliability* matrix, R

Step 5:   Generate the D matrix, such that $D(i) = \dfrac{R(i)}{C(i)}$ $\forall i$

Step 6:   Choose k such that $D(k) \geq D(i)$ $\forall i = 1,\ 2,\ ...,\ ST$ (# STs), Determine $C(k)$ and $R(k)$.

Step 7:   Compute the balance cost as $\left| Cost_{\max} - C(k) \right|$

$$\begin{cases} if & \left| Cost_{\max} - C(k) \right| < 0, then\ D(k) = 0,\ go\ to\ step\ 6 \\ else-if\ \left| Cost_{\max} - C(k) \right| = 0, then\ \text{the } kth \text{ path is the optimum solution}, STOP \\ else-if\ \left| Cost_{\max} - C(k) \right| > 0, then\ go\ to\ next\ step \end{cases}$$

Step 8:   Remove used links and remove any STs whose cost exceed balance cost. If all STs are removed, then STOP; otherwise go to next step

Step 9:   Generate the *Distance* matrix

Step10:   Select the ST having the maximum *Distance(i)*. Break the ties in favor of the ST which increases the number of nodes with degree ≥ 2 the most. Augment the network with that ST. Go to Step 7.

End.

Fig. 7.15: Formal description of the network reliability optimization algorithm.

The computations made in this algorithm are as follows.

$$S_c(k, j) = \begin{cases} c(j), & \text{the cost of link } j \text{ if it exists in } \textit{Spanning Tree } k, \\ & \text{where } k = 1, 2, ..., ST \ (\# \text{STs}) \\ 0 & \text{otherwise} \end{cases}$$

$$p_r(i, j) = \begin{cases} p_j, & \text{the relaibility of link } j \text{ if it exists in } \textit{Spanning Tree } k, \\ & \text{where } k = 1, 2, ..., ST \ (\#\text{STs}) \\ 1 & \text{otherwise} \end{cases}$$

$$c(k) = \sum_{j=1}^{L} S_c(k, j), \text{ where } L \text{ is the number of links}$$

$$R(k) = \prod_{j=1}^{L} S_r(k, j)$$

$$D(k) = \frac{R(k)}{C(k)}$$

Distance(k) = Distance between the initial ST and ST k.

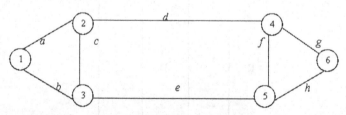

Fig. 7.16: Example network.

The S_r matrix

a	0.9	1.0	0.9	1.0	0.9	0.9	0.9	1.0	0.9	0.9	0.9	0.9	1.0	1.0	0.9	0.9	1.0	1.0	1.0	0.9	0.9	0.9	1.0	0.9	0.9	0.9	1.0	1.0	0.9	0.9
b	0.3	0.3	1.0	0.3	1.0	0.3	0.3	0.3	1.0	0.3	0.3	0.3	0.3	0.3	1.0	1.0	0.3	0.3	0.3	1.0	1.0	1.0	0.3	1.0	0.3	0.3	0.3	0.3	1.0	1.0
c	1.0	0.8	0.8	1.0	1.0	1.0	1.0	1.0	1.0	1.0	1.0	1.0	0.8	0.8	0.8	0.8	0.8	0.8	0.8	0.8	0.8	0.8	1.0	1.0	1.0	1.0	0.8	0.8	0.8	0.8
d	0.3	0.3	0.3	0.3	0.3	0.3	1.0	0.3	0.3	0.3	0.3	1.0	1.0	0.3	0.3	1.0	1.0	0.3	0.3	1.0	0.3	0.3	0.3	0.3	1.0	0.3	1.0	0.3	1.0	0.3
e	0.9	0.9	0.9	0.9	0.9	1.0	0.9	0.9	0.9	1.0	0.9	0.9	0.9	1.0	1.0	0.9	0.9	0.9	1.0	0.9	0.9	1.0	0.9	0.9	0.9	1.0	0.9	1.0	0.9	1.0
f	1.0	1.0	1.0	0.8	0.8	0.8	0.8	1.0	1.0	1.0	1.0	1.0	0.8	0.8	0.8	0.8	1.0	1.0	1.0	1.0	1.0	1.0	0.8	0.8	0.8	0.8	0.8	0.8	0.8	0.8
g	1.0	1.0	1.0	1.0	1.0	1.0	1.0	0.7	0.7	0.7	0.7	0.7	1.0	1.0	1.0	1.0	0.7	0.7	0.7	0.7	0.7	0.7	0.7	0.7	0.7	0.7	0.7	0.7	0.7	0.7
h	0.8	0.8	0.8	0.8	0.8	0.8	0.8	0.8	0.8	0.8	1.0	0.8	0.8	0.8	0.8	0.8	0.8	1.0	0.8	0.8	1.0	0.8	1.0	1.0	1.0	1.0	1.0	1.0	1.0	1.0

The S_c matrix

a	2	0	2	0	2	2	2	0	2	2	2	2	0	0	2	2	0	0	0	2	2	2	0	2	2	2	0	2	2	2
b	3	3	0	3	0	3	3	3	0	3	3	3	3	3	0	0	3	3	3	0	0	0	3	0	3	3	3	3	0	0
c	0	3	3	0	0	0	0	0	0	0	0	0	3	3	3	3	3	3	3	3	3	3	3	0	0	0	0	3	3	3
d	3	3	3	3	3	3	0	3	3	3	3	3	0	0	3	3	0	3	3	3	3	3	0	3	3	3	0	0	0	3
e	4	4	4	4	4	4	0	4	4	4	4	4	0	4	4	4	0	4	4	4	0	4	4	4	0	4	4	4	0	4
f	0	0	0	3	3	3	3	0	0	0	0	0	3	3	3	3	0	0	0	0	0	0	3	3	3	3	3	3	3	3
g	0	0	0	0	0	0	0	4	4	4	4	4	0	0	0	4	4	4	4	4	4	4	4	4	4	4	4	4	4	4
h	3	3	3	3	3	3	3	3	3	3	0	3	3	3	3	3	3	0	3	3	0	3	0	0	0	0	0	0	0	0

The C matrix

$\frac{1}{5}$	$\frac{1}{6}$	$\frac{1}{5}$	$\frac{1}{6}$	$\frac{1}{5}$	$\frac{1}{4}$	$\frac{1}{5}$	$\frac{1}{7}$	$\frac{1}{6}$	$\frac{1}{5}$	$\frac{1}{6}$	$\frac{1}{6}$	$\frac{1}{6}$	$\frac{1}{5}$	$\frac{1}{4}$	$\frac{1}{5}$	$\frac{1}{7}$	$\frac{1}{7}$	$\frac{1}{6}$	$\frac{1}{6}$	$\frac{1}{6}$	$\frac{1}{5}$	$\frac{1}{7}$	$\frac{1}{6}$	$\frac{1}{6}$	$\frac{1}{5}$	$\frac{1}{7}$	$\frac{1}{5}$	$\frac{1}{6}$	$\frac{1}{5}$

$$
R = \begin{bmatrix}
0.05832 \\
0.05184 \\
0.15552 \\
0.05184 \\
0.15552 \\
0.01584 \\
0.15552 \\
0.04536 \\
0.13608 \\
0.04536 \\
0.05103 \\
0.13608 \\
0.13824 \\
0.04608 \\
0.13824 \\
0.41472 \\
0.12096 \\
0.04536 \\
0.04032 \\
0.36288 \\
0.13608 \\
0.12096 \\
0.04536 \\
0.13608 \\
0.13608 \\
0.04536 \\
0.12096 \\
0.04032 \\
0.28224 \\
0.12096
\end{bmatrix}
\qquad
D = \begin{bmatrix}
0.003888 \\
0.003240 \\
0.010368 \\
0.003240 \\
0.010368 \\
0.001131 \\
0.010368 \\
0.002668 \\
0.008505 \\
0.003024 \\
0.003189 \\
0.008505 \\
0.008640 \\
0.003072 \\
0.009874 \\
0.027648 \\
0.007115 \\
0.002668 \\
0.002520 \\
0.022680 \\
0.008505 \\
0.008064 \\
0.002668 \\
0.008505 \\
0.008505 \\
0.003024 \\
0.007115 \\
0.002520 \\
0.017640 \\
0.008064
\end{bmatrix}
$$

From the above matrices, it is clear that spanning tree *acefh* has the best reliability to cost ratio (0.41472/15 = 0.027648). Thus, *ST acefh* is selected. The balance cost is 5. No more *ST* can be added. The algorithm stops. The ST is shown below.

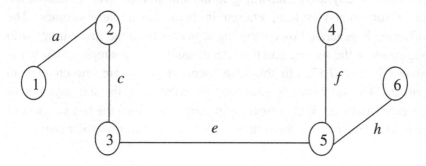

7.4.2 *Iterative Techniques*

A number of iterative algorithms have been used for solving the topological optimization of networks subject to reliability. The hard nature of the topological optimization problem calls for the need to use iterative algorithms. This is because these algorithms are capable of efficiently searching for a near optimal solution in a large solution space. Among the iterative techniques used are the Tabu Search (TS), Simulated Annealing (SA), and Genetic Algorithms (GAs). In this Section, we review the basic concepts of the GAs and show how it can be used to solve the topological optimization network problem.

A Genetic Algorithm (GA) is an iterative evolutionary technique that mimics the process of natural evolution. According to this technique, a solution of a problem is encoded in the form of a string of symbols, called the *genes*. A string of genes is called a *chromosome*. In the search for a solution to a given problem, an initial solution, called a *population* is chosen. The solution process goes through a number of iterations, known as *generations*. In each iteration, individual chromosomes in the population are evaluated according to what is called a *fitness function*. First two chromosomes having the highest fitness values are selected from the population and used as *parents*. Out of these parents, offspring are generated (evolved) using a number of possible operations, e.g., *crossover*, *mutation*, and *inversion*.

A number of forms exist for the crossover operation, e.g., simple, ordered, cycle, and partially mapped. Among these, the simple crossover has been widely used. According to the simple crossover, a random cut point (or points) is (are) chosen in both parent chromosomes. The offspring is generated by combining segments from the first parents with segments of the second parents. An example of the simple crossover is shown in Fig. 7.17. In this case, two cut points are chosen in both parents. The offspring is generated by combining the left segment of parents 1 with the right segment of parents 2 and then the last segment of parents 1.This form of the simple crossover is called *two-point crossover*.

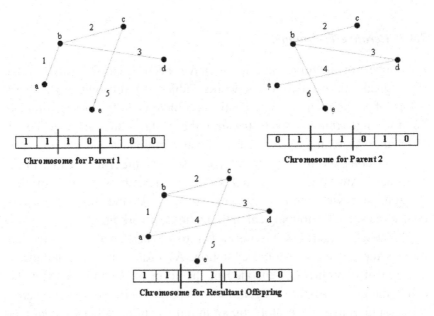

Fig. 7.17: Two-point crossover.

An offspring could be generated using a mutation process. The simplest form of a mutation process is to flip a single gene in the chromosome of a given parent. This is shown in Fig. 7.18.

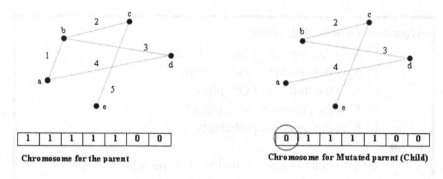

Fig. 7.18: The mutation process.

The quality of solution obtained using the GA algorithm depends on a number of parameters. These are the population size, crossover and mutation rates, and the type of crossover operation used. The selection of values for these parameters is problem specific. A GA technique can be used to obtain a near-minimal solution to the network topological optimization problem. A general outline of the GA algorithm is shown in Fig. 7.19.

Example

Consider the case of having a network population $N_p = 4$ and a number of offspring $N_o = 2$. Figure 7.20 illustrates example iteration for the GA. As can be seen in the figure, two offspring have resulted after applying the two-point crossover operations on each pair of parents. Having applied the crossover operations, the mutation can then be applied. This is shown in Fig. 7.21. This will result in six possible solutions. Only four out of these will have to be selected. This is because $N_p = 4$. This is done using the selected process explained before. The new selected four solutions will represent the starting point for the next iteration, and so on.

Algorithm Genetic Algorithm;
        (* N_p is the population size of the network*)
        (* N_g is the number of Generations*)
        (* N_o is the number of Offspring*)
        (* P_c is the crossover probability*)
        (* P_μ is the mutation probability*)
Begin
        Construct an initial population of N_p possible network
topologies;
        For (j = 1 to N_p)
            Evaluate Fitness (Population[j])
        End For
        For (i = 1 to N_g)
            For (j = 1 to N_o)
                Select parent topologies for Crossover
                (x,y) ← parent topologies;
                Perform Crossover with probability P_c
                Offspring[j] ← Crossover (x,y);
                Perform Mutation with probability P_μ;
                Evaluate Fitness (Offspring[j])
            End For
            Population ← Select N_p topologies for the next
iteration;
        End For
        Return highest scoring topology amongst the population
topologies;
End (**Genetic Algorithm***)

Fig. 7.19: Genetic Algorithm (GA) for the topological Optimization problem.

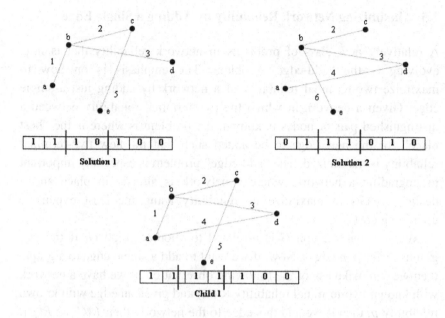

Fig. 7.20: Crossover example.

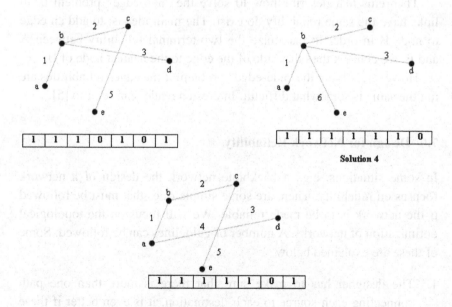

Fig. 7.21: Mutation operation.

7.5   Maximizing Network Reliability by Adding a Single Edge

A relatively new class of problems in network reliability that is now evolving is the "add-edge" problem. The emphasis is on how to maximize two-terminal reliability of a network by adding just a single edge. Given a network in which the two-terminal reliability between a distinguished pair of nodes is known, the problem is where is the "best place" for the new edge to be added such that the new two-terminal reliability is maximized. The "add-edge" problem is especially important in upgrading a network, where a network is already in place and a designer seeks to maximize its reliability using the least expensive upgrading cost.

We say that a graph G is n-related to another graph G^* if the two graphs differ in n edges. Now, if we want to add a single edge to a graph, then we can make use of the following observation: if we have a network with known two-terminal reliability R (G) and given an edge with known reliability p, then if we add this edge to the network, then $R(G^*) \geq R(g)$; Where G^* is the new network.

Theorems that describe how to solve the "add-edge" problem if all links have the same reliability do exist. The main idea is: to add an edge to node B in order to maximize the two-terminal reliability between A and B, we connect the other side of the edge to the nearest node of B.

However, solving the "add-edge" problem if the edges reliabilities are not the same is somewhat difficult. Interested reader can refer to [5].

7.6   Design for Network Reliability

In some situations, e.g., a backbone network the design of a network focuses on reliability. There are some simple rules that must be followed if the network is to be made reliable. We will focus on the topological optimization of networks. A number of guidelines can be followed. Some of these are explained below.

1.   The designer has to make sure that there is more than one path connecting each source to each destination. It is even better if these paths are non-overlapping. Of course this rule contradicts the cost

reduction rule. The designer needs to make some tradeoff between the two objectives, i.e., cost and reliability. According to this rule, tree networks are the least reliable in terms of the topological design.

2. Another important rule is to reduce the number of hops between each pair of nodes in the network as much as it is possible. If there are too many hops between a given source and destination, the reliability of the path might be very small even if the individual reliability of links is high. For example, if there are 150 hops between node A and node B and assuming that nodes are perfect and that links have reliability of 0.99% each, then the reliability of the path connecting A and B is $R = (0.99)^{150} \approx 0.22145$. It is clear from the example that it is a good design rule to keep the diameter of the network as small as possible.

3. Yet a third general rule that is useful for complex networks is to use different technologies in its design. Diversity usually (but not always) makes the network more robust.

7.7 Summary

Computer networks reliability and fault tolerance are becoming integral network design issues. A number of techniques are currently in use for designing reliable and fault-tolerant networks. A number of algorithms have also been introduced to calculate or estimate the reliability of a network. A number of other algorithms have been introduced attempting at maximizing the reliability and fault tolerance of a network given some cost constraints. Some other algorithms attempt at minimizing the cost of a network subject to reliability and fault tolerance constraints. The discussion in this chapter has focused on the topic of computer network reliability and fault tolerance. After introducing a number of basic background material and terminology, we introduced the topic of fault tolerance and reliability of loop (ring) networks. This was followed by a discussion on the issues of fault tolerance and reliability of general graph networks. In this regard, two main approaches have been introduced. These are the enumerative and the iterative techniques. The important issues related to the topological optimization of networks for improved reliability & fault tolerance have also been covered in some details. This was followed by an introduction to the issue of maximizing network reliability by adding a single edge and design for reliability of networks.

References

[1]   Abd-El-Barr, M., Zakir, A., Sait, Sadiq, and Almulhem, A., "Reliability and fault Tolerance based Topological Optimization of Computer Networks - Part I: Enumerative Techniques", IEEE Pacific Rim Conference, held August 30-31, 2003, Victoria, BC, Canada, pp. 732-735.

[2]   Abd-El-Barr, M., Zakir, A., Sait, Sadiq, and Almulhem, A., "Reliability and fault Tolerance based Topological Optimization of Computer Networks - Part II: Iterative Techniques", IEEE Pacific Rim Conference, held August 30-31, 2003, Victoria, BC, Canada, pp. 736-739.

[3]   R. G. Addie, "Algorithms and Models for Network Analysis and Design", http://www.sci.usq.edu.au/courses/CSC3413/netanal.pdf

[4]   Tongdan Jin & David W. Coit, "Network Reliability Estimates using Linear and Quadratic Unreliability of Minimal Cuts", Rutgers University, Piscataway, NJ 08854.
      www.rci.rutgers.edu/~coit/IEWP00-110.pdf

[5]   Klaus Dohmen, "Inclusion-Exclusion and Network Reliability", Humboldt-University, Berlin, Germany.
      http://www.combinatorics.org/Volume_5/PDF/v5i1r36.pdf

[6]   Michael Krivelevich, Benny Sudakov and Van H. Vu "A sharp threshold for network reliability",
      http://math.ucsd.edu/~vanvu/papers/random/sharpthreshold.pdf

[7]   Tony White, "Evolving Optimally Reliable Networks by Adding an Edge" School of Computer Science, Carleton University.
      http://www.scs.carleton.ca/~arpwhite/documents/Reliability%20_PDPTA%202002_.pdf

[8]   V.G. Krivoulets, V.P. Polesskii, "What is the Theory of Bounds for Network Reliability?", *Moscow Institute of Physics and Technology, Moscow, Russia.* http://www.jip.ru/2001/POL-22.pdf

[9]   Nozer D. Singpurwalla. & Andrew Swift, "Network Reliability and Borel.s Paradox", George Washington University, Washington, D.C
http://www.seas.gwu.edu/~irra/Downloads/3-borelsparadox.pdf

[10] Deepankar Medhi, "Network Reliability and Fault Tolerance", Department of Computer Networking, University of Missouri–Kansas City.
http://www.cstp.umkc.edu/public/papers/dmedhi/m_jweee99.pdf

[11] Berna Dengiz and Fulya Altiparmak, "Genetic Algorithms Design of Networks Consedering All terminal reliability", Department of Industrial Engineering, Gazi University. Turkey.
http://www.pitt.edu/~aesmith/postscript/ierc97org.pdf

Chapter 8

Fault Tolerance in High Speed
Switching Networks

This chapter introduces the main issues related to the design and analysis of fault tolerant switching architectures that are used in high speed networks. We put more emphasis on the switch fabrics used in designing the core of switch architectures. The techniques used in designing these switch fabrics are of general interest and should be useful in understanding and appreciating the basics of high speed network switch architectures. Our coverage in this chapter starts with an introduction to the main features of high speed switch architectures. We then provide a fault tolerance-based classification schemes for Switch Architectures (FTSAs). We finally discuss the design and analysis of a number of switching architectures with emphasis on their fault tolerance and reliability characteristics.

8.1 Introduction

High speed networks (HSNs) have various features that extend the capabilities of current packet-switching networks toward incorporating some of the desired features of circuit-switching networks. This is done in order to support real-time and variable bit-rate traffic most efficiently. Several switch architectures (SAs) have been introduced in the literature.

There are basically two main classes of SAs fabrics, i.e., time-division and space-division. Time-division architectures are further classified as shared-memory and shared-medium. In time-division architectures, the traffic from all N input lines is multiplexed into a single resource of bandwidth equal to N times the bandwidth of a single line. This resource is shared by all input and output ports and can be a common memory or a shared medium, such as a bus.

In space-division architectures, multiple concurrent paths are established from the input to the output lines. Each path has the same data rate capacity as an individual line. In addition, the control of the switch can be either centralized or distributed throughout the switch fabric, thereby reducing its design complexity. Space-division architectures are classified based on their structures as crossbar, banyan-based and N^2 disjoint paths.

Space-division switch fabrics have an inherent problem called internal blocking. This problem occurs when multiple disjoint paths can not be established simultaneously to route messages to their proper destinations. The internal blocking problem limits the throughput of the switch fabric. Many switch fabric designs are proposed to minimize the effect of the internal blocking problem.

The crossbar switch fabric is a non-blocking switch fabric. A main limitation of the crossbar switch fabric is that it can not switch more than one input message destined to the same output port simultaneously. This problem is called output contention. It severely affects the performance of the switch fabric when the destination patterns traffic is modeled as a hot-spot input traffic where most of the input messages are destined to a specific output port that is highly demanded, e.g., a file server. Another disadvantage of the crossbar switch fabric is the exponential increase in its size (the required number of cross-point switches) with the number of input lines. The crossbar switch fabric is therefore not recommended for large-size networks.

To solve the internal blocking and output contention problems in space-division switch fabrics, N^2 disjoint paths switch architecture switch fabrics have been introduced. This is the most efficient, yet very expensive, $N \times N$ switch fabric where it is possible to establish N^2 disjoint paths from the input to the output lines simultaneously.

Banyan-based switch architectures are more practical than the crossbar switch fabric for large size networks. At the same time, they are not as expensive as the N^2 disjoint paths switch fabrics. They are based on multi-stage interconnection networks (*MINs*). The simplest banyan-based switch fabric is the Baseline Banyan Network. There is at most one path connecting any input to any output lines. This network has two problems: internal blocking and output contention.

A buffered-banyan network based on a banyan network with buffers in each switching element is effective for uniform traffic since it resolves the blocking problem in the Baseline Banyan Network. It, however, introduces other problems for non-uniform traffic such as Head-Of-Line (HOL) blocking, large buffers requirement, and random delays within the switch fabric causing high jitter. HOL happens when one message is waiting its turn for access to an output port and the other messages behind it are blocked and forced to wait despite the fact that their output ports are possibly idle.

To resolve HOL blocking, Double Banyan Network (DBN) has been introduced. The network is based on cascading two buffered banyan networks: a distribution network followed by a routing network. While the DBN minimizes HOL blocking, it increases random delays within the switch fabric causing high jitter problem.

Bypass Queues-Banyan Network is proposed to resolve the internal and HOL blocking problems by allowing other messages in the input buffers, called bypass queues, to be transmitted when the leading message is blocked. It was shown that 90% throughput can be achieved for large-size switch fabric by using four banyan planes in parallel with bypass queues.

To resolve internal blocking without introducing the high jitter problem, Batcher-Banyan Network has been proposed. This switch architecture consists of two consecutive networks: batch sorting and banyan networks. Messages are first fed to a batch sorter in which they are sorted according to their destination address, and then routed by a banyan self-routing network.

In general, a network is called *i*-fault-tolerant if any set of *i* faults within the network can be tolerated. To improve the switch fabric reliability and fault tolerance, most of the banyan-based networks use one or more of the following strategies: (1) switch size and internal links expansion, (2) switching fabric duplication, (3) use of additional switching elements in each stage, (4) use of additional input/output ports, (5) use of buffers in each switching element, and (6) enhancement of the internal links speed relative to the input/output ports.

Extra-Stage Shuffle-Exchange Network uses an extra stage to the basic Shuffle-Exchange Network to improve its fault tolerance. This is achieved by providing two paths for each input-output pair. The main problem with this network is that the two paths of each input-output pair are not totally disjoint.

MD-Omega Network is a single fault-tolerant switch architecture that is based on a banyan network. It provides two disjoint paths throughout all network stages by using multiplexers at the input stage and de-multiplexers at the last stage. The Extra Stage Cube Network also provides two disjoint paths throughout all network stages. The Benes Network resolves the internal blocking problem and improves the fault tolerance. It consists of two baseline networks mirrored to each other sharing the middle stage. However, the internal blocking problem and the fault tolerance are not improved throughout all stages of the switch architecture. The transmission latency is doubled and the routing complexity is increased.

Itoh Network increases the number of paths from any input to any output pair. It consists of a modified version of the baseline network with added sub-switches between stages. The internal blocking problem and the switch element fault tolerance are resolved at the expense of losing the messages sequence and increasing transmission latency. In addition, the resulting switch architecture is not modular and does not have a regular structure.

The parallel-banyan network provides two disjoint paths without increasing the transmission latency and/or losing the message sequence. It consists of two parallel baseline networks (planes) connected using input and output routers. Internal blocking and output contention problems are not resolved within each plane.

The Network due Tagle and Sharma resolves the internal blocking and fault tolerance of each plane of the parallel-banyan network. This architecture allows routing from one plane to the other plane if there is message contention or switch element faults.

Tandem-Banyan Network (TBN) has been proposed in order to resolve the internal blocking, fault tolerance and output contention problems. It consists of multiple cascaded banyan networks. Unfortunately, the TBN achieves this at the expense of an increase in transmission latency and out-of-order message delivery.

The Baseline-Tree Network resolves internal blocking, fault tolerance, and output contention problems. It is based on multiple interconnected banyan networks to provide multiple paths from any input to any output pair with minimum message loss. The Baseline-Tree and Baseline Networks have the same transmission latency.

The Pipeline-Banyan Network (PBN) is based on the use of parallel banyan data planes controlled by a control plane. The control plane is for path reservation and the data planes are for messages routing. This switch architecture achieves a close to 100% maximum throughput, delay that is independent of the switch size, and in-sequence delivery of messages. Fault tolerance is not considered in the design of PBN.

The Network due to Lin and Wang Banyan resolves internal blocking and achieves fault tolerance by providing large number of paths between each input-output pair. This architecture provides two access points to the output ports to resolve the output contention problem. However, it does not preserve messages sequence in addition to introducing high jitter.

The Parallel-Tree Banyan Switch Fabric (PTBSF) resolves internal blocking and output contention. It is based on parallel banyan networks interconnected in a tree topology. This architecture consists of several levels. Messages sequence is not guaranteed when contended messages go through several levels in the tree.

Reliable And Zealous Network (RAZAN) resolves internal blocking, achieves fault tolerance and resolves output contention by providing disjoint paths and large number of redundant paths between each input-output pair. RAZAN and Baseline Networks have the same transmission latency. However, RAZAN's main disadvantage is the lack of scalability. This is because the size of the switching element increases as the network size increases.

8.2 Classification of Fault-Tolerant Switching Architectures

In this section, we provide a fault tolerance-based classification of switching architectures. According to this classification, switches are grouped based on the degree of fault tolerance they provide. A zero-fault tolerance switch architecture is defined as one that provides a single unique path from input to output such that if a switch and/or link along that unique path is faulty, then this path becomes inoperable and the input and output ports at the ends of this path cannot communicate. The Shuffle-Exchange multi-stage interconnection network is an example of a zero-fault tolerance switch architecture.

Based on the above criterion for switch architecture classification, we have identified one-, two-, and $\log_2 N$ –fault tolerance architectures. Table 8.1 shows examples for each switch class. It should be noted that in providing this classification, we assume that input and output switches are fault-free.

Table 8.1: Switch architecture fault tolerance-based classification.

Class	Examples
Zero-FT	Shuffle Exchange (SEN)
One-FT	Extended SEN, Benes, Itoh, Parallel Banyan, Tagle & Sharma, B-Tree
Two-FT	BTBN
$\log_2 N$ – FT	LN, ILN, RAZAN
Architecture-Dependent	FAUST, FTSS

8.3 One-Fault Tolerance Switch Architectures

8.3.1 *Extra-Stage Shuffle Exchange*

This network (see Fig. 8.1) has an extra stage in the front of a shuffle-exchange network. The first stage SEs broadcast the cell to both output links. In this way, two paths are established. However those paths are not disjoint in the first and last stages. This network is assumed to be one-fault -tolerant (assuming that the first and last stages of SEs are always fault-free). This network is simple and cost effective but it suffers from internal blocking. Terminal reliability of 8×8 network = (R^2) $(1 - (1 -$

$R^2)^2$), where R is the reliability of a SE and assuming that links among stages are fault-free.

It should be noted that Fig. 8.1 shows the channel graph of the SEN. This is a graph showing the possible paths in the network between each pair of input-output nodes.

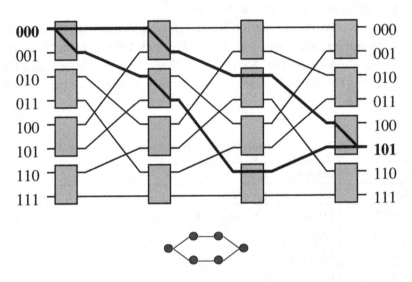

Fig. 8.1: An 8×8 extra stage shuffle-exchange network.

8.3.2 *Itoh Network*

This switch (see Fig. 8.2) uses extra sub-switches to accomplish multiple paths between input and output nodes. It consists of (Log_2N) stages. The switching elements are 3×3 and have different size sub-switches. The routing of this network follows a baseline algorithm. The difference is that if a contention or fault occurs in a given link, a R1 sub-switch is chosen. If the R1 sub-switch is faulty or congested, then a R2 sub-switch is chosen instead. This network has five redundant paths for 8×8 architecture. The degree of fault tolerance is one if the input and output stages are considered fault free. The out of sequence problem and jitter are the price of achieving fault tolerance in this network. The upper bound on the terminal reliability of 8×8 network $= 1 - (1 - R^5)^2 (1 - R^3)$ $(1 - R^4) (1 - R^6)$, where R is the reliability of a switching element.

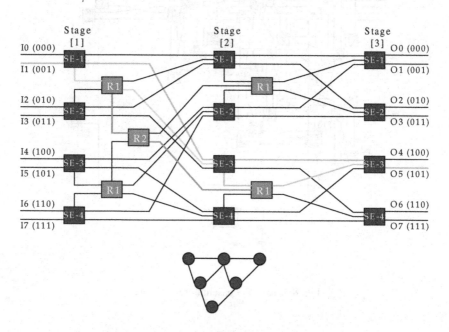

Fig. 8.2: An 8×8 Itoh's network.

8.3.3 *The B-Tree Network*

This architecture (see Fig. 8.3) consists of interconnected baseline networks to achieve multiple paths. The switching elements are 2×4. Two of the output links of each SE are called *formal links* and the other are called *redundant links*. The output multiplexers of a single output port are connected to N links. Each SE has the capability to route 4 cells if there is no contention, or faults. The routing of cells is done according to the baseline algorithm. If a faulty link or contented one is encountered, the cell is routed through alternative links. The routing of cells should pass through ($Log_2 N$) stages. This network has 8 redundant paths for 8×8 architecture. There are two disjoint paths without considering the input stage SEs. This network is single-FT if input stage SEs assumed to be fault free.

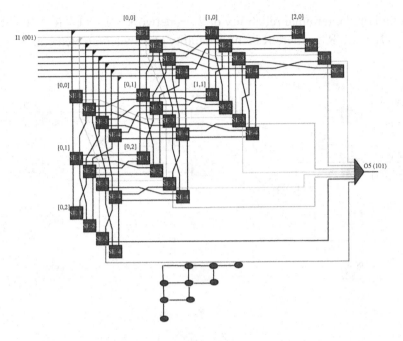

Fig. 8.3: An 8 × 8 baseline-tree network.

8.3.4 *Benes Network*

This network (see Fig. 8.4) consists of $(2Log_2N)-1$. The architecture of the switch is two baseline networks mirrored to each other and share the middle stage. Each stage consists of $N/2$ 2×2 SEs. The firs $(Log_2N)-1$ stages follow the baseline routing (with some modifications). If the chosen link causes contention or is faulty the other link is chosen. In this way the first $(Log_2N)-1$ stages can be considered as fault-tolerant stages. The rest (Log_2N) stages have a unique path to the destination. So if a fault or contention occurs, the cell is lost. This switch is single-FT assuming the first and last stage SEs are fault free. The number of stages is almost double which increase the cell delay. The internal blocking probability holds in the last (Log_2N) stages. Terminal reliability of network size 8×8 is given by: $(R^2) [1- [1 - (R^2)(1 - (1 - R)^2]]^2$

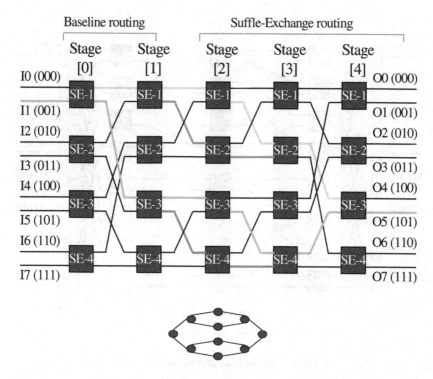

Fig. 8.4: An 8 × 8 Benes' network.

8.3.5 *Parallel Banyan Network*

This network has two disjoint paths (see Fig. 8.5). It is considered as single-FT. Routing in this network is the same as a regular baseline network. The input multiplexers can duplicate the cell to both planes so that the throughput doubles. If the link connected by the multiplexers is faulty or contented, the cell is routed through the other link. If a fault or contention occurs in any plane, the cell will be lost. The network delay is low since the cell goes through only (Log_2N) stages. However, the internal blocking problem is unsolved. Terminal reliability for an 8×8 network is given by: $(R^2)(1 - (1 - R^3)^2)$

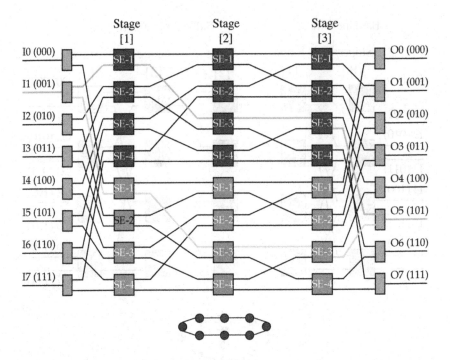

Fig. 8.5: An 8 × 8 parallel banyan network.

8.3.6 *Tagle & Sharma Network*

This network (see Fig. 8.6) is similar to the parallel banyan. The difference here is that this network uses a 4 × 4 SEs. The input and output stages SEs are 2 × 4 and 4 × 2. An input multiplexers and output demultiplexers are used.

In every stage, including the input multiplexers, a non-faulty link, is chosen. In this way eight redundant paths are possible for 8 × 8 architecture. The last stage switching elements has only one path to rout the cell.

This network solves the problem of internal blocking. It also has a large number of redundant paths with few stages to pass, (Log₂N). This network can be considered as single-FT including the ability of input/output stages failure.

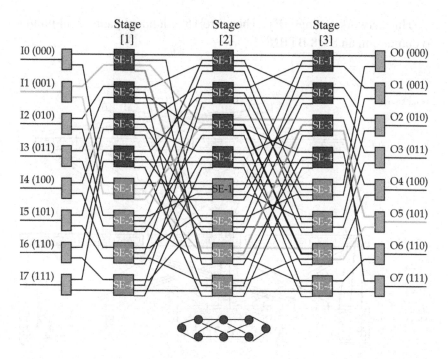

Fig. 8.6: An 8 × 8 Tagle & Shama's network.

8.4 Two-Fault Tolerance Switch Architectures

8.4.1 *Binary Tree Banyan Network*

This network (See Fig. 8.7) consists of two parallel interconnected banyan networks. The number of stages is $(Log_2N)-1$ and the interconnection between stages can be baseline. This network uses two types of switching elements: 4×4 & 4×6. There are three types of links: formal links, redundant links and standby links. Every output port has $2(Log_2N + 1)$ access points. This network uses an output buffer. The routing algorithm is the same as that of baseline with some modification in case of contention or fault. If the designated link is faulty or congested, the redundant link is used. If the redundant link is also congested or faulty, the standby link is used.

This network is single-FT. There are 16 redundant paths from input 0 to output 0 in an 8×8 BTBN.

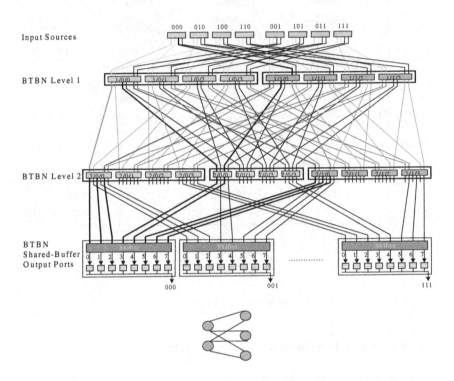

Fig. 8.7: 8×8 BTBN.

8.5   Logarithmic-Fault-Tolerance

8.5.1   *RAZAN*

This network (See Fig. 8.8) is a derivation of logical neighborhood network architecture. It consists of (Log_2N) stage with every stage having N SEs. The switching elements are $(n+1) \times (n+1)$ where n = (Log_2N). The switch elements are connected to SEs in the next stage whose binary address differs at most by one bit.

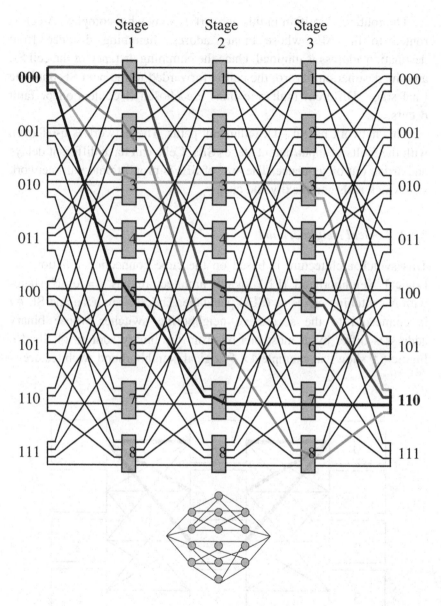

Fig. 8.8: An 8 × 8 RAZAN network.

The routing algorithm in this network is somewhat complex. A cell is routed to the SEs whose binary address hamming distance from destination address is minimal. Once the hamming distance of the cell SE and the destination is zero, the cell is forwarded to the next SE until the final stage. Different fault free links are chosen if contention or fault occurs.

This network has $(n + 1)!$ redundant paths. The network is n-FT even with the faults of input/output stages SEs. Cells can have different delays and arrive out of sequence. The size of SEs is proportional with network size which adds complexity and cost.

8.5.2 *Logical Neighborhood*

This switch architecture is based on the cube connection functions. A Logical Neighborhood (LN) switch architecture has $n = \log_2 N$ stages with N switching elements (SEs) per stage. The SEs are $n \times n$ and SE # i is connected to the successive neighboring switches whose binary addresses differ by at most one bit from the binary address of SE # i. Figure 8.9 shows an example 4×4 Logical Neighborhood Architecture.

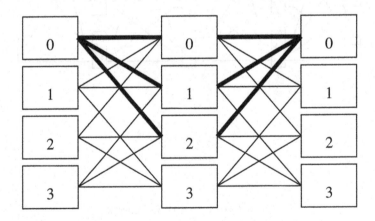

Fig. 8.9: A 4×4 Logical Neighborhood Architecture.

8.5.3 *Improved Logical Neighborhood*

This is an improved version of the LN switch. An $N \times N$ ILN consists of $n + 1$ stages excluding the input and output, where $n = \log_2 N$ and each stage has N elements as illustrated in Fig. 8.10. Input switching elements at stage 0 are $1 \times (n + 1)$. Switching elements at stages 1 to $(n + 1)$ are $(n + 1) \times (n + 1)$ each. The elements at the output stage, $n + 2$, are of $(n + 1) \times 1$. Each output element can receive up to $(n + 1)$ messages in one routing cycles. The received messages are buffered at their output queues. Switching elements in stage i are connected to the ones in stage $i + 1$ such that their binary addresses differ by at most one bit. For example, for $N = 8$, switch 001 in stage 1, will be connected to switches 000, 001, 011 and 101 in stage 2. The ILN is n-fault-tolerant and $(n + 3)!/6$ redundant paths exist between source-destination pairs. It also has $n + 1$ disjoint path from any source to any destination.

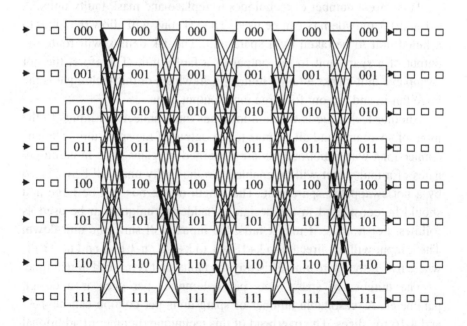

Fig. 8.10: An 8×8 ILN switch architecture.

Assume that the reliability of a switch or link is R, then the terminal reliability is given by $R = (1 - (1 - R)^{n+1})^{n+1}$. That is because among the $(n+1)$ paths, one path is sufficient to establish a route between a source and destination.

8.6 Architecture-Dependent Fault Tolerance

FAUST (See Fig. 8.11) is a framework architecture that can be applied to design fault-tolerant switch architectures. This framework provides a multi-plane (slices) network with extra units per column. The switching unit could be a single cross-point switch or sub-network of any kind. The idea of making the framework fault-tolerant is to incorporate hot swappable units at strategic places in the network. The spares can be placed in column wise, slice wise of both. Those spare units will replace faulty ones.

There are a number of techniques to replace and mask faulty units. A k:1 and 1:k mux/demux can be used. The k:1 mux will allow the input to a failed unit to be taken by a spare unit. The 1:k demux will route the output of a spare unit to the output of a faulty unit. Therefore, the hot swappable unit masks a faulty unit. The drawback of this technique is the large fan-in and fan-out for large input/output units.

Another technique is to use a long bus that connects all inputs to the input of spare unit and all outputs to the output of the spare unit. The bus connections with input/outputs are governed by gates. The input/output gates of a faulty unit will be enabled. So the faulty unit will be replaced by a hot swappable spare unit. The length of the bus can be large and should be considered in the design. A ladder technique can be used as follows. For n units, if unit k fails, the inputs will shift one unit down. The k input will be directed to k+1, k+1 to k+2 ... n-1 to n and n to n+1, where n+1 is the spare unit. This way the faulty unit is masked in real time.

The number of spare units per column or per slice is a design parameter. A reasonable number of spare units per column can be 4-32 and 4-16 for slices. The overhead of this technique (number of additional slices) is 25-40%. The degree of fault tolerance is dependent on the parameters chosen.

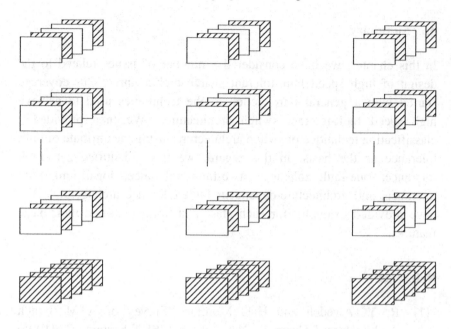

Location of spare units (shaded) in FAUST

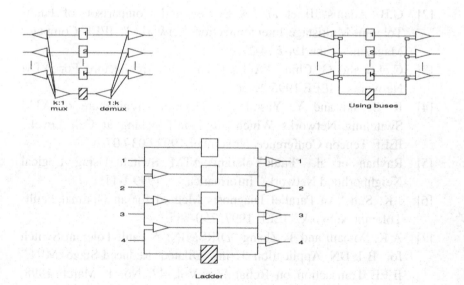

Fig. 8.11: FAUST architecture.

8.7 Summary

In this chapter, we have considered a number of issues related to the design of high speed fault-tolerant switch architectures. Our coverage started with a general introduction to the techniques used to achieve high speed fault-tolerant switch architectures. We then provided a classification technique of switch architectures using the attribute of fault tolerance as the basis. In this regard, we have identified zero-fault tolerance, one-fault tolerance, two-fault tolerance, logarithmic-fault tolerance, and architecture-dependent fault tolerance architectures. We have provided examples for each class and have identified their basic features.

References

[1] R. Y. Awedeh and H.T. Mouftah "Survey of ATM Switch Architectures." Computer Networks and ISDN Systems, 27 (1995) 1567-1613.

[2] G.B. Adams III et al. "A Survey and Comparison of Fault-Tolerant Multistage Interconnection Networks." IEEE Computer Magazine, June 1987 14-27.

[3] C. Lo and C. Chiu "A Fault-Tolerant Architecture For ATM Networks." IEEE 1995 29-36.

[4] K. Sezaki and Y. Yasuda "A General Architecture of ATM Switching Networks Which are Non-Blocking at Call Level." IEEE Tencon Conference, November 1992 603-607.

[5] Rayhan et al. "Fault-Tolerant ATM Switch Using Logical Neighborhood Network." Informatica 17, 1999 1-11.

[6] J.K. Suh "An Parallel Diagnosis Method for an Optimal Fault-Tolerant Network." IEEE 1997, 750-755.

[7] A.K. Somani and T. Zhang "DIRSMIN: A Fault-Tolerant Switch for B-ISDN Application Using Dilated Reduced-Stage MIN." IEEE Transaction on Reliability, Vol. 47, No. 1, March 1998, 19-29.

[8] K. Padmanabhan "An Efficient Architecture for Fault-Tolerant ATM Switches." IEEE/ACM Transaction on Networking Vol.3, No. 5, October 1995 527-537.

[9] L. Dittmann "The Kaleidoscope Switch a New Concept for Implementation of a Large and Fault-Tolerant ATM Switch System." IEEE 1997 683-690.

[10] Bachtiar, T.M., and Abd-El-Barr, M.H., "Logical Neighborhood Network for Fault Tolerance in Packet Switching Networks" International Conference on Microelectronics (icm'93), Dec. 14-16, 1993, Dhahran, Saudi Arabia, 287-293.

[11] S.B. Choi and A.K. Somani "Design and Performance Analysis of Load-Distributing Fault-Tolerant Netowrk." IEEE Transaction On Computers Vol.45 No. 5, May 1996 540-551.

[12] W. Stallings "High Speed Networks: TCP/IP and ATM Design Principles." Prentice Hall 1998.

[13] G. Al-Hashim "Design and Analysis of A High-Performance Fault-Tolerant ATM Network." MS. Thesis, KFUPM, May 1998.

[14] Abd-El-Barr, M.H., K. Al-Tawil, and T. Al-Jarad, "RAZAN: A High Performance Switch Architecture for ATM Networks", International Journal of Communication Systems, vol. II, pp. 275-285, November 1998.

[15] L. Ciminiera and A. Serra "A Connecting Network with Fault Tolerance Capabilities." IEEE Transactions on Computers, Vol.C-35, No.6, June 1986.

[16] Abd-El-Barr, M.H. and Abed, Osama, "Fault Tolerance and Terminal Reliability for a Class of Data Manipulator Networks", IEEE 37th Midwest Symposium on Circuits and Systems, August 3-5 1994, Lafayette, Louisiana, U.S.A. pp. 225-229.

[17] J. Lin and S. Wang "A High Performance Fault-Tolerant Switching Network for ATM." IEICE Transaction on Communication, Vol. E78-B, No. 11, November 1995.

[18] Y. Liao et al. "The Palindrome Network for Fault-Tolerant Interconnection." IEEE, pp.556-561, 1996.

[19] W. Chen et al. "A Fault-Tolerant Shuffleout ATM Switch." IEEE, pp.491-495, 1996.

[20] G. Adams and H. Siegel "The Extra Stage Cube: A Fault-Tolerant Interconnection Network for Supersystems." IEEE Transactions on Computers, Vol. C-31, No. 5, May 1982.

[21] S. Seo and T. Feng "The Composite Banyan Network." IEEE Transaction on Parallel and Distributed Systems, Vol. 6, No. 10, October 1995.

[22] D. Parker and C. Raghavendra "The Gamma Network." IEEE Transactions on Computers, Vol. C-33, No. 4, April 1984.

[23] N. Tzeng and P. Chuang "Fault-Tolerant Gamma Interconnection Networks." IEEE, pp.282-289, 1991.

[24] G. Biase et al. "An $O(\log_2 N)$ Depth Asymptotically Nonblocking Self-Routing Permutation Network." IEEE Transactions on Computers, Vol. 44, No. 8, August 1995.

Chapter 9

Fault Tolerance in Distributed and Mobile Computing Systems

This chapter is dedicated to a discussion on the different techniques used for achieving fault tolerance in distributed computing systems. In particular, we put emphasis on checkpointing techniques. The features of mobile hosts (*MHs*), in a mobile computing system, put a number of additional constraints, such as low communication bandwidth of a wireless channel and energy conservation. This requires adapting conventional checkpointing techniques to fit into mobile computing environments. We present a number of recently introduced checkpointing techniques that suit mobile distributed systems. These include Minimal Snapshot Collection, Mutable Checkpoints, Adaptive Recovery Techniques Message-logging based checkpoints, and Hybrid checkpoints. We end our discussion in the chapter with an overall comparison among these different techniques. In the next chapter, we provide more coverage of the issues related to fault tolerance in mobile distributed computing systems.

9.1 Introduction

A distributed system is viewed as a collection of processes that are used to run application(s) concurrently. These processes communicate with each other using *message-passing* protocols. During error-free operation all processes are assumed to have consistent information. But in the case of failure, some processes must restart its operation from the last point before failure. In order to be able to restart a failed process, we need to save the process state, i.e. variables and messages, during the error free period into a *stable storage*. The latter should be capable of storing the states of all processes as well as being safely accessible. A state should include information required to replay the process. The process of saving the states into a stable storage is called *checkpointing*.

Several protocols have been introduced in order to achieve checkpointing in distributed processes. These can be categorized as: *uncoordinated* and *coordinated protocols*. *Uncoordinated protocols* allow each process to take its local checkpoint independently and without coordination with other processes.

Coordinated protocols force each process to coordinate with other processes to take consistent checkpoints. The set of all local checkpoints is called *global checkpoint*. Coordinated checkpoints protocols can be further divided into *blocking* and *non-blocking algorithms*. Blocking algorithms suspend the underlying computations during checkpointing while *non-blocking algorithms* allow a process to continue its underlying computation. Blocking algorithms guarantee checkpoints consistency but are time-consuming (more overhead), while non-blocking algorithms are faster but are vulnerable to inconsistency. Coordinated checkpoints protocols suffer from high overhead. This is because each process needs to send a checkpoint request to all relevant processes to force them to take checkpoint.

Mobile computing systems consist of processes that communicate using wireless networks beside being able to move from one place to another while running. The moving processes (clients) are called *Mobile Hosts (MHs)*. To communicate with *MHs*, *Mobile Support Stations (MSSs)* are needed. A MSS must cover MHs. While moving, a *MH* may exit from one *MSS* coverage area and enter another. *MSSs* are connected by a static wired network, which provides reliable delivery of messages, while *MHs* are connected with *MSSs* via a wireless network.

Mobility features of mobile hosts, such as limited bandwidth, highly unreliable wireless links, power restriction, and limitation of storage space, necessitate the development of new checkpoint-recovery schemes for mobile networks.

In this chapter, we first present some background material on conventional checkpointing techniques. This is followed by a discussion on some of the recent algorithms developed for checkpointing in mobile computing systems.

9.2 Background Material

Figure 9.1 shows an illustration of three processes P_0, P_1, and P_2 that are running concurrently. The free running horizontal axis in the figure represents time. Messages are exchanged among the three processes as shown using single head arrows. For example, the arrow designated by the letter m indicates a message m sent from process P_1 to process P_2.

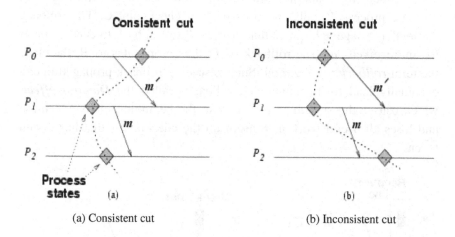

(a) Consistent cut   (b) Inconsistent cut

Fig. 9.1: Different types of cuts.

In this representation, an **Orphan message** is defined as a message whose *receive* event is recorded in the state of the destination process, but its *send* event is lost. Consider, for example, the cut (dashed line) in Fig. 9.1(a). This line represents a timeline showing the record of the state of the three processes. As can be seen, the line in Fig. 9.1(a) represents a consistent state of three processes. This is because the send and receive events of the two messages, m' and m are recorded. This is not the case for the cut (dashed line) in Fig. 9.1(b). This cut line shows an inconsistency since process P_2 is shown to have received message m but P_1 state does not reflect sending message m. A system is said to be *consistent* if it contains no orphan messages.

A *Consistent global checkpoint* refers to a set of N local checkpoints, one from each process, which forms a consistent system state. Any consistent global checkpoint can be used for system state restoration upon a failure.

A *Recovery line* is the most recent consistent global checkpoint. It should be noted that rolling back to a *recovery line*, which preserves global consistency, will minimize the amount of lost useful work in case of failure.

Consider, for example, the set of processes shown in Fig. 9.2. Suppose process P_2 fails and rolls back to checkpoint C. The rollback "unsent" message m requires that process P_1 to roll back to checkpoint B to "un-received" m. The rollback of P_2 thus propagates to P_1, therefore the term *rollback propagation*. Such cascading rollback propagation can eventually lead to an unbounded rollback, called the *Domino effect*, which causes the system to roll back to the beginning of its execution and loses all useful work in spite of all the checkpoints that have been taken.

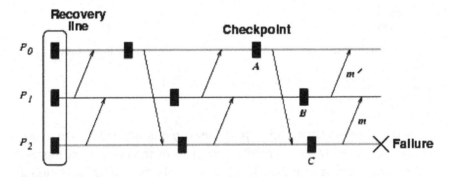

Fig. 9.2: Recovery line, rollback propagation and domino effect.

An *Avalanche effect* is the case when processes ask (request) each other to take a checkpoint in a recursive manner leading them to enter an infinite loop.

Uncoordinated checkpointing allows each process to take checkpoints independently. The main advantage of this protocol is that each process may take a checkpoint when it is most convenient. For example, a process may reduce the overhead by taking checkpoints when the amount of state information to be saved is minimal. Uncoordinated checkpointing has the following drawbacks.

(1) The possibility of occurrence of a domino effect.
(2) The possibility of a process taking a *useless* checkpoint that will never be part of a global consistent state.
(3) The need to maintain multiple checkpoints, and to periodically invoke a garbage collection algorithm to reclaim the checkpoints that are no longer useful.

In order to determine a consistent global checkpoint during recovery, the processes record the dependencies among their checkpoints during failure-free operation by storing the checkpoint interval index and the source addresses of incoming messages with the checkpoint. This is called the state dependency information, see Fig. 9.3.

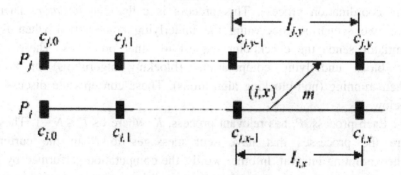

Fig. 9.3: Checkpoint index and checkpoint interval.

If a failure occurs, the recovering process initiates rollback by broadcasting a *dependency request* message to collect all the state dependency information maintained by each process. When a process receives this message, it stops its execution and replies with the state dependency information saved on stable storage as well as sending the state dependency information. The initiator then *calculates* the recovery line based on the global dependency information and broadcasts a *rollback request* message containing the recovery line. Upon receiving this message, a process whose current state belongs to the recovery line simply resumes execution; otherwise it rolls back to an earlier checkpoint as indicated by the recovery line.

One way to avoid the domino effect is to perform *coordinated checkpointing*. Coordinated checkpointing requires processes to coordinate their checkpoints in order to form a consistent global state. Coordinated checkpointing simplifies recovery and is not susceptible to the domino effect. This is because every process always restarts from its most recent checkpoint. Also, coordinated checkpointing requires each process to maintain only one permanent checkpoint on stable storage, reducing storage overhead and eliminating the need for garbage collection. The main disadvantages of the coordinated protocols are the high overhead and the large latency involved in committing output, since a global checkpoint is needed before determining the recovery line.

Coordinated protocols require a coordinator process to initiate the coordination process. This process is called the *initiator*. There are two scenarios concerning the underlying computation when the initiator sends the checkpoint request to other processes. These are to block underlying computations (blocking algorithms) or keep them running (non-blocking algorithms). These concepts are discussed below.

Each process, P, has relevant process, K, where $1 \leq K \leq N - 1$. These are the processes that have sent messages to P in the current checkpointing interval. In other words, the computation performed by P depends on the messages received from its relevant processes during the current checkpointing interval.

Coordinated algorithms (blocking and non-blocking) consist of two phases in which they save two kinds of checkpoints: *tentative* and *permanent*.

Phase I: The initiator process takes a tentative checkpoint and forces all relevant processes to take tentative checkpoints. Each process informs the initiator whenever it succeeds in taking a tentative checkpoint. A process may refuse to take a checkpoint depending on its underlying computation.

After the initiator has received positive replies from all relevant processes, the algorithm enters the second phase.

Phase II: If the initiator learns that all processes have successfully taken tentative checkpoints, it asks them to commit, i.e. make their tentative checkpoints permanent.

In case of blocking checkpointing algorithms, a process takes a tentative checkpoint in the first phase, and remains blocked (block underlying computation) until it receives the commit from the initiator in the second phase.

A non-blocking checkpointing algorithm does not require any process to suspend its underlying computation in phase I. When processes do not suspend their computations, it is possible for a process to receive a computation message from another process which is already running in a new checkpoint interval. If this situation is not properly handled, it may result in an inconsistency. Most non-blocking algorithms use what is called a Checkpoint Sequence Number (CSN) to avoid inconsistencies.

Communication-induced checkpointing (*CIP*) protocols avoid the domino effect without requiring all checkpoints to be coordinated. In these protocols, processes take two kinds of checkpoints, *local* and *forced*. Local checkpoints can be taken independently, while forced checkpoint *must* be taken to guarantee the eventual progress of the recovery line.

Log-based protocols assume that all events can be identified and logged to stable storage. During failure-free operation, each process logs all messages onto stable storage. Additionally, each process also takes checkpoints to reduce the extent of rollback during recovery. After a failure occurs, the failed processes recover by using the checkpoints and logged messages to replay its computations as they occurred during the pre-failure execution. This protocols require a minimum overhead.

9.3 Checkpointing Techniques in Mobile Networks

In this section, we present a general model of a distributed system in a mobile network, see Fig. 9.4. A mobile network consists of a large number of *mobile hosts* (*MHs*) and relatively fewer static *MSSs*, also called *base stations* (*BSs*) or *access points* (*APs*). These *MSSs* are equipped with wireless interfaces, and they act as gateways providing reliable communication between the wireless and the static wired networks.

Due to the limited coverage of wireless networks, a *MH* can only communicate with a *MSS* within a limited geographical distance, called a *cell*. Wireless communication channels between *MHs* and *MSSs* are assumed to be reliable where transmission delays are finite. A *MH* can reside in the *cell* of a *MSS* at any given time. As each *MH* is mobile, it can move from a *cell* to another. To provide the support of communication with mobility, a Mobile IP protocol is used.

We consider a distributed system consisting of N processes denoted by $P_0, P_1, P_2..., P_{N-1}$ running concurrently on *MHs* in the network. The processes do not share a common memory and message passing is the only way for them to communicate with one another.

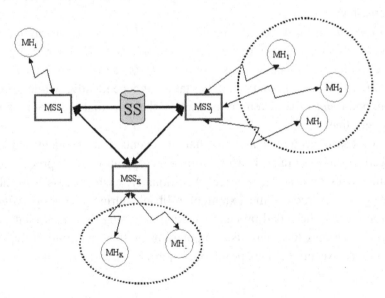

Fig. 9.4: Model of distributed network with mobile hosts.

9.3.1 *Minimal Snapshot Collection Algorithm*

This algorithm combines two approaches. It neither forces every node to take a local checkpoint nor blocks its underlying computation. The algorithm consists of two parts: a *minimal checkpoint collection* part and a *lazy checkpoint* part.

A minimal checkpoint collection is achieved using message-dependent concept. When a process *Pi* initiates a checkpoint collection, it takes a tentative local checkpoint and then sends a *request* message to its dependent processes. Upon receiving a checkpoint request, if the dependent process *Pj* hasn't taken any checkpoint associated with this initiator, it will take a tentative checkpoint and recursively sends *request* messages to its dependent processes. Otherwise, it will not take a checkpoint. A *trigger, which contains the latest initiator's* process ID (*PID*) and the initiator's checkpoint sequence number (*CSN*) will be piggybacked with the *request* message. The *trigger* carried by the *request* message prevents a process from taking multiple checkpoints when the process has already received the request for the same global checkpoint initiator.

Every process keeps a record of expected values of all other processes. When a distributed application sends out a message, it piggybacks its *CSN* and *trigger* information. A receiving node will decide whether to take tentative checkpoint before processing this message based on its own *trigger* information, expected *CSN* and message's *CSN* and *trigger* information.

When the initiator receives all the reply messages from its dependent processes, it will send *commit* messages to force them to turn their tentative checkpoints into permanent ones. The Minimal Snapshot Collection process will then terminate and the older permanent local checkpoints at those processes are discarded.

Once the *coordinated* checkpoint terminates, those processes, which are not initiator-dependent, take checkpoints in a *lazy* fashion. That is, it takes checkpoint when it receives the first computation message whose piggybacked *CSN* is higher than expected *CSN*, as a means to provide consistent checkpoint with the rest of checkpoints. The lazy phase lets mobile hosts take checkpoint in a *quasi-asynchronous* fashion. As the lazy phase advances checkpoint slowly, this avoids contention for the low bandwidth channels.

Consider, for example, the processes shown in Fig. 9.5. In this figure, P2 initiates the checkpointing interval by sending requests to all relevant processes, i.e., P1 and P3. After receiving reply from P1 and P3, P2 terminates the checkpointing processes by broadcasting *commit* message to all processes. When a commit message is received by other processes, P0 in this case, they will take their checkpoints in a lazy fashion without coordinating with other processes. This is done in order to reduce the bandwidth overhead. But this lazy phase may cause inconsistency between P0 and other processes.

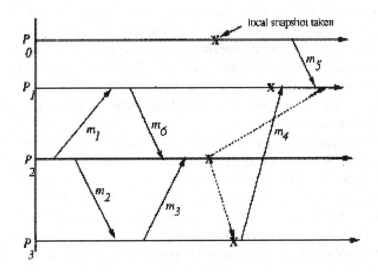

Fig. 9.5: Minimal snapshot algorithm.

To recover from a failure, process *Pi* rolls back to its latest checkpoint and sends rollback requests to all the processes to which *Pi* has sent computation messages. After each process's rollback is over, it replies to the initiator *Pi*. When initiator gets all the replies, rollback phase terminates. Each process maintains *sent*[1..*n*] and *received*[1..*n*] vectors in stable storage and logs the order of the received message in a *queue* to be used to resend the old (recomputed) messages again.

When a consistent state is reached, processes start recomputing. When process *Pi* starts recovery, it broadcasts a *recovering*(*i*) message to the processes indicated by *received* vector. When a process *Pj* receives the *recovering*(*i*) message, it retransmits the copies of the messages meant to *Pi*.

9.3.2 *Mutable Checkpoints*

Since Minimal Snapshot Collection algorithm might result in inconsistency, it is not a reliable scheme. Mutable Checkpoints algorithm is an enhanced scheme of the Minimal Snapshot Collection algorithm. It uses mutable checkpointing to avoid inconsistency and avalanche effect (processes in the system recursively ask others to take checkpoints). This algorithm tries to achieve the same goal of power and control overhead minimization by neither blocking the underlying computation nor forcing all processes to take checkpoints. In order to avoid inconsistency, processes need to keep its necessary checkpoints. In order to take minimum number of checkpoints, processes need to discard unnecessary but unavoidable checkpoints. A mutable checkpoint is neither a tentative checkpoint nor a permanent checkpoint, but it can be turned into a tentative checkpoint. For example, suppose a process *Pi* has taken a mutable checkpoint. When *Pi* receives a checkpoint request, it transfers the mutable checkpoint to the stable storage and forces all dependant processes to take tentative checkpoint. If *Pi* does not receive checkpoint request, it discards the mutable checkpoint after the checkpointing activity terminates.

The difference between the Mutable Checkpoint algorithm and the Minimal Snapshot Collection algorithm is in the operation performed upon a reception of a computation messages during checkpointing. When a process Pi receives a computation message from *Pj*, it will compare the message's checkpoint sequence number ($m.csn$) with its expected *csn* from process *Pj* ($csni[j]$). If $m.csn < csni[j]$, the message is processed and no checkpoint is taken. Otherwise, it will make a decision to take mutable checkpoint based on the following conditions.

1) *Pj* is in the checkpointing process before sending m
2) *Pi* has sent a message since last checkpoint
3) *Pi* has not taken a checkpoint associated with the initiator.

If all the conditions are met, mutable checkpoint is taken. If only condition 1 is satisfied, *Pi* only increases its *csn*. By taking mutable checkpoint, process *Pi* does not send checkpoint requests to other processes and it does not need to save the checkpoint on the stable storage.

The basic idea of the algorithm can be better explained through the example shown in Fig. 9.6. To initiate a checkpointing process, P2 takes its own checkpoint and sends checkpoint requests to P1, P3, and P4 since $R_2[1] = 1$, $R_2[3] = 1$, and $R_2[4] = 1$. When P2's request reaches P4, P4 takes a checkpoint and sends message m_3 to P3. When m_3 arrives at P3, P3 takes a mutable checkpoint before processing the message since $m_3.csn > csn_3[4]$ and P3 has sent a message during the current checkpoint interval. For the same reason, P1 takes a mutable checkpoint before processing m_2.

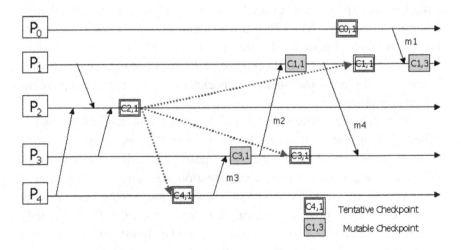

Fig. 9.6: An example of mutable checkpoints.

P0 did not communicate with another process before it took the local checkpoint. Later, it sends a message m_1 to P1. If P0 has finished its checkpointing process before it sends m_1, P1 does not need to take the checkpoint C1,2. Otherwise, P1 takes a mutable checkpoint C1,2 before processing m_1.

When P1 receives the checkpoint request from P2, since C1,1 is a mutable checkpoint associated with P2, P1 turns C1,1 into a tentative checkpoint by saving it on the stable storage. Similarly, P3 converts C3,1 to a tentative checkpoint when it receives the checkpoint request from P2. Finally, the checkpointing initiated by P2 terminates when the checkpoints C1,1, C2,1, C3,1, and C4,1 are made permanent. P1 discards C1,2 when it makes checkpoint C1,1 permanent or receives P0's commit, whichever is earlier.

9.3.3 *Adaptive Recovery*

As we discussed above, both Mutable Checkpoints Algorithm and Minimal Snapshot Collection Algorithm initiate checkpointing via sending *request* message. Time based checkpoint algorithm uses timers to avoid exchanging messages during the checkpoint creation. So, each process will advance a checkpoint independently (uncoordinated) from other processes when its local timer expires. The algorithm keeps the various timers almost the same to make sure that processes' states are stored at almost the same time. There are two issues associated with the algorithm. One is the *timing inaccuracies* issue and the other is *inconsistency* issue.

A resynchronization mechanism is used to solve problems related to initial timer inaccuracies and other causes of timer inaccuracies. Each process will piggyback each message with a Time-To-Next Checkpoint (*TTNC*) variable. When *Pj* receives this message, it will compare *own_TTC* (Time-To-Checkpoint) with *msg_TTNC*. If *own_TTC* is bigger than *msg_TTNC*, it sets *own_TTC to msg_TTNC*.

Inconsistency issue can be solved by using Checkpoint Sequence Number (*csn*) same as what has been used in both Mutable Checkpoints Algorithm and Minimal Snapshot Collection Algorithm. So each process will maintain a *csn* variable. The *csn* variable will be increased by one when checkpoint is advanced. When a process *Pj* receives a message, it checks its csn information (*own_csn*) with message's csn information (*msg_csn*). If *own_csn* < *msg_csn*, *Pj* takes a checkpoint and resets the timer to *msg_TTNC*.

Consider, for example, the execution of the three processes shown in Fig. 9.7. Processes create their checkpoints at different instants, because timers are not synchronized. After saving its *CN* checkpoint, process *P1* sends message *m1*. When *m1* arrives, process *P3* is still in its *CN-1* checkpoint interval. To avoid a consistency problem, *P3* first creates its *CN* checkpoint, and then delivers *m1*. *P3* also resets the timer for the next checkpoint. Message *m2* is an in-transit message that has not been acknowledged when process *P2* saves its *CN* checkpoint. This message is logged in the checkpoint of *P2*. Message *m3* is a normal message that indirectly resynchronizes the timer of process *P2*. It is possible to observe in the figure the effectiveness of the resynchronization mechanism.

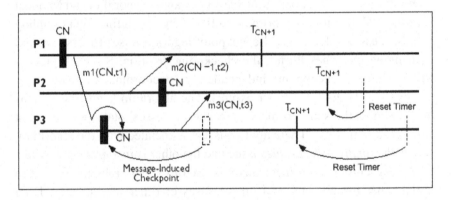

Fig. 9.7: Time based championing.

In mobile systems, some failures are permanent, and it is necessary to save checkpoints on stable storages. However, transient failures can be recovered locally to avoid the overhead of transferring checkpoints to the stable storage. The Adaptive Checkpoint algorithm creates two checkpoint schemes: soft checkpoints which are saved locally in the *MH* and hard checkpoints which are saved in the stable storage in the Base

Station (*BS*). Soft checkpoints are less reliable than hard checkpoints but they cost less than hard checkpoints. By changing the number of soft checkpoints that are created per hard checkpoints, this algorithm can adapt (hence the name) to different networks. For example, if the wireless channel is unreliable, the protocol saves many soft checkpoints. If high degree of fault tolerance is required, more hard checkpoints are taken instead. When a failure occurs, all processes rollback to the latest global consistent state to re-compute their work.

9.3.4 *Message Logging Based Checkpoints*

This scheme relies on the existence of Mobile IP architecture where three main structures are involved: *Mobile Hosts (MHs), Base Stations (BSs) and Home Agents (As)*. *A* is a *BS* that provides local communication for a *MH* and acts as a forwarding agent to messages that are intended for the *MH*, and re-route them to the appropriate *BS* which the *MH* has moved to.

Every message that is sent or received by a *MHi* is tagged and saved (logged) in the home agent *Ai*. *Ai* needs to keep a record for each *MHi* it covers to store all its incoming and outgoing messages. Consistency is guaranteed since all messages are logged and can be restored at any time.

Although, Ai receives all messages sent and received by MHi, it is imposible for Ai to store messages in the same order as MHi transmit or receive them. To solve this problem, they use the following protocol:

- Assign a buffer *mbuf$_i$* for *MHi* in *Ai*. Theses buffers are used to reorder the messages.
- An order information << *messages sent and received by MHi* >> is attached with each message sent by MHi.

As an example, consider the processes shown in Fig. 9.8. There are three mobile stations *Mi, Mj, Mk*. First *Mi* sends a message m1 to *Mj*. Next, *Mk* send a message m2 to *Mj*. These messages arrive at *Ai* in different order. So, *Ai* will use the buffer, *mbuf* to reorder them before

storing them as permanent messages. Later, when *Mj* wants to send
any message, say m3, it will piggyback it with the order information
$<<r(m1), r(m2), r(m3)>>$ since it knows the order.

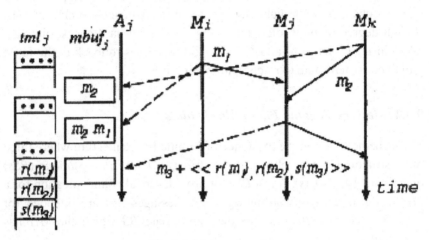

Fig. 9.8: Message logging.

9.3.5 *Hybrid Checkpoints*

As the name hybrid implies, this scheme combines coordinated and
uncoordinated checkpoint into one protocol. Coordinated checkpoint is
known for its advantage that stations can recover from their most recent
local checkpoints as all recent checkpoints are globally consistent
without domino effect. However, it is difficult for MHs to take local
checkpoints in coordinated bases.

A Hybrid technique can be summarized in the following steps:

*   Due to high cost of communication overhead, each *MH* takes its
    local checkpoint, *CMi* independently (uncoordinated) and sends it to
    its associated MSS. By this way the minimum overhead is sent
    through the wireless network since there is no coordination.
*   Mobile support stations, take local checkpoints, *CFi*, by using
    coordinated checkpointing protocol, which has higher overhead than
    uncoordinated protocol, but it preserve the global consistency.

To maintain consistency with *CFs* checkpoints among MSSs, log-based restart protocol is used. Messages exchanged between a mobile host *MH* and another host or *MSS* are stored in a stable storage of its associated *MSS*. Due to non-deterministic nature of message transmission, it is not possible to determine the order of messages sent and received by the *MH*. To solve this problem, messages logged at each *MSS* are stored temporary in a buffer *mbuf* for each *MH*. *MSS* is able to listen to all message sent or received by the *MH* through broadcasting property of wireless 802.11 LAN protocol. Order information of messages sent and received by *MH* is then piggied back to another message transmitted from the *MH*. *MSS* then uses this information to reorder the messages before permanently save them.

9.4 Comparison

Minimal Snapshot Collection and Mutable Checkpoints successfully make use of the idea of checkpoint overhead reduction by taking fewer numbers of synchronous checkpoints. This will avoid domino effect within the set of synchronous checkpoint, and overhead cost that would incur in sending message exchanges to all processes. By allowing non-blocking checkpoint, it keeps the failure-free overhead of the algorithm low, thus improve the checkpoint overhead. However, the two algorithms suffer from the need to provide more and larger control messages to avoid checkpoint inconsistency that comes with non-blocking checkpoint.

Adaptive checkpoint, on the other hand, can achieve low-cost wireless fault tolerance through eliminating checkpoint control messages, using Time-based synchronous checkpointing. As wireless bandwidth is limited, reduction in control messages largely reduces contention in the network. Small overhead is needed to resynchronize the checkpoint. What makes adaptive checkpoint an attractive scheme is the simplicity of its algorithm while achieving relatively good performance with low fail-free overhead. No coordination is needed as each process takes checkpoint independently. It also provides the option of mixing soft and hard checkpoints to achieve different Quality of Service (QoS) requirements. This can be applicable to all other schemes.

The main advantage of message logging protocols is that only the failed process needs to rollback and re-execute. These achieve recovery fast, and save bandwidth and power consumption in mobile hosts. The main drawback is the need for large storage to store all messages in the home agencies.

Hybrid checkpoint also achieves lower overhead by minimizing control messages through sending the checkpoints from MHs to MSSs independently without coordination between MHs. This eliminates the need to send requests from MHs to other MHs. The disadvantage is that the MSSs should perform a considerable amount of computations causing them to be over loaded.

Other issues related to the comparison of these algorithms, such as existence of domino effect and/or global consistency, are shown in Table 9.1.

Table 9.1: Comparing checkpoint schemes fore wireless networks.

Comparing issue ↓ Scheme ➡	Minimal snapshot collection	Mutable checkpoint	Adaptive checkpoint	Message logging	Hybrid checkpoint
checkpoint/process	1	1	1	1	several
Domino effect	No	no	No	no	no
Avalanche effect	No	no	No	no	no
Global checkpoint	Can be inconsistent	consistent	consistent	consistent	consistent
Non-blocking	Yes	Yes	Not mentioned	Yes	Yes(MHs), No (MSS)
Checkpoint control message (requests)	Many and large	Many and large	Almost non except for time synchronization	Fewer and small	Fewer and very small
Checkpoint complexity	High (due to dependency check)	high (due to dependency check)	low (simple periodic)	low (simple periodic)	Medium (periodic(MHs) non-periodic (MSS))
Checkpoint overhead (No. of checkpoints)	Small no. of checkpoints taken	Small no. of checkpoints taken	High All processes need to take checkpoints	High All processes need to take checkpoints	High All processes need to take checkpoints

9.5 Summary

In this chapter, we have discussed a number of checkpointing techniques used for distributed systems. We started by introducing a number of conventional checkpointing techniques that can be used in wired distributed systems. We then proceeded to discuss a number of recent checkpointing algorithms that can be used in mobile computing systems. These include Minimal snapshot collection, Mutable checkpoints, Adaptive recovery; Message-logging based checkpoints, and Hybrid checkpoints. We also provided an overall comparison among these different techniques. In the next chapter, we provide more coverage of the aspects of fault tolerance in mobile computing systems including software and hardware techniques.

References

[1] E. Elnozahy, D. Johnson, and Y.-M. Wang, "A Survey of Rollback-Recovery Protocols in Message-Passing Systems," Tech. Rep. CMU-CS-96-181, School of Computer Science, Carnegie Mellon University, October 1996.

[2] Y. Deng and E.K. Park, "Checkpointing and Rollback-Recovery Algorithms in Distributed Systems," J. Systems and Software, pp. 59-71, Apr. 1994.

[3] G. Cao and M. Singhal, "On Coordinated Checkpointing in Distributed Systems," IEEE Trans. Parallel and Distributed System pp. 1213-1225, Dec. 1998.

[4] D. Johnson, "Distributed System Fault Tolerance Using Message Logging and Checkpointing," PhD Thesis, Rice Univ., Dec. 1989.

[5] G. Cao and M. Singhal, "On the Impossibility of Min-Process Non- Blocking Checkpointing and an Efficient Checkpointing Algorithm for Mobile Computing Systems," Proc. 27th Int'l Conf. on Parallel Processing, pp. 37-44, Aug. 1998.

[6] Gouhong Cao and M. Singhal, "Mutable Checkpoints: A new Checkpointing approach for Mobile Computing Systems", IEEE Trans. On Parallel and distributed systems, Vol. 12, No. 2, Feb 2001.

[7] G. Cao and M. Singhal, "Low-Cost Checkpointing with Mutable Checkpoints in Mobile Computing Systems," Proc. 18th Int'l Conf. Distributed Computing Systems, pp. 464-471, May 1998.

[8] N. Neves, and W.K. Fuchs, "Adaptive Recovery for Mobile Environments," communications of the ACM, Vol. 40, No. 1, pp. 69-74, 1997.

[9] B. Crow, I. Widjaja, J. Kim, and P. Sakai, "IEEE 802. 11 Wireless Local Area Networks," IEEE Comm. Magazine, pp. 116-126, Sept. 1997.

[10] R. Koo and S. Toueg, "Checkpointing and Rollback-Recovery for Distributed Systems," IEEE Trans. Software Eng., pp. 23-31, Jan. 1987.

[11] T.H. Lai and T.H. Yang, "On Distributed Snapshots," Information in Parallel and Distributed System, Oct. 1993. Processing Letters, pp. 153-158, May 1987.

[12] D. Manivannan and M. Singhal, "A Low-Overhead Recovery Technique Using Quasi-Synchronous Checkpointing," Proc. 16th Int'l Conf. Distributed Computing Systems, pp. 100-107, May 1996.

[13] R. Prakash and M. Singhal, "Low-Cost Checkpointing and Failure Recovery in Mobile Computing Systems," IEEE Trans. Parallel and Distributed Systems, pp. 1035-1048, Oct. 1996.

[14] P. Ramanathan and K.G. Shin, "Use of Common Time Base for Checkpointing and Rollback Recovery in a Distributed System," IEEE Trans. Software Eng., pp. 571-583, June 1993.

[15] G. Cao and M. Singhal, "On Coordinated Checkpointing in Distributed Systems," IEEE Trans. Parallel and Distributed System pp. 1213-1225, Dec. 1998.

[16] G.H. Forman and J. Zahorjan, "The Challenges of Mobile Distributed Systems, pp. 86-95, Oct. 1992. Computing," Computer, pp. 38-47, Apr. 1994.

[17] R. Prakash and M. Singhal, "Low-Cost Checkpointing and Failure Recovery in Mobile Computing Systems," IEEE Trans. Parallel and Distributed Systems, pp. 1035-1048, Oct. 1996.

[18] T. Quahtani, "A Survey of Checkpointing Techniques in Distributed Mobile Computing Systems", Project Report, Department of Computer Engineering, KFUPM, 2003.

Chapter 10

Fault Tolerance in Mobile Networks

In Chapter 9, we have introduced the basic issues related to fault tolerance in distributed systems. In particular, we have emphasized the use of checkpointing techniques. We have also introduced a number of checkpoint-based techniques that are used in achieving fault tolerance in mobile distributed computing systems. In this chapter, we provide further coverage of the techniques used in mobile computing systems to tolerate the failure of MSSs. We start our coverage by introducing some background material. We then cover a number of the checkpoint-based (software-based) techniques. We follow that with coverage of what is called the hybrid (hardware-based) technique. The reader is advised to review the material covered in Chapter 9 before proceeding with this chapter.

10.1 Background Material

In presenting the techniques for fault tolerance in mobile networks, we adopt a general model for a distributed system as shown in Fig. 10.1. According to this model, a mobile network consists of a large number of *mobile hosts* (*MHs*) and relatively fewer static *MSSs*, also called *base stations* (*BSs*) or *access points* (*APs*). These *MSSs* are equipped with wireless interfaces, and they act as gateways providing reliable communication between the wireless networks and the static wired networks.

Due to the limited coverage of the wireless networks, a *MH* can only communicate with a *MSS* within a limited geographical called a *cell*. The wireless communication channels between *MHs* and *MSSs* are assumed to be reliable where transmission delays are finite. A *MH* can reside in the *cell* of a *MSS* at any given time. As each *MH* is mobile, it can move from a *cell* to another. To provide the support of communication with mobility, Mobile IP protocol is used.

We consider a distributed system as consisting of N processes denoted by $P_0, P_1, ..., P_{N-1}$ running concurrently on *MHs* in the network. The processes do not share a common memory and message passing is the scheme according to which they communicate with one another.

Since the state information of a MH is usually stored in a supposedly stable storage of the associated MSS, therefore a failure of a MSS can become catastrophic for the associated MHs. The state information of a *live* MH stored in a failed MSS is potentially lost. The time taken by a failed MSS to recover can be unacceptably long for a MH. It is therefore necessary to have a fault-tolerant mobile computing environment: one which provides uninterrupted service despite the failure of some MSSs.

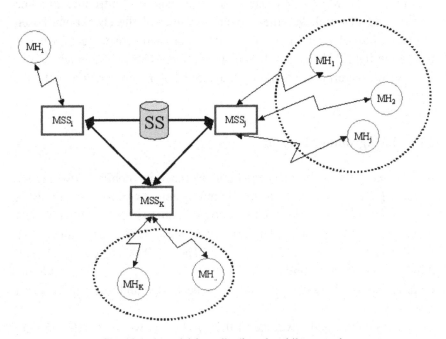

Fig. 10.1: A model for a distributed mobile network.

A number of schemes have been used for tolerating the failure of MSSs. In this chapter, we introduce a number of techniques used in mobile networks to tolerate the failure of MSSs. In particular, we cover a number of the checkpoint-based (software-based) techniques in addition to covering of is called the hybrid (hardware-based) technique.

The state of a message passing system is the collection of the individual states of all participating processes. Intuitively, a consistent system state is one that may occur in a legal execution of a distributed computation. A system is said to be consistent if it contains no orphan message, i.e. a message whose receive event is recorded in the state of the destination process, but its send event is lost (see Chapter 9).

10.2 More on Mutable Checkpoint Techniques in Mobile Networks

In Chapter 9, we have presented a number of recently introduced checkpoint-based techniques for achieving fault tolerance in mobile computing systems. In particular, we have presented the Minimal Snapshot Collection, Mutable Checkpoints, Adaptive Recovery Techniques, Message-logging based checkpoints, and Hybrid checkpoints. Among these techniques, the mutable checkpoint-based techniques seems to have caught the attention of a number of researchers. We therefore, provide in this section elaborate coverage of the mutable checkpoint-based techniques. The reader is advised to review the basic principles of the mutable checkpoint techniques before proceeding with the material covered in this section.

In mobile computing system, MSSs are connected by a static wired network, which provides reliable FIFO delivery of messages. A *cell* is a logical or geographical area covered by an MSS. An MH can directly communicate with an MSS by a reliable FIFO wireless channel only if it is present in the cell supported by the MSS. The distributed computation we consider consists of N processes denoted by P0, P1, P2, ..., P_{N-1} running concurrently on fail-stop MHs or MSSs in the network. The processes do not share a common memory or a common clock. Message passing is the only way for processes to communicate with each other. The messages generated by the underlying distributed application will be referred to as *computation messages*. Messages generated by processes to advance checkpoints will be referred to as *system messages*.

Each checkpoint taken by a process is assigned a unique sequence number. The ith ($i \geq 0$) checkpoint of process Pp is assigned a sequence number i and is denoted by $C_{p,i}$. The ith *checkpoint interval* of process Pp denotes all the computation performed between its ith and $(i+1)^{th}$ checkpoint, including the ith checkpoint but not the $(i+1)^{th}$ checkpoint.

10.2.1 *Handling Mobility, Disconnection and Reconnection of MHs*

A MH may get disconnected from the network for an arbitrary period of time. At the application level, the checkpointing algorithm may generate a request for the disconnected MH to take a checkpoint. Delaying a response to such a request until the MH reconnects at some MSS may significantly increase the completion time of the checkpointing algorithm. So, the following solution to deal with disconnections is proposed. Note that only local events can take place at an MH during the disconnect interval.

Disconnection of MH from MSS

First MH_i takes a local checkpoint and then transfers its local checkpoint to MSS_p as *disconnect-checkpoint$_i$*. If MH_i is asked to take a checkpoint during the disconnect interval, MSS_p converts *disconnect-checkpoint$_i$* into MH_i's new checkpoint and uses the message dependency information of MH_i to propagate the checkpoint request. MH_i also sends a *disconnect(sn)* message to MSS_p on the MH-to-MSS channel supplying the sequence number *sn* of the last message received on the MSS-to-MH channel. On receipt of MH_i's *disconnect(sn)*, MSS_p knows the last message that MH_i received from it and buffers all computation messages received until the end of the disconnect interval.

Reconnection of MH

Suppose MH_i reconnects at say MSS_p. If MH_i knows the identity of its last MSS, say MSS_p, it sends a *reconnect*(MH_i, MSS_p) message to MSS_p through MSS_p. If MH_i lost the identity of its last MSS for some reason, MH_i's *reconnect* request is broadcast over the network. On receiving the *reconnect* request, MSS_p transfers all the support information (the checkpoint, dependency vector, buffered messages, etc.) of MH_i to MSS_p and removes all the information related to the disconnection. Then, MSS forwards all the support information to MH_i. When the data sent by MSS_p arrives at MH_i, MH_i processes the buffered messages. If MSS_p has taken a checkpoint for MH_i, MH_i clears its message dependency information before processing the buffered messages. After these activities, the reconnect routine terminates and the relocated mobile host MH_i resumes normal communication with other MH_s (or MSS_s) in the system.

10.2.2 *A Checkpointing Algorithm Based on Mutable Checkpoints*

The Basic Scheme

The proposed non-blocking scheme for checkpointing can be explained as follows: When a process P_i sends a message, it piggybacks the current value of $csn_i[i]$. When process P_j receives a message m from P_i, P_j processes the message if $m.csn \leq csn_j[i]$, otherwise, P_j takes a checkpoint, updates its csn ($csn_j[i] = m.csn$), and processes the message. This method may result in a large number of checkpoints. Moreover, it may lead to an *avalanche effect* in which processes in the system recursively ask others to take checkpoints. For example, in Fig. 10.2, to initiate a checkpointing process, P2 takes its own checkpoint and sends checkpoint requests to all processes it depends on (i.e. it has received messages from them) which are P1, P3 and P4. When P2's request reaches P4, P4 takes a checkpoint and sends message m_3 to P3. When m_3 arrives at P3, P3 takes a checkpoint before processing it since $m_3.csn > csn_3[4]$. For the same reason, P1 takes a checkpoint before processing m_2.

Until now P0 has not communicated with other processes. Later, it takes a local checkpoint and then sends message m_1 to P1. P1 takes the checkpoint C1,2 before processing m_1 since P0 has taken a checkpoint which has a checkpoint sequence number larger than P1 expected. Then, P1 requires P3 to take another checkpoint (not shown in the figure) due to receiving m_2 from p3 before. P3 in turn asks P4 to take another checkpoint (not shown in the figure) due to m_3. If P4 had received messages from other processes after it sent m_3, those processes would have been forced to take checkpoints. This chain may never end.

In Fig. 10.2, if m_4 does not exist, it is not necessary for P1 to take C1,2 since checkpoint C1,1 is consistent with the rest of checkpoints. Based on this observation, they get the following scheme: When a process P_j receives a message m from P_i, P_j only takes a checkpoint when m.csn > $csn_j[i]$ and P_j has sent at least one message in the current checkpoint interval. However, if m_4 exists, the revised scheme still results in a large number of checkpoints and may result in an avalanche effect.

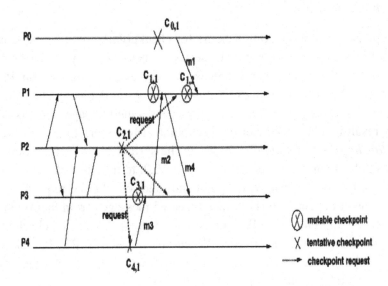

Fig. 10.2: An example of checkpointing.

Enhanced Scheme

Observation 1: It is not necessary to take checkpoint C1,2 even though m_4 exists since P1 will not receive a checkpoint request associated with Ć,1. Note that m_4 will not become an orphan even though it does not take checkpoint C1,2.

Observation 2: P1 does not have enough information to know if it will receive a checkpoint request associated with Ć,1 when P1 receives m1. also, since there is no previous communication between P0 and P1, P1 does not know whether it will receive a checkpoint request from P0 in the future or not.

These observations imply that C1,2 is unnecessary but still unavoidable. Therefore, upon receiving computation message there are two kinds of response checkpoints. For example, checkpoint C1,2 is different from C2,1. C1,1 is a checkpoint associated with the initiator P2 and P1 will receive a checkpoint request for the checkpointing initiated by P2 in the future. C1,2 is a checkpoint associated with P0, but P1 will not receive a checkpoint request from P0 in the future. However, P1 can discard C1,2 after the checkpointing initiated by P0 terminates (C1,1 becomes a permanent checkpoint) since at that time P1 is sure that it will not receive any checkpoint request initiated from P0.

A new concept called *"Mutable Checkpoint"* have been introduced to deal with checkpoints such as C1,1 and C1,2. A mutable checkpoint is neither a tentative checkpoint nor a permanent check-point, but it can be turned into a tentative checkpoint. When a process takes a mutable checkpoint, it does not send checkpoint requests to other processes and it does not need to save the checkpoint on the stable storage. It can save the mutable checkpoint anywhere, e.g., in the main memory or the local disk of MHs. When a process P_i receives a checkpoint request after it has taken a mutable checkpoint, it transfers the mutable checkpoint to the stable storage and forces all dependent processes to take tentative checkpoints. In this way, P_i turns its mutable checkpoint into a tentative checkpoint. If P_i does not receive the checkpoint request after the checkpointing activity terminates it discards the mutable checkpoint.

To show how this scheme avoids the avalanche effete and reduce the number of checkpoints, consider the following scenario. In Fig. 10.2, upon receiving m_2 at P1, it takes a mutable checkpoint C1,1 before processing it since $m_2.csn > csn_1$. C1,1 is turned into a tentative checkpoint when P1 receives the checkpoint request sent by P2. If P0 has finished its checkpointing activity before it sends m_1, P1 does not need to take a mutable checkpoint C1,2. Otherwise, P1 takes a mutable checkpoint C1,2, which will be discarded when P0's checkpointing terminates. Since C1,2 is a mutable checkpoint, it does not force P3 to take a new checkpoint. By this way and doing the same process with similar checkpoints, the number of checkpoints is significantly reduced.

Further Reduction in the Number of Checkpoints

Still a process may receive unnecessary checkpoint requests and may take unnecessary checkpoints. As shown in Fig. 10.3, P2 initiates a checkpointing process by taking a checkpoint C2,1 and forces P1 to take a checkpoint C1,1 (due to m_2). Later, to initiate a checkpointing process, P3 takes a checkpoint C3,1 and sends a request to P2 due to m_1. When P2 receives the request, it takes a checkpoint C2,2 and forces P1 to take a checkpoint C1,2. However, C2,2 and C1,2 are not necessary since m1 is not an orphan even though C1,2 and C2,2 do not exist.

These unnecessary checkpoints can be avoided by the following method: When a process P_i sends a checkpoint request to Pj, it attaches $csn_i[j]$ to the request. On receiving the request, P_j compares the attached $csn_i[j]$ (req-csn) with its own $csn_j[j]$. If $csn_j[j] >$ req-csn (i.e., P_j has recorded the sending of the message which creates the dependency between P_i and Pj), P_j does not need to take a checkpoint, otherwise, it takes a checkpoint. In Fig. 10.3, when P3 sends a request to P2, it attaches $csn_3[2] = 0$ to the request. When P2 receives the request, $csn_2[2]$ has been increased to 1 due to C2,1. thus P2 ignores this request and does not take checkpoint C2,2 and subsequently, P2 does not force P1 to take checkpoint C1,2.

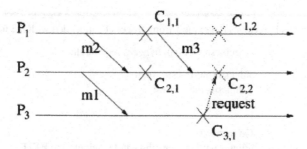

Fig. 10.3: Further reduce the number of checkpoints.

The Algorithm

This section describes the checkpointing algorithm based on the new concepts discussed so far. We start with the checkpoint initiation and then proceed to explain the response to checkpoint requests (system messages) and the response to the checkpoint request associated with computation messages. The algorithm is described by splitting it into its detailed steps.

Checkpointing Initiation

Checkpoint request can be started by any process. When that process, say Pi, sends the request, it does the following:

(1) take a local checkpoint
(2) increase $csn_i[j]$ by 1
(3) set the weight to 1 and cp- $state_i$ to 1
(4) set *trigger*.pid = its identifier and *trigger*.inum = $csn_i[i]$
(5) send checkpoint request to each P_j wher $R_i[j] = 1$
(6) resume underling computation.

Reception of a Checkpoint Request

Recall that this part deals with the response to the checkpoint request due to system messages, i.e., not due to computation messages.

Step 1: Process P_i receives the request from process P_j appended with the following:

$$req.csn\ (= csn_j),\ trigger_j,\ req.weight$$

Step 2: if req.csn >= old_csn (old Pj.csn), then
- P_i inherits the request
- Go to step 4

else
- Go to step3.

Step 3: Reply to the initiator with weight (the whole weight) and EXIT.

Step 4: in case of inherting the request, P_i do the following:
- Update its csn: $csn_i[i] = req.csn$
- Update its state to checkpointing in progress: $cp\_state_i = 1$
- Advanced to step5.

Step 5: if $trigger_i = req.trigger$, then P_i has already process the same
request before:
- Go to step6

else
- Take tentative checkpoint
- Increase $csn_i[i]$ by 1
- Go to step7

Step 6: if there is a mutable checkpoint where mut.trigger = req.trigger
then :
- Convert mutable checkpoint to permanent checkpoint
- Save it in the stable storage
- Propagate the request: go to step 7

else
- Go to step3

Step7: Propagating the request: for every process, P_k, that P_i depends on ($R_i[k] = 1$), if the csn attached with request about P_k ($req.csn_j[k]$) is greater than the csn expected by P_i ($csn_i[k]$, then this means that P_k will inherit the request from another way rather than through Pi, and hence no need to propagate the request to P_k. This can be represented as follows:

if $((R_i[k] = 1$ AND req. $csn_j[k] >= csn_i[k])$ OR ($R_i[k] = 0$) then
- Go to step 8

else ($R_i[k] = 1$ AND req. $csn_j[k] < csn_i[k]$)
- Propagate the request to P_k appended with the following:
  - req.trigger (=$trigger_i$)
  - req.weight – w_i) / number of requests
  - csni
- Goto step7

Step8:
- Reply to P_j with portion of the weight, w_i, and Exit
- Resume underlying computations

Note that step 7 is performed by sending the request to every process P_k that P_i depends on but P_j (initiator) does not. But this may result in inconsistency because receiving the request does not mean that the process will inherit the request.

Reception of Computation Messages

Upon receiving a computation massage, m, P_i performs the following steps.

Step 1: receive message, m, appended with the following: M.csn, cp-
state$_j$ and m.trigger.

Step 2: P_i compares its local expected csn, which is $csn_i[i]$ with m.csn
    If m.csn <= $csn_i[j]$ then
- No checkpoint is taken
- Go to step 4

    else
- $csn_i[j]$ = m.csn
- Goto step3

Step 3: Condition1: P_j is in the checkpointing process before sending m
        (m.cp-state = 1)

   Condition2: P_i has sent any computation message since the last
        checkpoint interval

   Condition3: P_i has not taken a checkpoint associated with the
        initiator P_j (*trigger$_i$* <> m.trigger)

   If Condition1 AND Condition2 AND Condition3 then
- Take a mutable checkpoint
- csn = m.csn
- cp_i = m.cp
- cp- *state$_i$* = 1
- sent$_i$ = 1
- Go to step4

   else (If Condition1 ONLY)
- $csn_i[i] = csn_i[i] + 1$
- Cp-satei = 1
- Go to step4

Step 4:
- Process the message m
- EXIT

Termination and Garbage Collection

The initiator adds weights received in all reply messages to its own weight. When its weight becomes equal to 1, it concludes that all processes involved in the checkpointing have taken their tentative checkpoints and, hence, it broadcasts commit messages to all processes in the system. If a process has taken a tentative checkpoint, on receiving the commit message, it makes its tentative checkpoint permanent and clears cp state. Other processes also clear their cp state and discard mutable checkpoints if there is any. Note that, when a process discards its mutable checkpoints, it updates its R and sent.

Example

The basic idea of the algorithm can be explained through the example shown in Fig. 10.3. In this figure, process P2 initiates checkpointing by taking its own checkpoint and sending checkpoint requests to P1, P3, and P4 since $R_2[1] = 1$, $R_2[3] = 1$, and $R_2[4] = 1$. When P2's request reaches P4, it takes a checkpoint and sends message m_3 to P3. When m_3 arrives at P3, it takes a mutable checkpoint before processing the message since $m_3.csn > csn_3[4]$ and P3 has sent a message during the current checkpoint interval. For the same reason, P1 takes a mutable checkpoint before processing m_2. On the other hand, P0 did not communicate with another process before it took the local checkpoint. Later, it sends a message m_1 to P1. If P0 has finished its checkpointing process before it sends m_1, P1 does not need to take the checkpoint C1,2. Otherwise, P1 takes a mutable checkpoint C1,2 before processing m_1.

When P1 receives the checkpoint request from P2, since C1,1 is a mutable checkpoint associated with P2, P1 turns C1,1 into a tentative checkpoint by saving it on the stable storage. Similarly, P3 converts C3,1 to a tentative checkpoint when it receives the checkpoint request from P2. Finally, the checkpointing initiated by P2 terminates when the checkpoints C1,1,C2,1,C3,1, and C4,1 are made permanent. P1 discards C1,2 when it makes checkpoint C1,1 permanent or receives P0's commit, whichever is earlier.

Multiple Concurrent Initiations

When a process P_j receives a checkpoint request from P_j while executing the checkpoint algorithm, P_i ignores P_j's checkpoint request or defers the request until it finishes its current checkpointing. If Pi's checkpoint request is ignored by a process, P_i has to abort its checkpointing efforts, which results in poor performance.

As multiple concurrent checkpoint initiation is orthogonal to our discussion, we only briefly mention the main features. When a process receives its first request for the checkpointing initiated by another process, it takes a local checkpoint and propagates the request. All local checkpoints taken by the participating processes for a checkpointing initiation collectively form a global checkpoint. The state information collected by each independent checkpointing is combined. The combination is driven by the fact that the union of consistent global checkpoints is also a consistent global checkpoint. The checkpoint thus generated is more recent than each of the checkpoints collected independently. Therefore, the amount of computation lost during rollback, after process failures, is minimized.

Handling Failures during Checkpointing

Due to the nature of mobile computing system, the possibility of failure of a process during checkpointing exists. The failed process can be the initiator process or intermediate process. Dealing with these failures differs based on the type of the failed process. The simplest way is to discard that process and its relevant processes by using abort message. However, this technique may cause a poor performance since the whole checkpointing aborts even when only one process fails.

10.2.3 *Performance Evaluation*

Simulation Results

The algorithm is evaluated in two cases: point-to-point communication and group communication.

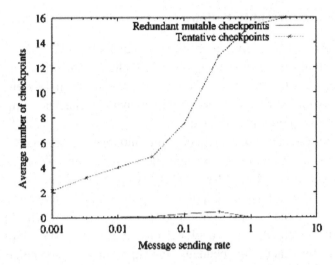

Fig. 10.4: The number of checkpoints in a point-to-point communication environment.

Point-to-Point Communication

In Fig. 10.4, when the message sending rate increases, the number of redundant mutable checkpoints for each checkpoint initiation increases at first and then decreases and it is always less than 4 percent of the number of tentative checkpoints. This can be explained as follows: A process takes a mutable checkpoint only when it receives a computation message before it receives the checkpoint request during the checkpointing time. It takes a tentative checkpoint if it has received messages that created dependency relationships with the initiator during the checkpoint interval. Since the checkpointing time (at most 2 * 16 = 32s long) is much less than the checkpoint interval (900s), in general, a process takes much fewer redundant mutable checkpoints. If the message sending rate is low, processes have low probability of sending messages and they have low probability of receiving messages during the checkpointing time. Thus, they have low probability of taking mutable checkpoints. If the message sending rate is high, it is more likely for a process to receive a message and take a mutable checkpoint during the checkpointing time. The mutable checkpoint is also more likely to be turned into a tentative checkpoint and then it is not a redundant mutable checkpoint. According to our algorithm, the initiator quickly propagates the checkpoint request; thus, a process is less likely to receive a computation message before the checkpoint request during the checkpointing time and it is less likely to take a mutable checkpoint.

Group Communication

Figure 10.5 shows the number of checkpoints in a group communication environment. Besides changing the intra-group message sending rate, a group leader also changes its inter-group message sending rate. For a group leader, the intra-group message sending rate is 1000 times faster than the inter-group message sending rate. On the right figure, the intra-group message sending rate is 10000 times faster than the inter-group message sending rate. sending rate is 1,000 times faster than the inter-group message sending rate; while on the right side of Fig. 10.5, the intra-group message sending rate is 10,000 times faster. As can be seen, with group communication, the number of tentative checkpoints and redundant mutable checkpoints on the right graph is less than that on the left graph and they are smaller than those in the point-to-point communication. In a group communication, when a process initiates a checkpointing process, processes in other groups have low probability of receiving messages from any process in the initiator's group. Thus, they are less likely to have dependency relationships with the initiator; that is, they have low probability of taking tentative checkpoints or redundant mutable checkpoints.

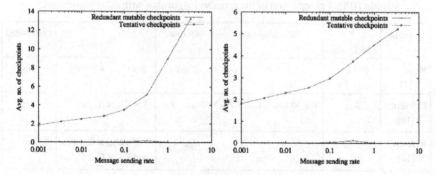

Fig. 10.5: The number of checkpoints in a group communication environment.

Comparison

As shown in Table 10.1, when compared to the algorithm in [10], the algorithm presented above reduces the message overhead from $3 * N_{min} * N_{dep} * C_{air}$ ($1 \leq N_{dep} \leq N - 1$) to $2 * N_{min} * C_{air} + min(N_{min} * C_{air}, C_{broad})$. When $N_{min} = N$, the message reduction can be from $O(N^2)$ to $O(N)$. The algorithm reduces the blocking time from $N_{min} * T_{ch}$ to 0. In the worst case, $N_{min} = N$. Compared to existing techniques, this last algorithm [18] forces only a minimum number of processes to take their checkpoints on stable storage. Note that there may be many applications running in the system: Some of them have higher reliability requirement and others do not. In a heterogeneous environment, some MHs may be more prone to failures than others. Moreover, different processes may run at their own speed and they may only communicate with a group of processes. As a result, some processes may need to take checkpoints more frequently than others. However, the algorithm presented in [1] forces all processes in the system to take checkpoints for each checkpoint initiation. Thus, this algorithm significantly reduces the message overhead and checkpointing overhead compared to [1]. Furthermore, in the case of output commit, the algorithm has much shorter delay compared to [1] since it requires fewer processes to take checkpoints before committing to the outside world. It seems that the algorithm needs more system messages than [1]. However, the algorithm in [1] is a centralized algorithm and there is no easy way to make it distributed without significantly increasing message overhead.

Table 10.1: A comparison of the proposed algorithm with other algorithms.

Algorithm	# Chickpoints	Blocking time	Output commi.		Distributed
Reference [1]	N	0	$N \times T_{ch}$	$2 \times C_{broad} + N \times C_{air}$	No
Reference [10]	N_{min}	$N_{min} \times (T_{msg} + T_{data} + T_{dist})$	$N_{min} \times T_{ch}$	$3 \times N_{min} \times N_{dep} \times C_{air}$	Yes
Reference [18]	N_{min}	0	$\approx N_{min} \times T_{ch}$	$2 \times M_{min} \times C_{air} + min(N_{min} \times C_{air}, C_{broad})$	Yes

The algorithm in [18] has the following advantages:

(1) It is a non-blocking algorithm.
(2) It tries to minimize the number of checkpoints by using the new concept, "mutable checkpoints". Mutable checkpoints does not send checkpoint request to the all processes that its process depends on. It propagates the requests to selected processes.
(3) The mutable checkpoint overhead is very small. Recall that mutable checkpoints are taken as a response to computational messages only. The overhead due to system messages is still high.
(4) It is distributed since mutable checkpoints are taken based on local decisions. Later, these checkpoints either converted to tentative checkpoints or canceled based on local decision also.
(5) It reduces the load sent to the stable storage since mutable checkpoints can be saved any where else.

The only disadvantage that can be observed is the high system messages overhead. This is because in order to reduce the number of checkpoints due to checkpoint requests (system messages), it needs to send the whole *csn* vector which contains the *csn* expected values of all other processes that the current process expect. The receiver will store that vector in RT record and then use it to select the processes that it should propagate the request to them as explained in setp 7 of reception process of the algorithm. This consumes more transmission time and needs more storage space.

10.3   Hardware Approach for Fault Tolerance in Mobile Networks

In this section, we present some hardware techniques that are used to achieve fault tolerance in mobile networks.

State Information Replication

Since power and resources of a MH are limited, part or all of its state information are stored in its MSS. Updating *st_info*(*h*) is easy for a primary MSS, since each message sent by Ito a MH *h* is sent through the primary MSS. Upon failure of a MSS, the state information (of the MHs in its cell) is lost. As a result, the MHs in MSS's cell will be unable to continue their operation until the state information is restored. Thus, the MHs are forced to wait until the recovery of MSS is completed. This can be overcome by maintaining *st_info(h)* at a number of *sec_mss(h)*. Two different techniques are employed. They are discussed below.

Pessimistic State Information Replication

In the pessimistic scheme, the primary MSS sends *st_infa(h)* to all SMSSs and does not update its own *st_infa(h)* unless it has received the acknowledg- ments from all the SMSSs indicating that they have updated their *st_infa(h)*. No message is delivered from the MSS to a destination MH unless the MSS has received acknowledgements from all SMSSs. This increases the overhead (in terms of number of acknowledgments) as well as the delay in updating the *st_infa(h)* and hence the delivery of message m to its destination is delayed. This is a disadvantage of this scheme. However, the scheme has an advantage in situations whereby the primary MSS fails, in which case the MH *h* moves to a SMSS and continues its operation without any delay. This is because an updated copy of *st_infa(h)* is already available in all SMSSs.

Optimistic State Information Replication

In the optimistic scheme, the primary MSS sends *st_info(h)* to all SMSSs and does not wait for the acknowledgements to arrive before it updates its *st_info(h)*. Thus, the message is delivered to the destination without any de- lay. However, the optimistic scheme has the disadvantage that in the case of primary MSS failure, MH *h* moves to a MSS, but it may not have the up-dated copy of *st_info(h)* and a recovery procedure has to be run which causes interruption in the operation of MH *h*.

Observations

Certain factors, such as mobility patterns of MHs, network topology, and frequency of migration of MHs affect the selection of SMSSs. One possible strategy to deal with such factors is as follows. If a MH *h* moves within a certain vicinity, then the MSSs within that locality are the most probable candidates for SMSSs of *h*. When failure of *pri_mss(h)* occurs, MH *h* switches to another MSS (call it MSS B) in *sec_mss(h)*, assigns B as *pri_mss(h)*, and proceeds with the computation. Moreover, migration of *h* to another cell during normal operation does not require additional handoff steps since there is already a copy of *st_info(h)* in its new MSS. This strategy is efficient if the movement of MH *h* is limited within a subset of cells, e.g., som MHs may have their movement frequently within one vicinity and seldom move to other areas.

Based on the characteristics of the pessimistic and the optimistic schemes, a hybrid scheme, which combines the features of both schemes, is presented below.

Hybrid State Information Replication

The overall organization of the MSSs in the hybrid scheme is depicted in Fig. 10.6.

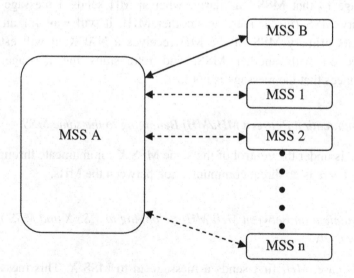

Fig. 10.6: Hybrid pessimistic-optimistic scheme.

In this scheme, a number of potential SMSS are identified for a Primary MSS, say 'A'. Pessimistic protocol is implemented between MSS 'A' and a subset of selected SMSS (solid arrow in Fig. 2). The selection of pessimistic SMSSs is done randomly from a set of potential SMSSs. An optimistic protocol is implemented between MSS A and the remaining SMSS of the selected set. Thus, for MSS A, we have a total of S SMSS, out of which T (where $T < S$) are pessimistic while the remaining $S - T$ stations are optimistic. In the following subsections, we provide detailed explanation of the system's operation.

Normal Operation

MSS/MH Communication

During normal operation, when MSS X sends a message (whose destination is h) to $pri\_mss(h)$, X stores the message in a buffer. This buffer is cleared when an ACK signal is received from the $pri\_mss(h)$. If X receives a NACK (indicating failure of primary MSS for h), X will identify the new primary MSS of h (call it B) and retransmits the message to that MSS. Similarly, when a MH sends a message to its primary MSS (for delivery to another MH), it will wait for an ACK from its primary MSS. If the MH receives a NACK, it will establish connection with another MSS, and retransmits the message. This guarantees that the message is not lost.

Communication Between MHi/MHj Belonging to the same MSS

All MHs under the control of the same MSS X communicate through this MSS. There is no direct communication between the MHs.

Communication Between MHi/MHj Belonging to MSS X and MSS Y Respectively

In this case, *MHi* first sends a message m to MSS X. This message is then stored in a buffer and is sent to MSS Y. When the message is received by MSS *Y*, it is delivered to *MH j* and an ACK is sent to MSS *X*. At that time the message m is cleared from the buffer of MSS *X*. Let m be the message such that either *sender(m)* = *h* or *dest(m)* = *h*. *st_info(h)* may be updated when *pri_mss(h)* receives m, and copies of this updated *st_info(h)* are sent to all SMSS (*sec_mss(h)*). This is done only if *st_info(h)* has to be updated. Upon reception of updated *st_info(h)* at all *sec_mss(h)*, they update their *st_info(h)*. ACKs from SMSS working as pessimistic is required by the *pri_mss(h)* to confirm that the SMSSs have updated the information. After receiving ACKs, *pri_mss(h)* updates *st_info(h)*, and sends the updated *st_info(h)* to all the remaining SMSS (optimistic protocol). The primary MSS then delivers the message to *dest(m)*, and sends an ACK to *sender(m)*. On the other hand, for SMSSs that operate under optimistic protocol, following procedure takes place. When a message m is received, it is stored in a *log* without processing the copy message immediately. The SMSS processes the messages in the log for MH *h* and updates *st_info(h)* occasionally (whenever the SMSS is idle or after a predetermined time interval). A SMSS is not required to send ACKs to primary MSS. The above process is depicted in Fig. 10.7, where, for illustration, four SMSS are shown, one of which operates under pessimistic protocol and the rest operate under optimistic protocol.

Handoff Procedure

If a MH *h*, initially in the cell of MSS A, wants to move to the cell of MSS B, it establishes communication with MSS B by using the beacon protocol (see Section 2). *h* sends the identity of its old MSS (MSS A) to MSS B. A handoff procedure takes place between A and B. MSS B notifies A by sending *handoff-begin* (*h*) message to A that *h* has changed its cell. MSS A waits for any pending ACKs from SMSS (the ones using pessimistic protocol), updates *st_info(h)*, and then sends *st_info(h)* to B. Any pending messages in A for *h* are also sent to B. A then sends *handoff_over(h)* message to B. If B belongs to *sec_mss(h)*, then *st_info(h)* need not be sent to B, so A just sends *handoff_over(h)* to B. The handoff procedure is depicted in Fig. 10.8.

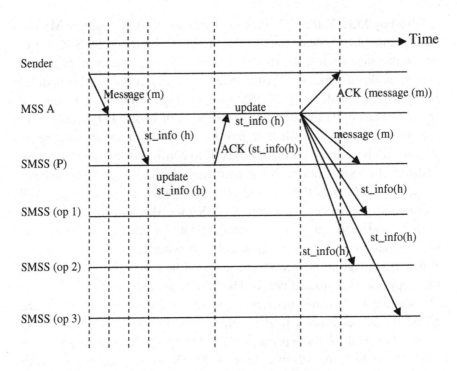

Fig. 10.7: Normal operation under the hybrid scheme.

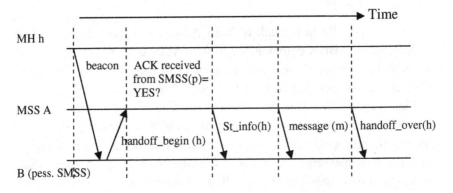

Fig. 10.8: Handoff procedure under the hybrid scheme.

If the set *sec_mss(h)* changes, MSS B sends *st_info(h)* to all the new MSSs in *sec_mss(h)* and notifies MSS A and the old MSSs in *sec-mss(h)* to delete *st_info(h)* from their storage.

Operation after Failure

Case 1: In case of failure of primary MSS A, hswitches to any of the MSSs operating as pessimistic, say MSS B, and notifies MSSB about the failure. IfB *Esec_mss(h)*, then *h* can continue its operation since a copy of *sf_in/ark)* is already stored in B, otherwise MH *h* also sends the set *sec_mss(h)* to MSS B.

Case 2: If the updated copy of *st_info(h)* is not present in **B,** then B acquires a copy of *st_info(h)* from one of the MSSs in *sec_mss(h)*. This causes MSS B to become the primary MSS of *h*. A new set of SMSS may emerge, deleting some old and adding some new SMSS. These SMSSs update their *st_info(h)* accordingly. This process is depicted in Fig. 10.9.

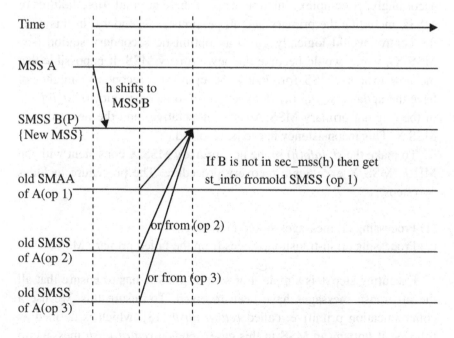

Fig. 10.9: Operation after failure of hybrid scheme.

Case 3: If a MSS fails during handoff, then *h* switches to the pessimistic SMSS in the set of its primary MSS and initiates a new handoff procedure (see above).

Case 4: If pessimistic SMSS has also failed, then the new MSS of *h* will acquire *st_injo(h)* from one of the optimistic SMSS of *h*.

With respect to the above cases, some points need clarification. Prior to all the above steps, the MH *h* is constantly updated with a list of secondary MSSs that satisfy the requirements of place and accessibility for being its future primary MSS. If only primary (say MSS A) fails, then the control goes to a pessimistic secondary (say MSS B). This station then becomes the primary station, and starts providing services to MH without any delay, since a copy of updated *st_info(h)* is already available to it. Now, this new MSS (i.e. MSS B) becomes the primary MSS for mobile host *h*. This information (i.e. MSS B is the new primary MSS) is sent to other MSS of mobile host *h*. These SMSS update their records accordingly. A complex situation arises if there are mul- tiple failures of MSSs, including the primary and all pessimistic secondary. In this case, the control would logically go to an optimistic secondary station (say MSS X), which would become the new primary MSS. It is possible that the new primary MSS (originally the optimistic secondary) might not have the updated *st_info(h)*. This may lead to inconsistency of *st_info(h)* in the original primary MSS A (now inoperative) and the new primary MSS X. This inconsistency has to be resolved.

To make the *st_info(h)* in the new primary MSS X consistent with the MH *h*, MSS X executes a recovery procedure. The procedure includes two steps:

(1) Processing all messages stored in the log for *h*.
(2) Processing all in-transit messages from the failed primary MSS A.

Executing step 1 is simple. For step 2, MSS X has to ensure that all the in- transit messages have been received. To ensure this, we use a communication primitive, called *return flush* [18], which is defined as follows. If host *p* (an MSS in this case) sends a *return flush* message to host q (primary MSS A in this case) that is known to have failed, the communication network will return the message to p after delivering all other in-transit messages from q to p.

Thus, MSS X sends a return flush to MSS A and starts processing the messages stored in the log for h. Once the stored messages are processed, it processes in-transit messages received and updates $st\_info(h)$. On receiving the return flush from the network, $st\_info(h)$ is considered to be consistent with the state of MH h. This completes the recovery procedure, and MH h can continue with the computation [3].

10.4 Summary

In this Chapter, the use of the concept of "mutable checkpoint" in the context of mobile distributed systems is explained. Mutable checkpoints can be saved anywhere, e.g., the main memory or local disk of MHs. In this way, taking a mutable checkpoint avoids the overhead of transferring a large amount of data to the stable storage at MSSs over the wireless network. The mutable checkpoint algorithm is non-blocking, reduces the number of checkpoints significantly and is distributed. Three different algorithms that use mutable checkpoint have been explained and compared. The hybrid pessimistic-optimistic scheme presented in this chapter maintains replicas of state information of the mobile hosts at various secondary mobile support stations. The scheme also allows the migration of mobile host from one cell to another while the state information of a mobile host is being replicated. Simulation results have shown that the hybrid scheme performs better than either of the optimistic and the pessimistic techniques both in terms of delay as well as storage capacity.

References

[1] E. Elnozahy, D. Johnson, and Y.-M. Wang, "A Survey of Rollback-Recovery Protocols in Message-Passing Systems," Tech. Rep. CMU-CS-96-181, School of Computer Science, Carnegie Mellon University, October 1996.

[2]   Y. Deng and E.K. Park, "Checkpointing and Rollback-Recovery Algorithms in Distributed Systems," J. Systems and Software, pp. 59-71, Apr. 1994.

[3]   G. Cao and M. Singhal, "On Coordinated Checkpointing in Distributed Systems," IEEE Trans. Parallel and Distributed System pp. 1213-1225, Dec. 1998.

[4]   D. Johnson, "Distributed System Fault Tolerance Using Message Logging and Checkpointing," PhD Thesis, Rice Univ., Dec. 1989.

[5]   G. Cao and M. Singhal, "On the Impossibility of Min-Process Non- Blocking Checkpointing and an Efficient Checkpointing Algorithm for Mobile Computing Systems," Proc. 27th Int'l Conf. on Parallel Processing, pp. 37-44, Aug. 1998.

[6]   Gouhong Cao and M. Singhal, "Mutable Checkpoints: A new Checkpointing approach for Mobile Computing Systems", IEEE Trans. On Parallel and distributed systems, Vol. 12, No. 2, Feb 2001.

[7]   G. Cao and M. Singhal, "Low-Cost Checkpointing with Mutable Checkpoints in Mobile Computing Systems," Proc. 18th Int'l Conf. Distributed Computing Systems, pp. 464-471, May 1998.

[8]   N. Neves, and W.K. Fuchs, "Adaptive Recovery for Mobile Environments," communications of the ACM, Vol. 40, No. 1, pp. 69-74, 1997.

[9]   B. Crow, I. Widjaja, J. Kim, and P. Sakai, "IEEE 802. 11 Wireless Local Area Networks," IEEE Comm. Magazine, pp. 116-126, Sept. 1997.

[10] R. Koo and S. Toueg, "Checkpointing and Rollback-Recovery for Distributed Systems," IEEE Trans. Software Eng., pp. 23-31, Jan. 1987.

[11] T.H. Lai and T.H. Yang, "On Distributed Snapshots," Information in Parallel and Distributed System, Oct. 1993. Processing Letters, pp. 153-158, May 1987.

[12] D. Manivannan and M. Singhal, "A Low-Overhead Recovery Technique Using Quasi-Synchronous Checkpointing," Proc. 16th Int'l Conf. Distributed Computing Systems, pp. 100-107, May 1996.

[13] R. Prakash and M. Singhal, "Low-Cost Checkpointing and Failure Recovery in Mobile Computing Systems," IEEE Trans. Parallel and Distributed Systems, pp. 1035-1048, Oct. 1996.

[14] P. Ramanathan and K.G. Shin, "Use of Common Time Base for Checkpointing and Rollback Recovery in a Distributed System," IEEE Trans. Software Eng., pp. 571-583, June 1993.

[15] G. Cao and M. Singhal, "On Coordinated Checkpointing in Distributed Systems," IEEE Trans. Parallel and Distributed System pp. 1213-1225, Dec. 1998.

[16] G.H. Forman and J. Zahorjan, "The Challenges of Mobile Distributed Systems, pp. 86-95, Oct. 1992. Computing," Computer, pp. 38-47, Apr. 1994.

[17] R. Prakash and M. Singhal, "Low-Cost Checkpointing and Failure Recovery in Mobile Computing Systems," IEEE Trans. Parallel and Distributed Systems, pp. 1035-1048, Oct. 1996.

[18] T. Quahtani, "A Survey of Checkpointing Techniques in Distributed Mobile Computing Systems", Project Report, Department of Computer Engineering, KFUPM, 2003.

Chapter 11

Reliability and Yield Enhancement of VLSI/WSI Circuits

The ever increasing demand of new functionality and specifications to be put in a system has made designers to increase the scale of integration in the Very Large Scale Integration (VLSI) circuits. As the feature size of transistors has been reduced into submicron level, VLSI manufacturers produced chips with smaller size to reduce the cost of manufacturing. Both the higher density of VLSI circuits and the smaller feature sizes imply that even tiny imperfections can corrupt a significant portion of the chip area. This in turn will increase the probability of having device failure.

There exists a number of ways for incorporating fault tolerance into VLSI circuits. This chapter is dedicated to a discussion on the reliability and yield enhancement of VLSI/WSI circuits. Our coverage starts with an introduction to the cause of defects and failures in VLSI systems. Yield and defect model of VLSI circuits will then be highlighted. Finally, techniques to improve yield and reliability of these circuits will be introduced.

11.1 Defect and Failure in VLSI Circuits

The active area of monolithic VLSI chips has always been limited by the random fabrication defects, which appear impossible to eliminate in even the best manufacturing process. The larger the circuit, the more likely it will contain such type of defects and consequently will fail to operate correctly. There exists a number of possible causes for defects. In addition, with the advance of technology and due to the higher level of integration, new types of defects may occur.

VLSI circuits are mass produced in a series of very complex processes. The chances that all devices will function according to the given specification depend on the control exercised in their manufacture. When some of the manufacturing parameters are not set properly then they result in many defective chips on a wafer.

Defect is defined as any physical anomaly on a chip (wafer) which may or may not cause improper functioning of VLSI circuits. A basic preliminary classification of defects can be made based on the fault distributions in *wafers* during fabrication. These faults affect the *yield* of VLSI/WSI circuits and can be classified as *gross failures* and *random failures*.

Gross defects are caused by manufacturing errors as a consequence of which wafers or at least major parts of wafers have no functioning chips (see Fig. 11.1). They are associated with the fact that the devices parameters are completely out of the acceptable bounds. It is evident that faults in this class can be overcome only at the processing level, by adopting the most careful control process in what is basically a fault avoidance approach. Statistics indicate that gross defects count only for about 15-17% of losses in VLSI circuits. On the other hand, random defects account for 85-83% of losses and responsible for run-time failures. Thus, random defects will be the emphasis of our discussion here.

Random defects are mostly caused by unwanted chemical and airborne particles that are deposited during the various steps of the process. Some of the random defects affect relatively large areas and can be identified by visual inspection: these are typically area and line defects. Other defects are characterized as spot defects and are considered to be localized and randomly distributed over the whole wafer. Spot defects are responsible for about 60% of faults occurring in VLSI/WSI circuits. Spot defect types include pinhole defects, photo defects, leakage defects, to name a few. Pinhole defects and photo defects contribute to a major portion of yield loss.

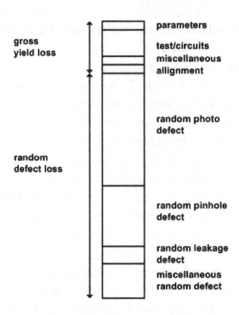

Fig. 11.1: Relative yield loss on logarithmic scale for DRAM.

Some spot defects might cause missing patterns or open circuits, while others cause extra patterns of short circuits. However, not all random defects results discrete faults such as line breaks or short circuits. A defect causes a discrete fault only if it is large enough to connect two disjoint conductors or disconnect a continuous pattern.

It is observed that defects tend to group together on VLSI/WSI circuits. This is called clustering. A *cluster* is a region, which encloses all the defects that demonstrate dependence on each other in the same location. This behavior causes damage in a small region on a VLSI/WSI circuit. There may be more than one cluster source on a chip. Figure 11.2 shows an example of a defect map of a wafer. Having all the defects closely clustered causes damage in a small region on the VLSI/WSI circuit. This will introduce faults in the circuits. Existence of faults on a chip makes the chip function improperly. Faults manifest itself in the form of system failure.

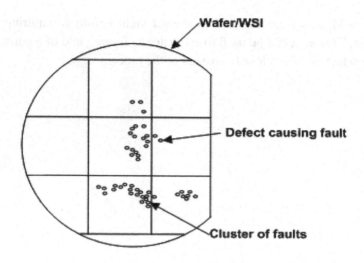

Fig. 11.2: A defect map of VLSI/WSI circuit.

11.2   Yield and Defect Model in VLSI/WSI Circuits

Among the performance indices for successful IC manufacturing, *yield* is regarded as the most important one. *Yield* is defined as the average fraction of good chips delivered by a production line. In other word,

$$\text{Yield} = \frac{\text{total number of good chips delivered}}{\text{total number of chips produced}}$$

Because of yield, even with 24 hours of operation, the equipment utilization will be low. In addition to the exponentially growing cost of manufacturing equipment, the profit margin for each IC manufacturer is decreasing. Therefore, improving yield is a key competitive issue for all IC manufacturers.

Yield models are used to predict manufacturing cost for products under development by determining the amount of chips that have to be manufactured to get the desired amount of good chips. Yield models are used to define the maximum level of integration possible for a given VLSI/WSI implementation.

A yield model can be used to predict yield before committing to a product. That is, it can be used to estimate the future yield of a current or new product and yield loss from each of the process steps.

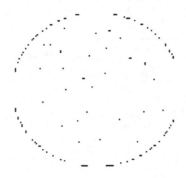

Fig. 11.3: A defect map showing a Poisson distribution.

It is commonly assumed that failure rate of a VLSI system follows a certain probability distribution function. At first, a Poisson probability distribution function was used for this purpose. The Poisson distribution makes a random distribution of defects, thus causing scattered defects on the circuits (see Fig. 11.3). Therefore, the average number of failures of the chip is formulated as follows:

$$\lambda_i = A_i\, D_i \qquad\qquad (11.1)$$

where λ_i is the average number of failures or defect caused by a defect type indicated by the index i. The quantity A_i is the critical area. The defect density is designated by D_i and has the units of defects per unit area. The overall average number of defects λ is the summation of defect average during all steps. The defect distribution model is given by the following equation:

$$P(i) = e^{-D_o\, A_{chip}}\, \frac{[D_o\, A_{chip}]}{i!} = e^{-\lambda}\, \frac{\lambda^i}{i!} \qquad\qquad (11.2)$$

where P(i) is the probability of finding i defects on a chip, D_o is the average defect density and A_{chip} is the area of the chip.

It has been observed that the above formula is too pessimistic and leads to predicted chips lower than actual yields. As the chip size continued to escalate, the Poisson model became increasingly inaccurate and tended to underestimate the yield for large dies. Consider, for example, a condition in which one half of a wafer is completely defect-free, so that the chip yield on that half is 100%. Let the other half be very defective, with an average of ten faults per chip. Let the faults within this half is also randomly distributed. This distribution therefore has a parameter $\lambda = 10$. The yield for this half is then 0%, and the combined yield for both halves is equal to 50%. Using the normal Poisson distribution function, the average number of faults per chip (for both halves) is equal to five. According to tables of cumulative Poisson distribution, it can be determined that the expected chip yield is 44%. Thus, the Poisson distribution function fails to accurately model the yield if clustering of faults occurs on a chip, a situation that has been repeatedly observed.

A yield model which gives similar results to those obtained using the Poisson distribution is the Binomial distribution. Like the former one, this distribution is also inaccurate. One of the main reasons that lead to the inaccuracy is clustering of manufacturing defects.

A good defect model for integrated circuit chips has to take two important factors into account: the variation from wafer to wafer of defect densities and defect clustering. A good way of integrating those effects is to use compound Poisson statistic. The Poisson distribution is compounded with a function f(D), which represents the normalized distribution of chip defect densities.

$$P(I, D_o, A) = \int_0^\infty \frac{(D_oA)^i e^{-DA}}{i!} f(D) d(D) \qquad (11.3)$$

This function is also known as Murphy's formula. The function f(D) is, in effect, a weighting function which accounts for the non-random distribution defect.

Different functions have been proposed and used for f(D). Some of these functions are the *delta*, *triangular*, *exponential*, *rectangular*, and *gamma* distribution functions. Using gamma distribution function as f(D) results in the following well known formula.

$$P(i, \alpha, D_0, A) = \frac{\Gamma(i + \alpha)(AD_0/\alpha)^i}{(i!)\Gamma(\alpha)(1 + AD_0/\alpha)^{i+\alpha}} \tag{11.4}$$

where α is the clustering parameter.

Substituting $\lambda = AD_0$, the negative Binomial distribution function is obtained as follows.

$$P\{X = i\} = \frac{\Gamma(\alpha + i)(\bar{\lambda}/\alpha)^i}{i!\Gamma(\alpha)(1 + \bar{\lambda}/\alpha)^{\alpha+i}} \tag{11.5}$$

where $[(\bar{\lambda})]$ is the grand average of λ of all areas on the chip.

Using Eq. (11.5), the formula for yield estimation becomes as follows.

$$Y = (1 + \bar{\lambda}/\alpha)^{-\alpha} \tag{11.6}$$

It can be shown that $[(\lambda)]$ is, in effect, the expected value of 1. When the clustering parameter α is large, i.e., $\alpha \to \infty$, the yield in Eq. (11.6) becomes equal to the yield in Eq. (11.1). This represents the case of random faults without any clustering. Smaller values of α indicate increased clustering. Experimentally derived values for α typically range between 0.3 and 5.

Yield formula shown in Eq. (11.6) accounts only for faults resulting from spot defects. Usually, a gross yield factor Y_0 must be included in the yield model. Gross yield losses are usually the result of systematic processing problems that affect whole wafer or parts therein. Introduction of the gross yield into the yield formula leads to

$$Y = Y_0(1 + \bar{\lambda}/\alpha)^{-\alpha} \tag{11.7}$$

Defect Modeling Based on Clustering

An important source of clustering is the radial variation in the average number of defects per chip. Clusters that occur on VLSI chips can be categorized into three classes. The first class includes clusters that are larger than the chip size, i.e., *large size clustering*. The second class deals with defect clusters that are smaller than chip area, i.e., *small size clustering*. The third class contains clusters with the same size as that of the chip area, i.e., *medium size clustering*.

In large size clustering, the size of a cluster is comparable to the size of the wafer, implying that the number of defects in any sub-area of the wafer has a negative Binomial distribution, and that the parameter α is constant for any sub-area of the wafer. In small size clustering, the wafer is divided into small modules (considered unit size) that are statistically independent. Any sub-area of the wafer is assumed to consist of a whole number of these modules, and hence defects in any disjoint sub-areas are independent. In addition, the number of defects in any sub-area has a negative Binomial distribution, and the parameter α is proportional to the area.

Medium size clustering is an intermediate method, in which the basic unit is a block consisting of R rows and C columns of $R \times C$ modules. The number of defects in a block has a negative Binomial distribution, and the defects in distinct blocks are statistically independent. The size of the block has to be chosen such that it encompasses a cluster.

A unified approach to the three distribution schemes is considered in a model that considers a chip as consisting of a basic unit called a module. A module is a circuit block such as a memory sub-array or a digital logic macro that is replicated on a chip. The area of a module is assumed to be the unit area, and all other areas are measured in these units. Therefore, a block is composed of B modules and the wafer of W modules. There are W/B blocks on the wafer. It is assumed that the number of defects per wafer has a negative Binomial distribution with parameter (λ_W, α_W). It has been shown that the number of defects in a block has a negative Binomial distribution with parameter (λ_b, α_b), where

$$\lambda_b = \frac{\lambda_w}{W/B}; \quad \alpha_b = \frac{\alpha_w}{W/B} \qquad (11.8)$$

For any area of size A contained in one block, the number of defects has a negative Binomial distribution with parameters

$$\left(\frac{A}{B}\lambda_b, \alpha_b \right) \tag{11.9}$$

Therefore, the module parameters (λ_m, α_m) are given by

$$\lambda_m = \frac{\lambda_b}{B} = \frac{\lambda_w}{W}; \quad \alpha_m = \alpha_b = \frac{\alpha_w}{W/B} \tag{11.10}$$

For any area consisting of C blocks, the number of defects has a negative Binomial distribution with parameters

$$(C\lambda_b, C\alpha_b) \tag{11.11}$$

Let E be the size of an area which is divided among K blocks such that

$$E = \sum_{i=1} KA_i \tag{11.12}$$

where A_i is the size of sub-area contained in block *i*. The number of defects in area E has a negative Binomial distribution if and only if $A_1 = A_2 = \cdots = A_K = E/K$; otherwise, it is the sum of K statistically independent negative Binomial random variables.

11.3 Techniques to Improve Yield

Due to the presence of faults, yield at the time of manufacturing falls. Improving yield can be done by defect avoidance, repairing process or introduction of redundant elements.

The first chips to have exploited fault tolerance techniques commercially have been memory chips. Some of the techniques used are spare-row and/or column organization, error correcting codes, associative approach and partially good chips.

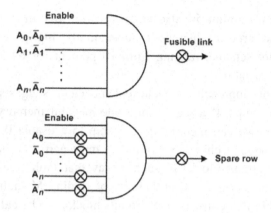

Fig. 11.4: A simple row replacement circuit.

The simplest circuit for substituting spare row for defective row is shown in Fig. 11.4. Fault tolerance is introduced by putting a fusible element in every row. In the case of the main array rows the fuse is used to disable the row when it is defective, and in the case of the spare rows it is used to enable the row when it is required. In addition, the decoding circuit of each spare row is connected by fuses to the true and complement values of all the row address bits so that its address can be defined. This approach has been adopted by a number of IC manufacturers.

Error correcting codes (ECC) is used in large memory systems to mask intermittent faults. Thus, using ECCs for yield enhancement can contribute to reliability improvement as well. However, the associated area overhead is much higher than the simple row (column) scheme.

The spare row (column) approach applies only to the replacement of individual faulty rows (columns). If we need to replace larger blocks of cells, as might happen with clustered rather than uniformly distributed defects, the address of the defective blocks is stored in an associative memory. This way, any incoming request to an address within the defective block will be redirected to a spare block. The spare block has a smaller size compared to the main memory array and consequently, its access time is substantially smaller. Thus, even with the additional time required to access the associative memory before spare block can be accessed, the overall time increase is less than two percent. The increase in power consumption is also insignificant (less than 0.6 percent). However, the area is increased substantially higher than the row (column) spare scheme, ranging from 10 percent for 64 kilobits to 27 percent for 1 megabit.

A different approach to yield enhancement suggests the use of partially good chips. If a section in a one megabit memory is defective beyond repair, we can reconfigure the chip to a usable 0.5 megabit or even a 0.25 megabit chip. To do this we must partition the circuitry of the chip into circuit blocks in such a way that fault free sections can function independently. The probability of finding M fault-free circuits blocks in a chip that consists of N circuits blocks can be calculated using Binomial coefficient. The partially good yield is formulated as

$$Y_{MN} = \frac{N!}{M!(N-M)!} \sum_{n=M}^{N} (-1)^{n-M} \frac{(N-M)!}{(n-M)!(N-n)!} Y_{nCB} \qquad (11.13)$$

where Y_{nCB} is the probability of finding n fault-free circuit blocks, obtained using the formula

$$Y_{nCB} = (1 + n\overline{\lambda}_{CB}/\alpha)^{-\alpha} \qquad (11.14)$$

where $[(\overline{\lambda})]_{CB}$ is the average number of faults per circuit block and α is the cluster parameter.

A wide variety of techniques have been used to repair integrated circuits. Many of these are similar to those techniques used for programmable integrated circuits. Some of the known techniques are metallization technique, laser surgery, electrical surgery, packaging technique and programmable technique.

11.4 Effect of Redundancy on Yield

Consider a chip with a single type of identical modules. Let N denotes the number of these modules. Define the following probability

$a_{M,N}$ = Probability of exactly M out of N modules are fault free

Assuming large-area clustering and negative Binomial distribution, the formula $a_{M,N}$ is given by

$$a_{M,N} = \sum_{k=0}^{N-M} (-1)^k \binom{N-M}{k}\binom{N}{M}\left[1+\frac{\bar{\lambda}_{CK}+(M+k)\bar{\lambda}}{\alpha}\right]^{-\alpha} \quad (11.15)$$

where $[(\bar{\lambda}_{CK})]$ is the average number of *fatal faults* - or *chip kill* faults - in the support circuits.

We can use this probability to calculate the yield of chips having redundancy. The overall yield of chip with redundancy is then

$$Y = Y_0 \sum_{M=N-R}^{N} a_{M,N} \quad (11.16)$$

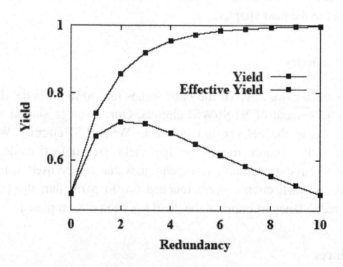

Fig. 11.5: Effective yield versus redundancy.

The yield expression in Eq. (11.16) can help finding the optimal amount of redundancy for a given fault-tolerant scheme. The optimal redundancy maximizes the number of acceptable chips per wafer. When the redundancy increases, the yield of the individual chip tend to increase, but the number of chips per wafer is decreased. Therefore, the term *effective yield* which is the chip yield multiplied by the ratio between the number of chips with and without redundancy is used.

Figure 11.5 shows the effective yield versus redundancy for a given gross yield. It is shown that the effective yield increases when redundancy is incorporated in the wafer until a certain point at which the effective yield declines. Therefore, depending on the amount of redundancy used and the chip area (including interconnections), the yield improvement will vary.

The most obvious candidates for yield enhancement using redundancy are those architectures which has a large number of identical cells and for which spare cells can be switched in to replace faulty ones. Memory chips certainly have such regular structure and are particularly suitable because there is no interaction between cells. Another possible architecture is in the form of VLSI/WSI processor arrays, which will be discussed in the next chapter.

11.5 Summary

In this Chapter, we covered the basic issues related to the reliability and yield enhancement of VLSI/WSI circuits. Our coverage started with an introduction to the defects and failure in WSI/VLSI circuits. We then introduced the issues related to the yield and defect modeling in VLSI/WSI circuits. A number of techniques that can be used to improve the yield of such circuits were touched on. In particular, the effect of adding redundancy to improve the yield has been contemplated.

References

[1]   C. H. Stapper and F. A. Armstrong and K. Saji. Integrated Circuits Yield Statistics. *Proceeding of the IEEE*, 17(4):453-470, April 1983.

[2]   T. E. Mangir and C. S. Raghavendra. Issues in the Implementation of Fault Tolerant VLSI and Wafer Scale Integrated System. *IEEE Proceeding ICCD'84*, 1984.

[3] C. H. Stapper. Large Area Fault Clusters and Fault Tolerance in VLSI Circuits: A Review. *IBM Journal Res. Develop*, 33(2):162-173, March 1989.

[4] C. H. Stapper. Small Area Fault Clusters and Fault Tolerance in VLSI Circuits. *IBM Journal Res. Develop*, 33(2):174-177, March 1989.

[5] G. Moore. VLSI: Some Fundamental Changes. *IEEE Spectrum*, 16(4), 1979.

[6] J. A. Cunningham. The Use and Evaluation of Yield Models in Integrated Circuit Manufacturing. *IEEE Trans. on Semiconductor Manufacturing*, 3(2):60-71, May 1990.

[7] T. J. Wallmark. Design considerations for integrated electron devices. *Proc. IRE*, 48:293-300, March 1960.

[8] C. H. Stapper. Effects of wafer to wafer defect density variations on integrated circuit defect and fault distributions. *IBM Journal of Research and Development*, 29(1):87-97, January 1985.

[9] C. H. Stapper. Correlation analysis of particle clusters on integrated circuit wafers. *IBM Journal of Research and Development*, 31(6):641-650, November 1987.

[10] T. L. Michalka and Ramesh C. Varshney and J. D. Meindl. A discussion of yield modelling with defect clustering, circuit repair, and circuit redundancy. *IEEE Trans. Semiconductor Manufacturing*, 3(3):116-127, Aug. 1990.

[11] I. Koren and Adit D. Singh. Fault tolerance in VLSI circuits. *Computer*, 23(7):73-83, July 1990.

[12] T. Yanagawa. Yield Degradation of Integrated Circuits Due to Spot Defects. *IEEE Trans. Electron Devices*, ED-19:190-197, Feb. 1972.

[13] D. M. H. Walker. *Yield Simulation for Integrated Circuits*. Kluwer, Norwell, MA, 1987.

[14] A. V. Ferris-Prabhu, L. D. Smith, and H. A. Bonges. Radial yield variations in semiconductor wafers. *IEEE Circuits and Devices Magazines*, 3:42-47, March 1987.

[15] Z. Koren, I. Koren, and C. H. Stapper. A statistical study of defect map of large area vlsi ic's. *IEEE Trans. on VLSI*, 2(2):249-256, June 1994.

[16] Z. Koren, I. Koren, and C. H. Stapper. A unified negative binomial distribution for yield analysis of defect tolerant circuits. *IEEE Trans. Computers*, 42(6):724-733, June 1993.

[17] William R. Moore. A review of fault-tolerant techniques for the enhancement of integrated circuit yield. *IEEE Proceeding*, 74(5):684-698, May 1986.

[18] C. H. Stapper, Andrew N. McLaren, and Martin Dreckmann. Yield model for productivity optimization of VLSI memory chips with redundancy and partially good product. *IBM Journal of Research and Development*, 24(3):398-409, May 1980.

[19] D. K. Pradhan and I. Koren. Yield and performance enhancement through redundancy in vlsi and wsi multiprocessor system. *IEEE proc.*, 74(5), May 1986.

[20] T. E. Mangir and A. Avizienis. Fault-tolerant design for vlsi: Effect of interconnection requirements on yield improvement of vlsi designs. *IEEE Trans. Computers*, 31(7):609-615, July 1982.

Chapter 12

Design of Fault-Tolerant Processor Arrays

In this chapter, we consider the issues related to the design of fault-tolerant processor arrays. Our coverage starts by providing some background material and useful terminology. Hardware redundancy techniques used in processor arrays are introduced in Section 2. The techniques covered include local, global, and the hybrid techniques. The issues related to self reconfigurable systems are covered in Section 3. These include the biologically inspired and the artificial neural network-based techniques.

12.1 Introduction

With the present VLSI/WSI technology, it is economically feasible to implement massively parallel processor arrays consisting of a large number of fine-grained regular processing elements (PEs). The advantages offered by PEs include low assembly cost, high reliability and high performance. Figure 12.1 shows a number of different topologies that are used in the manufacturing of processor arrays. Among these, hexagonal arrays are flexible and can be adopted for various algorithms. However, the inclusion of fault tolerance aspects in hexagonal arrays could be more complicated and less efficient since each PE is connected to six neighboring PEs. In this context, most fault-tolerant reconfiguration schemes assume the use of rectangular arrays.

Design Analysis

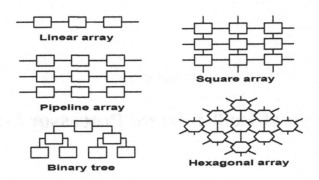

Fig. 12.1: Different topologies in processor arrays.

In general, the yield and/or reliability of a processor array can be enhanced by employing redundant Processing Elements (PEs) to replace faulty ones. The regularity of VLSI/WSI architectures allows fault tolerance to be achieved through redundancy in a cost-effective manner. Redundancy can be introduced by adding a limited number of redundant PEs that act as spares together with suitably augmented, but still regular, interconnection network.

One basic technique for introducing fault tolerance into processor arrays is through array reconfiguration. The rationale behind introducing reconfigureability into array architectures is twofold:

1. Yield enhancement to provide manufacturing cost-effectiveness
2. Reliability and performance enhancement to counter act the effects of operational faults.

A *fault-tolerant processor array* (FTPA) is a rectangular array of identical and regularly interconnected PEs incorporating redundant circuitry (spares) and hardware for reconfiguration. A FTPA can be considered as consisting of $(M+R) \times (N+C)$ PEs in which M and N represent, respectively, the number of rows and columns, while R and C represent, respectively, the number of spare rows and spare columns. A *cell* is a PE in a FTPA.

The structure of the processor array influences to a great extent the design of the reconfiguration scheme that can be used. The concept of logical array and physical array is defined as follows. A *physical FTPA* is a non-reconfigured FTPA that can contain faulty cells. A cell in physical FTPA is denoted by (i, j), where i and j represent the cells coordinates, $1 \leq i \leq (M+R)$, $1 \leq j \leq (N+C)$. A *logical FTPA* is a reconfigured FTPA that is fully operational. A cell in a logical FTPA is denoted by [i,j] where i and j represent its logical coordinates, $1 \leq i \leq M$, $1 \leq j \leq N$.

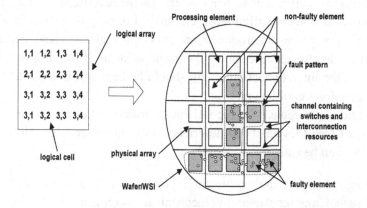

Fig. 12.2: Mapping of a logical array onto a physical array.

An *array reconfiguration* is a mapping Ψ of cells in the logical FTPA into functional cells in the physical FTPA. Thus $\Psi ([i,j]) = (k,l)$ if logical cell [i,j] corresponds to physical cell (k,l). If a mapping between all cells in a logical FTPA and cells in a physical FTPA exists, the reconfiguration is said to be successful. Figure 12.2 shows an example for mapping a logical array into a physical array.

There are two types of reconfiguration schemes, *static reconfiguration* and *dynamic reconfiguration*. Static reconfiguration is performed at array fabrication time and often uses hard (fixed) interconnections to bypass defective cells to enhance yield. Dynamic reconfiguration is performed during the operational lifetime of the array and uses soft (programmable) interconnections to logically replace faulty cells to improve reliability. Since failure can occur during the lifetime of FTPA, dynamic reconfiguration is more attractive than the static one. Moreover, dynamic reconfiguration offers the important characteristic of evolving with respect to failure, so that the system can adapt to the changing environment.

Evaluation of reconfiguration algorithms can be done using four figures of merit. These merits are: *complexity of the algorithm*, *utilization*, *area*, and *locality*. Utilization refers to spare usage. The term *harvesting* is used as a measure for utilization. Harvesting refers to the percentage of non-faulty cells that an algorithm is able to utilize in the array as active cells. Area refers to the overhead of the added interconnect and reconfiguration circuitry. Locality is measured as the length of physical interconnection between logically adjacent cells. Locality determines the delay between adjacent PEs. For real-time systems, the interconnection length should be kept within a limit, so that *hard deadlines* could be met.

Various strategies to reconfigure/restructure faulty physical PEs into fault free PEs has been described in the literature. Reconfiguration schemes can be categorized based on:

1. Logical array Topology: linear, rectangular, tree, or hexagonal
2. Logical array configuration mechanism: incremental or shifting
3. Logical cell Mapping domain: fixed or variable
4. Replacement unit: group of cells or a single cell
5. Hierarchy of reconfiguration: multi-level or single-level
6. Types of redundancy: hardware or time
7. Objective of reconfiguration: functionality or fault tolerance
8. Reconfiguration strategy: static, dynamic or hybrid

Each reconfiguration technique can be classified according to some (or all) of the above categories. In this Chapter, we focus the discussion on hardware redundancy techniques.

12.2 Hardware Redundancy Techniques

Hardware redundancy techniques, use large amount of spares to replace faulty PEs. Based on the allocation of spares, hardware redundancy is classified into local redundancy, global redundancy, hierarchical redundancy, or hybrid redundancy. These are explained below.

Local Techniques

In local redundancy techniques, structural regularity and locality of processing are the main objectives. The reconfiguration technique tends to preserve locality and therefore the number of spares introduced is considered to be high. The utilization of spares is forsaken and the yield improvement is expected to be limited. However, local techniques guarantee that the delay associated with the interconnection path after reconfiguration will be within a pre-defined limit.

In interstitial redundancy, locality is achieved by partitioning a given $N \times N$ array into smaller sub-arrays each of size $M \times M$ and confining spare cells inside each individual sub-array. For instance, a 25% interstitial redundancy array is shown in Fig. 12.3. In this case, each spare is assigned to a cluster of four primary cells. The spare cell in the interstice of a sub-array can be used only for that subarray. The failure of more than one cell in a sub-array will lead to failure of reconfiguration of that particular sub-array and consequently the unsuccessful reconfiguration of the whole array.

The analytical estimation of the yield for the interstitial shown in Fig. 12.3 can be carried out as follows. Assume that all cells have the same fault free probability, p, while the switch and interconnection network are fault free. For a sub-array, the yield will be given by:

$$y = p^5 + 5p^4(1-p)$$

For p = 0.9 the yield will be 0.92. If the array size is 8×8, then the yield of the array will become $(0.92)^{16} \cong 0.26$. As can be seen, increasing chip area through increasing the number of PEs together with the needed interconnection leads to a fall in the yield.

Interstitial redundancy requires the use of a supporting interconnection network. This is shown in part (b) of Fig. 12.3. Two types of switching elements are needed. Eight global switching elements (shown as a circle in Fig. 12.3) are needed, each can exist in one of two states. In addition, eight local switching elements (shown as square in Fig. 12.3) are needed, each can exist in one of four different states.

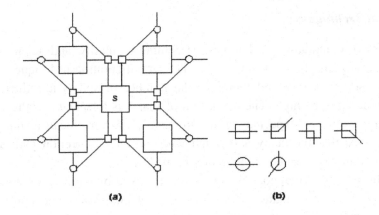

Fig. 12.3: Interstitial redundancy: (a) network structure (b) switch states.

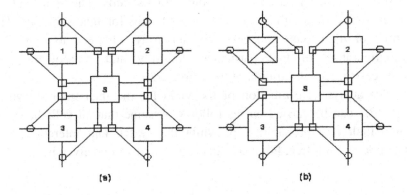

Fig. 12.4: Array configuration for different fault patterns (a) no cell is faulty (b) one cell is faulty.

Consider, for example, the fault-free and the faulty cases shown in Fig. 12.4. Part (a) of the figure shows array configuration when the sub-array is fault-free. In this case, the eight global switching elements are programmed so as to allow the four main PEs to communicate with their immediate neighbors in the neighboring sub-arrays. The spare PE is not used. This is to be compared to the case shown in part (b) of Fig. 12.4. In this case, PE #1 is assumed to be faulty. Accordingly, the array configuration will change such that PE#1 is bypassed and is replaced by the spare PE. That will require programming both global and local switching elements as shown in the figure. It should be noted that failure of another PE in the same sub-array cannot be accommodated and will result in the failure of the sub-array reconfiguration process. Thus, a 25% interstitial redundancy will fail to reconfigure the array if more than one cell per sub-array is faulty.

Interstitial redundancy techniques and the supporting interconnection network needed are considered to be simple. However, the spare utilization for this technique is considerably low.

Global Techniques

Global reconfiguration techniques make use of global redundancy by incorporating spare rows and/or columns to bypass faulty cells. A number of global-based techniques are discussed below.

Row/Column Elimination

In this technique, the processor array is provided with a number of spare rows as well as spare columns. A general outline of the problem is given as follows: All faulty cells are discarded by eliminating a suitable set of rows and columns containing them. The cost of this operation, defined as the number of fault free cells eliminated by the reconfiguration, must be minimized. The choice of the set of rows and columns that must be deleted (discarded from the working array) is proven to be an NP-complete problem. The problem can be solved by using the *association matrix* M_a or the *bipartite graph*.

An *association matrix* M_a is built such that any given row i in the matrix corresponds to one position of faulty cell; while each column corresponds, in order, to the rows $r_1,...r_N$ and the column $c_1...c_N$ of the physical array that contains faulty cells. Thus, row i represents the *i-th* faulty cell in the physical array, with coordinates (j, k). A set of column of M_a must be chosen so as to cover all its rows.

Consider, for example, the faulty array shown in Fig. 12.5. In this figure, blackened cells indicate faulty sells. Rows are numbered 1 to 6 from top to bottom and columns are numbered 1 to 6 from left to right. The corresponding association matrix M_a for the faulty array shown in Fig. 12.5 is shown in the Table 12.1. There are two marks in row i, one in correspondence to row r_j and the other one in correspondence to column c_k.

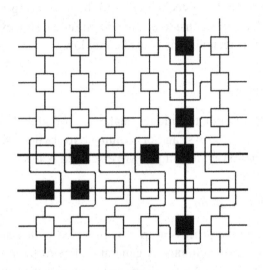

Fig. 12.5: Row/column elimination scheme.

To optimize the use of spares, we need to select the column in the association matrix that covers a large number of faulty cells. For example in Table 12.1, column c_5 covers 4 faulty cells, i.e. cell (1,5), (3,5), (4,5) and (6,5). If we take this column and replace it with a spare column (in the physical array), the columns under headings r_1, r_3, and r_6 of the association matrix can be eliminated, and one faulty cell in the column under heading r_4, i.e. cell (4,5) is also covered. Thus, by replacing columns under heading r_4 and r_5 of the association matrix with spare rows in the physical array and the column c_5 of association matrix with a spare column in the physical array, all faulty cells are covered and replaced, and the reconfiguration is successfully performed.

Table 12.1: Association matrix for the faulty array shown in Fig. 12.5.

	r_1	r_3	r_4	r_5	r_6	c_1	c_2	c_4	c_5
1,5	X	.	.	.	.	.	.	.	X
3,5	.	X	.	.	.	.	.	.	X
4,2	.	.	X	.	.	.	X	.	.
4,4	.	.	X	.	.	.	.	X	.
4,5	.	.	X	.	.	.	.	.	X
5,1	.	.	.	X	.	X	.	.	.
5,2	.	.	.	X	.	.	X	.	.
6,5	.	.	.	.	X	.	.	.	X

An alternative representation to the association matrix is to use a *bipartite graph*. For a graph G, let:

- The set of vertices V_r represents the rows of the array
- The set of vertices V_c represents the columns of the array
- A function f is defined so as to connect a vertex in V_r with a vertex in V_c if the corresponding cell in the array is faulty.

The reconfiguration scheme has to find the minimum number of vertices selected from the graph to cover all faulty cells.

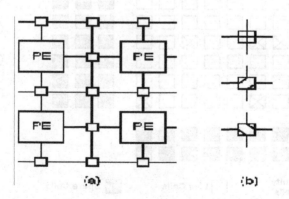

Fig. 12.6: Network supporting row/column elimination technique (a) interconnection (b) switch states.

The interconnection network required in order to support the reconfiguration according to this algorithm is shown in Fig. 12.6. In this case, one type of switching elements is needed. Each switching element can exist in one of three states as shown in part (b) of Fig. 12.6. As can be seen, the row/column elimination algorithm has the advantage of setting a predefined bound on interconnection links. However, the complexity of algorithm and the low spare utilization are the main drawback for this algorithm.

Selection of the minimum number of these vertices is shown to be an NP-complete problem. Some algorithms have been proposed to tackle the problem. A sub-optimal solution, the repair-most strategy, is discussed in the next section.

Repair-Most Strategy

The repair-most strategy is proposed to overcome the problem of the row/column elimination strategy. The philosophy can be described as to try to identify the rows and the columns with the largest number of faulty cells and eliminate them first.

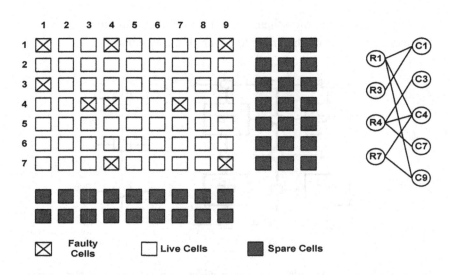

Fig. 12.7: Repair most strategy.

Consider, for example, the $(7+2) \times (9+3)$ FTPA shown in the Fig. 12.7. In the repair-most strategy, the array is represented in a bipartite graph whose two sets of vertices are the array rows and columns that contain faulty cells. The elimination starts from the row/column that contains the largest number of faults. In our case, the repair-most strategy replaces R_1 and R_4 with the two spare rows and C_1, C_4 and C_9 with the three spare columns, and the configuration algorithm is successful, as shown in Fig. 12.8 (with spares being omitted).

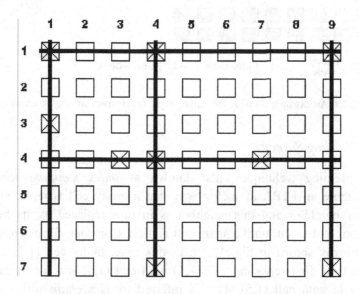

Fig. 12.8: Reconfigured array by repair most strategy.

The repair-most strategy does not, however, guarantee optimality. The algorithm may even fail with small number of faults if the faults are scattered thorough the array. Consider, for example, the faulty array shown in Fig. 12.9. It should be noted that although the number of faulty PEs in Fig. 12.9 is the same as those in the example shown in Fig. 8, however, the repair-most technique will fail to reconfigure the array. The algorithm replaces R_1 and R_4 with the two spare rows and C_1, C_4 and C_5 with the three spare columns. However, faulty cell (7,9) is left uncovered.

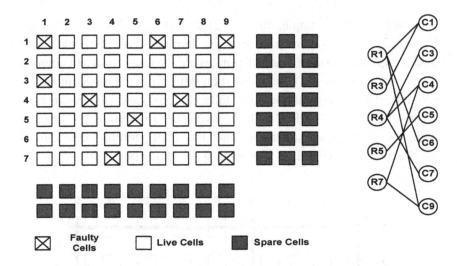

Fig. 12.9: An example showing the failure of the repair-most strategy to reconfigure.

Fault Stealing Strategy

Fault stealing techniques, also known as *index mapping* schemes, reconfigure an FTPA in such a way that a faulty cell is replaced by a healthy neighbor and this neighbor is in turn replaced by its healthy neighbor and so on, until a spare cell is used. Consider, for example, the faulty array shown in Fig. 12.10. In this case, faulty cell (1,3) can be replaced by first replacing cell (1,3) with cell (1,4) and then replacing cell (1,4) with cell (1,5). This is referred to as a *chain shift*. This is because the replacement consists of a chain of functional shifting from the fault site until a spare cell is reached.

There are two types of fault stealing: simple fault stealing (SFS) and complex fault stealing (CFS) algorithms. Each of these can be both with fixed and variable choice features. In what follows, we explain the simple fault stealing and complex fault stealing fixed choice algorithms.

In simple fault stealing (SFS) approach, (the function of) a faulty cell (i,j) can be shifted right to (that of) a fault free cell $(i,j+1)$ or down to $(i+1,j)$. The set consisting of cells $(i,j),(i,j+1)$ and $(i+1,j)$ is referred to as an *adjacency domain*.

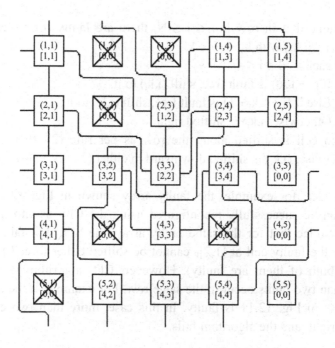

Fig. 12.10: Example of simple fault stealing (SFS).

In conducting a SFS, the array is scanned row-wise, the first faulty cell in a given row is defined as *horizontal fault*, while the second faulty cell in the same row is defined as *vertical fault*. Thus, for the array shown in Fig. 12.10, cells (5,1), (4,2), (1,3) and (4,4) are defined as *vertical faults* and other faulty cells are defined *horizontal faults*. To reconfigure the array, horizontal faults are chain-shifted right, and vertical faults are chain-shifted down. In Fig. 12.10, cells (1,2) and (2,2) are chain-shifted right, and cells (4,2), (1,3), and (4,4) are chain shifted down. The faulty array in the figure is successfully reconfigured using this SFS algorithm.

In complex fault stealing (CFS), the cell at $(i+1, j+1)$ is added to adjacency domain. Thus, unlike SFS, the fault in cell (i,j) can be shifted to $(i, j+1)$, $(i+1, j)$, and $(i+1, j+1)$. For an $(N+1) \times (N+1)$ array, the CFS is outlined below.

1. Assume that in row i, $1 \leq i \leq N$, there are faulty (or stolen) cells $(i,k_1)...(i,k_s)$ with $k_1 < \cdots < k_s$.
2. For each k_i, $0 < i < s$;
    a) If $(i+1,k_i)$ is fault free, shift (i,k_i) to it.
    b) Else if $(i+1,k_i+1)$ is fault free, shift (i,k_i) to it.
    c) Otherwise (i,k_i) is shifted right.
3. If no cell is shifted along the row as per rule (2), then (i,k_s) is, otherwise, (i,k_i) is shifted downward to either $(i+1,k_s)$ or $(i+1,k_s)$.

Consider, for example, the faulty array shown in Fig. 12.11. This array can be successfully reconfigured using the CFS as shown in the figure. Notice that for the same faulty array, the SFS will fail. This is because the faulty cell at $[1,2]_P$ cannot be shifted either to cell $[1,3]_P$ or $[2,2]_P$ (both of them are faulty). However, CFS algorithm will fail if more than two faults occur in the same row. For example, if the physical cell (2,4) in Fig. 12.11 is faulty. In this case, more than two cells are shifted right, and the algorithm fails.

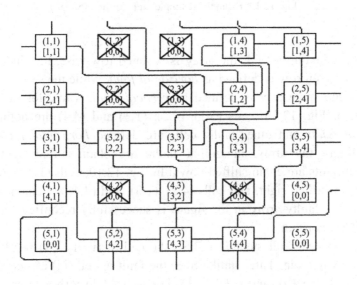

Fig. 12.11: Example of complex fault stealing (CFS).

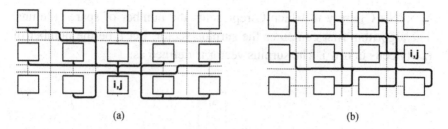

(a)   (b)

Fig. 12.12: Set of possible connections in CFS (a) vertical connection (b) horizontal connection.

The interconnection requirement for CFS becomes more complex than that required by all previous algorithms. Each cell may receive data from all its possible (alternative) *input adjacent*. The set possible connections between vertical and horizontal neighbors in CFS are shown in Fig. 12.12. The interconnection can be done by using switch bus architecture shown in Fig. 12.13.

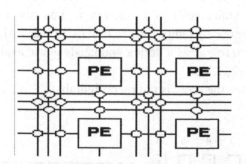

Fig. 12.13: Network supporting CFS.

FUSS (Full Use of Suitable Spare)

The FUSS is based on the fault shifting strategy. Non-faulty cells are shifted from regions with lesser faulty cells to regions with more faulty ones. The strategy uses an indicator vector called the *surplus vector*, to guide replacement of faulty cells. In FUSS-C the FTPA is an

$M \times (N + C)$ array in which C represents the number of spare columns. The algorithm first computes the surplus vector. Let f_i be the number of faulty cells in row i. The surplus vector is defined as:

$$S = \begin{bmatrix} s_1 \\ s_2 \\ \vdots \\ s_M \end{bmatrix}$$

where

$$s_i = \sum_{j-1}^{i} (C - f_i) = C_i - \sum_{j-1}^{I} f_i$$

is the surplus of row i. The rules of the algorithm are as follows.

1. If $s_i > 0$ the sum of spares in the row 1 through i is greater than the number of faulty cells in 1 through i, thus row i has extra cells available for use by faulty cells in row $i + 1, i + 2, \ldots M$.
2. If $s_i < 0$, then row i has a deficit and needs to use available cells from row $i + 1, i + 2, \ldots M$.
3. If $s_M < 0$, then the array is not reconfigurable.

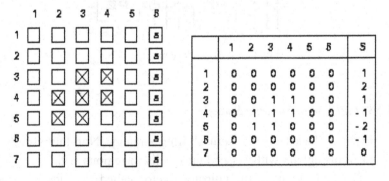

Fig. 12.14: Initial physical array.

Consider, for example, the array shown in Fig. 12.14, matrix A in the figure represents a $7 \times (5+1)$ array. The table given below shows a physical arrangement of cells where 1 represents a faulty cell. The surplus vector is obtained according to the Equation given before. With d denotes a shift down and a u denotes a shift up, the reconfiguration proceeds as follows:

1. Scan array upwards; when $s_i < 0$ shift a number equal to $|s_i|$ of faulty cells in row i to fault free cells in row $i+1$. When all $|(s_i)|$ cells are shifted successfully, s_i is reset to 0. For example in Fig. 12.14, one cell must be shifted from row 4 to row 5; cell (4,4) is shifted down to cell (5,4), which assumes the status code of d and s_4 is adjusted to 0. Cells (5,2) and (5,3) are also shifted down to cell (6,2) and (6,3), and s_5 is adjusted to 0.

2. Scan array downward; when $s_i > 0$ shift a number equal to $|s_i|$ of faulty cells in row i+1 to fault free cells in row i. When all $|(s_i)|$ cells are shifted successfully, s_i is reset to 0. Thus, cell (4,2) is shifted up to cell (3,2), which assume the status code of u and s_4 is adjusted to 0. Cell (3,3) is also shifted up to cell (2,3); and s_3 is adjusted to 0.

Fault shifting is performed, such that $s_1, s_2, \ldots s_M$ are all zero as shown below.

	1	2	3	4	5	8	S
1	0	0	0	0	0	0	0
2	0	0	u	0	0	0	0
3	0	u	1	1	0	0	0
4	0	1	1	1	0	0	0
5	0	1	1	d	0	0	0
8	0	d	d	0	0	0	0
7	0	0	0	0	0	0	0

The reconfiguration result is shown in Fig. 12.15.

1,1	2,2	1,2	1,3	1,4	1,5
2,1	3,2	3,3	2,3	2,4	2,5
3,1	4,2	0,0	0,0	3,4	3,5
4,1	0,0	0,0	0,0	4,4	4,5
5,1	0,0	0,0	4,3	5,4	5,5
6,1	5,2	5,3	6,3	6,4	6,5
7,1	6,2	7,2	7,3	7,4	7,5

Fig. 12.15: Final reconfigured array using FUSS.

The size of horizontal connection window $|W_H|$ and the size of vertical connection window $|W_V|$ of cell are given by

$$|W_H| = 5(C + 1)$$

$$|W_V| = 4(2C + 1) - 1$$

Where C is the number of row(column) spares. The connection window for a FUSS-1 is shown in Fig. 12.16.

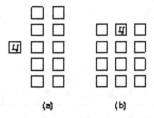

(a)   (b)

Fig. 12.16: FUSS-1 physical connection windows. (a) W_H. (b) W_V.

The algorithm ensures perfect fault coverage, under the assumption that all types of interconnections are possible. With switch interconnection resources shown in Fig. 12.17, successful reconfiguration in 90–98% of faulty cases is reported in the literature. The main drawback of this algorithm is the complexity of the algorithm that increases with the increase of the array size, and the interconnection delay that may not be limited.

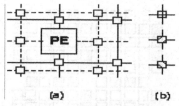

Fig. 12.17: FUSS: (a) switch and PEs interconnection (b) switch states.

The drawback of the global techniques approach is the relatively high requirements of interconnection and switching networks. The algorithm may result in high delay between cells in the array. Therefore, this approach is useful when delays due to interconnection are not crucial.

Hybrid Techniques

The hybrid approach is a slight deviation from the hierarchical approach with global redundancy in both levels. Instead of using dedicated spares in each block, the spares are shared between neighboring blocks as shown in Fig. 12.18. In this technique, the percentage of spare is expected to be higher than the one used in global techniques, but at the same time, higher percentage of array survivability is expected to be achieved. A number of hybrid techniques have been introduced in the literature. Among these, the array partitioning, single track switch, and the rule-based techniques are discussed below.

Array Partitioning

This algorithm partitions an $M \times N$ array into $M/L \times N/W$ identical $L \times W$ sub-arrays. Each sub-array (or block) is equipped with spare cells as illustrated in Fig. 12.18. The reconfiguration is performed locally inside each sub-array. Small target sub-arrays are thus created, and global reconfiguration is then accomplished by connecting the target sub-arrays according to a particular order. Since there is either a spare row or a spare column between neighboring (adjacent) sub-arrays, then both, or some, of these can be used by each of the neighboring sub-arrays.

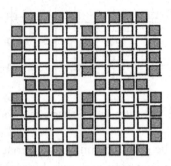

Fig. 12.18: Array structure for hybrid technique.

The reconfiguration of faulty elements is performed within each sub-array independently. Depending on the number of faulty elements in a sub-array, a faulty element is moved through a chain of replacements in one direction dictated by the following procedure. If cell $(r,c)_B$ in a block is faulty then count the total number of faulty cells at row r in the corresponding sub-array and represent it with p. Similarly, the total number of faulty cells in column c is represented as q. The replacement rules for replacing a faulty cell (r,c) by a fault-free spare located either in row r or in column c are given below.

1. case #1 (p=q): use the general rule: up $\rightarrow$ left $\rightarrow$ right $\rightarrow$ down sequence to borrow a spare cell to replace the faulty cell (r,c)
2. case #2 (p > q): use the column priority rule: up $\rightarrow$ down $\rightarrow$ left $\rightarrow$ right sequence
3. case #3 (p < q): use the column priority rule: left $\rightarrow$ right $\rightarrow$ up $\rightarrow$ down sequence

If for a faulty element a spare cannot be borrowed using the above three rules, the array reconfiguration fails. Consider, for example, the faulty sub-array shown in Fig. 12.19. According to the rules listed above, cell (1,1) is faulty. The number of other faulty cells in row 1 is one, i.e., p = 1 and the number of other faulty cells in column 1 is one, i.e., q = 1. This indicates that rule #1 is to be applied. According to this rule cell (1,1) will be replaced from the upward spare row while faulty cell (1,4) will be replaced from the left spare column. Similar manner is followed in replacing the remaining faulty cells in the sub-array. Part (b) of Fig. 19 illustrates the performed replacements following the rules. Part (c) of Fig. 19 shows the final indices assignment for this faulty sub-array. As can be seen, the supporting interconnection network needed for performing the array partitioning technique is in general expensive. Communication delay is bounded by the sub-array size.

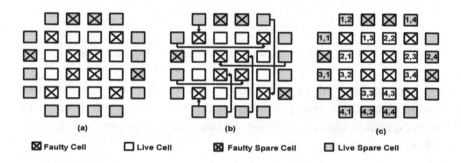

Fig. 12.19: Reconfiguration example of hybrid technique. (a) fault pattern. (b) reconfiguration. (c) final result.

Single Track Switch Reconfiguration

Single track means the existence of only one communication path along each horizontal/vertical channel. An example of an architecture that provides a single track switch is shown in Fig. 12.20. An important assumption made according to the single track switch reconfiguration is that faulty cells can be used as (converted into) connecting elements. This eliminates the requirement for interconnection resources (wires/switches) to bypass faulty cells. Thus, use of single track switch architecture not only saves area but also makes the assumption of fault free switches/wires more realistic, compared to other algorithms that use multiple-track switches.

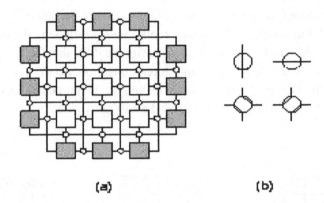

Fig. 12.20: Single track switch (a) physical array (b) switch states.

The structure of physical array used is the same as that used in the case of the array partitioning structure (see Fig. 12.20 (a)). The reconfiguration algorithm consists of two tasks: Placement and Routing. These are explained below.

1. **Placement:** A placement is defined using a one-to-one function, which maps all the logical indices to those of healthy cells in the physical array. A mapping $P(i,j) = (x,y)$ means that physical cell (x,y) is labeled with a logical index (i,j). Here the vertical axis uses x (i) index and the horizontal uses y axis (j) index.

2. **Routing:** On the physical array, a path linking $P(i,j)$ and $P(i+1,j)$ is called a *vertical link* and a path linking $P(i,j)$ and $P(i,j+1)$ is called a *horizontal link*. A *valid routing* means the establishment of all horizontal and vertical links in the physical array.

If no fault occurs, the logical indices will be the same as their physical indices, i.e., $(i,j) = (x,y)$. If a non-spare cell (x,y) is faulty, then it may be replaced by a healthy cell at say (x',y'), which in turn will be replaced by another cell at say (x'',y''), and so on. This replacement will eventually terminate when a spare cell is reached. The sequence of physical cells (x,y), (x',y'), (x'',y'')... involved in the chain reaction is called the *compensation path*. An example of a compensation path can be seen in Fig. 12.21(a).

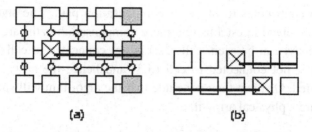

Fig. 12.21: Single switch track: (a) compensation path (b) near miss.

There should be as many compensation paths as there are faulty cells. These compensation paths have to be mutually exclusive, since a fault free cell cannot be used to replace more than one faulty cell. For each fault-free cell with physical location (x,y) there are four possible *straight compensation paths*: the *south, north, east* and *west*. These are respectively denoted as $[x^+,y]$, $[x^-,y]$, $[x,y^+]$, and $[x,y^-]$. Two horizontal compensation paths $[x_1,y_1^+]$ and $[x_2,y_2^-]$ are declared *near miss* if $|x_1-x_2| = 1$ and $y_1 < y_2$, see Fig. 12.21(b).

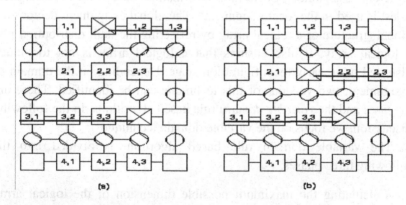

Fig. 12.22: Effect of near-miss on reconfiguration (a) A non near miss (b) An example of a near miss.

Consider the example shown in Fig. 12.22. Part (a) of the figure shows successful array reconfiguration when near miss condition does not exist. In part (b) of the figure, near miss condition occurs due to fault at $(2,2)_P$ and $(3,3)_P$. It is clear that the faulty cell in the second row contributes to the east compensation path, while the faulty cell in the third row contributes to the west compensation path. The states of the switches involved in establishing these compensation paths are shown in the figure. As can be seen, cell (2,2) is not connected to cell (3,2), and cell (2,3) is not connected to cell (3,3) and hence the array cannot be reconfigured. One can then conclude that the algorithm will successfully reconfigure a physical array if:

1. there exists a set of continuous and straight compensation paths covering all the faulty cells
2. there is neither intersection nor near miss among the compensation paths

Rule Based Algorithm

The main idea behind rule based reconfiguration technique is to identify a domain of assignment for faulty cells based on the fault distribution. According to this algorithm, fault distribution information is utilized in the global assignment. Local fault information, based on cell assignment rules, is used in the local assignment. The global assignment decides the global structure of a logical array by reflecting the fault distribution into a logical array. It also ensures that a logical array is not too much distorted in an early reconfiguration stage. Depending on the domain of assignment, two versions of this technique can be identified. These are the *fixed* and the *variable domain* rule based algorithms. In the following discussion, we focus on the variable domain technique.

The variable domain rule based algorithm is divided into the following three phases.

1. Calculating the maximum possible dimension of the logical array and determining the safe domains (see definition below). Each logical cell is assigned to its safe domain. If all cells are assigned, reconfiguration is successful.
2. Generating the *virtual spare tree* (see definition below) for the unassigned logical cell(s). If a virtual spare cell is in the safe domain, virtual spare assignment is applied. If all cells are assigned, reconfiguration is successful.
3. Applying the rule-based assignment for the remaining cells.

The algorithm starts by determining the safe domain for each logical cell. The *safe domain* of a logical cell is defined as the first domain of row and column range in the corresponding physical cell. Then, each logical cell is assigned to a fault free cell in each its safe domain. Any matching algorithm can be used for this purpose. However, since the matching problem is an NP-complete problem, a greedy method can be used whereby each logical cell is assigned by scanning its safe domain from the boundary inward to the center. Unassigned logical cells during this phase will be assigned in the local assignment phase.

Consider, for example, a faulty $(7+1) \times (7+1)$ array with 15 faulty cells ash shown in Fig. 12.23. A faulty cell is identified with index $(0,0)$ in the figure. The fault pattern, safe domain for each logical cell, and the result of the global assignment phase as explained above are shown in Fig. 12.23. Notice that logical cells $[2,4]_L$, $[3,4]_L$, and $[4,3]_L$ have not been assigned yet, while physical cells $[1,6]_P$, $[4,7]_P$, and $[8,3]_P$ are declared as spare cells.

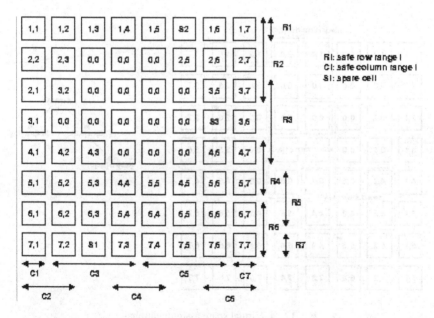

Fig. 12.23: Global assignment phase.

The *virtual spare assignment* is applied to match the unassigned logical cell (without violating the safe domain constraint). Virtual spare cells are generated first in the form of a tree data structure, called *virtual spare tree*, which has a spare cell as the root. Each child denotes a fault free cell whose previously assigned logical cell can be assigned to the parent node within its safe domain. Hence, *virtual spare cell* can be used as spare cells by assigning an already assigned logical cell to other fault free cell in its domain, until S (spare) is reached.

Consider the faulty array shown in Fig. 12.23. In this case, cell $[6,3]_L$ can be assigned to the spare cell $S_1 = [8,3]_P$ without violating the safe domain constraint. This is because S_1 is in the safe domain of $[6,3]_L$. If $[6,3]_L$ is assigned to S_1, then $[5,3]_L$ can now be assigned to $[7,3]_P$. Finally, the unassigned logical cell $[4,3]_L$ is matched to S_1 without violating the safe domain constraint. Cells $[5,3]_P$ and $[6,3]_P$ are called *virtual spare cells* since they act like spare cells for $[4,3]_L$. Figure 24 shows an example of virtual tree for S_1 and the result of the virtual assignment phase.

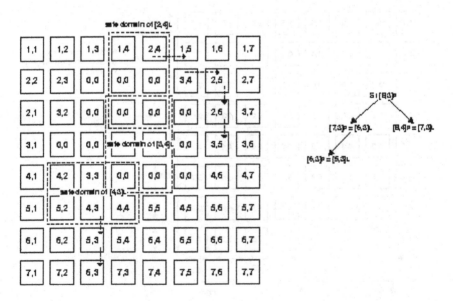

Fig. 12.24: Virtual spare assignment phase.

Since all logical cells have been assigned, the array is successfully reconfigured. However, if unassigned logical cells exist, the rule based assignment is applied. In this phase, the safe domain constraint is relaxed, and assignment rules are checked for cells in a higher domain level. The assignment of logical cell L to physical cell P must be done without causing a conflict. However, it can be observed that the assignment effect of L to P limits the span of logical rows which can be connected above, below, or to a neighboring cell of P. Hence, the assignment rules are decided by the interconnection resources. An in-depth explanation of the assignment rules can be seen in reference 15.

12.3 Self-Reconfiguration Techniques

Several reconfiguration techniques for mesh connected rectangular arrays have been described in the previous section. Unfortunately, all of these techniques lack the ability of self-reconfigureability. With the increasing need for adaptive and real-time systems in which human intervention is minimal, then reconfigureability becomes one important major criterion for fault-tolerant systems. Few reconfiguration techniques for fault-tolerant processor arrays emphasize the aspect of self-reconfigureability.

In order to be able to self-reconfigure a process array, the switch mechanism used has to know the status of each neighboring PE, i.e., either it is faulty or fault-free. Hence, each PE must have self-checking mechanism and send its status to the neighboring switches. Based on this information, a switch can adaptively change its state and perform self-reconfiguration. Two self-reconfiguration techniques are briefly discussed below.

Biologically Inspired Technique

This technique follows the hypothesis that one way to design long-life systems, is to seek inspiration from nature. In order to mimic emergent properties and behaviors in biological organisms, it is necessary to study their hierarchical organization. As we know, cells are the smallest indivisible living blocks out of which all organisms are built. During embryonic development, cells differentiate into different kinds. Groups of millions of specialized cells form organs and tissues (e.g. liver, kidneys and nerves). Each organ has a specific function that results from the activity of its constituent cells. Several organs constitute a system, e.g., the nervous system, the respiratory system and the lymphatic system. Systems are more complex organizations whose function is essential for the survival of the organism. An organism is a collection of systems that interact with each other.

The *Embryonic system* introduces a new family of fault-tolerant systems inspired by nature. Its main ideas come from the mechanisms sustaining the embryonic development of multi-cellular organisms. Similar to natural cellular systems, every one of the embryonic array's cells performs the same basic operation independent of the particular logic function it is involved with, i.e., each cell interprets one of the configuration registers allocated in its memory to perform the logic operations needed for the correct implementation of the system's specification. Which configuration register is selected will depend on the coordinates of the cell determined by those of its neighbors. Embryonic cellular arrays share the following properties with their biological counterparts: Multi-cellular organization (the PEs), cellular differentiation (every cell has a unique set of co-ordinates) and cellular division (every cell is configured by only one configuration register). Figure 12.25 shows the architecture of a generic embryonic system.

In this figure, the address generator assigns to each cell an individual set of co-ordinates, which depend exclusively on the co-ordinates of the nearest south and west neighbors. The logic block is controlled by a configuration register which is selected by the corresponding co-ordinates. When a fault is self-detected by a cell, it becomes transparent for the calculation of co-ordinates allowing another cell to take its coordinates and therefore its function. Digital data are transmitted from one cell to its neighbors through a North-East-West-South (NEWS) connection. The I/O router block allows the spread of information over the whole array. This block is controlled by one section of the corresponding configuration register.

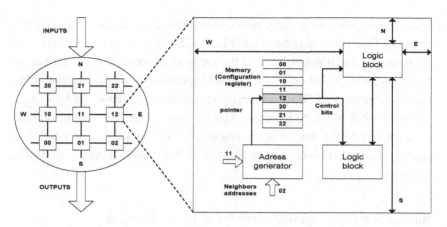

Fig. 12.25: Basic components of an embryonic system.

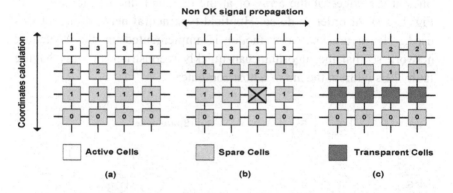

Fig. 12.26: Reconfiguration in embryonic array a) co-ordinate calculation b) Fault. detection c) Transparent cells.

Every embryonic cell performs self checking continuously. If a failure is detected, the faulty cell will become transparent allowing another cell to take its co-ordinates and therefore its function. It then issues a status signal that eliminates some cells according to the reconfiguration mechanism in use, e.g. cell elimination or row elimination. Surviving cells recalculate their co-ordinates and select a new configuration register (see Fig. 12.26). By doing so, every cell performs a new function and, if the amount of spare cells is enough to replace all the failing cells, the overall functionality of the original array should be preserved. Thus, the reconfiguration is implemented by using a different local memory location. The strategy is far from being optimal with respect to the use of spare resources, but the short time needed to recover from a failure makes it attractive in implementing real-time systems.

Built-in Self Reconfiguring Array Using Neural Network

According to this technique, faulty PEs are directly replaced through a self-reconfiguring mechanism using spare PEs placed at two orthogonal lines at the edges of the array or at the diagonal line of the array (see Fig. 12.27). In order to do so, Hopfield-type neural network model was used. The neural network model is implemented in the switching network so that the algorithm can quickly reconstruct an array having faulty PEs without the aid of a host computer.

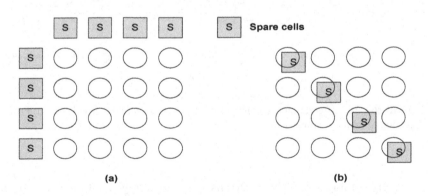

Fig. 12.27: Built-in Self Reconfigurable Array a) Orthogonal spare scheme b) Diagonal spare scheme.

The repairability condition is defined as follows. Let $G = (V, E)$ be a bipartite graph such that $V = V_1 \cup V_2$, $V_1 \cap V_2 = \emptyset$ and $E \subseteq V_1 \times V_2$ where the degree of any vertex in V_1 is equal to or less than 2. The maximal sub-graph G is partitioned with the vertex set $V_1 \cup \psi(V_1)$ into connected components and denote the vertex sets in V_1 of the connected components as $C_1, C_2,\dots C_m$ (for each C_p, $C_p \subseteq V_1$, $\psi(C_p) \subseteq V_2$, and for $i \neq j$ $(C_i \cup \psi(C_i)) \cap (C_j \cup \psi(C_j)) = \emptyset$). The repairability is given if there exists a matching from V_1 to V_2 if and only if $|C_i| \le |\psi(C_i)|$ for each C_i holds where $|C|$ means the number of elements in C.

The reconfiguration proceeds as follows:

1. For a given array with faulty PEs, construct a fault graph G from the fault set F.
2. Denote each connected component as $CC_i = C_i \cup \psi(C_i)$. If each connected component satisfies the reconfigureability condition, the array is repairable and goto 3. Otherwise, it is not repairable and the algorithm terminates.
3. For each CC_i and while there is a vertex with degree 1 in $\psi(C_i)$, make a vertex v with degree 1 in $\psi(C_i)$ match to its adjacent vertex in w in C_i, remove v, w and the edges incident to them. Note that the remaining CC_i, that is $(C_i - v) \cup (\psi(C_i) - w)$ is connected.
4. If all the degrees of the vertices of CC_i are equal or more than 2, CC_i becomes an *Euler Graph* and hence, just two matching are obtained. Then choose one of them and the algorithm ends.

The neural network model is used to calculate the maximum matching where the variable x_{ij} denotes the state of the neuron n_{ij}, that is, fire ($x_{ij} = 1$) and non-fire (x_{ij} 0). By setting the appropriate parameters, the structure of the digital neural circuit for orthogonal and diagonal spare schemes can be built. The detailed explanation of the neural network model is given in reference 29.

12.4 Summary

Array processors are massively parallel processors consisting of a large number of fine-grained regular processing elements. In this chapter, we have discussed a number of issues related to fault-tolerant arrays processors. Our coverage in this chapter focused on the hardware redundancy techniques that can be used in order to improve the reliability and the fault tolerance aspects of array processors. In particular, we have covered the local, global, the hybrid hardware redundancy techniques. In each technique, we have presented a number of ways to achieve the objectives of that particular technique supported with simple examples for illustration. The issue of self-reconfiguration has been discussed briefly at the end of the chapter.

References

[1] Kenneth E. Batcher. Design of a massively parallel processor. *IEEE Transactions on Computers*, C-29(9):836-840, September 1980.

[2] S.Y. Kung. *VLSI Array Processors*. Prentice Hall, 1988.

[3] D.K. Pradhan and I. Koren. Yield and performance enhancement through redundancy in vlsi and wsi multiprocessor system. *IEEE proc.*, 74(5), May 1986.

[4] I. Koren and D.K. Pradhan. Modeling the effect of redundancy on yield and performance of vlsi. systems. *IEEE Trans. Computers*, pages 344-355, March 1987.

[5] M. Chean and J.A.B. Fortes. A taxonomy of reconfiguration techniques for fault-tolerant processor arrays. *IEEE Computer*, pages 55-68, Jan. 1990.

[6] R. Negrini, M.G. Sami and R. Stefanelli. *Fault Tolerance Through Reconfiguration in VLSI and WSI Arrays*. The MIT Press, Cambridge, Massachusetts, London, England, 1989.

[7] A. Rosenberg. The diogenes approach to testable fault-tolerant arrays of processors. *IEEE Trans. Computers*, 32:902-910, 1983.

[8] A.D. Singh. Interstitial redundancy: An area efficient fault tolerance scheme for large area vlsi processor arrays. *IEEE Trans. Computers*, 37(11):162-173, March 1988.

[9] K.S. Hedlund and L. Snyder. Wafer scale integration of configurable highly parallel (chip) processors. *Proc. Conf. Parallel Processing*, pages 262-264, 1982.

[10] M. Chean and J.A.B. Fortes. The full use of suitable spares (fuss) approach to hardware reconfiguration for fault-tolerant processor arrays. *IEEE Trans. Computers*, 39(4):564-571, Apr. 1990.

[11] M. Sami and R. Stefanelli. Reconfigurable architectures for vlsi processing arrays. *IEEE proceeding.*, pages 712-722, 1986.

[12] Sy Yen Kuo and W.K. Fuchs. Efficient spare allocation for reconfigurable arrays. *IEEE Design and Test*, pages 24-31, Feb. 1987.

[13] M. Wang, M. Cutler and S.Y.H. Su. Reconfiguration of vlsi/wsi mesh array processors with two level redundancy. *IEEE Trans. on Computers*, 38(4):547-553, Apr. 1989.

[14] Jung H. Kim and Phill K. Rhee. The rule-based approach to reconfiguration of 2-d processor arrays. *IEEE Trans. on Computers*, 42(11):1403-1408, Nov. 1993.

[15] Phill K. Rhee. *On the Reconfiguration of VLSI Processor Arrays*. PhD thesis, Center of Advanced Computer Studies, University of Southwestern Louisiana, 1990.

[16] Shann Ning Jean Sun Yuan Kung and Chih Wei Chang. Fault-tolerant array processors using single track switches. *IEEE Trans. Computers*, 38(4):500-514, Apr. 1989.

[17] Shann Ning Jean, H.C. Fu and Sun Yuan Kung. Yield enhancement for wsi array processors using two and half track switches. *IEEE Int'l Conf. on WSI*, pages 243-250, 1990.

[18] S.Y. Kung, S.N. Jean and C.W. Chang. Fault-tolerant array processors using single track switches. *IEEE Trans. Computers*, 38(4):501-514, Apr. 1989.

[19] Y.Y. Chen, Yung Shiuan Shyu and Ching Hwa Cheng. An effective framework for fault tolerant vlsi/wsi arrays based on hybrid redundancy approach. *IEEE Int'l Conf. on WSI*, pages 1531-1542, 1994.

[20] T. Horita and I. Takanami. Fault-tolerant processor array based on the 1 1/2 track switches with flexible spare distributions. *IEEE Trans. on Computers*, 49(6):542-552, June 2000.

[21] M.D. Smith and P. Mazumder. Generation of minimal vertex covers for row/column allocation in self repairable arrays. *IEEE Trans. Computers*, 45(1):109-115, Jan. 1996.

[22] F. Lombardi and R. Negrini and R. Stefanelli. Reconfiguration of VLSI Arrays by Covering. *IEEE Trans. on Computers*, 8(9):952-965, September 1989.

[23] F. Distante, F. Lombardi and D. Sciuto. Array partitioning: A methodology for reconfigurability and reconfiguration problems. *Proc. Int'l Conf. Computer Design*, pages 564-567, 1988.

[24] Y.Y. Chen, Sau Gee Chen and Jiann Cherng Lee. Yield and performance issues in fault-tolerant wsi array architectures. *IEEE Int'l Conf. on WSI*, pages 319-328, 1995.

[25] Stephen Pateras and Janusz Rajski. Design of a Self Reconfigurating Interconnection Network for Fault-Tolerant VLSI Processor Arrays. *IEEE Trans. on Reliability*, 38(1):40-50, April 1989.

[26] Pinaki Mazumder and Y. S. Jih. Restructuting of Square Processor Arrays by Built-in Self-Repair Circuit. *IEEE Trans. on Computers Aided Design*, 12(9):1255-1265, September 1993.

[27] Lizy Kurian John and Eugene John. A Dynamically Reconfigurable Interconnect for Array Processors. *IEEE Trans. on VLSI Systems*, 6(a):150-157, March 1998.

[28] Cesar Ortega and Andy Tyrrell. Biologycally Inspired Real Time Reconfiguration Technique for Processor Arrays. *Proceeding of 5th IFAC Workshop on Algorithms and Architectures for Real Time Control*, 1998.

[29] Itsuo Takanami. Built-in Self-Reconfiguring Systems for Fault-Tolerant Mesh Connected Processor Arrays by Direct Spare Replacement. *Proceeding of the 2001 IEEE Symposium on Defect and Fault Tolerance in VLSI Systems (DFT'01)*.

[30] J.S.N. Jean, H.C. Fu and S.Y. Kung. Yield enhancement for wsi array processors using two and half track switches. *Proc. IEEE Int'l Conf. WSI*, pages 243-250, 1990.

[31] Vwani P. Rowchowdhury and Theodora A. Varvarigou and Thomas Kailath. A Polynomial Time Algorithm for Reconfiguring Multiple-Track Models. *IEEE Trans. on Computers*, 42(4):385-395, April 1993.

[32] Vwani P. Rowchowdhury and Theodora A. Varvarigou and Thomas Kailath. Reconfiguring Processor Arrays Using Multiple-

Tracks Model: The 3-track-1-spare Approach. *IEEE Trans. on Computers*, 42(11):1281-1293, November 1993.

[33] Nobuo Tsuda. Fault-Tolerant Processor Arrays Using Additional Bypass Linking Allocated by Graph Coloring. *IEEE Trans. on Computers*, 49(5):433-442, May 2000.

[34] Fabrizio Lombardi. Reconfiguration of VLSI Arrays by Covering. *IEEE Trans. on CAD*, 8(9):952-965, September 1989.

[35] Yung-Yuan Chen. A Comprehensive Reconfiguration Scheme for Fault-Tolerant VLSI/WSI Array Processors. *IEEE Trans. on Computers*, 46(12):1363-1371, December 1997.

[36] L.M. J and J. Grinberg. The 3-d computer: An integrated stack of wsi wafers. *Wafer Scale Integration*, pages 253-317, 1989.

[37] Carl McCrosky and Mostafa Abd-El-Barr and Machdum Bachtiar. Fault-Tolerant Wafer Scale Arrays trough Wafer Stacking. Technical Report, Department of Computer Science, University of Saskatchewan, Oct 1992.

[38] M.G. Sami and R. Stefanelli. Fault Tolerance of VLSI Processing Arrays: The Time Redundancy Approach. *Real Time Systems Symposium*, pages 200-207, Dec 1984.

[39] J.A.B. Fortes and C.S. Raghavendra. Gracefully Degradable Processor Arrays. *IEEE Trans. on Computers*, C-34:1033-1044, Nov. 1985.

[40] C.P. Low and H.W. Leong. On the reconfiguration of degradable vlsi/wsi arrays. *IEEE Trans. Computer Aided Design*, 16(10): 1213-1221, Oct. 1997.

[41] Salih Y. and Fabrizio L. Reconfiguration of Two Dimensional VLSI Array by Time Redundancy. *IEEE Conference on Computer Design*, pages 210-219, 1992.

[42] Chor Ping Low. An efficient reconfiguration algorithm for degradable. vlsi/wsi arrays. *IEEE Trans. on Computers*, 49(6): 553-559, June 2000.

Chapter 13

Algorithm-Based Fault Tolerance

The demand for large amount of computation power to solve computation-intensive scientific/engineering problems is increasing at a high pace. Matrix computation forms the core of computation-intensive tasks, such as image processing and finite elements analysis. The computational power needed for these tasks can be obtained through the use of multiple low-cost high performance processors. These processors have been made available by the rapid progress in the VLSI/WSI technologies. The need for fault-tolerant, highly reliable processors to perform these tasks is a must. Algorithm-based fault tolerance (ABFT) is a system-level methodology for achieving highly reliable and fault-tolerant computation. ABFT techniques can detect (and correct) errors concurrently while operations such as matrix addition, multiplication, and scalar product are in progress. The use of ABFT allows us to detect failures within a single processor in multiple processor systems.

ABFT techniques are characterized by encoding of the input data, tailoring the algorithm used, and distributing the computation steps among processing units used. Data encoding can be performed at the word level in order to protect against bit errors. A faulty processing unit can affect all bits of a word. Therefore, data encoding at the word level is performed in ABFT. A basic requirement in this process is that the information portion of the encoded data must be easy to recover. Existing matrix algorithms must be redesigned (modified) in such a way that they can operate on the encoded data. A modified algorithm is expected to take longer time to operate on the encoded data. This time overhead must not be excessive. A third requirement is that computation must be well distributed among the processing units. This is needed such that the failure of any processing unit can affect only a portion of the correct data. Error detection and correction schemes used must therefore be such that a faulty unit will not be able to mask the effect of error(s).

This Chapter is dedicated to a discussion on ABFT techniques. Our coverage in this chapter starts with a discussion on ABFT for matrix operations. We consider operations such as matrix addition and multiplication. We then discuss ABFT fault detection and correction methods. We also conduct a discussion on ABFT on a hypercube and mesh-connected multiprocessors. Sample matrix problems and their ABFT solutions are provided at the end of our discussion in the chapter.

13.1 Checksum-Based ABFT for Matrix Operations

In order to allow for ABFT in matrix operations, the involved matrices are encoded in what is known as checksum matrices. An extra row and/or an extra column are appended to the original matrix. Each Element in the extra row represents the sum of the elements in the columns above it. Each Element in the extra column represents the sum of the elements in the row to which it is appended. Different encodings are defined below. In presenting these encodings, we assume that the original matrix, A, has n rows and m columns (n × m matrix).

A Column Checksum matrix A_c is (n + 1) × m *such that*

$$a_{n+1,j} = \sum_{i=1}^{n} a_{i,j} \quad 1 \leq j \leq m$$

A Row *Checksum matrix A_r is* n × (m + 1) *such that*

$$a_{i,m+1} = \sum_{j=1}^{m} a_{i,j} \quad 1 \leq i \leq n$$

A Full Checksum *matrix A_f is* (n + 1) × (m + 1) *and it is the column checksum matrix of the row checksum matrix, A_r.*

Figure 13.1 shows example for the three checksum matrices encodings mentioned above.

$$\begin{bmatrix} 2 & 4 & 6 & 8 \\ 1 & 3 & 5 & 7 \\ 3 & 5 & 7 & 9 \\ 4 & 7 & 9 & 8 \end{bmatrix}\begin{bmatrix} 20 \\ 16 \\ 24 \\ 28 \end{bmatrix} \qquad \begin{bmatrix} 2 & 4 & 6 & 8 \\ 1 & 3 & 5 & 7 \\ 3 & 5 & 7 & 9 \\ 4 & 7 & 9 & 8 \end{bmatrix} \qquad \begin{bmatrix} 2 & 4 & 6 & 8 \\ 1 & 3 & 5 & 7 \\ 3 & 5 & 7 & 9 \\ 4 & 7 & 9 & 8 \end{bmatrix}\begin{bmatrix} 20 \\ 16 \\ 24 \\ 28 \end{bmatrix}$$

$$\qquad\qquad\qquad\qquad [10\ 19\ 27\ 32] \qquad\qquad\qquad [10\ 19\ 27\ 32][176]$$

(a) *Row checksum matrix*   (b) *Column checksum matrix*   (c) *Full checksum*

Fig. 13.1: Checksum matrices.

An important property of the checksum encoding is that it is preserved under matrix addition, multiplication, LU decomposition, scalar product, and matrix transposition. Table 13.1 illustrates this observation.

Table 13.1: Checksum encoding preservation.

Matrix operation	Example	Checksum encoding
Addition	$C = A + B.$	$C_f = A_f + B_f.$
Multiplication	$C = A \times B$	$C_f = A_c \times B_r$
Decomposition	$C = LU$	$C_f = L_c U_r$
Scalar Product	$C = a \times A$	$C_f = a \times A_f$
Transposition	$C = A^T$	$C_f = A_f^T$

Example: Matrix addition.

Consider the case of two full checksum matrices **A** and **B**. The two matrices were originally 4×4 each. They were made full checksum matrices by adding an extra row and an extra column in each of them, i.e., each of the full checksum matrices A_f and B_f is a 5×5 matrix satisfying the checksum property. Matrix C_f is obtained by adding A_f and B_f as shown below.

$C_f = A_f + B_f$

$$
\begin{bmatrix}
6 & 12 & 15 & 19 & 52 \\
6 & 6 & 11 & 18 & 41 \\
11 & 13 & 7 & 17 & 48 \\
18 & 11 & 25 & 23 & 77 \\
41 & 42 & 58 & 77 & 218
\end{bmatrix}
=
\begin{bmatrix}
4 & 9 & 11 & 14 & 38 \\
3 & 2 & 6 & 12 & 23 \\
7 & 8 & 1 & 10 & 26 \\
13 & 5 & 18 & 15 & 51 \\
27 & 24 & 36 & 51 & 138
\end{bmatrix}
+
\begin{bmatrix}
2 & 3 & 4 & 5 & 14 \\
3 & 4 & 5 & 6 & 18 \\
4 & 5 & 6 & 7 & 22 \\
5 & 6 & 7 & 8 & 26 \\
14 & 18 & 22 & 26 & 80
\end{bmatrix}
$$

It should be noted that the elements in the last row (column) of C_f represent the sum of the elements in the corresponding columns (rows). This clearly shows that C_f preserves the checksum property, i.e., the matrix addition operation preserves the checksum property.

The following example shows that the matrix multiplication operation also preserves the checksum property.

Example: Matrix multiplication

Consider the case of two full checksum matrices **A** and **B**. The two matrices were originally 4×4 each. They were made full checksum matrices by adding an extra row and an extra column in each of them, i.e., each of the full checksum matrices A_f and B_f is a 5×5 matrix satisfying the checksum property. Matrix C_f is obtained by multiplying A_f and B_f as shown below.

$C_f = A_f \times B_f$

$$
\begin{bmatrix}
20 & 20 & 20 & 20 & 80 \\
28 & 28 & 28 & 28 & 112 \\
36 & 36 & 36 & 36 & 144 \\
44 & 44 & 44 & 44 & 176 \\
128 & 128 & 128 & 128 & 512
\end{bmatrix}
=
\begin{bmatrix}
1 & 2 & 3 & 4 & 10 \\
2 & 3 & 4 & 5 & 14 \\
3 & 4 & 5 & 6 & 18 \\
4 & 5 & 6 & 7 & 22 \\
10 & 14 & 18 & 22 & 64
\end{bmatrix}
\times
\begin{bmatrix}
2 & 2 & 2 & 2 & 8 \\
2 & 2 & 2 & 2 & 8 \\
2 & 2 & 2 & 2 & 8 \\
2 & 2 & 2 & 2 & 8 \\
8 & 8 & 8 & 8 & 32
\end{bmatrix}
$$

Having shown that matrix operations preserve the checksum property, we now illustrate the error handling capability of the ABFT.

13.2   Checksum-Based ABFT Error Handling

It was mentioned in the introduction that ABFT can be used to detect, locate and correct errors in data. In order to show that, we define the matrix distance between two matrices as the number of elements in which they differ. The minimum matrix distance of a set of full checksum matrices is the minimum of the matrix distances between all possible pairs of full checksum matrices in the set.

Consider the set of all (unique) full checksum matrices, $S_{r \times c}$, of size $r \times c$. It can be shown that the minimum matrix distance of $S_{r \times c}$ is 4. Thus, a single erroneous element can be detected and corrected in a full checksum matrix. This is because the minimum distance needed to detect and correct a single error, e, should be $\geq 2e + 1$. When a single element in a full checksum matrix is in error, then this element can be located by identifying the row and the column to which it belongs. The erroneous element exists at the intersection of this row and that column. This is to be contrasted to the single error detection capability of a system using only row (column) checksum matrices.

In the case of full checksum matrices, erroneous element detection can be done by computing the sum of the information elements in each row and column and comparing the computed sum with the corresponding checksum value. Any discrepancy will indicate an error. The location of the erroneous element can be determined by intersecting the inconsistent row and the inconsistent column. Correction of the erroneous element can be made by adding the difference between the computed sum of the row (column) data elements and the checksum to the erroneous element in the information part. Correction can also be made by replacing the checksum by the computed sum (this can only be done in the case where the checksum is incorrect).

Example: Consider the shown matrix multiplication

$$
\begin{bmatrix}
20 & 20 & 20 & 20 & 80 \\
28 & 28 & 20 & 28 & 104 \\
36 & 36 & 36 & 36 & 144 \\
44 & 44 & 44 & 44 & 176 \\
128 & 128 & 120 & 128 & 504
\end{bmatrix}
=
\begin{bmatrix}
1 & 2 & 3 & 4 & 10 \\
2 & 3 & 4 & 5 & 14 \\
3 & 4 & 5 & 6 & 18 \\
4 & 5 & 6 & 7 & 22 \\
10 & 14 & 18 & 22 & 64
\end{bmatrix}
\times
\begin{bmatrix}
2 & 2 & 2 & 2 & 8 \\
2 & \boxed{2} & 2 & 2 & 8 \\
2 & 2 & 2 & 2 & 8 \\
2 & 2 & 2 & 2 & 8 \\
8 & 8 & 8 & 8 & 32
\end{bmatrix}
$$

The computed summation indicates a discrepancy in row #2 and column #3. This indicates the existence of an erroneous element at the intersection of row #2 and column #3, i.e. element (2,3). In order to find the correct value of the element we add 8 (112-104) to the erroneous element (20) to get a 28, the correct value of the element.

13.3 Weighted Checksum Based ABFT

The weighted checksum encoding scheme is used to increase the error correction capability of systems. The main idea is that with the introduction of d weighted checksum rows (columns) and for a suitably chosen weight vector, it is possible to make a given system d-error detectable and $\left\lfloor \dfrac{d}{2} \right\rfloor$-error correctable.

A weighted row-checksum matrix is defined as follows

$$
A_r = \left[A\, Aw^{(1)}\, Aw^{(2)} \ldots Aw^{(d)} \right]
$$

In the case when $d=2$, where $w^{(1)} = e = [11\ldots1]^T$ and $w^{(2)} = w = [123\ldots n]$, if the erroneous element is a_{lm}, then the possible erroneous version of a_{ij}, call it a'_{ij}, $1 \le i, j \le n$. If we define the following two values (see Reference 5)

$$
s_1 = \sum_{k=1}^{n} a'_{km} - (e^T A)_m
$$

$$
s_2 = \sum_{k=1}^{n} w_k a'_{km} - (w^T A)_m
$$

Examination of $s_2/s_1 = l$ can help locating the error in the (l,m) position of A. In order to correct this error, we use $a_{lm} \leftarrow a'_{lm} + s_1$.

Example (see Reference 5):

Consider the case of a 2×2 matrix A. The following weighted checksum matrix is obtained from A as a result of performing some operations on other weighted checksum matrices.

$$A_{rw} = \begin{bmatrix} 1 & 2 & 3 & 5 \\ 2 & 3 & 7 & 10 \\ 3 & 0 & 3 & 3 \end{bmatrix}$$

It should be noted that the erroneous element must be in the second row. This is because the checksum elements in that row do not satisfy the checksum property. One can also compute $s_1 = 2$ and $s_2 = 2$, therefore $s_2/s_1 = 1$. This indicates that the erroneous element must be in column #1. Hence a_{21} must be the erroneous element. Correction can be made to that element by adding $s_1 = 2$ to the value of a_{21}, which will result in a correct value for $a_{21}=4$.

13.4   ABFT on a Mesh Multiprocessor

In this section, we explain the application of the ABFT for a matrix multiplication on an $n \times n$ mesh-connected multiprocessor system (see Fig. 13.2). The matrices to be multiplied are A and B. The resultant un-encoded matrix is $C \leftarrow A \times B$. The input matrices are encoded to become A_c (column checksum) and B_r(row checksum). The resultant encoded matrix is $C_f \leftarrow A_c \times B_r$. In the figure, each square represents a processing element (PE). Processing element $PE_{i,j}$ performs the operation $c_{i,j} \leftarrow c_{i,j} + a_{i,k} \times b_{k,j}$. After n steps, each processor calculates an element of the full checksum matrix C_f. The existence of any single erroneous element can then be detected and corrected as shown in the previous section.

After having all the elements of C_f, the first n processors of the $(i + 1)$th row can be used to compute the sum of the ith row of the matrix C using a tree-like scheme in $\log_2 n$ time units (ignoring the data transfer time among processors). In a similar way, the $(n + 1)$th row of C_f can be computed by the first row of the processor array. The computed sum can then be compared to the corresponding element in the checksum row. A similar procedure is needed to check the consistency of the columns of C_f.

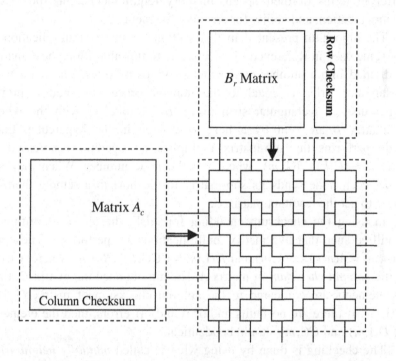

Fig. 13.2: Matrix multiplication on a mesh-connected multiprocessor.

It should be noted that the amount of hardware redundancy, measured in terms of the number of extra processing elements needed, in the above mesh-connected multiprocessor system is $(2n + 1)$. The amount of time redundancy, measures in terms of the extra time units needed to check for the correctness of the resultant matrix is $2 \times \log_2 n$ (assuming that addition and multiplication times needed by a processing element are equal).

13.5   Checksum-Based ABFT on a Hypercube Multiprocessor

In this section, we explain the application of the ABFT for a matrix multiplication on a hypercube multiprocessor system. In particular, we consider the problem of matrix multiplication expressed as $C(n,m) = A(n,k) \times B(k,m)$. There exist a number of algorithms for performing matrix multiplication using hypercube architecture. These differ in terms of their speed, memory requirements, inter-processor communication, and ability for error confinement.

The algorithm presented in this section for matrix multiplication is the same used in Reference #1. According to this algorithm, the A matrix is divided into a number of rectangular strips by rows. The number of rectangular strips is equal to the number processors (nodes) in the hypercube. A rectangular strip of matrix A together with the whole of matrix B are sent by a host to a node in the hypercube. Each node performs the sub-matrix multiplication operation expressed as $C(i,m) = A(i,k) \times B(k,m)$, where i is the node number. When they are done, each node sends its sub-matrix to the host to assemble them in order to get the resultant matrix C.

In using the checksum encoding for ABF, the above algorithm is modified such that two matrix multiplications are performed. These are $C(n,m) = A(n,k) \times B(k,m)$ and $D(1,m) = CC(1,k) \times B(k,m)$ where, $CC(A)$ is the *column checksum* of matrix A. Having obtained the matrix D, then its elements are compared to the column checksum of matrix C, i.e., $C(1,m)$. If there are no faults and/or round-off errors, then the elements of $D(1,m)$ and $C(1,m)$ should be identical.

The checking is done by using what is called *mutually neighboring* concept. According to this concept, the nodes of the hypercube are divided into groups each consisting of two mutually neighboring nodes (mates). A checking is done between a node and its mate as follows.

1. Node i computes the column checksum of A strip and the D strip of its mate
2. Node i obtains the C strip of its mate
3. Node i compares the C strip of its mate with the D strip and based on the outcome of the comparison, it send the results (pass or fail) to the host.

4. If all nodes "pass" the test, then the host concludes that the computation is error-free; otherwise the computation is concluded as erroneous.

The following example (quoted from Reference 5) illustrates the above procedure.

Example

Consider the case of a 4-node hypercube (node 0, node 1, node 2, and node 3), see Fig. 13.3. In this figure, items shown in continuous lines are computed locally while those shown in dashed lines represent those that are received by the node.

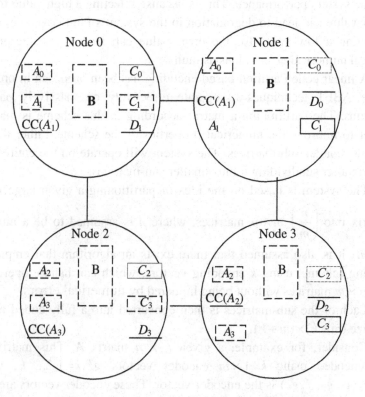

Fig. 13.3: Checksum-based matrix multiplication on a four-processor hypercube.

For example, node 0 will receive strip A_0, stripe A_1, and the matrix B. It will compute $C_0 = A_0 \times$ B, $CC(A_1)$, and $D_1 = CC(A_1) \times$ B. It will receive C_1 from its mate, node 1, compute $CC(C_1)$ and compare it to D_1.

13.6 Partition-Based ABFT for Floating-Point Matrix Operations

The two encoding techniques discussed in Sections 13.2 and 13.3, i.e., Checksum and Weighted-Checksum, can be classified as *linear coding techniques*. These techniques can be used in providing effective ABFT for fixed-point (integer) matrix operations. Their use in providing ABFT for floating-point matrix operations introduces a serious complications, i.e., the need for tolerating a certain error (a deviation from zero) in the values of s_1 and s_2. Selection of this error value has a detrimental effect on the system performance. This is because selecting a high value for the error value can lead to degradation in the system's fault coverage, while selecting a low value for the error value can lead to misinterpreting typical numerical error values as faults.

A linear code Partition-based encoding has been proposed in order to scale ABFT techniques to operate effectively on massively parallel systems. The partitioning a matrix according to this scheme is made in order to improve the numerical properties of the scheme, rather than to handle smaller sub-matrices. The system will operate on the entire large matrix after subdividing it into smaller sun-matrices.

The system is based on the idea of partitioning a given large $n \times n$ matrix into $\left(\dfrac{n}{m}\right)^2$ $m \times m$ matrices, where n is assumed to be a multiple of m. It is also assumed that there exists an algorithm that employs a coding scheme, using k encoding vectors, which can handle operations on $m \times m$ matrices without being hindered by numerical errors.

Each of the sub-matrices is then converted into a fully coded matrix of size $(m+k) \times (m+k)$.

Consider, for example, a given $n \times n$ matrix A. This matrix can be encoded using k $1 \times m$ encoder vectors $g_i^T, i = 1, 2, ..., k$, where $g^T = (g_1, g_2, ..., g_n)$ is the encoder vector. These encoder vectors are used to encode the A matrix as shown below.

$$\begin{bmatrix} A_{11}^c & A_{12}^c & A_{13}^c & \cdots & A_{1p}^c \\ A_{21}^c & A_{22}^c & A_{23}^c & \cdots & A_{2p}^c \\ \cdot & \cdot & \cdot & & \cdot \\ \cdot & \cdot & \cdot & & \cdot \\ A_{p1}^c & A_{p2}^c & A_{p3}^c & \cdots & A_{pp}^c \end{bmatrix}$$

It is assumed that $n = pm$, and each A_{ij}^c is an $(m+k) \times (m+k)$ encoding of the $m \times m$ sub-matrix A_{ij} of A such that A_{ij}^c is given by the following.

$$A_{ij}^c = \begin{bmatrix} A_{ij} & A_{ij}g_i & \cdots & A_{ij}g_k \\ g_1^T A_{ij} & g_1^T A_{ij}g_i & \cdots & g_1^T A_{ij}g_k \\ \cdot & \cdot & \cdot & \cdot \\ \cdot & \cdot & \cdot & \cdot \\ g_{k1}^T A_{ij} & g_k^T A_{ij}g_i & \cdots & g_{k1}^T A_{ij}g_k \end{bmatrix}$$

Example

Consider the case of an $n \times n$ matrix A, where $n = 2m$ and $k = 1$. According to the partitioning scheme, the A matrix is subdivided into four sub-matrices as shown below.

$$\begin{bmatrix} A_{11} & A_{12} \\ A_{21} & A_{22} \end{bmatrix}$$

The partitioned encoded matrix for A will be as shown below.

$$\begin{bmatrix} \begin{bmatrix} A_{11} & A_{11}g \\ g^T A_{11} & g^T A_{11}g \end{bmatrix} & \begin{bmatrix} A_{12} & A_{12}g \\ g^T A_{12} & g^T A_{12}g \end{bmatrix} \\ \begin{bmatrix} A_{21} & A_{21}g \\ g^T A_{21} & g^T A_{21}g \end{bmatrix} & \begin{bmatrix} A_{22} & A_{22}g \\ g^T A_{22} & g^T A_{22}g \end{bmatrix} \end{bmatrix}$$

There is hardware overhead of partitioning the encoding scheme with respect to the regular encoding technique by comparing the number of elements in both cases. This can be done as follows. Assume that the partitioned encoded matrix with k encoder vectors has H times more elements than the regular encoded matrix. Then H is calculated as follows.

$$H = \frac{((\sfrac{n}{m})(m+k))^2 - (n+k)^2}{(n+k)^2} = \left(\frac{1+\sfrac{k}{m}}{1+\sfrac{k}{pm}}\right)^2 - 1 \cong \frac{2k}{m}, \text{ independent of } n.$$

The approximation above assumes that $p \gg 1$ and $\sfrac{k}{m}$ is small.

Consider, for example, that a weighted checksum scheme capable of handing matrices of size 100×100 and that two encoder vectors are used, i.e., $k = 2$. In this case, the partitioned checksum matrix will have only 4% more elements than the regular full checksum matrix. This also indicates that the time required to operate on the partitioned matrix is not significantly larger than that required to operate on the regular encoding scheme.

It should be noted that the implementation of an ABFT for an $n \times n$ matrix on a two-dimensional mesh of processors for the case $k = 1$ requires a $\left(\frac{n}{m}\right)(m+1) \times \left(\frac{n}{m}\right)(m+1)$ processor array. This is about $\sfrac{2}{m}$ times more hardware as compared to the regular checksum encoding scheme. No additional hardware is required to compute the checksums for rows/columns. This is because these checksums can be computed by processing elements in other rows/columns. In terms of fault coverage, the non-partitioned scheme can detect and correct a single fault. On the other hand, the partitioned two-dimensional mesh array can detect and correct a single fault or alternatively it can detect three faults in each $m \times m$ sub-matrix. Therefore, the partitioned scheme can detect and correct up to $\left(\frac{n}{m}\right)^2$ faults, if each $m \times m$ sub-matrix contains no more than one fault, or detect up to $3\left(\dfrac{n}{m}\right)^2$ faults, if each $m \times m$ sub-matrix contains no more than 3 faults.

13.7 Summary

This chapter is mainly concerned with the basic issues related to algorithm based fault tolerance. Our coverage in this chapter started with the basic technique of checksum-based ABFT for matrix operations. We then discussed some check-sum ABFT error handing techniques. This was followed by a discussion on the weighted checksum based ABFT. Two examples were then discussed: ABFT on a mesh of multi-computer and checksum –based ABFT on a hypercube multi-computer network. Our coverage in the chapter concluded with a brief discussion on the technique that uses partitioning for ABFT floating-point matrix operations.

References

Books

[1] Pradhan, D., (Editor) "Fault-Tolerant Computer System Design", 1996, Prentice-Hall Publishing Company.

Journal and Conference Papers

[1] Huang, K. and Abraham, J., "Algorithm-Based Fault Tolerance for matrix Operations", IEEE Transactions on Computers, vol. C-33, no. 6, pp. 518-528, June 1984.
[2] Jou, J. and Abraham, J., "Fault-Tolerant Matrix Arithmetic and Signal Processing on Highly Concurrent Computing Structures", Proceedings IEEE, vol. 74, pp. 732-741, May 1986.
[3] Anfinson, C. and Luk, F., "A Linear Algebraic Model of Algorithm based Fault Tolerance", IEEE Transactions on Computers, vol. 37, no. 12, pp. 1599-1604, December 1988.

[4] Prata, P. and Silva, J., "Algorithm-Based Fault Tolerance Versus Result-Checking for Matrix Computations", International Symposium on Fault Tolerance Computing (FTCS)-29, pp. 4-11, 1999.

[5] Vijay, M. and Mittal, R., "Algorithm-based faulty tolerance: a review", Microprocessors and Microsystems, 21 (1997), 151-161.

[6] Milovanovic, E. Milovanovic, I. Stojecev, M. and Jovanovic, G., "Fault-Tolerant Matrix Inversion on Processor Array", Electronic Letters, pp. 1206-1208, June 1992.

[7] Reddy, A., Banerjee, P., "Algorithm-Based Fault Detection for Signal processing Applications", IEEE Transactions on Computers, vol. 39, no. 10, pp. 1304-1308, October 1990.

[8] Vinnakota, B. and Jha, N., "Synthesis of Algrothm-Based Fault Tolerance Systems from Dependence Graphs", IEEE Transactions on Parallel and Distributed Systems, vol. 4, no. 8, pp. 864-874, August 1993.

[9] Banerjee, P., et al., "Algorithm-Based Fault Tolerance on a Hypercube Multiprocessor", IEEE Transactions on Computers, vol. 39, no. 9, pp. 1132-1145, September 1990.

[10] Yeh, Y. and Feng, T., "Algorithm-Based Fault Tolerance for Matrix Inversion with Maximum Pivoting", Journal of Parallel and Distributed Compting, vol. 14, pp. 373-389, 1992.

[11] Choi, Y-H. and Malek, M., "AZ Fault-Tolerant Systolic Sorter", IEEE Transactions on Computers, vol. 37, no.5, pp. 621-624, May 1988.

[12] Rexford, J. and Jah, N., "Algorithm-based Fault Tolerance for Floating-Point Operations in Massively Parallel Systems", http://citeseer.ist.psu.edu/42575.html

[13] Kim, Youngbae, « Fault-Tolerant matrix Operations for Parallel and Distributed Systems », http://citeseer.ist.psu.edu/kim96fault.html

[14] Kim, Youngbae, cc, "Fault-Tolerant Matrix Operations Using Checksum and Reverse Computation", http://citeseer.ist.psu.edu/60979.html

Chapter 14

System Level Diagnosis-I

Advances in semiconductor technology have made it feasible to implement high performance parallel computing systems consisting of a large number of processing elements on a single chip. These complex computing systems can be used in solving real-time applications as well as computation-intensive engineering/scientific problems. Some of these problems are mission-critical systems. A small mistake in such systems can lead to devastating human life loses. It is therefore prudent to incorporate a sizeable degree of fault tolerance and reliability in these systems. Incorporating redundant processing elements has been the most widely adopted technique for achieving such level of fault tolerance and reliability. These redundant elements can be used to replace faulty ones. In performing such replacement, the system needs to be switched periodically to what is known as *diagnostic mode*. During this mode, detection of faulty processing element(s) is performed. A straightforward way for implementing this strategy is to have each processing element performs a scheduled diagnosis process using specific test vectors. These test vectors can then be analyzed in order to determine the faulty processing element(s). As the complexity of the diagnosed systems increases, so does the amount of data that need to be analyzed.

An alternative to the above strategy is to make use of the inherent parallelism built into the system under diagnosis. In this case, each processing element (unit) should be capable of testing a number of other designated units and produces a test outcome. Test outcomes are produced by a central unit that monitors the tested unit outputs. The system can then be viewed as a directed graph. Units are the vertices of the graph while each test forms a directed edge from the testing vertex (unit) to the tested vertex (unit). A test result of 1 (0) is generated if the tested unit is found faulty (fault-free). The test result is used as the weight (label) of the corresponding edge in the graph. It is possible that either, or both, of the testing and the tested units is (are) faulty. Faulty testing unit may generate arbitrary test results whose interpretation may vary. The collection of all test results is called a *syndrome*. A syndrome can be decoded to identify faulty and fault-free units. This strategy is called *System Level Diagnosis* (*SLD*).

This chapter deals with the issues related to system level diagnosis. We start our coverage by introducing some basic terminology and background material. This is followed by a detailed discussion on diagnose-ability models. In particular, we introduce five models. These are the PMC (Preperata, Metz, and Chein) model, the BGM (Barsi, Grandoni, and Maestrini) model, the comparison model, the distribution model, and the probabilistic model. Next, we introduce a number of diagnosable systems together with their respective diagnose-ability algorithms. We conclude our discussion by presenting a number of example diagnosis systems and show how to develop their diagnosis algorithms. The application of the concepts introduced in this chapter is covered in the next chapter.

14.1   Background Material and Basic Terminology

A diagnosable system S consisting of n units is denoted by the set $U = \{u_1, u_2, ..., u_n\}$. Each unit $u_i \subseteq U$ is capable of testing a subset of units $X \in U - \{u_i\}$. A *test link*, t_{ij}, indicates that unit u_j is tested by unit u_i and a test a_{ij} is produced. The complete collection of tests in S is called the *test connection assignment* (*TCA*) of S. The TCA is represented by a directed graph $D = (U, E)$, where each unit $u_i \in U$ is represented by a vertex and an edge $(u_i \rightarrow u_j) \in E$ if t_{ij} is a test in the *TCA*.

A faulty unit is assumed to contain one of two possible types of faults. These are *permanent fault* or *intermittent fault*. An intermittently faulty unit can behave either as a fault-free unit of as a faulty unit, when tested by different units or at different times by the same unit, i.e., its test result could differ from one test to the other. Unless otherwise mentioned, all diagnosis algorithms presented in this Chapter apply to permanent faults.

A *fault set*, $F \subseteq U$, is the subset of the faulty units in S. The set of syndromes $S(F)$, corresponding to a fault set F, contains those syndromes that are producible by a system in the presence of F. A *diagnosis* is defined as the identification of the set F on the basis of a given syndrome. In the presence of a set F, there exist two types of syndromes. A *Single producible syndrome (SPS)* can be attributed to only one unique set of faulty units. A *multi-producible syndrome (MPS)* can be attributed to more than one fault set, making it impossible to identify uniquely the actual fault set causing it.

Diagnosis is defined as the determination of the fault situation in a given system consisting of a number of units given its syndrome. In representing systems, each unit is assigned a state such that if the unit is fault-free, then its state is "0" and if the unit is faulty, then its state is "1". Figure 14.1 shows an example system consisting of five units, two of which are identified as faulty. A link from unit u_i to unit u_j indicates that unit u_i tests unit u_j. The test result is shown next to the link according to the convention indicated above.

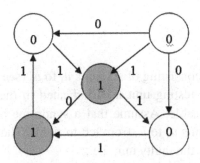

Fig. 14.1: Example diagnosed system.

A family of *allowable fault sets (AFS)*, $F = \{F_1, F_2, ..., F_k\}$, is defined as the fault sets that could be handled by a system level diagnosis procedure. Two fault sets are called *distinguishable* if there exists at least one test whose outcome is different in the presence of the two fault sets.

The *t-fault-class* is a AFS that includes all possible fault sets with cardinality $\leq t$. The maximum value of t, called the *degree of diagnose-ability (DOD)* is defined as the maximum number of faulty units that a system can guarantee to diagnose. A fault set $F_i \in F$ is said to be *uniquely diagnosable (UD)*, if any syndrome $s_i \in S(F_i)$ is not producible in the presence of any other $F_j \in F$; $s_i \notin S(F_j) \ \forall \ F_j \in F$ and $F_j \neq F_i$.

A *distinguishing test* is a test whose outcome is different in the presence of two fault sets F_i and F_j. A *complete diagnosis* is that in which all faulty units can be identified based on a given syndrome in the presence of such fault set; otherwise the diagnosis is *incomplete diagnosis*. A *correct diagnosis* is one in which no fault-free units are identified as faulty. If fault-free units are identified as faulty, then we have an *incorrect diagnosis*.

A system is said to be t-diagnosable if a syndrome produced by any fault set from the t-fault class can be uniquely associated with the same fault set by a diagnosis algorithm operating under the assumption that the fault set belongs to the t-fault class. A *one-step t-fault diagnosis* (also called diagnosis without repair) refers to the identification of all t faulty units in one instance, without modifying the system, from a given syndrome.

Example

Consider a system consisting of six units u_1 to u_6 (see Fig. 14.2). The test outcome of unit u_i testing unit u_j is indicated in the figure as a_{ij}. This system is 1-diagnosable. Assume that a syndrome of the form 000001 (representing the units u_1 to u_6 from left to right). The 1 in that syndrome represents correctly the faulty unit, i.e., u_1.

As a general rule, for a system having n units, N number of testing links, d degree of diagnostic graph, and t faulty units to be *t-diagnosable*, then the system must satisfy three conditions, namely $n \geq 2t + 1$, $d \geq t$ and $N \geq nt$. These conditions are sufficient if and only if no two units test each other and that each unit is tested by at least t other units.

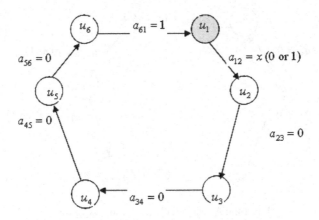

Fig. 14.2: One-step 1-diagnosable system.

A sequential t-fault diagnosis (also called diagnosis with repair) refers to the identification of at least one of the t faulty units, if there exists any, from a given syndrome. The diagnosis is carried out in sequential rounds, during each at least one faulty unit is guaranteed to be identified. An identified faulty unit is replaced (or repaired). The process is repeated until all faulty units are identified and replaced.

Example

Consider the system shown in Fig. 14.3. In this system, units u_1 and u_2 are faulty. The test outcome is $(a_{12}, a_{23}, a_{34}, a_{45}, a_{56}, a_{61}) = (x,x,0,0,0,1)$. Notice that this syndrome mimics the case of a single u_1 fault, i.e., $(a_{12}, a_{23}, a_{34}, a_{45}, a_{56}, a_{61}) = (0,0,0,0,0,1)$. However, the pattern (001) indicates that unit u_1 is faulty. Thus removing u_1 will results in the system shown in Fig. 14.4. The syndrome of this new system is $(a_{23}, a_{34}, a_{45}, a_{56}, a_{62}) = (x,0,0,0,1)$. This new syndrome has also the pattern $(0,0,1)$, which indicates that unit u_2 is faulty. The removal of unit u_2 will result in a fault-free system. This indicates that the system in Fig. 14.3 is a sequentially 2-diagnosable system.

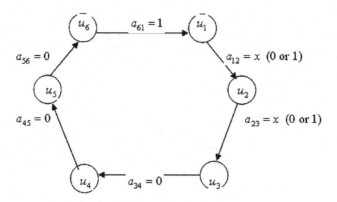

Fig. 14.3: A sequentially 2-diagnosable system.

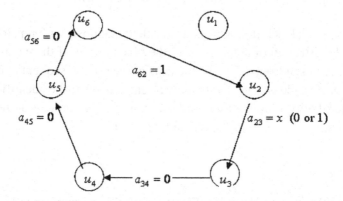

Fig. 14.4: The sequentially 2-diagnosable system in Fig. 14.2 with unit u_1 removed.

In general, a system is said to be sequentially t-diagnosable if the following conditions are satisfied: $n \geq 2t + 1$ and $N \geq n + 2t - 2$.

In addition to the above two main system diagnoses, a n number of other systems exist. These are introduced in Section 14.3.

Given a test assignment for a system, the diagnose-ability problem aims at characterizing the family of allowable fault sets (AFS) for a given diagnose-ability measure. Determining the diagnose-ability of a system depends also on the diagnosis model used. Diagnosable systems can be classified based on a number of criteria. These criteria include the following.

1. Faults and their categories: This includes the types of faults covered (permanent, intermittent, or hybrid) and the allowed fault sets.
2. Test Result interpretation: This includes symmetric invalidation, asymmetric invalidation or comparison model.
3. Number of steps used for diagnosis: This includes one-step or multi-step diagnosis.
4. Availability of Maintenance: This includes isolate, reconfigure, replace or repair during the diagnosis process.
5. Comprehensiveness of diagnosis: This includes complete and correct diagnosis.

There are basically three system-level diagnosis problems that are considered in the literature. These are the Characterization Problem, the diagnose-ability problem, and the diagnosis problem. The characterization problem is concerned with determining the necessary and sufficient conditions for a system to be diagnosable. Such condition for a one-step t-diagnosable system is $n \geq 2t + 1$ given that each unit is tested by at least t distinct other units. Given a test assignment for a system, the diagnose-ability problem is concerned with determining its one-step and sequential diagnose-ability. This translates to determining the maximum number t of arbitrary units that can be faulty such that the set of faulty units can be uniquely identified on the basis of a given syndrome. It has been shown that an algorithm with a complexity of $O(nt^{2.5})$ can calculate the t-diagnose-ability of a given test assignment. Given a test assignment and a syndrome for a system, the diagnosis problem is concerned with determining a consistent fault set of minimum cardinality, i.e. finding an algorithm for identifying such faulty set. It has been shown that an algorithm with a complexity of $O(n^{2.5})$ can be found to solve this problem.

14.2 System-Level Diagnosis Models

In this section, we review a number of the system-level diagnosis models. A diagnosis model describes the way faulty and fault-free units behave, the way tests' results are obtained, and the way diagnosis is carried out.

PMC (*Symmetric Invalidation*) Model

This model is named after **Preperata**, **Metz** and **Chein**. It was introduced in order to identify faulty units in a distributed system. According to the PMC, the diagnosed system is modeled as a directed graph $G(V, E)$. The units are the vertices V and the tests correspond to the edges E. An edge (u, v) exists in E if and only if u tests v. The PMC assumes that when a unit tests another unit, then the test outcome is either *pass* (tested unit is fault-free) or *fail* (tested unit is faulty). The PMC model assumes that all faults are permanent. The PMC also assumes that the test outcome is accurate as long as the testing unit is fault-free. According to the PMC model all test data are gathered and analyzed by a central unit and that the diagnosis is distributed back to the system units.

According to the PMC, unit u tests unit v in three steps as follows.

1. Unit u sends a test input sequence to v.
2. Unit v performs some computation on the test sequence and returns an output to u.
3. Unit u compares the output produced by v with the expected results and produces an outcome: 0 means *pass* (tested unit is fault-free) while 1 means *fail* (tested unit is faulty).

It should be noted that if the testing unit u is faulty, then the test outcome could be any value irrespective of the status of the tested unit v. Table 14.1 summarizes the different test outcome possibilities as explained above.

Table 14.1: PMC test outcome rules.

Testing unit (u)	Tested unit (v)	Test outcome
Fault-free	Fault-free	0
Fault-free	Faulty	1
Faulty	Fault-free or faulty	x (0 or 1)

A system consisting of n units is *t-diagnosable* if $n \geq 2t + 1$ given that each unit is tested by at least t distinct other units. The PMC model is called a symmetric invalidation model since a faulty unit produces unreliable test result when testing either faulty or fault-free units (see Table 14.1). The best known algorithm for determining the diagnose-ability of one-step t-diagnosable system under the PMC model has a time complexity given by $O(nt^{2.5})$.

GM (Asymmetric Invalidation) Model

This model is attributed to **B**arsi, **G**randoni, and **M**aestrini. It is considered as a modification of the PMC model with a more realistic representation of systems. According to this model, a faulty unit v will be always identified as faulty regardless of the state of the testing unit u. Table 14.2 summarizes the different test outcome possibilities as explained above.

Table 14.2: BGM test outcome rules.

Testing unit (u)	Tested unit (v)	Test outcome
Fault-free	Fault-free	0
Fault-free	Faulty	1
Faulty	Fault-free	x (0 or 1)
Faulty	Faulty	1

The BGM is called *asymmetric model*. This is because a faulty unit will produce a "1" when testing another faulty unit while producing an "x" when testing a fault-free unit. Except for the last observation, the BGM model is based on the same assumptions made by the PMC model.

From the diagnose-ability view point, the BGM model is considered to be relatively simpler. This is because according to this model, if the test outcome is 0, then the tested unit is considered as fault-free. In addition, if the test interconnection assignment of a system is a fully connected graph and there exists at least two fault-free units, then there exists a test for each other producing a test result of 0. This makes such units identifiable and accordingly their test outcomes can be used to diagnose all other units correctly and completely. That will make the condition $n > t + 1$ sufficient for the diagnose-ability of the system. It should also be noted that according to this model, each unit should be tested by at least t other units.

According to the BGM model, one-step diagnosis is possible if the cardinality of the fault set is as large as $(n\text{-}2)$ in a fully-connected diagnostic graph. Sequential diagnosis becomes trivial according to the BGM model. This is because any unit that passes the test is fault-free and if the diagnostic graph is strongly connected, then from that unit it is possible to determine the state of at least one faulty unit. The BGM model differs from the PMC model in that it restricts the set of the possible syndromes originated by a fault set. The best known algorithm for determining the diagnose-ability of one-step t-diagnosable system under the BGM model has a time complexity given by $O(nt^2/\log t)$.

The Comparison Model

This model is attributed to Malek. According to this model, the diagnostic graph is undirected, each edge (u_i, u_j) represents the comparison between unit u_i and unit u_j. The binary label used represents the comparison outcome such that it is a "0" if the two units agree and "1" otherwise. The basic assumption in this model is that two faulty units will never agree and likewise a faulty unit will never agree with a fault-free one. Table 14.3 summarizes the different test outcome possibilities according to the comparison model.

Table 14.3: Comparison model test outcome rules.

First unit (u_i)	Second unit (u_j)	Test outcome
Fault-free	Fault-free	0
Fault-free	Faulty	1
Faulty	Fault-free	1
Faulty	Faulty	1

It should be noted that when comparing more than two results, then up to $\lceil \frac{n}{2} \rceil - 1$ units can be diagnosed. Unlike the PMC model in which tests are performed in rounds between the execution of system tasks, the comparison model allows comparisons to be performed simultaneously with the system tasks. Thus, according to this model, a fault is detected when it occurs. In addition, a system's ability to contain faults is higher compared to those handled using the PMC model.

The above approach does not take into consideration the problem of which module performs the comparison. A more general model would be to assume that comparisons are performed by independent units which themselves may be subject to faults. The main assumptions here is that two faulty units never produce the same output and that a faulty comparator invalidates the comparison (see Table 14.4). It should be noted that although comparisons are distributed in this modified model, diagnoses are still performed in a centralized unit as before.

Table 14.4: A more general comparison model.

Comparator	1st Compared unit	2nd Compared unit	Comparison outcome
fault free	fault free	fault free	0
fault free	fault free	faulty	1
fault free	faulty	fault free	1
fault free	faulty	faulty	1
faulty	fault free	fault free	x (0 or 1)
faulty	fault free	faulty	x (0 or 1)
faulty	faulty	fault free	x (0 or 1)
faulty	faulty	faulty	x (0 or 1)

The Distributed Model

A major drawback of the PMC model is the need for a centralized diagnose system that decodes the test syndromes. This diagnose system must be reliable and must be able to communicate with each and every unit in the system. The distributed model avoids this drawback by having the syndrome be decoded in a distributed manner by the units themselves. According to this model, each unit collects information about other units in two ways: a test done by itself on its neighbors or information received from its neighbors about other units in the system.

At the end of the diagnosis process, all fault-free units in the system must agree on the diagnosis of the system. According to this model, units can make the following assumptions.

1. Fault-free units accept diagnostic information only from fault-free neighbors
2. Use the same test outcome rules as in the PMC model (see Table 14.1)
3. A faulty unit could corrupt a message sent by a fault-free unit
4. Faults do not occur during diagnosis.

The Probabilistic Model

According to this model each unit is assigned a probability (reliability) index. The goal of the diagnosis is to find the most likely fault set that is consistent with the obtained syndrome. A *p-t-diagnosable* system is one in which there exists a unique consistent fault set whose probability of occurrence is greater than *p*.

14.3 Diagnosable Systems

Two basic diagnosable systems were introduced in Section 14.1. These are the *t-diagnosable* and the *sequentially-diagnosable* systems. In this section, we review a number of other diagnosable systems. In particular, we review the *excess-diagnosable, partially-diagnosable, adaptively-diagnosable*, and the *incrementally-diagnosable* Systems.

Excess-Diagnosable Systems

This approach is meant as a way to increase the degree of diagnose-ability of a given system in spite of the availability of limited interconnections among its units. The main idea is to allow some of the fault-free units to be incorrectly diagnosed as faulty. By doing so, it will be possible to use fewer number of tests to quickly isolate the set of all faulty units together with some incorrectly diagnosed fault-free units. This way the remaining part of the system can restart its operation while a more comprehensive diagnosis process is independently applied in order to identify the incorrectly diagnosed fault-free units and maybe put them back to work. Excess-diagnose-ability is further classified into two sub-categories. These are the *t-s-diagnose-ability* and the *t-k-diagnose-ability*. These two sub-classes are introduced below assuming the PMC (symmetric invalidation) model.

t/s-faulty Diagnosable Systems

A system is said to be t/s-diagnosable if any set of up to t units can be diagnosed and repaired by replacing at most s units. In other words, in a t/s-diagnosable system, up to $s - |F|$ units may be incorrectly diagnosed, where $|F|$ is the actual number of faulty units. The main drawback of the t/s-diagnosable system is that the upper bound on the number of incorrectly diagnosed units is s-1 (in the case of having only one faulty unit), which can be large in comparison with the actual number of faulty units.

A special case of the t/s-diagnosable system is the t_1/t_1 – diagnosable system. In this special system ($s = t = t_1$), almost 50% reduction in the number of test links can be achieved for the same degree of diagnose-ability, compared to the number of tests required in a *t*-diagnosable system. For a system to be t_1/t_1 – diagnosable, every set of units with size $2(t_1 - p)$, $0 \le p < t_1$ should be tested by more than p units. This requirement implies that $n > 2t$. There is no test requirement for a single unit in a t_1/t_1 – diagnosable system. It is interesting to notice that in a t_1/t_1 – diagnosable system, all faulty units except at most one can be correctly identified and that all faulty units can be isolated within a set of t_1 or less units, of which at most one can possibly be fault-free, i.e., at most one unit can be incorrectly diagnosed as faulty. The following example shows the advantages of the t_1/t_1 – *diagnosable* system as compared to the *t-diagnosable* system.

Example (from Reference 9)

Consider the system consisting of 13 units as shown in Fig. 14.5.

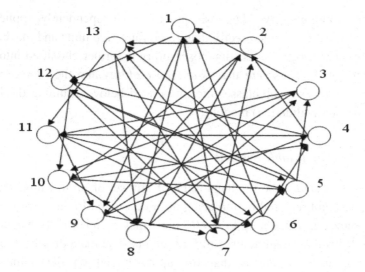

Fig. 14.5: An example D(13,3,{2,5,6}) system.

This system is denoted as $D(n,t,\{k_1,k_2,...,k_t\})$ where n is the total number of units and each unit i is tested by t other units given by $(i+k_1)\bmod n,(i+k_2)\bmod n,...,(i+k_t)\bmod n$. According to the given notation, the system in Fig. 14.5 is characterized as D(13,3,{2,5,6}). This system is t_1/t_1 – diagnosable for $t_1 = 5$ while the same system is t-diagnosable for $t \le 3$.

t/k-diagnosable Systems

This system is similar to the previous in allowing certain number of incorrectly diagnosed units. However, the t/k-diagnosable system puts an upper bound, k, on the number of incorrectly diagnosed units regardless of the number of actual faulty units (upper-bounded by t) that exists in the system.

A system is said to be t/k-diagnosable if given any test syndrome produced by the system under the presences of a fault set F, all faulty units can be isolated to within a set of F', out of which at most k units can possibly be fault-free, i.e., incorrectly diagnosed, where $|F'| \le |F| + k$, provided that the number of faulty units does not exceed t. Therefore, in the t/k-diagnosable system, the degree of diagnose-ability is maintained the same as in the *t*-diagnosable system however at a substantial reduction in the required number of test links. In other words, for the same number of tests, the value of *t* can be substantially increased at the expense of allowing some small number of incorrectly diagnosed units, *k*.

A necessary and sufficient condition for a system to be called *t/k-diagnosable* is that every set of units having size $2(k + p)$, where $1 \leq p \leq t - k$ should be tested by more than $t-(k + p)$ units. It is also necessary that every set of units having size between $k + 1$ and $2k + 1$ should be tested by at least $t-k$ units, whereas it is sufficient that every set of units having size $k + 1$ should be tested by at least t units. It should be noted that *t/k-diagnosable* system requires that $n > 2t$, the same as required by the $t_1/t_1 - diagnosable$ system.

It is interesting to notice that the class of *t/k-diagnosable* systems can be viewed as a generalization of the *t-diagnosable* systems ($k = 0$) and the $t_1/t_1 - diagnosable$ systems ($k = 1$).

The attractiveness of the t/k-diagnose-ability can be demonstrated by considering the hypercube architecture. A *d*-dimensional cube has $n = 2^d$ node and is *t*-diagnosable for $t = d$. The diagnose-ability of the same cube under the t/k-diagnose-ability is given by $[(k + 1)d - (k + 1)(k + 2)/2 + 1]$, where k is the maximum number of possible incorrectly diagnosed units. Consider, for example, a 10-cube. This architecture is 10-diagnosable under the *t-diagnose-ability* condition. The same cube is 31 diagnosable if up to 3 units are allowed to be incorrectly diagnosed.

Partially Diagnosable Systems

The classical approach of *t*-diagnosable systems will fail to identify those fault sets of sizes larger than *t* and which are also uniquely diagnosable. This in addition to the fact that in a given application, one may not always be interested in diagnosing all fault sets uniquely, indicate the need for a more general framework for fault diagnose-ability. In this framework, the ability to determine whether a given critical fault set F_k is uniquely diagnosable with respect to a given family of allowable fault sets $F = \{F_1, F_2, ..., F_f\}$ is possible.

Somani, Agarwal and Avis introduced the *single fault set diagnosis* (sf-diagnosis) system. This class of systems can be classified as partially diagnosable systems. The family of allowable fault sets which was considered in their work is similar to the *t*-fault class, which they called n_f -fault class to avoid confusion with *t*-diagnose-ability. However, the value of n_f is chosen arbitrarily based on maximum expected fault set size. The goal is to determine whether a given fault set can be diagnosed with respect to the n_f -fault class. Thus, a given fault set F is sf-diagnosable if, given any syndrome and assuming that the fault set belongs to the n_f -fault class, it can be uniquely diagnosed.

The basic requirement for unique diagnosis of any fault set is that either all fault-free units should remain strongly connected or, if a partition of fault-free units is created by the faulty units, then each partition should be such that diagnosis can be completed within each partition independently. Otherwise, unique diagnosis cannot be guaranteed. This diagnosis is always correct but may be incomplete. The same authors also showed that the sf-diagnosis problem is co-NP-complete both in the PMC and the BGM model. The sf-diagnose-ability problem has a polynomial solution for the PMC model and it is co-NP-complete for the BGM model.

Adaptively Diagnosable Systems

In non-adaptive diagnosis, all tests must be scheduled in advance. According to these systems, the diagnosis algorithm operates once the tests have been executed and the syndrome has been collected by the central unit. However, not all the tests are always necessary for the diagnosis. To reduce the burden of unnecessary tests, Nakajima introduced the adaptive tests model. In this approach, it is assumed that any unit is capable of testing any other unit in the system. Hence the test graph should be a complete graph. The main idea is that tests can be determined dynamically depending on the previous test results. Thus, the unit performing the diagnosis chooses the order of the tests to be executed by the units during the diagnosis process adaptively. According to the adaptive diagnosis, it is required that $t < \frac{n}{2}$ but only n + t − 1 tests (lower bound) are sufficient for a system consisting of *n* components with at most *t* faulty units. It has been shown that an adaptive diagnosis algorithm for a system consisting of *n* units and modeled by a hypercube with at most *t* faulty units uses $n + t - 1$ tests if $t = \log_2 n$ and $n + t$ tests if $t < \log_2 n$.

Incrementally Diagnosable Systems

In most practical systems, especially mission-oriented ones, when a faulty unit is identified, then the system is reconfigured in such a way that the faulty unit is isolated. It is only when maintenance facilities become available that such faulty unit(s) is (are) repaired. The system may be allowed to function in a degraded mode and with reduced capabilities. Motivated by this, Somani introduced the idea of incrementally diagnosed systems. A system is said to be incrementally k/t-diagnosable if the following constraints are satisfied.

1. Faults occur sequentially,
2. No more than *k* faults can occur between two diagnosis steps,
3. Faults are diagnosed and system is reconfigured before new faults occur, and
4. The total number of faulty units does not exceed *t*.

Example (from Reference 5)

Consider the case of a fully connected system having six units (see Fig. 14.6).

Assuming that $k = 1$, the system shown in Fig. 14.6 is $\frac{1}{(n-2)} = \frac{1}{4} -$ incrementally diagnosable, i.e., it can tolerant up to four faulty units. The same system is only $\left\lfloor \frac{(n-1)}{2} \right\rfloor = 2$-diagnosable, i.e. it can only tolerant up to two faulty units according to the *t*-diagnose-ability characterization.

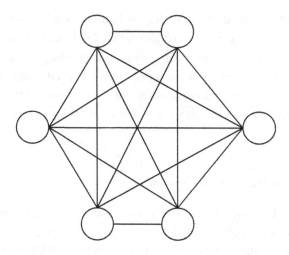

Fig. 14.6: A completely connected system with 6 units.

Safe System Diagnosis

The concept of *safe system level diagnosis* which combines diagnosis and detection was introduced by Vaidya and Pradhan. The safe diagnosis approach ensures that at most t faulty nodes can be located and at most u faulty nodes (with u > t) can be detected. Safe diagnosis attempts to locate the most likely fault patterns while detecting the less likely fault patterns. It is shown that a large fault detection capability, along with the existing fault location capability, can be achieved with minimal additional testing overhead. A system is t–FL–u–FD with u > t + 1 is a (t + 1)-diagnosable system. The converse of this statement is not true. This means that the u > t + 1 is the lower bound and u cannot be lower than this. When a t–FL–u–FD system is used for fault location, it can be at most $\lfloor (t + 1)/2 \rfloor$-diagnosable.

14.4 Diagnose-Ability Algorithms

A diagnosis algorithm decodes a syndrome produced by a system in order to identify faulty and fault-free units. The set of inputs needed by any diagnosis algorithm are as follows.

1. Test digraph $D = (U, E)$ of the system.
2. System class (t-diagnosable, t/s-diagnosable, or t/k-diagnosable, etc.).
3. Model for the interpretation of test outcomes (PMC, BGM, Comparison, etc.)
4. Fault set(s) whose unique diagnose-ability is(are) to be established.
5. Allowable fault set(s)

A diagnosis algorithm should determine the diagnose-ability of a fault set F (or a family of fault sets) from the allowable fault set(s). It should also determine the degree of diagnose-ability of the system. A number of practical algorithms that deal with the diagnosis problem in both general and specific systems have been developed over the years. In what follows, we discuss two types of diagnosis algorithms developed for general systems. These are the centralized and the distributed diagnosis systems.

14.4.1 *Centralized Diagnosis Systems*

In a centralized diagnosis algorithm, the syndrome is analyzed by one single central unit using global system information. Therefore, test results produced by all system units should be transmitted to the central unit for analysis. Syndrome decoding/analysis outcomes should then be transmitted back from the central unit to the individual units. As can be seen, such centralized arrangement can require massive input/output transactions, especially for systems consisting of large number of units. In addition, the existence of a single central unit causes the system to become a single point failure.

A straightforward way of performing such centralized diagnosis is for the central unit to use comparison among tests produced by individual unit in order to identify the faulty units. Consider the following diagnosis algorithm for *t-diagnosable* systems. Let $a(i, j)$ be the test outcome and B_i be the test table produced by unit u_i, $i = 1, 2, ..., (n-1)$. Each B_i consists of $B_{i,0}, B_{i,1}, B_{i,2}, ..., B_{i,(n-1)}$ where $B_{i,j}$ represents the test results of u_i on u_j. If unit u_i is fault-free, then its testing table B_i will be correct. There are at most t faulty units and therefore, there exists at least $(n-t)$ B_i that are identical. If there is one set of identical tables $B_{i,1}, B_{i,2}, ..., B_{i,s}$

such that s ≥ (n - t) then each of these tables in the set correctly identifies the existing faulty unit. Let $i \in [0,1,...,(n-1)]$ and $t \in [1,2,...,(n-1)]$, the algorithm proceeds as follows.

1. Set $B_{i,m} = 0$ for $m = 0,1,...,(n-1)$
2. Set $(j$-$k, k) = i + 1$ and $N_F = 0$.
3. If $N_F \geq t$ or $k = i$ then stop; else go to step 4
4. If $a(j, k) = 1$ then set $B_{i,k} = 1$, $N_F = N_F + 1$ and go to step 5; else set $j = k$
5. Set $k = k + 1$ and go to step 1.

Example

Consider the system shown in Fig. 14.7. The system consists of six units U_0 to U_5. Assume that at most two units may be faulty, i.e., $t = 2$. Assume also that the interconnection pattern is $D_{1,2}$. Let us assume that the syndrome is as shown in Table 14.5 (x in the table is assumed to be any value). It should be noted that a unit test itself as fault-free. Units U_0 and U_1 are the faulty units in this system.

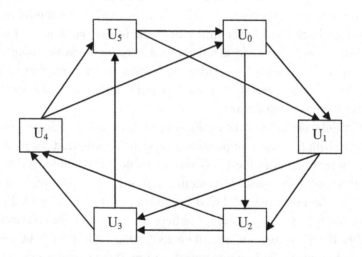

Fig. 14.7: Example system.

Table 14.5: Syndrome for the example system.

Unit	0	1	2	3	4	5
0	0	0	1	X	X	X
1	X	0	1	0	X	X
2	X	X	0	0	0	X
3	X	X	X	0	0	0
4	1	X	X	X	0	0
5	1	1	X	X	X	0

Using the algorithm presented above, the generated B matrix consisting of the B_0, B_1, ..., B_5 tables will be as shown below. In this matrix, each table is generated depending on the syndrome. For example, unit U_2 concludes that units 2 (which is U_2 itself), 3 and 4 are fault-free. This means that it can use their conclusion about the other units to generate its own table. So, it is clear that both test 5 as fault free and unit 4 test unit 0 as faulty. Since unit 5 is faulty so it can use its result for the state of unit 1 which believes that it is faulty and the table of unit U_2 is complete. All the other tables are done in this way.

K	0	1	2	3	4	5
B_i						
B_0	0	0	1	0	0	0
B_1	1	0	1	0	0	0
B_2	1	1	0	0	0	0
B_3	1	1	0	0	0	0
B_4	1	1	0	0	0	0
B_5	1	1	0	0	0	0

As can be seen, there are four identical tables, i.e., n-t = 4. If we have less than this number then it means that there are more than t faulty nodes. Therefore, the algorithm will not work in this case. From the table of U_2 we can conclude that units 0 and 1 are faulty under the assumption that U_2 is fault-free. Let's apply the algorithm step by step to generate the table of U_2. Here i = 2.

Step 00: $B_2=[0\ 0\ 0\ 0\ 0\ 0]$; $j=i=2$; $k=i+1=3$; $N_f=0$;

Step 1a: $N_f=0$ which is not greater than or equal to $t=2$;
           $k=3$ which is not equal to $i=2$; so go to step 2;

Step 2a: $a(2,3)=0$; so $j=k=3$; go to step 3;

Step 3a: $k=k+1=4$; go to step 1;

Step 1b: $N_f=0$ which is not greater than or equal to $t=2$;
           $k=4$ which is not equal to $i=2$; so go to step 2;

Step 2b: $a(3,4)=0$; so $j=k=4$; go to step 3;

Step 3b: $k=k+1=5$; go to step 1;

Step 1c: $N_f=0$ which is not greater than or equal to $t=2$;
           $k=5$ which is not equal to $i=2$; so go to step 2;

Step 2c: $a(4,5)=0$; so $j=k=5$; go to step 3;

Step 3c: $k=k+1=0$ (since modulo 6); go to step 1;

Step 1d: $N_f=0$ which is not greater than or equal to $t=2$;
           $k=0$ which is not equal to $i=2$; so go to step 2;

Step 2d: $a(5,0)=1$; $B_{2,0}=1$; so $B_2=[1\ 0\ 0\ 0\ 0\ 0]$
           $N_f=N_f+1=1$; go to step 3;

Step 3d: $k=k+1=1$; go to step 1;

Step 1d: $N_f=1$ which is not greater than or equal to $t=2$;
           $k=1$ which is not equal to $i=2$; so go to step 2.

Step 2d: $a(5,1)=1$; $B_{2,1}=1$; so $B_2=[1\ 1\ 0\ 0\ 0\ 0]$;
           $N_f=N_f+1=2$; go to step 3;

Step 3d: $k=k+1=2$; go to step 1;

Step 1e: $N_f=2=t$; so stop.

Now the table of unit U_2 is $B_2 = [1\ 1\ 0\ 0\ 0\ 0]$. This means that under
the assumption that U_2 is fault-free the table B_2 is correct and specifies
exactly the faulty units, which is the case. According to B_2 units U_0 and
U_1 are the faulty set. Let's look to some of the steps to see how the table
was constructed. Steps 00 and 1a are straight forward. If we look at step
2a, we see that $a(2,3) = 0$ means that unit 2 tests unit 3 to be fault free. So
j is now updated to 3 ($j = 3$) so that we can use the tests performed by
unit 3. This is done because unit 3 is fault-free from unit 2 point of view.
At step 3a k is now updated to 4. Step 1b is clear so let's go to step 2b.
We can see that $a(3,4) = 0$ so unit 4 is fault-free from unit 3 point of view

and as a result from unit 2 point of view. So the same thing is done meaning that $j = 4$ and $k = 5$. Notice that we did not change any value in the table because all elements are initiated to zero and we did not find any faulty unit till this point. The same procedure is done till step 3c. The only thing here is that $k = 0$ since $5 + 1(modulo6) = 0$. Step 1d is clear so go to step 2d. Notice here that $a(5,0) = 1$; this means that unit 0 is faulty from unit 5 point of view and indirectly from unit 2 point of view. This means that we cannot use its tests because it is faulty. That is why j is not updated to 0 here. Therefore the element $B_{2,0} = 1$ since unit 2 tests unit 0 to be faulty in an indirect way. B_2 is updated accordingly, i.e $B_2 = [1\ 0\ 0\ 0\ 0\ 0]$. $N_f = 1$. Step 3d updates k to 1. In step 1e we see that $N_f = 1$ which is not greater than or equal to 2. So continue with step 2d. Here we are using the results of unit 5 on unit 1 not the results of unit 0 because it is faulty. $a(5,2) = 1$ so $B_{2,1} = 1$ and $B_2 = [1\ 1\ 0\ 0\ 0\ 0]$. The value of j is not updated as we see since unit 1 is faulty. $N_f = N_f + 1 = 2$ in this step and then we will go to step 3d. At this step k is updated to 2 and we will continue with step 1e. In this step the condition that $N_f = 2 = t$ is satisfied so we have to stop the algorithm at this point. The final table of B_2 is $B_2 = [1\ 1\ 0\ 0\ 0\ 0]$. As we said if unit 2 is fault free then B_2 describes exactly the faulty set.

All the tables, i.e B_i, are generated in the same way regardless of the state of unit i. So after the construction of all the tables we will check if we have n-t or more identical tables. If we have, then these identical tables contain the faulty set. This is the case illustrated in this example; we have four identical tables of the form $B_i = [1\ 1\ 0\ 0\ 0\ 0]$, and two other tables. This means that from this table we have units 0 and 1 as the faulty units. In the program we have to check this case so, we have to search for at least n-t identical tables. Here comes the time complexity of the program. So we have to check at least n-t possible tables and this is the best case. In each of these comparisons we have to check that element by element increasing the time complexity more and more.

Meyer and Masson have suggested an accelerated algorithm. As we said, the diagnosis of the faulty set requires that the tables B_i's for $i = 0, 1, 2, ..., $ n-1 be compared. This has a high time complexity. The authors have suggested the following. For each $j = 0, 1, ..., $ n-1, let v_j be the number of indices for which $B_{i,j} = 1$. This means that: v_j = cardinality of $\{i \in [0, 1, ..., n\text{-}1] \mid B_{i,j} = 1\}$.

In other words, v_j is the summation of ones in the jth column of the full B matrix. For example, from the table above the v_j's are $v_0 = 5$, $v_1 = 4$, $v_2 = 2$, $v_3 = 0$, $v_4 = 0$ and $v_5 = 0$. These quantities can be used for diagnosis as discussed in the Chapter 16.

A central disagreement graph-based algorithm is presented below.

Disagreement Graph-Based Algorithm

This algorithm has also been developed for *t-diagnosable* systems. The algorithm represents the disagreements among the units in the test graph in the form of an undirected graph, called the *disagreement* graph of the *L-graph*. For each unit u_i, a set of units $L(u_i)$ is defined consisting of all those implied faulty units if u_i is considered to be fault-free. Two units disagree if directly, or indirectly, they produce contradictory test results. The nodes of the *L-graph* are the nodes of the original test graph. An edge exists from node u_i to another node u_j in the *L-graph* if $u_j \in L(u_i)$. Thus, an edge exists between those pair of nodes for which the assumption that one unit is fault-free directly or indirectly implies that the other unit is faulty. The steps of the algorithm are as follows.

1. Construct the *L-graph*.
2. Find V_f the minimum cover set of the graph (finding V_f in an NP for general graphs)
3. Find a maximum matching in the *L-graph*. This will match a faulty and a fault-free unit in the system
4. Visit the *L-graph* starting from a unit that is not included in the matching.

Example

Consider the system graph shown in Fig. 14.8. Part (a) of the figure depicts the system test graph and a generated syndrome. Part (b) of the figure shows the corresponding disagreement graph and part (c) depicts the maximum matching of the disagreement graph, which leads to the minimum vertex cover of the graph, i.e., the set of faulty units.

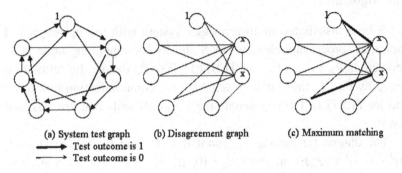

(a) System test graph   (b) Disagreement graph   (c) Maximum matching
➤ Test outcome is 1
→ Test outcome is 0

Fig. 14.8: Example centralized diagnosis systems.

14.4.2 *Distributed Diagnosis Systems*

Contrary to central diagnosis algorithms, a distributed diagnosis algorithm is executed on many or all the units in the system simultaneously. A distributed diagnosis algorithm depends on the interconnection network of the system. If the interconnection network of a system is any general graph, then the distributed diagnosis algorithm may be very complex and may require too much information flow among the processors executing such an algorithm. However, if the interconnection network is regular in nature, then the diagnosis algorithm may be much simplified.

One of the early distributed diagnosis algorithms for t-diagnosable systems was developed by Kuhl and Reddy. In this algorithm, each unit in the system determines the status of every other unit based on the information it collects through distribution of test results information. Each unit tests a number of pre-designated neighbors and disseminating diagnostics messages. Each test result is broadcasted by the testing unit to all the other units. Intermediate nodes on a path from one unit to another unit in the system graph are used to transmit messages. A diagnostic message reaching a unit from another unit may not be entirely correct or reliable because this message may be routed through a faulty unit or link. The algorithm is explained next.

The Algorithm

Let S be a distributed multi-processor system with testing graph T. Let each unit (processing element) of S and its corresponding node in T be denoted as P_0, P_1, ..., P_n. Let TESTED_BY (P_i) denote the set of all unit tested by P_i, i.e., those units reachable by a communication link from P_i, and let TESTED_OF (P_i) denote the set of all units that are assigned to test P_i.

The diagnostic message is denoted as D_0 and D_1, where D_0 and D_1 are sets of integers in the range [0, n]. Each P_i will compute a fault vector $F_i = f_i^1 \ f_i^2 \dots f_i^n$ where $f_i^j = 1$ if P_i concludes that P_j is fault free and $f_i^j = 0$ if P_i determines P_j to be fault free. Assume that a round of testing has been completed (recall that the test result of a test of P_j performed by P_i is denoted as $a_i^j \in \{0, 1\}$). Then each P_i can compute its fault vector F_i according to the following algorithm.

---

1. Initialize set D_0, D_1 to null. Let $f_i^1 = 0$ and let f_i^j be unspecified for $j \neq i$.
2. For each $P_r \in$ TESTED_BY (P_i) do
   a. Let $f_i^r = a_i^r$
   b. If $a_i^r = 0$ then add r to the set D_0 else add r to D_1.
3. Broadcast message D_0, D_1 to all $P_j \in$ TESTED_OF(P_i).
4. For each message received from neighbor P_j, where $P_j \in$ TESTED_BY(P_i) and $a_i^j = 0$, until F_i is completed do
   a. Reinitialized D_0 and D_1 to null.
   b. For each $k \in D_0{}' \cup D_1{}'$ such that f_i^k is not yet specified do
      i. If $k \in D_0{}'$ then add k to D_0 else let $f_i^k = 0$.
      ii. Else add k to D_1 and let $f_i^k = 1$.
   c. If $D_0 \cup D_1$ is not null then broadcast message D_0 and D_1 to all processors P_t such that $P_t \in$ TESTED_OF(P_i) - $\{P_j\}$ and $a_i^t \neq 1$.
5. Let any still unspecified positions of F_i be 0.

The diagnose-ability of distributed system (k(G)) depends on the connectivity of the system. Using algorithm SELF, it can be shown that the system is t-fault self-diagnosis if and only if k(T) ≥ 2. Hosseini, Kuhl and Reddy proposed another algorithm called NEW_SELF. This algorithm is an improvement over the above algorithm and includes failure and recovery during diagnosis.

It was shown that the implementation of the above algorithm is impractical in real systems due to high resource requirements. Therefore, the following adaptive distributed system diagnosis was proposed.

Adaptive Distributed System Diagnosis

There are two significant drawbacks to the SELF algorithms. The first drawback concerns with limited diagnose-ability. If there exist two consecutive faulty nodes, test result reports that are not forwarded to all fault-free nodes. The second major drawback of the algorithm concerns redundancy, in terms of both inter-node testing and report forwarding. For t-diagnosable systems, each node must be tested by at least $t+1$ other node. Ideally, each node must be tested by only one fault-free node to ensure correct diagnosis, thus all but one of the $t+1$ tests and information forwarding are redundant.

The Adaptive DSD (ADSD) algorithm differs considerably from the above shown algorithm in that the testing assignment is adaptive and determined by the fault situation. Node failures and repairs are considered; link failures are not. The Adaptive DSD algorithm further differs from the above algorithm in that the number of nodes in the fault set is not bounded. The remaining fault-free nodes correctly diagnose the fault states of all nodes in the system.

In ADSD, an array called TESTED_UP$_x$ is maintained at each node n_x. The array contains N elements, indexed by node identifier, i, as TESTED_UP$_x$[i], for $0 \leq i \leq N-1$. Each element of TESTED_UP$_x$ contains a node identifier. The entry TESTED_UP$_x$[i] = j indicates that n_x has received diagnostic information from a fault-free node specifying that n_i has tested n_j and found it to be fault-free. Consider the example shown in Fig. 3.8. The TESTED_UP$_2$ array maintained at n_2 for an eight node system with n_1, n_4, and n_5 faulty is shown in Fig. 14.9(b). Note that "x" represents an entry that is arbitrary.

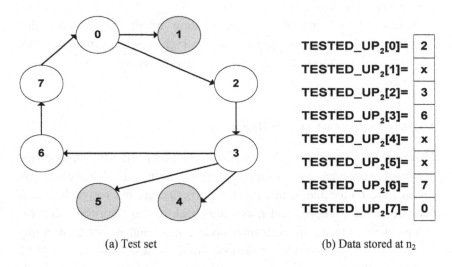

(a) Test set	(b) Data stored at n_2

Fig. 14.9: Adaptive DSD.

The ADSD algorithm executes at each node by first identifying another unique fault free node and then updating local diagnostic information with information received from that node. Functionally, this is accomplished as follows. List the nodes in sequential order, as $(n_0, n_1, ..., n_{N-1})$. Node n_x identifies the next sequential fault-free node in the list, sequentially testing consecutive nodes n_{x+1}, n_{x+2}, etc., until a fault-free node is found. Diagnostic information received from the tested fault-free node is assumed to be valid and is utilized to update local information. All addition is modulo N so that the last fault-free node in the ordered list identifies the first fault-free node in the list. This proceeds as follows.

1. Let y=x
2. repeat
    a. $y = (y+1) \bmod N$
    b. request n_y to forward $TESTED\_UP_y$ to n_x
3. until n_x tests n_y as fault free
4. $TESTED\_UP_x[x] = y$.
5. for i=0 to N−1
    a. if $(i \neq x)$ then $TESTED\_UP_x[i] = TESTED\_UP_y[i]$

The Adaptive DSD algorithm specifies that a node sequentially tests consecutive nodes until a fault-free node is identified. For the example shown in Fig. 14.8, n_0 tests n_1, finds it to be faulty and continues testing. Subsequently, n_0 tests node n_2, finds it to be fault-free and stops testing. Node n_2 finds n_3 to be fault-free and stops testing immediately. Node n_3 must test three nodes before it tests a fault-free node.

Diagnosis is accomplished at any node n_x by following the fault-free paths from n_x to other fault-free nodes. The algorithm uses the information stored in $TESTED\_UP_x$ to diagnose the system. Its results are stored in an array, $STATE_x$, where $STATE_x[i]$ represents the diagnosed state of node n_i. For correct diagnosis, $STATE_x[i]$ must equal s_i for all i. The diagnose algorithm to be executed by a node n_x is given as follows.

1. for i = 0 to N−1
    a. $STATE_x[i]$ = faulty
2. node_pointer = x
3. repeat
    a. $STATE_x$[node_pointer] = fault-free
    b. node_pointer = $TESTED\_UP_x$ [node_pointer]
4. until (node_pointer = x);

Testing round is defined as the maximum time interval needed by the fault-free units to test another fault-free unit, or test all units as faulty. In ADSD, the value of testing round is proven to be O(N), with the maximum number of test O(N). In addition, the diagnose-ability of ADSD is (N–1)-diagnosable as compared to the t-diagnosable of SELF algorithm.

Hierarchical-Adaptive Distributed System Diagnosis (Hi-ADSD)

Consider a system S consisting of a set of N nodes, n_0, n_1, ..., n_{N-1}. The system is assumed to be fully connected, i.e., there is a communication link between any two nodes (n_i, n_j). Each node n_i is assumed to be in one of two states, faulty or fault free. A combination of the state of all nodes constitutes the system's fault situation. Nodes perform tests on other nodes in a testing interval, and fault-free nodes report test results reliably.

Nodes are grouped into clusters for the purpose of testing. Clusters are sets of nodes. The number of nodes in a cluster, its size, is always a power of two. Initially, N is assumed to be a power of 2, and the system itself is a cluster of N nodes. A cluster of n nodes n_j, ..., n_{j+n-1}, where j MOD n = 0, and n is a power of two, is recursively defined as either a node, in case n = 1; or the union of two clusters, one containing nodes nj, ..., $n_{j+n/2-1}$ and the other containing nodes $n_{j+n/2}$, ..., n_{j+n-1}.

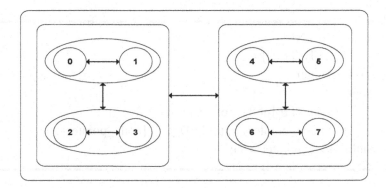

Fig. 14.10: A hierarchical approach to test clustered system.

Figure 14.10 shows a system with eight nodes organized in clusters. In the first testing interval, each node performs tests on nodes of a cluster that has one node, in the second testing interval, on nodes of a cluster that has two nodes, in the third testing interval, on nodes of a cluster that has four nodes, and so on, until the cluster of $2^{\log N-1}$, or N/2, nodes is tested. After that, the cluster of size 1 is tested again, and the process is repeated. The lists of ordered nodes tested by node i in a cluster of size 2^{s-1}, in a given testing interval, are denoted by $c_{i,s}$. When node i performs a test on nodes of $c_{i,s}$, it performs tests sequentially until it finds a fault-free node or all other nodes are faulty. Supposing a fault-free node is found; from this fault-free node, node i copies diagnostic information of all nodes in $c_{i,s}$. Using function $c_{i,s}$, when two different nodes test the a given cluster, they will start testing different nodes. If all nodes in $c_{i,s}$ are faulty, node i goes on to test $c_{i,s+1}$ in the same testing interval. Again, if all nodes in $c_{i,s+1}$ are faulty, node i goes on to test $c_{i,s+2}$, and so on, until it finds a fault-free node or all nodes are found to be faulty.

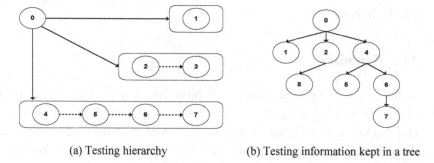

(a) Testing hierarchy   (b) Testing information kept in a tree

Fig. 14.11: Adaptive DSD.

Consider, for example, the system shown in Fig. 14.11. Part (a) of the figure shows the testing hierarchy for eight nodes, from the viewpoint of node 0. When node 0 tests a cluster of size 2^2, it first tests node 4. If node 4 is fault-free, node 0 copies diagnostic information regarding nodes 4, 5, 6, and 7. If node 4 is faulty, node 0 tests node 5, and so on. Hi-ADSD uses a tree to store information about the tests in all clusters. Part (b) of the figure shows the tree for node 0, for the case that all nodes are fault-free.

The following is the Hi-ADSD algorithm.

[1] for s = 1 TO log N DO
[2] repeat
       a. node_to_test = next in $c_{i,s}$
       b. if node_to_test is fault-free
    then update cluster diagnostic information
[3] until (node_to_test is fault-free) OR (all nodes in ci,s are faulty)
[4] if all nodes in $c_{i,s}$ are faulty
    then erase cluster diagnostic information
[5] end for

The Hi-ADSD algorithm has the latency of log N testing rounds, with maximum number of test of $O(N^2)$. The diagnosability of the system is (N−1)-diagnosable.

14.5 Summary

In this chapter, we have covered the basic issues related to system level diagnosis. In particular, we have first introduced some basic terminology and background material. We have followed that up with a detailed discussion on diagnose-ability models. Along that line, we have introduced five models. These are the PMC (Preperata, Metz, and Chein) model, the BGM (Barsi, Grandoni, and Maestrini) model, the comparison model, the distribution model, and the probabilistic model. A number of diagnosable systems together with their respective diagnose-ability algorithms have also been introduced. We concluded our discussion by presenting a number of example diagnosis systems and show how to develop their diagnosis algorithms. In the next chapter, we will elaborate on the application of the concepts introduced in this chapter in the context of regular and grid-connected structures.

References

[1]   F.P. Preparata, G. Metz and R.T. Chien, "On The Connection Assignment Problem of Diagnosable Systems," IEEE Transactions on Electronic Computers, vol. EC-16, pp 848-854, Dec 1967.

[2]   S.L. Hakimi and A.T. Amin, "Characterization of Connection Assignment of Diagnosable Systems," IEEE Transactions on Computers, pp 86-89, Jan 1974.

[3]   G.L. Meyer and G.M. Masson, "An Efficient Fault Diagnosis Algorithm for Symmetric Multiple Processor Architectures," IEEE Transactions on Computers, vol. c-22, no. 11, pp 1059-1063, Nov. 1978.

[4]   F.P. Preparata and G. Metze and R.T. Chien. On the connection assignment problem of diagnosable systems. *IEEE Trans. Electr. Computer*, EC(16):848-854, 1967.

[5]   Arun K. Somani. System-level Diagnosis: A Review. http://www.google.com/search?hl=en&ie=UTF8&q=%22System+Level+Diagnosis%3A+A+Review%22+

[6]   S.L. Hakimi and A.T. Amin. Characterization of connection assignment of diagnosable systems. *IEEE Trans. Computer*, C(23):86-88, Jan 1974.

[7]   F. Barsi and F. Grandoni and P. Maestrini. A theory of diagnosability without repairs. *IEEE Trans. Computer*, C(25):585-593, 1976.

[8]   K.Y. Chwa and S.L. Hakimi. Schemes for fault-tolerant computing: a comparison of modularly redundant and t-diagnosable systems. *Information and Control*, 49:212-238, 1981.

[9]   K.Y. Chwa and S.L. Hakimi. On Fault identification in diagnosable systems. IEEE Transactions on Computers, vol. C-30, 1981, pp. 414-422.

[10] J.G. Kuhl and S.M. Reddy. Fault diagnosis in fully distributed systems. *IEEE Symp. Fault-Tolerant Computer*, pages 100-105, 1981.

[11] J. Xu and S. Huang. Sequentially t-diagnosable Systems: A Charaterization and Its Applications. *IEEE Trans. Computers*, 44(2):340-345, Feb. 1995.

[12]   Somani, A., K. and Agarwal, V., K. and Avis, D.,. A Generalised
       Theory for System Level Diagnosis. *IEEE Transactions on
       Computers*, C-36(5):538-546, May 1987.

[13]   Kreutzer, S. and Hakimi, S., L. Adaptive Fault Identification in
       Two New Diagnostic Models. *Proceedings of the 21st Allerton
       Conference on Communication, Control and Computing*, pages
       353-362, 1983.

[14]   M. Malek. A Comparison Connection Assignment for Diagnosis
       of Multiprocessor Systems. *Proceedings of the 10th Symposium on
       Computer Architecture*, pages 31-35, May 1980.

[15]   Chwa, K., Y. and Hakimi, S., L. Schemes for Fault-Tolerant
       Computing: A Comparison of Modulary Redundant and t-
       Diagnosable Systems. *Information and Controls*, 45(3):212-238,
       1981.

[16]   Maeng, J. and Malek, M. A Comparison Connection Assignment
       for Self-Diagnosis of Multicomputer System. *Proceedings of the
       11th Fault-Tolerant Computing Symposium*, pages 173-175, June
       1981.

[17]   Maheshwari, S., N. and Hakimi, S., L. On Models for Diagnosable
       Systems and Probabilistic Fault Diagnosis. *IEEE Transactions on
       Computers*, C-25(3):228-236, March 1976.

[18]   Fujiwara, H. and Kinoshita, K. Connection Assignement for
       Probabilistic Diagnosable Systems. *IEEE Transactions on
       Computers*, C-27(3):280-283, March 1978.

[19]   G. Sullivan. System Level Fault Diagnosability in Probabilistic
       and Weighted Models. *Proceedings of the 17th Fault-Tolerant
       Computing Symposium*, pages 190-195, 1987.

[20]   Blount, M., L. Probabilistic Treatment of Diagnosis in Digital
       Systems. *Proceedings of the 7th Fault-Tolerant Computing
       Symposium*, pages 72-77, 1977.

[21]   Blough, D., and Sullivan, G., and Masson, G., M. Almost Certain
       Diagnosis for Intermittently Faulty Systems. *Proceedings of the
       18th Fault-Tolerant Computing Symposium*, pages 260-271, 1988.

[22]   G. Sullivan. A Polynomial Time Algorithm for Fault Diagnosability.
       Annual Symposium on Foundations of Computer Science, pages
       148-156, 1984.

[23] A.T. Dahbura and G.M. Masson. An $O(n^{2.5})$ fault identification algorithm for diagnosable systems. *IEEE Transactions on Computers*, C-33:486-492, 1984.

[24] F.J. Allan and T. Kameda and S. Toida. An approach to the diagnosability analysis of a system. *IEEE Transactions on Computers*, C-24:1040-1042, 1975.

[25] T. Kohda. On one step diagnosable systems containing at most t faulty units. *Systems, Computers, Controls*, 9(5), 1978.

[26] Raghavan, V. and Tripathi A., R. Improved Diagnosability Algorithms. *IEEE Transactions on Computers*, 40(2):143-153, Feb 1991.

[27] Raghavan, V. and Tripathi A., R. Sequential Diagnosability is co-NP Complete. *IEEE Transactions on Computers*, 40(5):584-595, May 1991.

[28] Preparata, F., P. Some Results on Sequential Diagnosable Systems. *Proceedings of the Hawaii International Conference on Systems Science*, pages 623-626, Jan 1968.

[29] Maestrini, P. and Liu., C., L. On the Sequential Diagnosability of a Class of Digital Systems. *Proceedings of the 11th Fault-Tolerant Computing Symposium*, pages 112-115, June 1981.

[30] Ciompi, P. and Simoncini, L. The Boundary Graphs: An Approach to the Diagnosability with Repair of Digital Systems. *Proceedings of the 3rd Texas Conference of Computer Systems*, pages 931-939, Nov 1974.

[31] Ciompi, P. and Simoncini, L. Analysis and Optimal Design of Self-Diagnosable Systems with Repair. *IEEE Transactions on Computers*, C-28(5):362-365, May 1979.

[32] A.D. Friedman. A new measure of digital system diagnosis. *IEEE Symp. Fault-Tolerant Computing*, pages 167-169, 1975.

[33] S. Karunanithi and A.D. Friedman. Analysis of digital systems using a new measure of system diagnosis. *IEEE Trans. on Computers*, C-25:121-133, 1979.

[34] C.L. Yang and G.M. Masson and R.A. Leonetti. On fault isolation and identification in t_1/t_1-diagnosable systems. *IEEE Transactions on Computers*, C-35:639-643, 1986.

[35] C.L. Yang and G.M. Masson. An Efficient algorithm for multiprocessor fault diagnosis using the comparison approach. *IEEE Symp. Fault-Tolerant Computing*, pages 238-243, 1986.

[36] A.K. Somani and O. Peleg. On Diagnosability of Large fault Sets and Its Applications to Regular-Interconnected Computer Systems. *IEEE Transactions on Computers*, 45(8):892-903, Aug 1996.

[37] A.K. Somani, V.K. Agarwal and D. Avis. A generalized theory for system level diagnosis. *IEEE Transactions on Computers*, C-36:538-546, 1987.

[38] Somani, A., K. and Agarwal, V., K., and Avis, D. On the Complexity of Single Fault Set Diagnosability and Diagnosis Problems. *IEEE Transactions on Computers*, 38(2):195-201, Feb 1989.

[39] Vaidya, N., H. and Pradhan, D., K. System Level Diagnosis: Combining Detection and Location. *Proceedings of the 21th Fault-Tolerant Computing Symposium*, pages 488-495, 1991.

[40] Vaidya, N., H. and Pradhan, D., K. Safe System Level Diagnosis. *IEEE Transactions on Computers*, 43(3):367-370, March 1994.

[41] K. Nakajima. A New Approach to System Diagnosis. *Proceedings of the 19th Allerton Conference on Communication, Control and Computing*, pages 697-706, 1981.

[42] L. Meyer and G.M. Masson. An Efficient Fault Diagnosis Algorithm for Symmetric Multiple Processor Architectures. *IEEE Transactions on Computers*, C-27(11):1059-1063, Nov 1978.

[43] Dahbura, A., T. and Masson, G., M. An $O(n^{2.5})$ Fault Identification Algorithm for Diagnosable Systems. *IEEE Transactions on Computers*, C-33(6):486-492, June 1984.

[44] Gregory F. Sullivan. An $O(t^3 + |E|)$ fault identification algorithm for diagnosable systems. *IEEE Transactions on Computers*, 37(4):388-397, April 1988.

[45] C.L. Yang and G.M. Masson. An efficient algorithm for multiprocessor fault diagnosis using the comparison approach. *IEEE Symposium Fault-Tolerant Computing*, pages 238-243, 1986.

[46] S.H. Hosseini and J.G. Kuhl and S.M. Reddy. A Diagnosis Algorithm for Distributed Computing Systems with Failure and Repair. *IEEE Transactions on Computers*, 33:223-233, 1984.

[47] R.P. Bianchini and R. Buskens. Implementation of On-Line Distributed System-Level Diagnosis. *IEEE Transactions on Computers*, 41(5):616-626, May 1992.

[48] R.P. Bianchini and R. Buskens. An Adaptive Distributed System Level Diagnosis Algorithm and Its Implementation. *Proceeding of FTCS-21*, pages 222-229, 1991.

[49] Elias P. Duarte and Takashi Nanya. A Hierarchical Adaptive Distributed System-Level Diagnosis Algorithm. *IEEE Transactions on Computers*, 47(1):34-45, Jan 1998.

Websites

[50] http://www.google.com/search?hl=en&lr=&ie=UTF8&q=Adaptiv ely+Diagnosable+Systems

[51] http://www.google.com/search?hl=en&ie=UTF8&q=%22System+ Level+Diagnosis%3A+A+Review%22+

[52] http://www.lab.ss.titech.ac.jp/ueno-lab/papers/Files/2001_03.pdf

[53] http://www.ewh.ieee.org/soc/icss/pdf/Thulasiraman2.pdf

Chapter 15

System Level Diagnosis-II

In Chapter 14, we have introduced the basic principles and techniques as applied to system level diagnosis. In this chapter, we continue our discussion on the system level diagnosis however with an emphasis on the application of the introduced principles in the context of regular structures and grid-connected systems. We emphasize these systems mainly because they represent the core of massively parallel computing machines.

15.1   Diagnosis Algorithms for Regular Structures

One of the main drawbacks of distributed diagnosis algorithms presented before is the need of fully connected network. Unfortunately, most of real life systems do not have that specification since the cost to implement such system will be very high. However, there is a class of systems having regularity in terms of its processing elements and interconnection networks. Although the connectivity between its elements is very limited, the regularity and hierarchical nature of these systems are very suitable for many applications. Grid processors (with mesh or torridly connection), hypercube and variant or enhanced hypercube are some example of those systems.

Unfortunately, with such interconnection structures, the one-step diagnose-ability is very small as compared to the number of units and, presumably, to the potential number of faults. For this reason, there has been a shift towards the probabilistic approach, which tolerates incorrect and/or incomplete diagnoses occurring with low probability.

378

Diagnose-ability of regular structures has been studied by many researchers in many published work. Their work is basically based on the PMC or comparison model, considering the regularity, limited interconnection network, and the hierarchical nature of regular structures.

Kavianpour and Kim introduced the *pessimistic* t/t-diagnosable system for hypercube. Somani and Agarwal and Huang introduced diagnosis algorithms for regular systems which provide complete diagnoses whose correctness is evaluated under a probabilistic model. LaForge et al. evaluated a diagnosis algorithm aiming at the identification of non-faulty units in a quasi-regular structure derived from grids. Chessa et al. and continued by Caruso et al. introduced some algorithms for regular structures based on *syndrome dependent bound*. Adaptive system level diagnosis has also been proposed. Other diagnosis algorithms can found in the literature. Some of the above mentioned algorithm will be presented in the following.

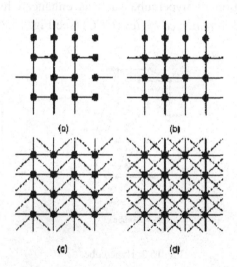

Fig. 15.1: Grids with L = 4 (a) triangular (b) square (c) hexagonal (d) octagonal.

15.2 Regular Structures

A grid structure of size $n = L^2$, where L is a positive, even integer, is composed of n units arranged in L columns and L rows. Each unit is indexed by a pair (x,y) of integers, with x = 0, ... L–1 and y = 0, ... L – 1. Units are connected to a constant number of neighbors. Depending on the number of neighbors (three, four, six, or eight), grids are called *triangular, square, hexagonal or octagonal,* respectively. Figure 15.1 shows these architectures. Simple grids may be derived from architectures of the same size by removing the wraparound links crossing the border. This implies that the degree of units lying on the border is smaller than the degree of internal units hence simple grids are quasi-regular structures.

A hypercube of dimension d, is composed of $n = 2^d$ units. Every unit u is labeled with a d-digits binary number. Units are connected based on the Hamming distance of their label. Edge (u,v) exists if and only if their distance is one. A hypercube of dimension d = 4 is shown in Fig. 15.2(a). It is immediate that hypercube are d-regular structures and the degree $d = \log n$ is an increasing function of the size. There exists some variation of hypercube such as enhanced hypercube (see Fig. 15.2(b)) or *cube connected cycles (CCC)* (see Fig. 15.2(c)).

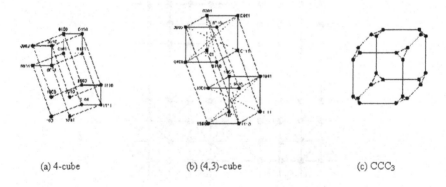

(a) 4-cube   (b) (4,3)-cube   (c) CCC₃

Fig. 15.2: Hypercube.

15.3 Pessimistic One-Step Diagnosis Algorithms for Hypercube

It has been long known that the diagnose-ability of an n-dimensional hypercube (called n-cube) is n. Under the normal (also called *precise*) one step diagnosis strategy, a situation where a good processor is completely surrounded by $t-1$ or less faulty processors, where t represents the fault bound, must not occur because the status of the isolated processor cannot be determined. Therefore, the degree of diagnose-ability under the precise strategy becomes low. Under the pessimistic strategy, such an isolated processor is treated as a potentially faulty processor and replaced. An important property common for both precise and pessimistic strategy is that no faulty processor will remain undetected and un-repaired. While the pessimistic might involve wasteful replacement of some operational processors, it has an advantage over the precise strategy in that the degree of diagnose-ability becomes higher.

The pessimistic t'/t' diagnosis strategy assumes that up to t' processors may be replaced/repaired where t' is the fault bound. A system S is pessimistically one-step t'/t' fault diagnosable if given the fault bound t' (>0), t' or fewer processors that include all the faulty processors present and possibly some processors of unknown status in S can be identified for replacement after a testing phase.

Consider the case of two arbitrarily selected processors v_i and v_j which are separated by distance d (that is in the range $1 \leq d \leq n$). There are n disjoint paths from processor v_i to processor v_j. Among these, there are d paths of length d and $n-d$ paths of length $d+2$ from v_i to v_j. Thus, on each of $n-d$ paths there are at least two processors one of which is connected to processor v_i and the other connected to processor v_j. Therefore, on the $(n-d)$ paths there are at least $2(n-d)$ processors of which at least $(n-d)$ processor can test v_i and at least $(n-d)$ other processors can test v_j. Also, on each of the other d paths there are 0,1, or 2 processors which can test processor v_i and v_j, or both, depending on whether d is equal to 1 or 2 or greater than 2. The total number of processors which can test processors v_i or v_j or both are thus as follows:

$$\text{for } d \geq 3; \ 2(n-d)+2d = 2n$$

$$\text{for } d = 2; \ 2(n-d) + d = 2n-d, \text{ and}$$

$$\text{for } d = 1; \ 2(n-d) \qquad = 2n-2d$$

Design Analysis

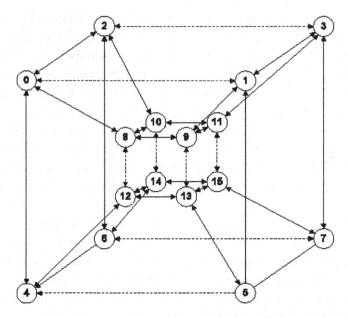

Fig. 15.3: Example of pessimistic one-step diagnosis strategy on 4-cube.

Therefore, given a faulty n-cube with the fault bound of $2n - 2$, where $n \geq 4$, all faulty processors can be removed by replacing at most $2n - 2$ processors. In a 4-cube, each of the 2^4 processors can test four immediate neighbors and vice versa. According to the above definition, a 4-cube is pessimistically one-step 6/6 fault diagnosable. Therefore, if the fault bound is 6, we can repair a faulty 4-cube in one step by replacing at most six processors. Consider, for example, the 4-cube shown in Fig. 15.3. Five processors 0,2,3,5, and 9 are faulty. An analysis of the syndrome shown in the figure (a bold line in the figure shows a testing connection while a dashed-line shows non-testing connection) indicates that the five processors 0,2,3,5, and 9 are definitely faulty and the status of processor 1 is unknown. Therefore, the system can be repaired by replacing six processors 0,1,2,3,5 and 9. The non-faulty processor 1 is replaced because it can be tested only by four other faulty processors and thus no reliable information about its status can be made available. Note that with a 4-cube the precise one-step diagnosis strategy can be used only when the fault bound is four of less.

15.4 Diagnosis for Symmetric Multiple Processor Architecture

In this Section, we show how to consolidate the knowledge generated in this Chapter in implementing a simple fault diagnosis system. The system selected consists of n units, denoted as U_0, U_1, U_2, ..., U_{n-1}. If U_i tests U_j to be fault-free, then $a(i,j) = 0$ while $(i,j) = 1$ if U_i tests U_j to be faulty. The test produced by U_i is reliable if and only if U_i is fault-free. But if U_i itself is faulty, then the output produced by this unit is unreliable and could be 1 or 0 regardless of the state of U_j. We associate a table B_i with each module U_i, where $i = 1,2,..., n-1$, such that B_i represents the conclusion of U_i regarding the state of all other modules. It should be noted that B_i is not the syndrome of the network but it is computed based on the syndrome of the system. The aim here is to find the faulty set from the existing network. We have to have some conditions to be satisfied so that the faulty set can be located. It is assumed that the system is t diagnosable and that each unit is tested by at least t other units, where t represents the maximum allowable number of faults that can occur in the network. It is also assumed that the system is symmetric (see Chapter 14). The interconnection network used is assumed to be of the form $D_{1,t}$. This means that there is a testing connection from $U_{i \text{ to}} U_j$ if and only if j-$i = m$ *modulo n* and that m takes values from 1 to t. It has been shown that if $n \geq 2t + 1$, then the system is t-diagnosable.

Diagnosis Algorithm

Each table B_i has n components $B_{i,0}$, $B_{i,1}$, ..., $B_{i,n-1}$ where $B_{i,j}$ represents the conclusion of U_i concerning the state of U_j. Having the complete set B_0, B_1, ..., B_{n-1} would mean that every module has made a conclusion about the state of all the other modules including itself. The assumption is that if U_i is fault-free, its corresponding table is correct. We offer the following Lemmas (proofs of these Lemmas can be found in References 10 and 12)

Lemma 1: There exists at least n-t of the B_i tables which are identical.

Lemma 2: If there exists only one set of identical tables $B_{i(1)}$, $B_{i(2)}$, ..., $B_{i(s)}$, such that $s \geq n\text{-}t$, then each of these tables correctly describes the existing fault situation.

It should be noted that if there is more than one set of identical tables with cardinality larger than or equal to *n-t*, no conclusion can be made about the fault set. This corresponds to the situation where there are more than *t* faults in the network.

Theorem 1: Suppose that $n \geq 2t + 1$; then there exists one and only one set of identical tables with cardinality greater than or equal to *n-t*.

We must have a procedure to build the complete *n* tables B_0, B_1, ..., B_{n-1}. If module U_i is fault-free, then table B_i contains the exact set of faulty units. The following algorithm is used to generate tables B_0, B_1, ..., B_{n-1}.

***Algorithm* 1:** Let i be in [0, 1, ..., n-1] and t in [1, 2, ..., n-1].

Step 0: Set all elements of B_i to zero, $j = i$, $k = i + 1$ and $N_F = 0$.
Step 1: If $N_F \geq t$ or $k = i$, then stop; else go to step 2.
Step 2: If $a(j, k) = 1$, set $B_{i,k} = 1$, $N_F = N_F + 1$ and go to step 3; else $j = k$ and go to step 3.
Step 3: Set $k = k + 1$ and go to step 1.

Notice here that all the additions performed are modulo n. Also, we have assumed that a $D_{1,t}$ interconnection design is used. We used the notation of $a(j, j + r)$ instead of $a(j,f(r,j))$.

Theorem 2: If a $D_{1,t}$ interconnection design is used with the condition that the maximum number of faulty units that can occur is *t* and the module U_i is fault-free, then table B_i constructed by the algorithm contains exactly all set of faulty units.

The algorithm is shown in the flowchart in Fig. 15.4.

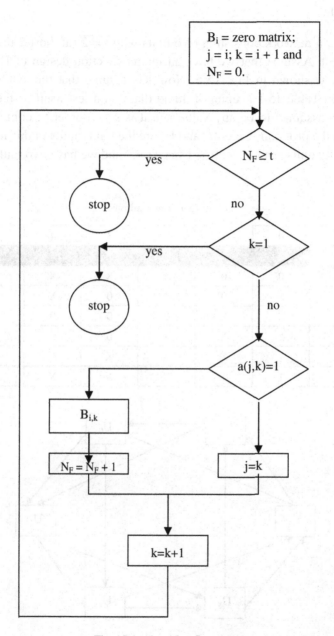

Fig. 15.4: Algorithm flowchart.

Example

Consider a network consisting of 6 units with t = 2 (at most 2 units may be faulty). Assume that we have an interconnection design of $D_{1,2}$. The network is shown in Fig. 15.5. Now lets assume that the syndrome is shown in Table 15.1 keeping in mind that a unit test itself as fault-free. The x is assumed to be any value and it is set in order to complete the array in the program. Units U_0 and U_1 are the faulty units in this network. The faulty units can be identified since t = 2 and we have two faulty units here.

Table 15.1: The syndrome.

K	0	1	2	3	4	5
J						
0	0	0	1	X	X	X
1	X	0	1	0	X	X
2	X	X	0	0	0	X
3	X	X	X	0	0	0
4	1	X	X	X	0	0
5	1	1	X	X	X	0

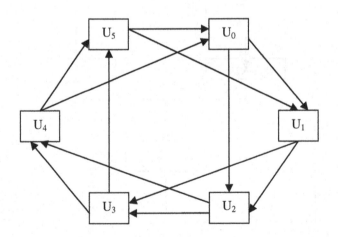

Fig. 15.5: Example network.

If we use the algorithm above, the generated B matrix consisting of $B_0, B_1, ..., B_5$ will be as shown in Table 15.2.

Table 15.2: Resulting matrix.

K	0	1	2	3	4	5
B_i						
B_0	0	0	1	0	0	0
B_1	1	0	1	0	0	0
B_2	1	1	0	0	0	0
B_3	1	1	0	0	0	0
B_4	1	1	0	0	0	0
B_5	1	1	0	0	0	0

We can see here that there are 4 identical tables, i.e., n-t = 4. Each table is generated depending on the syndrome. For example, processor U_2, concludes that units 2 (which is U_2 itself), 3 and 4 are fault-free. It means that it can use their conclusion about the other units to generate its own table. So, it is clear that both test unit 5 as fault free and unit 4 test unit 0 as faulty. Since unit 5 is faulty so it can use its result for the state of unit 1 which believes that it is faulty and the table of unit U_2 is complete. All the other tables are constructed in a similar way. From the table of U_2 we can conclude that units 0 and 1 are faulty under the assumption that U_2 is fault-free. Let's apply the algorithm step by step to generate the table of U_2. Here $I = 2$.

Step 00: $B_2=[0\ 0\ 0\ 0\ 0\ 0]$; j=i=2; k=i+1=3; N_f=0;
Step 1a: N_f=0 which is not greater than or equal to t=2; k=3 which is not equal to i=2; so go to step 2;
Step 2a: a(2,3)=0; so j=k=3; go to step 3;
Step 3a: k=k+1=4; go to step 1;
Step 1b: N_f=0 which is not greater than or equal to t=2; k=4 which is not equal to i=2; so go to step 2;
Step 2b: a(3,4)=0; so j=k=4; go to step 3;
Step 3b: k=k+1=5; go to step 1;

Step 1c: $N_f=0$ which is not greater than or equal to $t=2$;
           $k=5$ which is not equal to $i=2$; so go to step 2;
Step 2c: $a(4,5)=0$; so $j=k=5$; go to step 3;
Step 3c: $k=k+1=0$ (since modulo 6); go to step 1;
Step 1d: $N_f=0$ which is not greater than or equal to $t=2$;
           $k=0$ which is not equal to $i=2$; so go to step 2;
Step 2d: $a(5,0)=1$; $B_{2,0}=1$; so $B_2=[1\ 0\ 0\ 0\ 0\ 0]$
           $N_f=N_f+1=1$; go to step 3;
Step 3d: $k=k+1=1$; go to step 1;
Step 1d: $N_f=1$ which is not greater than or equal to $t=2$;
           $k=1$ which is not equal to $i=2$; so go to step 2.
Step 2d: $a(5,1)=1$; $B_{2,1}=1$; so $B_2=[1\ 1\ 0\ 0\ 0\ 0]$;
           $N_f=N_f+1=2$; go to step 3;
Step 3d: $k=k+1=2$; go to step 1;
Step 1e: $N_f=2=t$; so stop.

Now the table of unit U_2 is $B_2 = [1\ 1\ 0\ 0\ 0\ 0]$. This means that under the assumption that U_2 is fault-free the table B_2 is correct and specifies exactly the faulty units, which is the case. According to B_2, units U_0 and U_1 are the faulty set. Let's look at some of the steps to see how the table was constructed. Steps 00 and 1a are straightforward. If we look at step 2a, we see that $a(2,3) = 0$ means that unit 2 tests unit 3 to be fault free. So j is now updated to 3 (j = 3) so that we can use the tests performed by unit 3. This is done because unit 3 is considered fault-free from the point of view of unit 2. At step 3a k is now updated to 4. Step 1b is clear so let's go to step 2b. We can see that $a(3,4) = 0$ so unit 4 is fault-free from unit 3 point of view and as a result from unit 2 point of view. So the same thing is done, i.e., j = 4 and k = 5. Notice that we did not change any value in the table because all elements are initiated to zero and we did not find any faulty unit till this point. The same procedure is done till step 3c. The only thing here is that k = 0 since 5 + 1(modulo6) = 0. Step 1d is clear so go to step 2d. Notice here that $a(5,0) = 1$; this means that unit 0 is faulty from the point of view of unit 5 and indirectly from unit 2 point of view. This means that we cannot use its tests because it is faulty. That is why j is not updated to 0. Therefore, the element $B_{2,0} = 1$ since unit 2 tests unit 0 to be faulty in an indirect way. B_2 is updated accordingly, i.e $B_2 = [1\ 0\ 0\ 0\ 0\ 0]$. $N_f = 1$. Step 3d updates k to 1. In step 1e we see that $N_f = 1$ which is not greater than or equal to 2. So continue with step 2d. Here we are using the results of unit 5 on unit 1 not the results of unit 0 because it is faulty. $a(5,2) = 1$ so $B_{2,1} = 1$ and $B_2 = [1\ 1\ 0\ 0\ 0\ 0]$. The value of j is not updated as we see since unit 1 is faulty. $N_f = N_f + 1 = 2$ in this step and then we will go to step 3d. At this step k is updated to 2 and we will continue with step 1e. In this step the condition that $N_f = 2 = t$ is satisfied so we have to stop the algorithm at this point. The final table of B_2 is: $B_2 = [1\ 1\ 0\ 0\ 0\ 0]$. As can be seen, if unit 2 is fault free then B_2 describes exactly the faulty set.

All the tables, i.e B_i, are constructed in a similar way regardless of the state of unit i. So after the construction of all the tables we will check if we have n-t or more identical tables. If we have, then these identical tables contain the faulty set. This is the case illustrated in this example; we have 4 identical tables of the form:

$B_i = [1\ 1\ 0\ 0\ 0\ 0]$, and two other tables. It means that from this table we have units 0 and 1 as the faulty units. In the program we have to check this case so, we have to search for at least n-t identical tables. Here comes the time complexity of the program. So we have to check at least n-t possible tables and this is the best case. In each of these comparisons we have to check that element by element increasing the time complexity more and more.

Meyer and Masson have suggested an accelerated algorithm. As we said, the diagnosis of the faulty set based on the results of Lemmas 1 and 2 and theorem 2 requires that the tables B_i's for $I = 0, 1, 2, ..., n-1$ be compared. This has a large time complexity. The authors have suggested the following. For each $j = 0, 1, ..., n-1$, let v_j be the number of indices for which $B_{i,j} = 1$. This means that v_j = cardinality of $\{i \in [0, 1, ..., n-1] \mid B_{i,j} = 1\}$. In other words, v_j is the summation of ones in the *j*th column of the full B matrix. For example, from table 2 the v_j's are $v_0 = 5$, $v_1 = 4$, $v_2 = 2$, $v_3 = 0$, $v_4 = 0$ and $v_5 = 0$. These quantities can be used for diagnosis as discussed in the following algorithm.

> **Algorithm 2:** Let t in [1, n-1] be given.
> Step 0: Compute the tables B_0, B_1, B_2, ..., B_{n-1} by using algorithm 1.
> Step 1: Compute the quantities v_0, v_1, ..., v_{n-1}.
> Step 2: Let V={j ∈ [0, 1, ..., m-1] | $v_j \geq t + 1$}

Theorem 3: If a $D_{1,t}$ interconnection design is used, the maximum number of faulty units which can occur is t, and if $n \geq 2t + 1$, then U_j is faulty if and only if j is in V.

If we take our example from Table 2, $t + 1 = 2$ and $V = \{0,1\}$ as step 2 says. Therefore, the faulty units from theorem 3 are U_0 and U_1.

The code of algorithm 1 and 2 are combined in one program written in MATLAB (The MATLAB code for the two algorithms is shown in an Appendix at the end of the chapter). Symmetric networks and their syndromes are generated randomly. The B_i tables are generated using algorithm 1 and they are compared to conclude whether the system is diagnosable or not and if it is, the faulty units are identified. After that, the program uses algorithm 2 to identify the faulty units. The example that we discussed in tables 1 and 2 has been implemented using the code and the program gives identical results.

It is seen that when the program is run, the results are satisfied in many cases. Algorithms 1 and 2 can diagnose the faulty units in the system and they give identical results. If the system is not diagnosable, algorithm 1 works fine but algorithm 2 diagnoses some of the faulty units even if the number of faulty is greater than t, which should not be the case. We have seen that when the system is diagnosable both systems works. We will show two examples to illustrate the idea. One example will show that both algorithms cannot diagnose the system when it is not diagnosable, which is correct. The other example will show that when the system is not diagnosable, algorithm 1 works fine but algorithm 2 claims that the system is diagnosable and it states the faulty units from its point of view, which is an unreliable result. We can see this from Theorem 3. It states that the algorithm assumes that the number of faulty units occurring does not exceed t.

Example 2

Consider the following syndrome for 6 units and t = 2.

Table 15.3

K	0	1	2	3	4	5
J						
0	0	1	0	X	X	X
1	X	0	0	0	X	X
2	X	X	0	0	1	X
3	X	X	X	0	1	1
4	1	X	X	X	0	0
5	1	1	X	X	X	0

The B matrix is shown below:

Table 15.4

K	0	1	2	3	4	5
B_i						
B_0	0	1	0	0	1	0
B_1	1	0	0	0	1	0
B_2	1	0	0	0	1	0
B_3	1	0	0	0	1	0
B_4	1	1	0	0	0	0
B_5	1	1	0	0	0	0

Because we have only at most 2 identical tables corresponding to rows B_1 and B_2 and rows B_4 and B_5, the system is not diagnosable according to algorithm 1. We have to have at least n-t = 4 identical tables. The MATLAB output of this step is

> The number of faults is > t
> The Diagnosis Algorithm Does not Work

The values of v_j's are $v_0 = 5$, $v_1 = 3$, $v_2 = 0$, $v_3 = 0$, $v_4 = 3$ and $v_5 = 2$. We have three elements that have a value greater than or equal to $t + 1 = 3$. These could be the faulty set but because the number of units here is 3 which is greater than $t = 2$ (the maximum allowable faulty set), the system is not diagnosable. This condition is not stated in the paper but it is put to check the efficiency of the algorithm. The MATLAB output of this step is:

> Results of Accelerated algorithm is as follows:
> The number of faults>t
> The Diagnosis Algorithm Does not Work

Example 3

Consider the following syndrome for 6 units and $t = 2$.

Table 15.5

K	0	1	2	3	4	5
J						
0	0	1	0	X	X	X
1	X	0	1	1	X	X
2	X	X	0	0	1	X
3	X	X	X	0	1	1
4	1	X	X	X	0	0
5	0	1	X	X	X	0

The B matrix is shown below:

Table 15.6

\	0	1	2	3	4	5
B_i						
B_0	0	1	0	0	1	0
B_1	0	0	1	1	0	0
B_2	0	0	0	0	1	1
B_3	0	0	0	0	1	1
B_4	0	1	0	0	0	0
B_5	0	1	0	0	1	0

Algorithm 1 concludes that the system is not diagnosable, which is the case.

The output of the MATLAB program is:

```
The number of faults is > t
The Diagnosis Algorithm Does not Work
```

The values of v_j's are $v_0 = 0$, $v_1 = 3$, $v_2 = 1$, $v_3 = 1$, $v_4 = 4$ and $v_5 = 2$. It concludes that the faulty units are 1 and 4 since $t + 1 = 3$. The output of the MATLAB code is:

```
Results of Accelerated algorithm is as follows:
The faulty units are as follows:
V_results= 1     4
```

15.5 Summary

In this chapter, we conducted a discussion on the system level diagnosis with emphasis on the application of the introduced principles in Chapter 14 in the context of regular structures and grid-like connected systems. These systems were mainly emphasized because they represent the core of massively parallel computing machines.

References

[1] J.P. Hayes and T.N. Mudge and Q.F. Stout. Architecture of a Hypercube Supercomputer. *Proc.* 1986 *Int'l Conf. Parallel Processing*, pages 653-660, Aug. 1986.

[2] N.-F. Tzeng and S. Wei. Enhanced hypercubes. *IEEE Trans. Computers*, 40(3):284-294, Mar 1991.

[3] K. Efe. A Variation on the Hypercube with Lower Diameter. *IEEE Trans. Computers*, 40(11):1312-1316, Nov. 1991.

[4] K. Efe. The Crossed Cube Architecture for Parallel Computing. *IEEE Trans. Parallel and Distributed Systems*, 3(5):513-524, Oct. 1992.

[5] A. Kavianpour and K.H. Kim. Diagnosabilities of Hypercube under the Pessimistic One-Step Diagnosis Strategy. *IEEE Trans. Computers*, 40(2):232-237, Feb. 1991.

[6] D. Wang. Diagnosability of Enhanced Hypercubes. *IEEE Trans. Computers*, 43(9):1054-1061, Sept. 1994.

[7] S. Khanna and W.K. Fuchs. A Graph Partitioning Approach to Sequential Diagnosis. *IEEE Trans. Computers*, 46(1):39-47, Jan. 1997.

[8] Dajin Wang. Diagnosability of Hypercubes and Enhanced Hypercubes under the Comparison Diagnosis Model. *IEEE Trans. Computer*, 48(12), Dec. 1999.

[9] Jianxi Fan. Diagnosability of Crossed Cubes under the Comparison Diagnosis Model. *IEEE TRANSACTIONS ON PARALLEL AND DISTRIBUTED SYSTEMS*, 13(7), July 2002.

[10] Antonio Caruso, Stefano Chessa, Piero Maestrini, and Paolo Santi. Diagnosability of regular systems. *Journal of Algorithms, Elseview Science (USA)*, 45:126-143, 2002.

[11] J.R. Armstrong and F.G. Gray. Fault diagnosis in a Boolean n cube array of microprocessors. *IEEE Trans. Computers*, 30(8):587-590, Aug. 1981.

[12] A.K. Somani and V.K. Agarwal. Distributed Diagnosis Algorithm for Regular Interconnected Systems. *IEEE Trans. Computers*, 41(7):899-906, July 1992.

[13] K. Huang, V.K. Agarwal, L. LaForge, and K. Thulasiraman. A Diagnosis Algorithm for Constant Degree Structures and Its Application to VLSI Circuit Testing. *IEEE Trans. Parallel and Distributed Systems*, 6(4):363-372, Apr. 1995.

[14] L.E. LaForge, K. Huang, and V.K. Agarwal. Almost Sure Diagnosis of Almost Every Good Element. *IEEE Trans. Computers*, 43(3):295-305, Mar. 1994.

[15] S. Chessa and P. Maestrini. Correct and Almost Complete Diagnosis of Processor Grids. *IEEE Trans. Computers*, 50(10):1095-1102, Oct. 2001.

[16] Chao Feng, Laxmi N. Buyan, and Fabrizio Lombardi. Adaptive System Level Diagnosis for Hypercube Multiprocessors. *IEEE Trans. Computers*, 45(10):1157-1170, Oct. 1996.

[17] Sengupta and A. Dahbura. On Self-Diagnosable Multiprocessor Systems: Diagnosis by the Comparison Approach. *IEEE Trans. Computers*, 41(11):1386-1396, Nov. 1992.

[18] Abhijit Sengupta and Chung Rhee. On a generalization of the self implicating structures in diagnosable systems. *IEEE Trans. Circuits and Systems-1: Fundamental Theory and Application*, 40(4):239-245, April 1993.

[19] L. Baldelli and P. Maestrini. Self-Diagnosis of Array Processors. *Proc. Fault-Tolerant Computing Symp. (FTCS-24)*, pages 48-53, 1994.

[20] D.P. Bersekas and J.N. Tsitsiklis. *Parallel and Distributed Computation, Numerical Methods*. Prentice Hall Int'l, 1989.

[21] E.P. Duarte Jr and T. Nanya. An SNMP-based Implementation of the Adaptive Distributed System-level Diagnosis Algorithm for LAN Fault Management. *In NOMS'96 - IEEE/IFIP* 1996 *Network Operations and Management Symposium*, pages 530-539, April 1996. Kyoto, Japan.

[22] M. Bearden and R. Bianchini Jr. Efficient and fault-tolerant distributed host monitoring using system-level diagnosis. *Proceedings of the IFIP/IEEE International Conference on Distributed Platforms: Client/Server and Beyond, Dresden, Germany*, pages 159-172, Feb. 1996.

[23] C. Lamb and L. DeBrunner and J. Fagan and A. Das and K. Thulasiraman and R. Sexton. Fault Tolerance of the Global Navigation Satellite System Using System Level Diagnosis. *Asilomar Conference on Signals, Systems, and Computers, Pacific Grove, California*, pages 897-901, Nov. 1997.

[24] Wang, Hongjian and Bian, Xinqian and Ding, Fuguang and Han, Guiping. The application of a distributed system-level diagnosis algorithm in dynamic positioning system. *Proceedings of the 4th World Congress on Intelligent Control and Automation, Shanghai, China*, pages 2274-2278, June 2002.

[25] S. Chessa. *Self-Diagnosis of Grid-Interconnected Systems with Application to Self-Test of VLSI Wafers.* PhD thesis, University of Pisa, Italy, Department of Computer Science, March 1999.

[26] C. Fuhrman. Comparison-based Diagnosis in Fault-Tolerant Multiprocessor Systems. PhD thesis, Swiss Federal Institute of Technology in Lausanne (EPEL), Department of Computer Science, July 1996.

Websites

[27] http://www.google.com/search?hl=en&lr=&ie=UTF8&q=Adaptiv ely+Diagnosable+Systems

[28] http://www.google.com/search?hl=en&ie=UTF8&q=%22System+ Level+Diagnosis%3A+A+Review%22+

[29] http://www.lab.ss.titech.ac.jp/ueno-lab/papers/Files/2001_03.pdf

Appendix

```
%Generate Symmetric Networks of N Nodes
for N=6:15
    t=floor((N-1)/2);
    %Generate A Random Syndromes
    a=round(rand(N));
    %This is to assign the mumber 5 if unit i does not
test unit j
    %and to assign  a(i,i) to 0 since the assumptio is
that unit i
    %is assumed to test itself as falut free
    for i=1:N
        for j=1:N
            if mod((j-1)-(i-1),N) >t
                a(i,j)=5;
            elseif i==j
                a(i,j)=0;
            end
        end
    End
    %The Syndrome is now
    The_Random_Syndrome_is=a
    %Generate The Maximum Allowable Number Of Faults
        The_Maximmum_numberOfFaults_is=t
    i=0;
    B=zeros(N,N);%Generate an Empty Table

    %The Original Algorithm To Construct The Tables:
    for count1=1:N
        j=i; k=mod(i+1,N); Nf=0;
        while (Nf < t & abs(k-i)>0),
            if   a(j+1,k+1)==1
                B(i+1,k+1)=1;
                Nf=Nf+1;
            else
                j=k;
            end
            k=mod(k+1,N);
        end
        i=i+1;
    end
    The_Generated_Tables_are=B
```

```
%check if the number of equal tables are >=n-t
for i=1:N-1
    count=0;
    for j=i:N
        if B(i,:)==B(j,:)
        count=count+1;
        end
    end
    if count>= N-t
        i1=i
        break
    end
end
count
if count<N-t
    disp('The number of faults is > t')
    disp('The Diagnosis Algorithm Does not Work')
else
    c1=zeros(1,t);
    count1=0;
    for c=1:N
        if B(i1,c)==1
            c1(count1+1)=c-1;
            count1=count1+1;
        end
    end

    %Display the faulty units of Original Algorithm
    disp('The faulty units are:')
    c1(1,1:count1)
end
    %The Accelerated Algorithm
    for i2=1:N
        V(i2)=sum(B(:,i2));
    end
    count3=0;
    for i3=1:N
        if V(i3)>=t+1
            V_results(count3+1)=i3-1;
            count3=count3+1;
        end
    end
```

```
      Disp('Results of Accelerated algorithm is as
follows:')
      if count3>t
         disp('The number of faults>t')
         disp('The Diagnosis Algorithm Does not
Work')
      else
         disp('Thre faulty units are as follows:')
      %Results of Accelerated Algorithm
      V_results
      end
   pause
   clear all
end
```

MATLAB code

Chapter 16

Fault Tolerance and Reliability of the RAID Systems

Redundant Array of Independent Disks (RAID) systems have been proposed as a solution for the needed high performance and reliability of secondary storage systems. This chapter discusses basic design issues in RAID and describes the classic RAID level–0 to level–5 architectures. We also compare these designs in terms of reliability and performance. In addition, two advanced RAID systems are introduced and examined. Reliability of RAID systems is also discussed.

The first RAID system was originally proposed in the 1980s. The main objective then was to design a secondary storage system that would provide higher data transfer rates. The objectives have since then been expanded to include reliability and fault tolerance as well as performance.

Today, RAID is the state-of-the-art secondary storage solution provided by computer manufacturers for applications requiring high performance and reliability. One of main factors that drive the interest in RAID is the constant increase in the speed of microprocessors. It is recognized that increasing the speed of one part of the system (the microprocessor) without increasing the speed of some other parts (secondary storage) would force an upper bound on the increase of the overall performance of the system.

Another important factor driving the development of RAID is the increasing demands for more reliable and fault-tolerant secondary storage systems. As the dependence on computer systems increase, the reliability of such systems becomes crucial. For example, a database (DB) server for airline reservation cannot afford to be interrupted. Similarly, a bank cannot afford to loose data about customers' accounts.

Disk arrays provide an excellent solution to these problems. The basis upon which RAID is built is redundancy. Redundancy is utilized in a number of different ways to increase both reliability and performance.

16.1 Introduction

A simplified hard disk drive consists of a set of circular surfaces on top of each others. These are called *platters*. Each platter contains many concentric circular paths or rings called *tracks*. Furthermore, a platter is covered by a magnetic material used to store the data bits along each track. Each platter can be divided into angular sections called *sectors* by which data is organized and addressed, see Fig. 16.1.

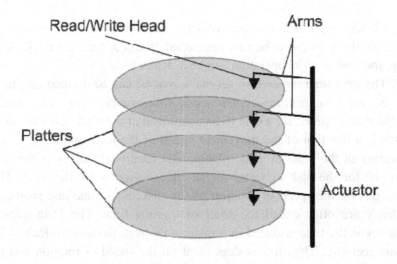

Fig. 16.1: A simplified hard disk drive.

Reading and writing to data sectors is done using special heads. Heads are held by arms which are moved across sectors using an *actuator* (see Fig. 16.2). Although all heads move together, only one of them actually reads or writes at the same time.

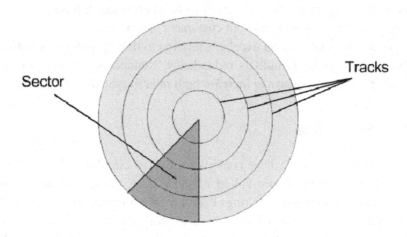

Fig. 16.2: Tracks and sectors.

Platters rotate in a constant velocity. So, when data is to be read or written, the head has to be first positioned on top of the right track. After that the read or write operation can be executed.

The total time required to service a request can be divided into three parts: *seek time, rotational latency and data transfer latency.* Seek time is the time required for a disk to be positioned at the right radial location. This is a function of the movement speed of the head and the previous location of the head over the platter. The rotational latency is the time needed for the disk to rotate to the right sector under the head. This depends on the speed of rotation of the disk. Seek time and rotational latency are often called the *head positioning* time. The Data transfer latency is the time required to transfer data from the disk surface to the main memory. This time is dependent on the speed of rotation and the capacity of the magnetic material (the number of bits per unit area).

It is worth mentioning that the head positioning time is relatively large. Sometimes it is ten times larger than the data transfer time. Yet, the head poisoning time varies significantly with the nature of I/O requests. For instance, requests for sequential large-sized blocks require much less head positioning delay than requests for random average-sized set of blocks.

Designing disk arrays in general comprises many decisions. Yet, these decisions can be categorized into two main types: *data organization and redundancy mechanisms.*

Data organization is the way logical addresses produced by the computer are mapped to physical addresses on the array. The two main options are *direct mapping* and *disk stripping*. In direct mapping (*often called independent addressing*) logical sectors are directly mapped to physical sectors on the disks. Here, the administrator of the system is responsible of distributing the data onto the various disks. Some disks might receive more requests depending on the data they hold. This may create what is called a "hotspot" where most of the load is concentrated on a small portion of the disks. In this approach, load balancing between disks is relatively difficult.

In disk stripping, the disk array represents a single address space to the host. This is achieved by dividing the address space into logical consecutive blocks (called *stripes*). These stripes are distributed onto the disks in a round-robin fashion.

Disk stripping can be performed in two ways. The first method is to make the stripes relatively small. This is often called *fine-grained stripping*. The other method is to divide the data into large or *coarse-grained stripes*. In fine-grained stripping, all disks participate in servicing an I/O request, while in coarse-grained stripping it is possible that only one disk would service a relatively small request. Fine-grained stripes are better for applications with high data rate (few but large requests). This is because all disks would participate in servicing the request in parallel producing a significant speedup. Coarse-grained stripping is appropriate for high I/O rate applications (many but small requests).

16.2 Redundancy Mechanisms

The reliability of a single disk is generally high. However, as the number of disks in a disk array increases, the reliability of the overall system decreases. For example, if the MTTF of a single disk ranges from 20 to 100 years, the MTTF of a disk array would only be few months or even weeks depending on the number of disks in the system. This reduction in the MTTF drives the need for redundancy in the system to provide higher fault tolerance.

Unfortunately, adding redundancy to a system often causes its cost to increase and its performance and capacity to decrease. Therefore, choosing the appropriate redundancy mechanism to be used is an important factor.

Redundancy can be added to the system in many ways. One mechanism is to duplicate data into redundant disks. The produced copy of the data serves as an online backup of the original one. If a disk fails, then its data can be retrieved from its duplicate (often called *mirror*). This added redundancy can also be utilized to enhance the performance of servicing read requests. Since any requested data unit is stored in two locations (disks), the one with least cost can be used to service the request. Unfortunately, this scheme would increase the delay of write requests since the data has to be written twice: the original data and the duplicate one.

Another way of adding redundancy is using *parity*. It has been shown that a single error can be recovered using a single parity bit and the correct data bits. In a system using a parity mechanism, the parity value is calculated from a group of data bits distributed over all protected disks. If a disk fails, the parity information along with un-corrupted data can be used to reconstruct the failing disk's content.

Data replication and parity mechanisms can recover only a single error. Alternative techniques are needed to tolerate two, or more, simultaneous faults.

To be able to analyze the performance of disk arrays, we first need to formally define the different types of I/O requests that would typically be serviced by a disk system. These are *small read, small write, large read and large write.*

A small read (or write) request is a request for a small data block. By small we mean that the requested data is small enough to be serviced by a single disk. In contrast, large requests are requests that require all disks to participate in the service.

Read requests performance generally differ from write requests performance because write requests would require extra operations to be performed to update the redundant disks.

RAID Level – 0

This level of RAID is not really redundant (see Fig. 16.3). Actually, all what it does is to distribute the data bits over several disks. This level of RAID does not target reliability. Rather, the main objective is performance. RAID level–0 is usually used along with supercomputers where performance is the main concern.

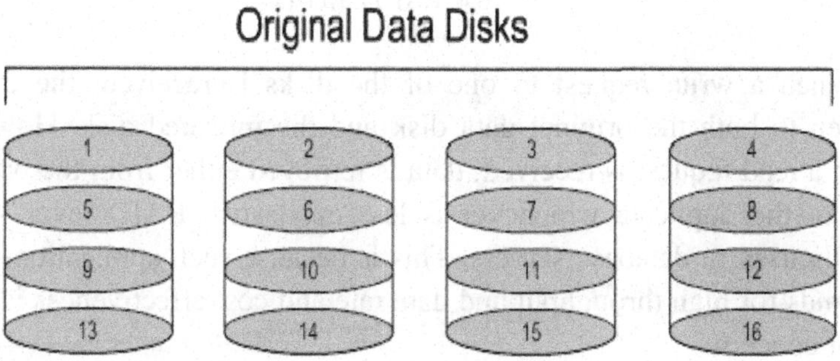

Original Data Disks

Fig. 16.3: Original data disks.

In this system where there is no redundancy, read and write requests are similar. A small read or write would be serviced from one disk and hence no speed-up is gained. On the other hand, large requests can be serviced from multiple disks simultaneously. So a speed-up equal to the number of participating disks can be gained. In the following analysis of the rest of RAID levels we will use the performance of RAID level – 0 as a reference.

RAID Level – 1

RAID level – 1 is based on mirroring or shadowing (see Fig. 16.4). One of the data disks is mirrored (or duplicated into another one). If one of the data disks fails, then data is retrieved from its mirrored disk.

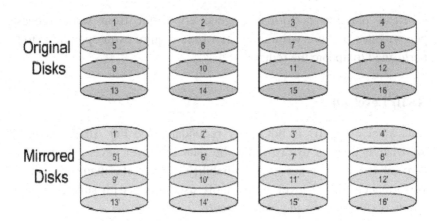

Fig. 16.4: RAID Level-1.

When a write request to one of the disks is received, the data is written to both the original data disk and the mirrored disk. However, when a read request is received, data is retrieved either from the original disk or the duplicate whichever is less expensive. RAID level – 1 is usually used in database servers. This is because such applications have demands for high throughput and data rate and cost effectiveness is not a major concern.

In this system where data disks are mirrored, read performance differ from write performance. A small read would be serviced from one disk and hence no speed-up is gained. On the other hand, large read requests can be serviced from multiple disks simultaneously. So a speed-up equal to the number of participating disks can be gained.

In the case of write requests (small and large), the data must be written twice: once to the original data disks and another to the mirrored ones. Therefore the performance of writes in this scheme is half that of RAID level – 0.

RAID Level – 2

RAID level – 2 (see Fig. 16.5) is based on Hamming encoding technique. It is an Error Correcting Code, which can be used to detect and locate a single error.

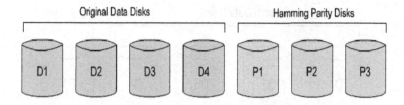

Fig. 16.5: RAID Level-2.

This technique is used in this RAID level by providing extra disks to store parity bits. If an error occurs in one of the disks, it can be corrected using the information in the rest of the disks (both data and parity disks). The data bits of each data word are distributed evenly on the data disks. The parity bits are calculated for each word and stored in their corresponding parity disks.

When a read request is serviced, all disks (data and parity) participate in the process. The validity of the data is checked using the parity values. When a write request is serviced then parity bits have to be calculated for each word and stored in their corresponding location in the parity disks. RAID level – 2 is rarely used because other levels provide a better alternative both in reliability and performance.

In this system, Hamming parity disks are used. Since the data is bit interleaved, a read request of any size would be serviced by all the data disks. This results in an increase in the bandwidth by a factor equal to the number of data disks. For write requests, we need to update the parity disks in addition to the data disks which degrade the performance.

RAID Level – 3

The relatively large number of bits required by Hamming is used to locate the error in addition to detecting it. However disk technology is different than memory and data communication technologies in that it is possible to identify a failing disk without requiring the help of codes. Therefore, it is possible to use a single parity disk instead of the many disks used in level – 2. This disk stores a parity bit that is used to detect the existence of a fault. If this occurs, the disk controller can easily identify the failing disk. RAID level – 3, 4 and 5 are based on this idea.

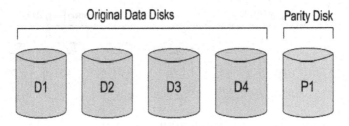

Fig. 16.6: RAID Level-3.

In RAID level – 3 (see Fig. 16.6), the bits of each data word are distributed onto each data disk. However, a single parity disk is used to store the parity bits. Consequently, all disks participate in servicing reads and writes operations. In a read operation, the parity bit is checked to verify the validity of data. The parity bit must be calculated and stored in a write operation.

RAID level – 3 is simple and therefore is appropriate for applications requiring high bandwidth or data rate but not high I/O rates.

In this system, one parity disks is used. Since the data is bit interleaved, a read (or write) request of any size would be serviced by all the data disks. This results in an increase in the bandwidth by a factor equal to the number of data disks over the bandwidth achieved in RAID level - 0.

However, throughput of small reads (or writes) in such a design is 1/N the throughput of a RAID level – 0 because only one request can be serviced at a time, where *N* is the total number of disks in the array. The throughput of large requests is slightly less than that of RAID level – 0 because the parity disk does not participate in servicing the request.

RAID Level – 4

RAID level – 3 can be called *Bit-Interleaved Parity* because the bits of each word are distributed onto all data disks and the parity is calculated for each single word. In contrast RAID level – 4 (see Fig. 16.7) is called *Block-Interleaved Parity* to indicate the fact that data is partitioned into blocks (e.g. of size 1KB) and each block is stored on a separate disk. Consequently, data from different (and sometimes independent) blocks participate in calculating the value of the parity.

Original Data Blocks   Parity Blocks

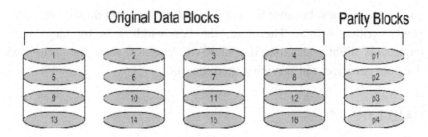

Fig. 16.7: RAID Level-4.

The main motivation behind moving from bit-interleaved parity to block-interleaved parity is to increase the throughput, i.e., the number of I/O requests serviced per second. Since data are stored in large blocks which are stored on separate disks, small read requests can be serviced from one or a subset of the total data disks. This way multiple read requests can be serviced simultaneously increasing the number of I/O operations per second.

Unfortunately, write performance is not as good. Modification of a block in a single disk requires the recalculation of the parity. This in turn requires the value of the old parity and the old value of the updated disk in addition to the new updated value. So, a single write operation requires first reading from two disks (one parity and one data). Then the parity is recalculated using the read information plus the new value. In fact, the new parity can be calculated by XORing all these values. Finally, the modified block plus the parity block is written into their corresponding disks. This whole operation is called *Read-Modify-Write*.

In this system, one parity disks is used but data is block interleaved. So, (N-1) small read requests can be serviced at the same time, resulting in a throughput slightly less than that of RAID level – 0. Similarly, the bandwidth seen by large read requests is slightly less than that of RAID level – 0 since the parity disk does not participate in servicing the requests.

To service a small write request, a read-modify-write operation must be performed. This operation requires reading two disks and writing two disks. So the throughput of a small write is 1/4 that of a RAID level – 0. Fortunately, we do not need this operation (i.e. read-modify-write) in a large write request because the parity can be calculated directly from the newly written values. Therefore, the bandwidth seen by large write requests is slightly less than that of RAID level – 0 since the parity disk does not participate in servicing the requests.

RAID Level – 5

Like RAID level – 4, RAID level – 5 (see Fig. 16.8) is a *block interleaved parity* disk array. Data is stored in blocks and parity is calculated for a parity group of blocks. The main difference between the two designs is that RAID level – 5 has a distributed parity design. Unlike level – 4, the parity blocks are not reserved to one single disk. Instead, the parity blocks are distributed onto all the disks. Consequently, the discrimination between data disks and parity disks diminishes.

Original Data Blocks & Parity Blocks Interleaved

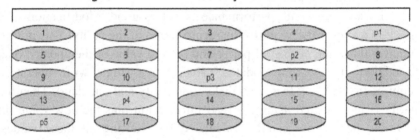

Fig. 16.8: RAID Level-5.

Like level – 4, this design can service multiple small read requests at the same time providing high I/O rate. Moreover, large read requests can be serviced from multiple disks increasing the data rate. Yet, any write operation still requires the use of the expensive *read-modify-write* operation.

An important advantage of RAID level – 5 over RAID level – 4 is that it removes the *"hotspot"* created in level – 4. A hotspot refers to a disk that is requested much more often than other disks, which is the parity disk in this case. RAID level – 5 alleviates this problem by distributing the parity over all disks.

RAID level – 5 is one of the best alternatives found in the RAID family. It provides a balanced choice between reliability, performance and cost. Therefore, it is the most widely used type of RAID.

The performance of this system, where data is block interleaved and parity is distributed, is very much similar to that of level – 4. The only difference is that this design can offer a slightly better large read performance. This can be achieved by placing the parity onto disks carefully such that all disks are able to participate in servicing the requests. Large write performance is still the same as that of level – 4 because we still need to *waste* a small portion of the bandwidth to update the parity block.

The cost of RAID systems can easily be calculated by determining the number of extra (redundant) disks required. Table 16.1 summarizes the cost of each disk compared to that of RAID level – 0 where N disks are used.

Table 16.1: Different RAID systems cost.

RAID level -1	RAID level -3	RAID level -4	RAID level -5
2 * N	N +1	N +1	N +1

16.3 Simple Reliability Analysis

As mentioned earlier, disk arrays were originally designed to provide higher bandwidth and throughput. Unfortunately, as the number of disks increase in the array, the reliability of the overall system decreases.

Consider, for example, the *Mean Time To Data Loss* (MTTDL). For a single disk, MTTDL = MTTF(disk). This value is typically around 200,000 hours (or about 23 years) which is relatively large. However, the MTTDL of a non-redundant disk array is given by this formula:

$$MTTDL = MTTF(sys) = MTTF(disk)/N.$$

where N is the number of disks in the array. So, for the previous MTTF value of a single disk and an array of 16 disks, the MTTDL of the system would be about 1.4 years.

This reduction in reliability justifies the need for redundancy. In 1-FT RAID like RAID level 1 to 5, the failure of a single disk can be tolerated. However, data will be lost if another disk fails before repairing the first one. It has been shown that the MTTDL of a RAID level – 5 system is given by:

$$MTTDL = \frac{MTTF\ (disk)^2}{N \times (G-1) \times MTTR(disk)}$$

where N is the total number of disks in the array, G is the parity group size and MTTR is the Mean Time To Repair. Therefore, for a system with 16 disks in total organized in parity groups of size 7 and MTTF(disk) = 200,000 hours and MTTR(disk) = 12 hours, the MTTDL is about 4000 years!!

Figure 16.9 compares the reliability of a single disk to that of the previously described RAID -5.

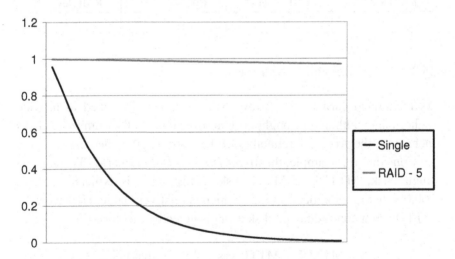

Fig. 16.9: Single disk versus RAID Level-5 reliability.

16.4 Advanced RAID Systems

RAID levels 1 to 5 can tolerate a single fault in the system. However, if another fault occurs before the first disk is repaired then data will be lost. Yet, our previous calculations show that such an event is so likely to happen given that the failure of another disk is independent of the failure of the first one.

Unfortunately, this last assumption is too optimistic. In reality, when one disk fails, the probability that another one would follow is higher. Given this, the reliability of such a system degrades significantly.

Moreover, data loss can occur even if no other disk fails because of uncorrectable bit errors. If this happens during the reconstruction process, then data would be lost.

There exist a number of applications that are very sensitive to data loss. Such applications require even more reliable secondary storage systems than what is provided by RAID levels 1 to 5. In this section we will introduce two advanced RAID architectures: RAID level – 6 and EVENODD. Both of these systems can tolerate two simultaneous disk failures providing an extremely high reliability.

RAID Level – 6

RAID level – 6 (see Fig. 16.10) is based on the Reed-Solomon (RS) codes. It is an optimal solution in terms of the number of redundant disks required: it requires only two redundant disks, P and Q. This scheme is very similar to the block interleaved distributed parity.

Original Data Blocks & P + Q Blocks Interleaved

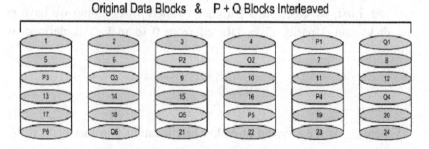

Fig. 16.10: RAID Level-6.

Like RAID level – 5, RAID level – 6 requires the use of read-modify-write procedure for small write operations. However, RAID level – 6 requires accessing 6 disks instead of 4 in the case of RAID level – 5. This is because we need to update the information in the P and Q blocks.

RAID level – 6 is based on Reed-Solomon codes, which require operations over finite fields. These operations need special hardware and cannot be implemented over standard RAID level – 5 disk controllers. Such controllers are optimized to do XOR operations that are heavily used in simple parity.

EVENODD

This is a newer design than RAID level – 6. Like level – 6, EVENODD is 2-FT system. The main objective behind developing this scheme was to simplify the hardware required and the coding decoding procedures. EVENODD is a RAID scheme that requires only XOR operations for encoding and decoding. So, it can be implemented over standard RAID level – 5 controllers. In addition, it provides a better performance for small write requests as will be discussed later.

Like RAID level – 6, EVENODD is an optimal solution in terms of the number of redundant disks required. To tolerate two disk failures, EVENODD requires 2 redundant disks only. The first disk stores the horizontal parity and the second stores the diagonal EVENODD parity.

The first disk is the simple parity disk in RAID level – 4. The value of parity is calculated simply by XORing the data bits that are in the same parity group. We call this disk the *Horizontal Parity Disk*.

The calculation of the second disk, *The Diagonal Parity Disk*, is more involved. First, we calculate a parameter called S. Assuming we have m data disks and 2 parity disks labeled from 0 to m-1, S is defined as follows.

$$S = \bigoplus_{t=0}^{m-1} a_{a-1-t,t}$$

Where $a_{x,y}$ is the element at disk x and location y in that disk. If we enumerate this equation we notice that the values participating in the calculation of S belong to the diagonal in the middle (see example below). We call this diagonal *the Main Diagonal*.

After that the values of the diagonal parity disk is calculated by XORing a certain diagonal of data bits and XORing the result with S. The values can be calculated formally using the following formula:

$$a_{l,m-1} = S \oplus \left(\bigoplus_{t=0}^{m-1} a_{<l-t>_m, t} \right), 0 < l < m - 2$$

Where $<x>_y = z$ means $z = x \bmod y$.

Depending on the value of S, the parity in the Diagonal parity Disk is either even or odd (hence the name EVENODD). If $S = 0$, we have even parity; otherwise, we have odd parity.

To clarify this, let us consider the following example. Suppose that we have 5 data disks plus two parity disks. Assume that we have 4 data elements in each disk. The following table represents the described system

1	0	0	1	**0**		
1	0	1	**0**	1		
0	1	**1**	1	1		
0	**1**	1	1	0		

We first calculate the values for horizontal parity disk to get:

1	0	0	1	**0**	0	
1	0	1	**0**	1	1	
0	1	**1**	1	1	0	
0	**1**	1	1	0	1	

The next step is to calculate the parameter S. S is calculated by XORing the values that are bolded in the table. So, S = 0. Therefore, we have even parity in the second parity disk. Next we calculate the parity for the diagonal parity disk:

1	0	0	1	0	0	1
1	0	1	0	1	1	0
0	1	1	1	1	0	1
0	1	1	1	0	1	0

Now let us assume that disk 0 and disk 2 has failed and try to reconstruct their values.

?	0	?	1	0	0	1
?	0	?	0	1	1	0
?	1	?	1	1	0	1
?	1	?	1	0	1	0

It can be shown that the parameter S can be obtained by XORing the bits in the two parity disks. So the first step is to find the value of $S = 0$. Since we have the value of S, we can find the missing value in the main diagonal. This can be calculated by XORing the correct values and S. This would give a value of 1 at location (2,2).

?	0	?	1	0	0	1
?	0	?	0	1	1	0
?	1	1	1	1	0	1
?	1	?	1	0	1	0

By finding this value we have row 2 complete but for the bit (2,0). The value of this bit can be calculated from the parity in the first parity disk. The resulting value of bit (2,0) is 0.

?	0	?	1	0	0	1
?	0	?	0	1	1	0
0	1	1	1	1	0	1
?	1	?	1	0	1	0

Finding the value of bit (2,0) makes the blue diagonal complete but for the bit at (0,2). This can be calculated by XORing the correct values in the blue diagonal with their corresponding bit in the second parity disk and with S. This results in a value of 0 at location (0,2).

?	0	**0**	1	**0**	0	1
?	0	?	**0**	1	1	0
0	1	1	1	1	0	1
?	1	?	1	0	1	0

Following the same logic, we use the horizontal parity to find the value at (0, 0) to be 1. Then we use the diagonal parity to find the missing bit in the green diagonal (i.e. bit (1, 0)) to be 1. This enables us to find bit (1, 2) using the horizontal parity to be 1. Similarly bit (3, 0) can be found from the pink diagonal to be 0. Finally we find the value at (3, 2) from the horizontal parity to be equal to1. The final result is as follows.

1	0	**0**	1	**0**	0	1
1	0	**1**	0	1	1	0
0	1	**1**	1	1	0	1
0	1	**1**	1	0	1	0

This is exactly equal to the original values and the failed disks are reconstructed successfully.

For EVENODD to work successfully, the number of data disks must be prime. Yet, if the number was not prime, then we can find the nearest larger prime and use it. For the additional disks, we use imaginary disks with all bits equal to 0.

In small reads, both RAID level – 6 and EVENODD perform the same. The request would be serviced from a single disk. Similarly, for large reads, (N-2) disks participate in servicing the requests providing a performance of (N-2/N) relative to RAID level – 0.

For small writes, both systems would use the read-modify-write operation. RAID level – 6 require 6 accesses. On the other hand, EVENODD performs differently depending on the location of the data block. As long as the data block is not on the main diagonal, then only 6 accesses are needed. Moreover, since the operations done in EVENODD are simpler than those in RAID level – 6, the speed of the update is about double that of RAID level – 6.

However, if the updated a block that was on the main diagonal, then we need to update the value of S and all the values in the second Parity disk. This is the main draw back of EVENODD.

For large writes in RAID level – 6, we need to update the two blocks corresponding to the updated row. Whereas in EVENODD, we need to update the horizontal parity block and all the blocks in the diagonal parity block. This is because a large write will definitely modify a block in the main diagonal.

The reliability of both systems is similar since both can tolerate two simultaneous disk failures. The MTTDL of such systems is given by

$$MTTDL = \frac{MTTF(disk)^3}{N \times (G-1) \times (G-2) \times MTTR(disk)^2}$$

16.5 More on RAIDs

This section discusses some of the advanced topics in the field of RAID. We start by taking a closer look at the reliability of RAID systems. Then we will investigate the effect of parity placement on the performance of the system. Finally we will discuss some implementation considerations for RAID systems.

Reliability of RAID Systems

In our previous discussions and calculations we have used a simplified model to investigate the reliability of RAID systems. In this section we revisit this issue with a more realistic view.

First, in our previous discussions, we assumed that only disks could fail. A disk array contains many parts other than the disks that are not perfect. These components include the power supply, disk controller, cables and fans. The reliability of these components should also be taken into consideration.

It has been shown that if we take all these supporting hardware into consideration then the resulting reliability of the system is 3% of the reliability estimated by the simplified model. Adding redundancy into the supporting hardware would increase the reliability of the system to 81% of the estimated reliability in the simplified model.

In the simplified model, we assumed that data could be lost only by components failures. Data loss can occur because of *uncorrectable bit errors*. These are bits that have been corrupted on the surface of the disk. They might be caused by the reading process or the writing process.

Typically uncorrectable bit errors occur once in $2.5 * 10^{10}$ accesses. This value seems reasonable. However if a disk fails in a parity-based disk array then we need to read all the data in all non-failing disks (about 300 million sectors) to be able to reconstruct the data in the failing disk. The probability of reading all the data correctly is $(1-1/2.5 * 10^{10})^{300,000,000} = 0.988$.

In the simplified model, we assumed that failures of disks are independent. In most cases they are not. For example, a power burst that damages one disk will likely also damage another one. Also, if a disk fails due to aging, then most likely other disks of the same age would have less reliability. Taking this into considerations, the MTTDL of 1-FT disk array becomes:

$$MTTDL = \frac{MTTF\ (disk1)\ \times MTTF\ (disk\ 2)}{N \times (G-1) \times MTTR(disk)}$$

Where MTTF(disk1) is different than MTF(disk2).

Parity Placement

RAID level – 5 is considered to be the most widely used scheme. In this scheme parity is block interleaved and distributed over all the disks. Parity Placement refers to the way the parity blocks are distributed over the disks.

Parity blocks can be grouped into a single disk (like in level – 4). Also, the parity blocks can be placed at the last row of the array (flat-left-symmetric). In addition, the parity blocks can be placed on the diagonals: either right or left. Moreover the organization can be symmetric or asymmetric. The following figures show an example of each possibility.

0	1	2	P0
3	**4**	5	**P1**
6	7	**8**	**P2**
9	10	11	P3

Level –4 design

0	1	2	**3**
3	**4**	5	6
6	7	**8**	9
P0	**P1**	**P2**	P3

Flat – left – symmetric

P0	0	1	2
3	P1	4	5
6	7	P2	8
9	10	11	P3

Right Asymmetric

P0	0	1	2
5	P1	3	4
7	8	P2	6
9	10	11	P3

Right symmetric

0	1	2	P0
3	**4**	P1	5
6	P2	**7**	8
P3	9	10	**11**

Left Asymmetric

0	1	2	P0
4	**5**	P1	3
8	P2	**6**	7
P3	9	10	**11**

Left symmetric

Edward and Katz have shown using simulation that Left Symmetric and Flat-Left-Symmetric outperform all the previously mentioned designs. It is worth mentioning that level – 4 placement was the worst in servicing writes requests due to contention over the parity disk. Yet it performed very well (compared to left symmetric) in servicing reads.

The followings are some suggested general guidelines for parity placement:

1. Avoid putting parity blocks in the same column.
2. Place the parity in such a way that if you have a large write request spanning a complete row then you can update the parity without reading old data.
3. Distribute parity and data over all disks
4. Maximize the distance between parity blocks.

Implementation Considerations

For a RAID to work properly some information that is neither data nor parity should be maintained. The most important information to keep is the validity of disk sectors. If a disk fails, then all its sectors must be marked invalid to prevent users from reading from them. Similarly, if a failed disk is reconstructed, its sectors must be marked valid again.

Another piece of information to keep is the consistency of parity blocks. If a data block is being updated, then the parity block corresponding to it should be marked inconsistent. This is especially important in the case of crashes to prevent using the inconsistent block in reconstruction.

RAID systems are supposed to continue to function when a disk fails. Yet, in such a case, the system is so vulnerable. If a system crashes while a user is performing a write operation, then the written data would be corrupted and the corresponding parity block would be inconsistent and cannot be used for reconstruction. If this happens, data will be lost. To avoid this, some type of logging should be done for operations performed by users in the reconstruction period.

Now, let us consider the problem of connecting the RAID system to the computer. The most common way is to divide the disks into smaller groups and connect each group of disks together with a *String Controller* to the computer. It is recommended to choose parity groups to be orthogonal to the string groups. This is called *Orthogonal RAID*.

16.6 Summary

In this chapter, we have discussed some basic decisions that should be considered when designing RAID systems. Six classic RAID designs (RAID level – 0 to 5) have been explained and compared in terms of performance and reliability. In addition, two advanced RAID schemes have been introduced: RAID level – 6 and EVENODD. Although both of these schemes can tolerate double disk failure, EVENODD provide a simpler encoding and decoding algorithms. The issue of RAID reliability has been discussed in some details. That was followed by an examination of the effect of parity placement on the performance of RAID together with some implementation considerations.

References

[1]   Blaum, M., Brady, J., Bruck, J., Jai Menon, "EVENODD: an efficient scheme for tolerating double disk failures in RAID architectures", IEEE Transactions on Computers, Volume: 44 Issue: 2, Feb 1995.

[2]   Edward K. Lee and Randy H. Katz, "The Performance of Parity Placements in Disk Arrays", IEEE Transactions on Computers, Vol. 42 No. 6, June 1993.

[3]   Ganger, G.R., Worthington, B.L., Hou, R.Y., Patt, Y.N., "Disk arrays: high-performance, high-reliability storage subsystems", IEEE Computer, Volume: 27 Issue: 3, Mar 1994.

[4]   Martin Schulez, Garth Gibson, Randy Katz and David Paterson, "How Reliable is A RAID?", Thirty-Fourth IEEE Computer Society International Conference, 27 Feb-3 Mar 1989.

[5]   Peter M. Chen, Edward K. Lee, Garth A. Gibson, Randy H. Katz and David A. Patterson, "RAID: High Performance Reliable Secondary Storage", ACM Computing Survey Journal, Vol. 26 No. 2 , 1994.

[6]   Dan Feng; Hai Jin; Jiangling Zhang, "Improved EVENODD code", 1997 IEEE International Symposium on Information Theory. 1997.

[7]   Franaszek, P.A.; Robinson, J.T., "On variable scope of parity protection in disk arrays", IEEE Transactions on Computers.

[8]   Menon, J.; Riegel, J.; Wyllie, J., "Algorithms for software and low-cost hardware RAIDs", Compcon '95.'Technologies for the Information Superhighway', Mar 1995.

[9]   Shenze Chen; Towsley, D., "A performance evaluation of RAID architectures", IEEE Transactions on Computers, Volume: 45 Issue: 10, Oct 1996.

[10] Sahai, A.K., "Performance aspects of RAID architectures", IEEE International Performance, Computing, and Communications Conference, 1997.

Websites

[11] http://whitepapers.informationweek.com/detail/RES/

[12] http://www.mysql.de/it-resources/white-papers/cluster.php

[13] http://itpapers.zdnet.com/search.aspx

[14] http://www.research.ibm.com/high_avail96/home.html

[15] http://infoweek.bitpipe.com/detail/RES/974223211_644.html

[16] http://whitepapers.informationweek.com/data/detail

[17] http://www.intel.com/business/bss/solutions/blueprints/pdf/cvic02 28.pdf

[18] http://eutaxy.net/franklin/papers/eutaxy.net~papers~discex01.pdf

[19] http://www.ganssle.com/articles/ahugedat.htm

[20] http://www.ee.ryerson.ca:8080/research/compsys/

[21] http://www.ee.ryerson.ca/~gnkhan/publications/iccd98.pdf

[22] http://bs.hhi.de/~wiegand/icip03_mcoder.pdf

[23] http://www-ree.jpl.nasa.gov/fy98_reports/rsft.html

[24] http://www.ece.jhu.edu/~gglm/Projects/fault.html

[25] http://www.necsam.com/servers/files/DRecovery_datasheet.pdf

[26] http://www.csr.city.ac.uk/people/lorenzo.strigini/FTcourse.html

[27] http://homepages.cs.ncl.ac.uk/mohammad.alsaeed/gpfi/index.php

[28] http://www.cs.uidaho.edu/~krings/CS449/Notes.F03/449-03-37.pdf

[29] http://www.cs.ucla.edu/~rennels/article98.pdf

[30] http://www.arcos.inf.uc3m.es/html_english/seminarios/20002001/ stf_english.html

[31]   http://www.cs.colostate.edu/~cs530/1intro.pdf
[32]   http://www.cs.kent.ac.uk/people/staff/rdl/EDCC-4/Papers/tyrrell.pdf
[33]   http://www.elec.york.ac.uk/bio/publications/dwb-caos-nasa2000.pdf
[34]   http://bees.jpl.nasa.gov/pdf/wadrian.pdf
[35]   http://www.md.kth.se/RTC/SC3S/papers/avizienis.pdf
[36]   http://www.ia-tech.com/publications/asset98.pdf
[37]   http://rac.alionscience.com/rac/jsp/webproducts/products.jsp
[38]   http://rac.alionscience.com/pdf/4Q2002.pdf
[39]   http://rac.alionscience.com/pdf/2Q2003.pdf

Chapter 17

High Availability in Computer Systems

This chapter is dedicated to a discussion on highly available systems. Our coverage starts with an introduction in which we conduct a discussion on the hardware and software requirements for achieving high availability. We then briefly review the basic concepts as applied to the Tandem highly available systems. Our coverage ends with a brief introduction to the availability issue as applied to the client/server computing paradigm.

17.1 Introduction

High availability refers to a system with a high probability of being working at any random instant of time and hence having a minimum downtime. There are certain computing applications where availability is a crucial requirement. These include healthcare, telecommunications, banking, and airline reservations. These applications/services require computing systems that are highly reliable, redundant, and available around the clock.

Highly available applications must have the ability to process transactions without interruption. Upon the occurrence of failure, recovery must occur instantly. The occurrence of failures and failure recovery must be transparent to the users. The operating system needs to continuously maintain the integrity of all data files, so that only recent operations need to be scrutinized upon restart. This requires, among others, the use of a well managed hot standby strategy for all critical components. A highly available computing system need also to be protected against data corruption and/or loss due to disk or controller

426

failures, and to ensure that transactions in-process can be reconciled and recovered.

In designing a highly available system, it is required to have both data and states be protected against any possible failures. A key principle in achieving this is the avoidance of single points of failure. This will require maintaining all processing and states on distributed systems. In addition, redundancy has to be incorporated at all critical points. Highly available systems require the use of suitable hardware and software.

High availability can be achieved via the use of some or a combination of the following hardware techniques.

(1) The use of redundant sparing techniques: These include the following techniques.

   (a) Cold Standby (CS): Following a component failure, an automatic fault detection and recovery mechanism is used to detect the fault, and bring into service a redundant component. This redundant component must be initialized. Once this is done, users are able to reconnect to it and begin processing again from the point of their rollback. Typically, the length of time required to detect the fault and invoke the redundant component is quite low (tens of seconds). However, the time required for the initialization of the redundant component can be much longer.

   (b) Warm Standby (WS): Following a component failure, an automatic fault detection and recovery mechanism detects the fault, and notifies the redundant component to take over. This redundant component has been actively running, and is partially initialized. Furthermore, it may already share some of the processing state of its failed peer. Hence, not all work in progress may have to be rolled back. Fault detection time for Warm Standby systems is similar to that in the case of Cold Standby systems, but the recovery time is dramatically lower than Cold Standby (typically tens of seconds), due to the partial initialization and state sharing.

(c) Hot Standby (HS)/Active Replication (AR): Active and redundant components are tightly coupled in groups and (logically) indistinguishable to the users of the component group. Following a component fault, users of the component are not disconnected and do not observe the fault in any way. Work in progress continues with the remaining redundant component(s) in the group providing the component functionality. In this model, the masking is complete and transparent and the users of the system are uninterrupted. Recovery time is instantaneous.

(2) Clustering represents two or more systems working together to provide availability or load balancing. Clustering enables high availability through distributed computing in which all the members of the cluster actively provide service but on failure of any single cluster element the load is redistributed over the remaining elements along with a corresponding degradation of performance. Clustered systems do not provide automatic correction of a failed node.

High-availability (HA) computing, as commonly practiced, utilizes the redundant resources of clustered (two or more) systems or components. Either a Dual-Redundant (D-R) approach is taken or a Live Insertion (L-I) approach is taken. D-R sparing strategy requires replication of the complete system so as to allow complete switching of the work load on failure of the active one. Live insertion involves replication of components so as to allow insertion of the spare component into the existing system on failure of its corresponding active component.

As far as software is concerned, high availability often requires software that requires a suite of management software that is aware-of and operates on the software itself. This includes at least three dimensions: configuration, instrumentation, and online upgrade. Configuration is frequently used for performance and scalability and instrumentation is required for both performance and availability. Online software upgrade (without shutting down the system) is essential to provide high availability. It involves, among others, online database evolution, and simultaneous operation of multiple versions of the software. It is often required to rollback to the old software version if something goes wrong with the upgrade process. A schematic of an online upgrade is shown in Fig. 17.1.

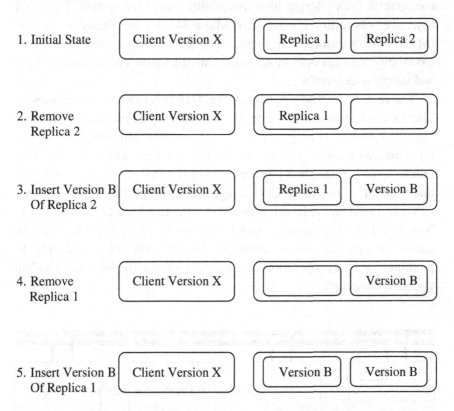

1. Initial State   Client Version X   Replica 1   Replica 2

2. Remove Replica 2   Client Version X   Replica 1

3. Insert Version B Of Replica 2   Client Version X   Replica 1   Version B

4. Remove Replica 1   Client Version X   Version B

5. Insert Version B Of Replica 1   Client Version X   Version B   Version B

Fig. 17.1: Steps for online software upgrade for availability purposes.

It should be noted that in order to achieve the above online software upgrading, server versions A and B must be sufficiently compatible to share processing state between them. Also, clients (which typically have an independent lifecycle, represented as Version X) must be able to transparently interoperate across server versions A and B. Similar issues arise when the clients are upgraded from X to Y. It should also noted that if the upgrade from Version A to B is significant enough (e.g. a large amount of new functionality added in Version B), it may not be possible at all.

17.2   Tandem High Availability Computers at a Glance

The Tandem NonStop system was introduced in 1976 as the first commercial fault-tolerant high availability computer system. The main objective was to provide a system whose Mean Time Between Failures (MTBF) is measured in years. The key design principles were modularity, fail-fast operation, single fault tolerance, online maintenance, and simple user interface.

The first TANDEM system was the **T/16** (later renamed **NonStop I**). The NonStop consisted of 2 to 16 processor modules, each capable of about 0.7 MIPS. The system used a custom bus connection called the **Dynabus**. Modules connected to the Dynbus were constructed so that failure would always leave at least one of the busses free for use by the other modules. The basic CPU design was patterned after the HP 3000 CPU, a 16-bit stack-based processor with 32-bit address space. The NonStop I used a custom operating system called the *Guardian* in which all operations used message passing with the use of check-pointing for every operation. Figure 17.2 shows the original Tandem system architecture.

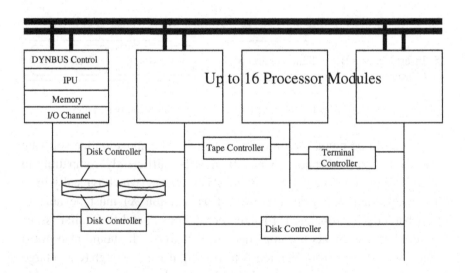

Fig. 17.2: Original Tandem system architecture.

In 1981, the NonStop I was followed by the **NonStop II** with a slight MIPs improvement from 0.7 to 0.8 and an upgrade in memory from a maximum of 384 KB per CPU in the NonStop I, to 2MB in the NonStop II. In 1983's the **NonStop TXP** system was introduced achieving a 2.0 MIPS and an upgrade in the physical memory to 8MB with the use of the same Dynabus system. Introduced along with the TXP was the fiber optic FOX bus system, which allowed a number of TXP and NonStop II systems to be connected together to form a larger system with up to 14 nodes.

In 1986, the **NonStop VLX** was introduced with the use of a new Dynabus, increasing speed from 13 Mbit/s to 40 Mbit/s (total, 20 Mbit/s per independent bus). Also introduced was the **FOX II**, increasing the size of the networks from 1Km to 4 Km. Introduced also in 1986, was the first in-house fault-tolerant NonStop SQL database. About a year later, CLX, a minicomputer sized machine was introduced. It was much smaller and less expensive compared to the TXP. By the end of its lifetime, the CLX achieved a performance that is more or less similar to that achieved by the VLX. Figure 17.3 shows a block diagram for the CLX.

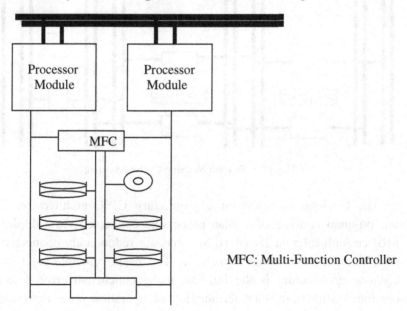

Fig. 17.3: CLX system diagram.

The **NonStop Cyclone** was introduced in 1989, introducing a new superscalar CPU design. The Cyclone was about four times as fast as the CLX 800, which Tandem used as their benchmark. Figure 17.4 shows the overall Cyclone system architecture.

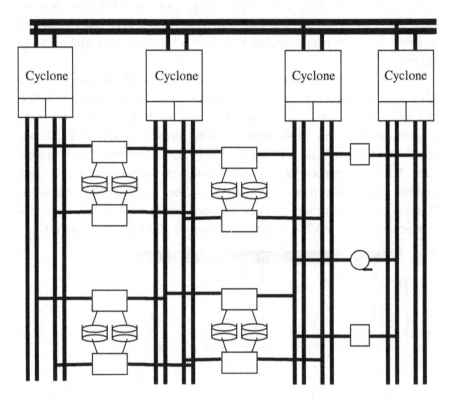

Fig. 17.4: Tandem NonStop Cyclone system.

The Cyclone is based on a proprietary CISC architecture. Each section-quad consists of a quad processors connected via a duplex 40 MB/sec fault-tolerant Dynabus. Sections are redundantly connected via fault tolerant fiber optics Dynabus+. The basic principle used in the Cyclone architecture is the fail fast using concurrent error detection combined with immediate termination of operation upon detection of error. This is in addition to the use of Double Error Detection Single

Error Correction (DED-SEC) in memories. A RISC implementation of the *Guardian* was introduced in 1991 running on the MIPS R3000 CPU resulting in code that was some 25% slower than the original Cyclone.

The *Guardian* operating system uses two basic fault tolerance protocols, i.e., consistency checking and the "I'm alive" message. Consistency checking is used to compare redundant data structures and kernel-level assertions in order to catch local software and/or hardware failures. In case of detecting an error, Guardian operating system is designed to halt the processor such that integrity can be ensured. The "I'm alive" message will be used by other processors in order to detect the halted processor. This is possible since each second every processor sends the "I'm alive" message over every bus to all processors in the system. Another feature of the Guardian operating system is that it creates and maintains a duplicate, backup process on a separate processor. If the primary process fails or fall victim to a hardware failure, the operating system automatically switches to the backup. Periodic check-pointing messages are used in order to maintain consistency checking between the primary and the backup processes. A Tandem system evolution is shown in Table 17.1.

Table 17.1: A Tandem system evolution.

Processor	NonStop I	NonStop II	TXP	VLX	CLX 600	CLX 700	Cyclone	K-10000
Cycle time	100 ns	100 ns	83 ns	83 ns	133 ns	91 ns	45 ns	6.3 ns
Proc/System	2-16	2-16	2-16	2-16	1-6	2-8	2-16	4/section (Up to 4080)
Memory	2MB	16MB	16MB	256MB	32MB	32MB	2GB	256MB/Proc
Bus speed	2×13M B/s	2×13M B/s	2×13M B/s	2×20M B/s	2×20M B/s	2×20M B/s	2×20M B/s	2×20MB/s
Channel speed	4MB/s	5MB/s	5MB/s	5MB/s	3MB/s	4.5MB/s	2×5MB/s	4×5MB/s

In 1993 the **NonStop Himalaya K-Series** using the MIPS R4400 was introduced Fig. 17.5 shows a Himalaya K10000 section.

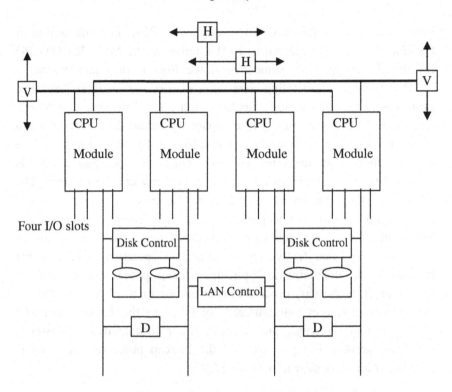

Fig. 17.5: Four-Processor Himalaya K10000 section.

The processors used are 150 MHz R4400 RISC processors with 32 KB of primary cache and 4MB of secondary cache. Each processor has its own main memory with 64-256 MB of error-correcting memory. In addition, each processor has dual connections to the inter-processor bus. The K10000 uses a 3-dimensional torus network called TorusNet. The inter-processor bus is connected to the TorusNet-H and the TorusNet-V fiber optic interfaces. Figure 17.6 shows a fault-tolerant four-CPU sections using the TorusNet.

In that arrangement, the horizontal controllers are used to connect four sections in a ring, called a node. The vertical controller is used to connect up to 14 nodes in a two-dimensional torus, called a domain. The depth controllers (labeled D in Fig. 17.5) are used to connect 16 domains together for a total of 4080 processors. This massively parallel multi-computer system is designed such that it eliminates single points of failure and prevents error propagation. This is achieved by having every component replicated and fail-fast.

The Himalaya family of processors specifications is shown in Table 17.2.

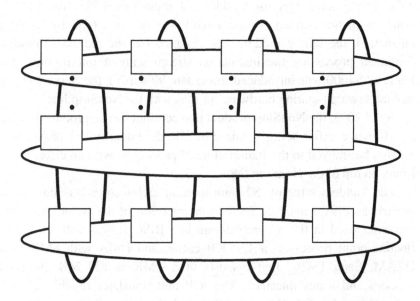

Fig. 17.6: TorusNet connection of 4-CPU sections of the Himalaya K10000.

Table 17.2: Summary of the Himalaya family of processors.

Specifications	K200	K2000	K20000 TorusNet Node	K20000 TorusNet Domain	K20000 Multidomain TorusNet
Processor type	MIPS R4400/125 MHz	MIPS R4400/125 MHz	MIPS R4400/200 MHz	MIPS R4400/200 MHz	MIPS R4400/200 MHz
Maximum # Processors	4	16	16	224	4080
Cache size/processor	1 MB	1 MB	4 MB	4 MB	4 MB
Maximum main memory size	512 MB	4096 MB	4096 MB	56 GB	1044 GB
Maximum disk storage	184 GB	3232 GB	64 TB	916 TB	16712 TB
Maximum # I/O Channels	4	16	64	896	16320

The Himalaya K-series was followed by the Himalaya **S-Series** in 1997. The S-Series machines continued the use of MIPS processors, including the R4400 and R10000.

The *Integrity* family of computers was also introduced in the early 90's. These computers used additional redundant CPUs running the same instruction stream. When a fault was detected (e.g. by lockstep mismatch), the failing module was disabled but the redundant module continued processing the instruction stream without interruption. The Integrity S4000 was introduced in the late 90's using the ServerNet and moving towards sharing hardware designs with the NonStop line.

As of 2003, the NonStop product line continues to be produced, under the HP name. After being acquired by HP, the Integrity line of NonStop Servers has moved to the Itanium line of processors with an effort to run Linux on top of the NonStop OS.

The Tandem integrity S2 fault-tolerant architecture was introduced as early as 1991. Figure 17.7 shows an overview of the architecture. The processor used in the S2 architecture is a RISC R4000 with an R4010 floating-point processor, a 128 KB cache, and DMA with 8MB local DRAM. Each TMRC unit consists of a TMR, a 128 MB of global memory and a bus interface. The IOP unit translates reliable I/O bus operations to NonStop-V+ operations and vice versa. It has also a set of interrupt registers in order to hold the interrupts issued by peripheral devices.

As can be seen in the figure, the basic architecture is based on the principle of triple modular redundancy (TMR). The main idea is to guarantee data integrity throughout the entire system. Three processor modules, each consisting of a CPU and a local memory are performing independently the same job until they need to access a doubly-replicated global memory. Two Triple Modular Redundant Controllers (TMRCs) are used to vote upon both the address and the data. The TMR configuration is used to guarantee protection against a single failure of any type (permanent, transient, of intermittent). The voting mechanism is such that it informs processor modules of existing discrepancy. The detection of an error will lead to the shutting down of the faulty processor. The DMA system uses checksum to provide data integrity

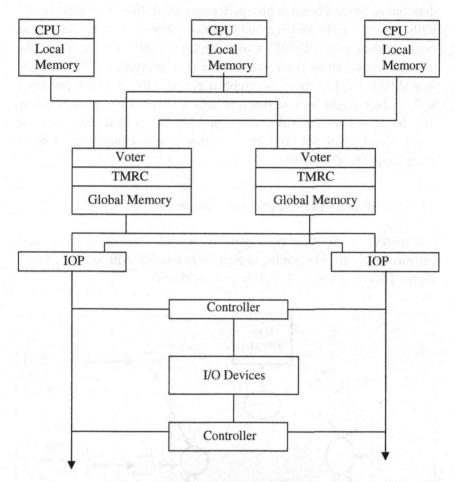

Fig. 17.7: Overview of the Tandem S2 Architecture.

during data transfer on the bus. The TMRCs are organized in a hot-spare configuration. Only one TMRC is connected to the bus at a given time. Each TMRC contains a self-checking logic for detection and fail-fast mode. Global memory is protected by a parity bit per byte. A bitwise majority voting is used and a vote analyzer is used in order to detect the faulty input. Each TMR contains a pair of voters for error detection within the voter. Parity checking is used in order to protect against errors on the data-paths inside the TMRCs. Not only is voting performed on data and addresses, but it is also performed on all I/O and interrupts. All IOPs are are self-checking and fail-fast. When an IOP detects an incorrect data from a TMRC, it asks the sapre TMRC for the same data, thus preventing faults from global memory to propagate to I/O devices. In addition, local memory is scrubbed periodically. A faulty processor will not be brought back to function until it passes a power-on self-test. The design of the S2 architecture guarantees that a fault that occurs on one processor will not propagate to other system components without being caught by the TMRC.

17.3   Availability in Client/Server Computing

Client/server computing paradigm has become the standard in most campus LAN and is beginning to be used in mission-critical applications. Figure 17.8 shows typical client/server architecture.

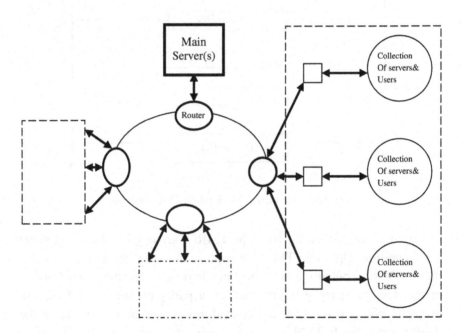

Fig. 17.8: Typical client/server architecture.

As can be seen from the figure, typical client/server architecture uses a LAN with main server(s) (communication, name, and security severs) for access to the outside world, e.g., a WAN. Servers are typically powerful workstations and clients can PCs or ATM devices. There is typically up to 50 clients per database server. In a typical client/server environment, hardware and software from different vendors are used. Applications are not confined to a given host, but rather are spread among clients and servers.

In a distributed system, such as the client/server model presented above, it is reasonable to think of a different way in which system availability is defined. This is because of the nature of the job performed by the clients and the servers. The failure of a client can lead to a single user outage while the failure of a server can lead to 50 user outage. It is therefore reasonable to assume that an appropriate client/server availability measure should into consideration both the duration of an outage and then number of users affected by such outage. This indicates that availability should be measured from the user's point of view rather than from the system point of view. User availability can be defined as user uptime/(user uptime + user downtime), averaged across all users. User availability will be measured in terms of the annual user outage minutes. This helps avoid having to artificially decide how many down users equates to a system outage. For example, an average of one user out of 10000 is down will lead to 99.99% user availability, or about 50 annual outage minutes per user.

To a first order approximation, the system unavailability can be computed assuming the outage causes are statistically independent and that they in series. In this case, the system unavailability can be approximated using the following equation:

$$U_s = 1 - A_s = 1 - A_1 \times A_2 \times ... = 1 - (1 - U_1) \times (1 - U_2) \times ...$$

In the above equation, we assumed the following:

U_s = System unavailability, A_s = System Availability,

A_i = Availability due to outage #i, and U_i = unavailability due to outage #i.

17.4 Chapter Summary

In this chapter, we have briefly covered some of the basic issues related to highly available systems. In particular, we provided a quick review of the Tandem highly available systems. We have also introduced the fundamental concept of availability in the Client/Server environment.

References

[1]   Alan Wood, "Predicting Client/Server Availability", IEEE Computer Magazine, April 1995, pp. 41-48.

[2]   Alan Wood, "NonStop Availability in a Client/Server Environment", Tandem Tech Report 94-1, Part No. 106404, 1994.

[3]   Priya Kothari, "Clustering: A High Availability Solution", A White paper, Wipro Infotech, 2002.

[4]   Jane Wright and Ann Katan, "High Availability: A Perspective", Garther Research, Technology Overview, June 15, 2001.

[5]   "Fault-Tolerant Servers: The Choice for Continuous Availability", A White paper, NEC Computers International, October 2001.

[6]   Joel Bartlett, et al., "Fault Tolerance in Tandem Computer Systems", Tandem Tech. Report 90.5, Part No. 40666, May 1990.

[7]   Jim Gray, "A Census of Tandem System Availability Between 1985 and 1990", Tandem Tech. Report 90.1, Part No. 33579, January 1990.

[8]   Daniel Lenoski, "A Highly Integrated Fault-Tolerant Minicomputer: The NonStop CLX", Tandem Tech. Report 87.5, Part No. 11640, November 1987.

[9]   Robert Horst and Sandy Metz, "A Technical Overview of the Tandem TXP Processor", Tandem Tech. Report No. 87606, April 1984.

[10] Alan Wood, "Software Reliability Growth Models", Tandem Tech. Part No. 130056, September 1996.